Truly Yours &c —
Justin Edwards

"LIGHT AND LOVE."

A SKETCH

OF

THE LIFE AND LABORS

OF THE

REV. JUSTIN EDWARDS, D. D.

THE

EVANGELICAL PASTOR;

THE ADVOCATE OF

TEMPERANCE, THE SABBATH, AND THE BIBLE.

BY REV. WILLIAM A. HALLOCK,
OF NEW YORK CITY.

PUBLISHED BY THE
AMERICAN TRACT SOCIETY,
NEW YORK: 150 NASSAU-STREET.
BOSTON: 28 CORNHILL.

CONTENTS.

CHAPTER I.

EARLY LIFE TO HIS ENTERING THE MINISTRY—1787-1812.

CHAPTER II.

HIS MINISTRY IN ANDOVER—FIRST FIVE YEARS, 1812-1817.

CHAPTER III.

HIS MINISTRY IN ANDOVER—FIVE YEARS, 1817-1822.

CHAPTER IV.

HIS MINISTRY IN ANDOVER—BIBLE VIEWS OF THE MINISTRY AND CHURCH OF CHRIST—1823, 1824.

CHAPTER V.

HIS MINISTRY IN ANDOVER—LAST THREE YEARS, 1824-1827.

CHAPTER VI.

HIS MINISTRY IN BOSTON—NEARLY TWO YEARS, 1828, 1829.

CHAPTER VII.

HIS LABORS IN THE TEMPERANCE REFORMATION—FIRST TWO YEARS, 1830, 1831.

CHAPTER VIII.

LABORS IN THE TEMPERANCE REFORMATION—TWO YEARS, 1832, 1833.

CHAPTER IX.

LABORS IN THE TEMPERANCE REFORMATION—THREE YEARS, 1833-1836.

CHAPTER X.

HIS PRESIDENCY IN THE THEOLOGICAL SEMINARY—SIX YEARS, 1836-1842.

CHAPTER XI.

HIS LABORS FOR THE SANCTIFICATION OF THE SABBATH—SEVEN YEARS, 1842-1849.

CHAPTER XII.

LABORS FOR THE SANCTIFICATION OF THE SABBATH—CONTINUED.

CHAPTER XIII.

HIS COMMENT ON THE BIBLE AS GOD'S GIFT FOR ALL MEN—FOUR YEARS, 1849-1853.

CHAPTER XIV.

THE CLOSING LABORS OF HIS LIFE.

OF

REV. JUSTIN EDWARDS, D. D.

CHAPTER I.

EARLY LIFE TO HIS ENTERING THE MINISTRY.

A. D. 1787-1812.

"The works of the Lord are great, sought out of all them that have pleasure therein." When by his grace he reaches the heart of a young man, enlightens him into the riches of his holy word, teaches him the salvation of Christ, and leads him to consecrate a long eventful life of unwearied usefulness to "Him who washed us from our sins in his own blood," and to the best interests of all for whom He died, a lesson is set before us by which all may profit.

The subject of this sketch, with characteristic modesty, prepared no written memorial of himself; and of many of the most laborious and useful portions of his life, the only record is in enduring results on earth and before the throne of God. His letters to his father's family, which had been carefully preserved, were destroyed by fire; and of his letters to his wife and children, and other relatives and friends, all of which seem to have been written in the midst of pressing public duties, probably not one was intended for the public eye. Of these letters only such passages have been retained as seemed to be of general interest.

JUSTIN EDWARDS was born April 25, 1787, in Westhampton, which until September, 1778, was a part of Northampton, Hampshire county, Massachusetts. He was the second son of Justin Edwards, and was a descendant of Alexander Edwards, who came from Wales in 1640, settled in Springfield, Massachusetts, and a few years after removed to Northampton, where the succeeding ancestors of the subject of this memoir resided till his father removed to Westhampton.*

* "Alexander Edwards came from a border town in Wales in 1640, and settled in Springfield. It appears from a deposition, that his minister in Wales was Mr. Wroth, a conspicuous Puritan preacher. He married a young widow, Sarah Searl, April 28, 1642. He removed to Northampton about 1655, where he died, September 4, 1690. He had eight children, the oldest of whom was Samuel, born March 7, 1643.

"Samuel Edwards, son of Alexander, married Sarah Boykin, daughter of Jarvis Boykin of New Haven, about 1675. He had six children, the eldest of whom was Samuel, born March 26, 1676. He died April 13, 1712.

"Samuel Edwards, son of Samuel, married first Mercy Pomeroy, 1708. She died 1712, and he married Sarah Pomeroy of Colchester, Connecticut. He died March 8, 1749. He had nine children, including Samuel, born September 12, 1716, and Noah, born June 6, 1722.

"Noah Edwards, son of the second Samuel, married Jerusha Alvord, June 28, 1749; she died 1798, and in his old age he married widow Elizabeth Wright, September 11, 1799. He died September 3, 1805. He had eight children; the second child was Justin, born in 1752.

His mother, Elizabeth Clark, was a devoted exemplary Christian, who had a word to speak for Christ as opportunity presented, and whose instructions and prayers, though she was removed by death when he was but five years old, he never forgot. He is remembered as a pleasant virtuous child who could be confided in; a kind, consistent, and industrious youth; assisting his father on the farm; in the district school esteemed by his mates, and showing a love of study, with an active vigorous mind; a good reader, and a fine proficient in arithmetic; avoiding contention; cautious in speaking of the faults of others; and having the friendship and confidence of all who knew him, when, at the close of 1804, he had reached the age of nearly eighteen.

The period in the religious history of our country was eventful, and struck its lines deep into the char-

"Justin Edwards, son of Noah, married Elizabeth Clark in 1778. He removed to Westhampton, where his wife died, December 6, 1792; and he married Mary Bartlet, January 1, 1795, a niece of Phebe Bartlet, whose early history is given in President Edwards' work on Revivals. He died October 6, 1816, aged sixty-four. His children by the first wife were Dotia, Jesse, Justin, (Rev. Dr. Edwards,) and Elizabeth; and by the second, Sarah, who died in infancy, Mary, and William.

"Samuel Edwards, born in 1716, brother of Noah, was the grandfather of the late Rev. Professor Bela B. Edwards.

"The ancestors of Rev. Dr. Justin Edwards were all farmers, industrious men, neither rich nor poor, and nearly all of them, male and female, were members of the church, and they were all persons of good character. I remember Justin Edwards, senior, of Westhampton. He was a quiet farmer that minded his own business, a man of few words, and perfectly honest.

"SYLVESTER JUDD.

"NORTHAMPTON, February 6, 1854."

acter and history of this worthy youth. As the triumphs of the gospel in the seventeenth century, in the days of Bunyan, Baxter, and Flavel, had been followed—partly through the blighting influence of the Act of Uniformity, which for twenty-five years banished from their pulpits near two thousand godly pastors—by a half century of spiritual dearth, when God again poured out his Spirit, both on the mother country and our own, in the days of Whitefield, Wesley, Lady Huntington, President Edwards, Brainerd, and the Tennents, about the year 1740; so, before the close of another half century, this later glorious work of God was succeeded by prevalent declension. These devoted servants of Christ had rested from their labors; men of zeal without knowledge had put a rash hand to the ark; our seven years' war of the Revolution, with its desolating moral effects, had intervened; French Infidelity had entered into high places, and threatened to pervade the community; the life-giving influences of the Spirit had been withdrawn; the greater part of our churches had sunk into formalism; in many of them the necessity of being born again by the renewing of the Spirit was overlooked; and men without prayer, without faith, or love, claimed admission to gospel ordinances on the so-called "half-way covenant" system, reserving to themselves the right of celebrating, or neglecting the Lord's supper at their own pleasure.

The church at Westhampton, through the period of the childhood and youth of the subject of this memoir, felt this unhappy, pervading influence: essentially evangelical in doctrine, but without revivals, without meetings for social prayer; vital piety, on the one hand, not being contemned, and on the other, not regarded as a prerequisite to membership. Sixty or seventy years had elapsed since President Edwards was laboring amid showers of mercy at Northampton; and preached the sermons constituting his "History of Redemption," and wrote his immortal treatises on Revivals. A majority of his own congregation, as early as 1750, undervaluing the richest gifts of divine grace, had effected his removal; and darkness and spiritual dearth again lamentably prevailed.

Yet the savor of the genuine work of God about 1740 remained in many churches; and multitudes of God's chosen ones were walking worthy of their high calling. At that day many an eye dimmed with age brightened, and many a furrowed countenance glowed with new life, in the recital of well-remembered scenes, when the thunders of Sinai, and the moving accents of the Saviour's love fell from the lips of Whitefield, or President Edwards, who had long since joined the assembly of the first-born in heaven.

In the wonderful providence of God, the death of one of these aged worthies was the means of life to the subject of this memoir. Those familiar with President Edwards' "Narrative of the surprising Work of God in Northampton," remember the prominence he gives to the narrative of "Phebe Bartlet," a dear child five years old, whom he could not but regard as savingly converted to God. She was born in March, 1731, adorned the gospel of Christ to advanced years, and in December, 1804, at the age of nearly seventy-four, went, with her pious husband, Mr. Noah Parsons, who was then nearly or entirely blind, to spend a few days with her son in Westhampton, who was a near neighbor of Mr. Justin Edwards. There she was taken sick, and died January 5, 1805. Young Justin kindly assisted in ministering to the wants of these aged servants of Christ; and as he heard their heavenly conversation, and saw the dying woman calmly trusting in her Saviour—willing to live, or go to be with Him, as should be his holy will—and saw the divine supports that sustained the bereaved and lonely husband, he said to himself, Here is a religion that I have not, and that I must have. For many weeks he said nothing to any one of his religious feelings; he betook himself to the faithful study of the word of God and to prayer, and at length believed that he had been enabled to cast himself on Christ as his only and all-sufficient portion. Thus he was one of the fruits, through the power and grace of Him "who worketh all things after the counsel of his own will," of "The Great Awakening of 1740."

But another heavenly influence was to come in to form his religious character. The great revival of the work of God which commenced about the year 1800, which exploded from all our evangelical churches the subterfuge of the "half-way covenant," and *gave rise to the missionary movements of the age*, was already working in many churches, not only at the north, but at the south in connection with the labors of Dr. Archibald Alexander and others, and extending westward, with calm but majestic power, characterized by a depth and thoroughness which caused the most incredulous to acknowledge, "This is the work of God." The "Connecticut Evangelical Magazine," issued at Hartford, which heralded the progress of this work, was widely circulated; Southampton was visited by the special influences of the Spirit; and soon the blessing fell on Westhampton. The pastor and members of the church were quickened; many mourned the low state into which they had fallen; and young Edwards gave joy to their hearts by relating, to the godly and the impenitent around him, what he hoped God had done for his own soul. He soon began to seek the salvation of others, and took part in religious meetings, including meetings of the young.

About this time he commenced teaching the centre school in Westhampton, which he daily opened and closed with prayer, and in which an unusual religious interest appeared. Calmly addressing the school one morning on their eternal interests, he found that sighs and sobs were pervading the room; and the pastor was sent for, to come in and address the school and pray with them. These facts were heard with wonder by the people; God was indeed among them by his Spirit, and "forty or fifty" were added to the church on the profession of their faith. A Christian lady, who about this time was visiting her friends in Westhampton, well remembers that "much was said of his extraordinary performances in the meetings for prayer and religious conference;" and to the questions, "When was he converted? How long has he been a Christian?" she heard the reply, "He has always been good—I think he was sanctified from his birth." She adds, "There was a great desire to see and hear him at the meetings; and *his mother's prayers* were often mentioned."

In April, 1806, about fifteen months after he witnessed the happy death of her that was Phebe Bartlet, we find he has solemnly consecrated himself to the service of his Redeemer—a service to which, for forty-seven years, he devoted his ceaseless energies, till it was said of him, "Blessed are the dead . . . . for *they rest.*" He had already placed himself under the instruction of his kind and worthy pastor, the Rev. Enoch Hale, an accurate scholar, who ministered to that church for fifty years from its formation in 1779, and who died among them in 1837 at the advanced age of eighty-three.

In this month we have the first record from his pen, in a small book of memoranda, and with it the following document written and subscribed by him.

"ETERNAL AND GLORIOUS JEHOVAH—Wilt thou permit me, who am a sinful worm of the dust, to present myself before thee, and enable me by thy grace, with the deepest humiliation, self-abasement, and contrition of soul, to surrender myself to thee, both soul and body, which is my most reasonable service. Through Christ Jesus, thy dear Son, who willingly laid down his life for sinners, and relying solely on his atonement and intercession, O enable me by faith to take hold of the new covenant of grace, and give myself up to thee, and cheerfully, sincerely, and unreservedly to consecrate all I am and all I have, faculties of both body and mind, to thy service; and may I be enabled by thy grace to renounce the world, with all its prospects, allurements, and vanities, to place no dependence upon them, and humbly accept of the *Lord Jehovah*, the ever blessed God,

Father, Son, and Holy Ghost, for my only hope and portion, both in this life and that which is to come.

"May I be sensible what a being Thou art, and know the way in which sinners may find mercy and acceptance in thy sight. Enable me to embrace Christ Jesus as he is offered in the gospel, and place my soul's immortal hope in Him, who is alone able to save. O wash my soul in the fountain of his blood, and interest me in thy covenant, ordered in all things, and sure. Use me as an instrument in thy hand of upbuilding the Redeemer's kingdom and advancing thy glory. May I now renewedly resolve, by thy grace, to live as becometh the gospel of Christ, sensible that I am not at home here in the body. And wilt thou clothe my naked soul with the righteousness of Christ, sanctify me by thy Spirit, and may I be united to the blessed Saviour as the branch is united unto the vine. May I not depend on my own strength, but on thy grace, by which alone I shall be enabled to perform my solemn vows. O, save me from the destroying sin of hypocrisy, and enable me to know my own heart; and wilt thou search and try me, and lead me in the way everlasting.

"Ever direct me in the way of duty; and when the all-trying hour of death shall come, whether sooner or later, O may I be found ready, with my loins girt about, my lamp trimmed and burning, and, through thy boundless grace in the Saviour, be received to thy heavenly kingdom, where thy saints worship thee with perfect and upright hearts.

"J. E. April 24, 1806."

The little book of memoranda referred to contains first a list of works read for one year, twenty-three in number, all religious, and most of them highly spiritual, including Baxter's Reformed Pastor, the Life of Brainerd, Backus on Regeneration, Doddridge's Rise and Progress, Edwards on the Affections, Fuller's Gospel its Own Witness, Willison on the Lord's Supper, West and Littleton on the Resurrection, and kindred works, with one of systematic theology. Such reading he continued diligently throughout the whole course of his literary and theological studies; and it is well known, that through life he took an active part in the wide diffusion of such religious works. The memoranda comprise also a record of all the sermons he heard during the year, the classical studies he pursued, and a few current incidents, among which are the following:

"April 1, 1806. I yesterday commenced studying Latin."

"April 27. I this day enter upon the twentieth year of my age. Nineteen years of my mortal life are gone, and how little of the great business of life has been performed!"

"May 4. Thirty-one persons were this day added to the church of Christ in Westhampton."

"May 10. Began to study Virgil."

"Aug. 22. Began the Greek Testament."

"May 18, 1807. Commenced the study of Hebrew."

"Oct. 3. Ended my studies with Rev. Mr. Hale."

"Oct. 8. Was examined and admitted into the Sophomore class in Williams college."

His father not only was unable consistently to support him in acquiring his education, but had a desire to retain him at home as the support of his own advancing years. His parents furnished his clothing, no small part of it made by the hands of his mother and sister, but for his pecuniary expenses he was mainly thrown upon his own resources. A memorandum gives these as $38 expended in the preparatory course, and $287 in college ; $55 70 as received from his father, and the remainder he paid chiefly by teaching, at intervals during the progress of his classical studies, and after their close. He often walked forty miles, from Westhampton to Williamstown, or returning, and so vigorous was his health, and so buoyant his spirits in view of the object before him, that he scarcely thought of its being a burden.

In the winter vacation of his first year in college, we find he was teaching in Easthampton; the succeeding winter, in Holliston, Mass.; and many are the evidences of the high estimation in which he was held by his pupils and their parents, and the pastors whose hands he strengthened by his consistent Christian deportment and influence.

In January, 1808, we find a letter of melancholy interest addressed to him by his class-mate, the late early fallen and lamented William H. Maynard, of the bar and senate of New York; Edwards and he having been regarded as holding the first standing in the class, and of course rivals for the highest honors. Maynard was then teaching in Plainfield, Mass., where he fitted for college with the Rev. Moses Hallock, whose hospitable abode was sometimes a half-way house for Edwards, as he walked to and from college. Maynard writes him a friendly letter, withal proposing that they should room together on their return to college; and though Maynard professed no special interest in religion, yet as he believed it would be gratifying to Edwards, he gives him, much as a minister might have done, in a page and a half of closely written foolscap, a minute description of a powerful revival of religion then enjoyed in Plainfield, describing the operation and fruits of the Spirit, and particular cases of decided conversion, though making no allusion whatever to the state of his own soul.

In college, he was a cheerful, intelligent, consistent Christian, universally respected and esteemed; but he was so constantly pressing forward his studies, his bodily frame being so energetic and his health so perfect as seemingly to require neither exercise nor relaxation, that the intimacies he formed were few. We have no letter from his pen written during his college course. His list of *books read* is continued, and shows a wide range of subjects; and he doubtless urged on his reading and studies, no less when he was absent in teaching, than when within the college halls. Besides all the studies and exercises of the three years' course, he read about two hundred volumes, embracing, beyond the range of strictly religious, devotional works, Lord Bacon's Essays, Newton on Prophecy, Prideaux and Shuckford's Connections, Locke on the Human Understanding, Robinson's Charles V. and America, Marshall's Life of Washington, Mavor's Universal History, Hume and

Gibbon, Reid and Stewart on the Mind, Edwards on the Will, Milner's Church History, Porteus' Lectures, Paley's Natural and Moral Philosophy, Butler's Analogy, Jews' Letters to Voltaire, Montesquieu's Spirit of Laws, Blackstone's Commentaries, Junius, Addison's, Franklin's, and Priestley's works, etc.

The orations and treatises he delivered or read in college, show also that his mind was not limited to a single range of subjects. Among the topics discussed, are the wonders of the human soul, whether certain crimes ought to be punished with death, love of country, instructions to representatives in Congress, the measures of the then existing political administration, the union of ecclesiastical and civil power, hereditary and elective monarchy contrasted, evidences of a divine Providence in the affairs of men, the work of redemption the greatest and most wonderful of the works of God, a funeral oration on the death of a class-mate, and the valedictory oration on the *Signs of the Times*, for he graduated with the highest honors of his class, September 5, 1810.

The "signs of the times" were indeed then portentous. Napoleon Buonaparte was subjugating kingdoms at his will; our country was on the eve of war with Great Britain; every man's heart quaked with terror; yet the speaker points to the great missionary movements of the age, and the promises of God, as indications that the world's redemption drew nigh.

Feeling the obligation to repay the money he had borrowed for his college course, he again devoted some months to teaching, in Athens, in the state of

New York, and, March 11, 1811, joined the theological seminary at Andover.

The same work of the Holy Spirit, beginning about the year 1800, which had reached the heart of young Edwards in Westhampton, and had produced glorious fruits in Western Massachusetts and Connecticut, of which the Rev. Dr. Griffin said, "I could stand at the door of my house in New Hartford, Connecticut, and count sixty churches laid down in one field of divine wonders," had also reached Eastern Massachusetts, where deadness and spiritual dearth had long and lamentably prevailed. The university at Cambridge, with its professor of theology, had gone over to the open denial of the divinity of Christ; in the city of Boston, only one of the Congregational churches, the "Old South," maintained the doctrines of the cross, and men of God were moved to found the Andover seminary, as a rampart for the truth. Its orthodoxy was so offensive, like that of the seminary at Geneva, under Dr. Merle D'Aubigné and Gaussen; or the burning zeal of Whitefield and his associates, about the year 1740, both in Old and New England; or of the Haldanes in Scotland, that the Legislature of the state of Massachusetts long hesitated to grant it the power of holding sufficient funds; it being placed under the direction of the trustees of Phillips' academy and a board of visitors. The day was one of trial. Churches were separating themselves from each other on the great doctrines centering in the supreme divinity of our Lord and Redeemer; and many were coming out, erecting new churches, and supporting themselves as separate organizations.

The professor of rhetoric elected at the organization of the seminary was the Rev. Dr. Griffin, who unsheathed the sword of truth, and wielded it with mighty power, as he had done for ten years previous, amidst wonderful displays of divine grace ; and when he was transferred to Boston, where he delivered his celebrated "Park-street Lectures," he was succeeded in the seminary by the Rev. Dr. Ebenezer Porter, who came also from the midst of the great revivals in Connecticut, and with his hallowed piety, and beautifully consistent and prayerful life, proclaimed Christ crucified with trumpet tongue, till he rested from his earthly labors. The other professors had devoted their lives to the seminary with kindred views.

In the interior of the seminary, the influence of the revival of the work of God was also manifest in the hallowed missionary spirit. Samuel J. Mills, Gordon Hall, and James Richards, all the fruits of that outpouring of the Spirit, were familiar associates of Edwards in Williams college. They had there privately consecrated themselves personally to foreign missions, and of them, with a few others, Dr. Griffin says, "On the banks of the Hoosac, under the haystacks, these young Elijahs prayed into existence the embryo of foreign missions." Arriving at Andover, Edwards rejoined these missionary pioneers, with Dr. Judson, late of Burmah, and Nott and Newell, who were the six men, as representatives of whom four of their number publicly offered themselves to the General Association of Massachusetts to go personally to the heathen, if means could be provided for their support, which was the commencement of the foreign missionary movement in this country. The heart of Edwards beat warmly with theirs; he united in their prayers and counsels, which embraced not only foreign missions, but plans for supplying our own new settlements, and western and southern frontiers. But before he had decided the question whether himself to go to the heathen, or to the remote destitute in our own country, divine Providence evidently called him to not less arduous labors in the field immediately around him. He was ardently attached to the missionary enterprise; he ever gave it his prayerful counsels and his faithful personal support; and his plans of usefulness through life had a reach as wide as the ruins of the fall.

In the seminary, he pursued his studies and prosecuted his reading with the same quenchless zeal as in college; and though at proper times, and especially in intimate discussions with his fellow-students, the late Rev. Professors Olds and Dutton, Dr. Timothy Woodbridge, and others, he broke many a friendly lance on the knotty and recondite points of divinity, yet the characteristic of his theological course, as of his future life, was, that he made THE BIBLE, in its plain, practical, and obvious import, his great textbook. In the public exercises of the seminary; in the Wednesday evening conference, when the professors and students met, and conversed freely on subjects of personal religion, and the practical duties and responsibilities of the ministry; in the devotional meetings of the students; in a weekly prayer-meeting at the centre of the town, where he frequently led in prayer and spoke of Christ and his salvation; in meetings in the neighboring towns, as there was opportunity; and in social intercourse with his brethren, he manifested a depth of piety, maturity of judgment, wisdom, and discretion, that won confidence, and indicated that God was preparing him for extensive usefulness in the church.

Not many months had elapsed, when the venerable Samuel Abbot, Esq., of Andover, the first of the princely donors who laid the foundations of the seminary, had fixed his eye on Edwards, in whom both he and Mrs. Abbot soon became deeply interested, and their endeared attachment to him was sundered only by death. The church in Andover, to which the venerable Rev. Samuel Phillips had ministered almost sixty years from its formation in 1711, and then the Rev. Jonathan French almost thirty-seven years, had now been nearly three years destitute of a pastor; and though for a considerable period the "half-way covenant" system had in this church been laid aside, those wishing to join, whose lives were inoffensive, and especially if they had family worship, were admitted without insisting on evidence of a vital union with Christ by faith; and a revival of religion like those in the days of President Edwards, and those which had already marked the beginning of this century, is not known to have been there enjoyed. A somewhat serious division was existing in the congregation, turning on the vital points of evangelical truth, and from time to time the pulpit had recently been supplied by men "denying the Lord that bought us." Mr. Abbot and others were alarmed for the interests of the congregation; and after becoming satisfied of the qualifications of Mr. Edwards, the wish was expressed to him, that he should leave the seminary, though scarcely half through the regular course, assume the charge of a congregation of not far from 2,000 souls, scattered over a large territory; attempt to heal their divisions; and all with the expectation that his revered instructors and his fellow-students would be among his constant hearers. The attachment of the evangelical part of the congregation increased; the more they knew and heard him, the warmer was their love; the professors, fearing the consequences if he denied their request, gave their unanimous consent; the students concurred in what they believed so wise a choice; and the young man was pressed above measure to know what truly were the "indications of Providence," which then and ever he sought to follow, with no contravening will of his own.

Having been licensed to preach, May 12, 1812, and the committee for supplying the pulpit having made some overtures with reference to a call, he wrote them the following letter, addressed to "Deacon Daniel Poor, chairman of the committee for supplying the pulpit in the south parish in Andover:"

"ANDOVER, June 29, 1812.

"DEAR SIR—It is undoubtedly the duty of every person, to pursue that course of conduct which will best advance the glory of God and the good of mankind; and the person whose heart is right, will resolve to follow the path of duty, wherever it may go. But where the path of duty leads, or what course of conduct will on the whole best advance the glory of God and the good of mankind, is a question sometimes difficult to decide. Upon this subject, as well as all others, every person stands in need of divine guidance and direction.

"God sees fit to leave the path of duty sometimes doubtful, that we may be sensible of our dependence, and that we need divine guidance, as well as divine support. This is especially the case with a minister of the gospel in this land at the present day, *when there are hundreds of churches which once had pastors, but now are destitute;* thousands of new settlements which never statedly enjoyed the ordinances of the gospel, and are literally starving for the bread of life. When there are thousands of heathen on our borders, millions in America, and hundreds of millions in other parts of the world, whose souls are as precious, and who need salvation as much as our friends and acquaintance, it is not easy for a minister to decide where he must labor, in order to do the most good. He must therefore seek for divine direction, and follow the indications of Providence. But a minister, in order to be useful and faithful to the souls of men in any place, needs much preparation. He must be a scribe well instructed into things which pertain to the kingdom of God; must be well acquainted with the Bible, with the character of man, and the way of salvation which he must preach to others. And at this day, when iniquity is coming in like a flood; when the Christian world is divided, both with respect to the character of God, and the character of man; when our American churches are rent into parties, and the watchmen do not see eye to eye, but preach different ways of salvation; and when there is and can be but one way of life, and that so strait and narrow, that our Saviour said, 'Few there be that find it;' it is especially necessary that a minister be well acquainted with divine truth, with the character of man, and the plan of salvation through a Redeemer.

"It has therefore been a question which has rested with great weight on my mind, since I engaged to preach in this place, whether I ought to go into the ministry immediately, or spend a longer time in preparation. But as I am a mere child in theology, and have lately begun to study it in a manner which I hope will be important to the church and the world, I think it my duty to pursue the course for the present, and spend a longer time in study, before I settle in the ministry. I therefore request that nothing be done towards giving me a call to settle in this place.

"But viewing your highly important situation in the church, the long time you have been without a minister, and the evils to which a people in this situation are always exposed; remembering also the kindness, respect, and affection, with which I have been treated while among you, and your ardent desires to obtain a minister of the gospel, my heart beats with emotion which can be felt, but never described. And I hope that I can join with you in looking to the great Head of the church, that you may have a faithful minister sent among you, one in whom your hearts can be united; who shall know the way of life, have an ardent love for souls, and who shall watch for them as one who expects to render an account; who shall be a rich blessing for a long time to come, and at last meet you and your children on the right hand of Christ.

'With great respect and esteem,

"Your brother in Christ,

"J. EDWARDS."

Notwithstanding the reception of the above letter, the church, on the 24th of July, gave him a call by a vote of "49, and 3 neuter," and on the 10th of August the parish united in it by a vote of "163, and 19 in the negative." A letter to him, September 1, from a deacon of the church, says, "It is impossible to conceive the evils which would probably result from a negative. While we wish your mind to be at liberty to weigh the important subject in all its bearings, we cannot refrain from expressing our own convictions, that the almost unanimous call of this church and society, so long distracted and in danger of dissolution, must be considered as the call of heaven." The following shows his acceptance of their call; and he was ordained and installed pastor on the 2d of December.

"ANDOVER, Oct. 3, 1812.

"To the Church and Society in the south parish of Andover:

"DEAR BRETHREN AND FRIENDS—The invitation which you gave me, to settle with you in the work of the gospel ministry, has been a subject of serious consideration. Although I had not intended to settle in any place at present, yet so unanimous a call, in so favorable circumstances, and from so important a society, could not but demand the most serious attention. I have therefore viewed the subject in its various bearings and relations, have consulted with friends of Christ in this and other parts of the country, and have often implored divine guidance and direction.

"After the most careful inquiry concerning the will of God, I have concluded to accept your invitation, and to labor for you, and for Christ, in this part of his vineyard. But on account of my present state of health, and the very short time which I have had to prepare for the ministry, I must accept your invitation under the following condition, namely, that I shall have opportunity to devote myself to study until the month of April.

"Brethren, I commend you and myself unto God, beseeching him that the consequences of this decision may be such as he shall approve, such as we shall review with pleasure in this life, and with unspeakable joy in the life to come.

"I ask also an interest in your prayers, that I may have the presence of God, the assistance of his Spirit, and a single eye to his glory; that I may feel the worth of souls, and watch for them as one who expects to render an account; that I may be faithful unto death, and at last meet you and your children on the right hand of Christ.

"With abiding affection,

"Yours, in the Lord,

"J. EDWARDS."

Ladies of the congregation having presented him garments which they deemed appropriate for the installation, he thus acknowledged their kindness.

"Feeling myself under peculiar obligations, I cheerfully express my warmest gratitude to the benevolent females who have manifested their kindness and liberality, in presenting me suitable garments for the ordination and other public occasions.

"I receive them as a new token of that kindness and respect which I have so frequently experienced since my residence in Andover. Although I came to this place a stranger, and expected to leave it in that character, yet that Being who should always be our director, appears at present to determine otherwise. And while I view the events of his providence, it kindles peculiar emotions to see him providing me, notwithstanding all my unworthiness, such a number of friends. And it affords great satisfaction to reflect, that although I may not be able to reward them for all their kindness, yet if it is the fruit of that disposition which charity hopes and the Saviour requires, it will meet an abundant reward.

"Knowing it to be necessary that all be provided with suitable garments, I have observed with the deepest regret that many appear to be destitute. They are provided with a suitable garment for the ordination, and such public occasions; but you recollect we are soon to assemble on another occasion, called 'the marriage supper of the Lamb,' where there will be a very large assembly not only of our friends and connections and the people in this vicinity, but all of every kindred and tongue and people and nation under heaven. For this important occasion many have no garment, and as they have only a few days to provide one, I fear they never will obtain it. Having had evidence of your kindness and liberality, I am encouraged to request you to afford them your united assistance. The garment for this occasion is peculiar, and is called the 'righteousness of Christ;' and he is the only person in the universe who can provide it. Viewing the distress and anguish which all will be in who are not clothed with this garment, he has kindly provided enough for us all. They are now all completed and deposited in Emmanuel's wardrobe, but they are so costly and valuable that not one can ever be purchased. The only way for a person to obtain one, is to feel his need of it; be sensible that he is altogether unworthy to receive it, and without it is undone; and in the character of a suppliant make application to Christ. But as this garment is worn only by a few, and is at present unfashionable, those who are destitute feel no need of it, and make no exertion to obtain it. This renders their case doubly distressing; for so long as they remain ignorant of their need, so long they will remain destitute of a garment for the great day.

"I therefore entreat you, dear friends, to compassionate their case, and propose that we all make a united application to Christ for them. And as the greater the number who at the same time make application, the greater will be the prospect of success, let us invite our friends and neighbors and acquaintances to join in the request. Although it be not necessary that a number be in the same place, yet it is desirable, and will increase the prospect of success, for all to make application at the same time and for the same object. I therefore propose that the time, or a part of it, between the hours of eight and nine, on Saturday evening, unless some other time be thought more convenient, be weekly and sacredly devoted to this benevolent object; that all who have a heart to feel, or a tongue to pray, may at the same time unite in fervent supplications to the Friend of sinners, that He would have compassion upon them, and lead them to see their condition while there is hope, and make application to Him before it be for ever too late; that He would give them repentance to salvation, and clothe them with the robe of his righteousness, which shall fit them to enter the gates of life, and sit down with his redeemed at the marriage-supper of the Lamb.

"The course here proposed is one that has been pursued with glorious success by multitudes who have gone before us, and we have the most abundant encouragement to follow their example. Should a single individual obtain a garment for the great day in consequence of our endeavors, we shall perform an act of charity which heaven will approve; and should the hand which procures the favor at present be concealed, eternity will acknowledge the deed."

CHAPTER II.

HIS MINISTRY IN ANDOVER.

FIRST FIVE YEARS, 1812—1817.

In a few transient leaves of memoranda of pastoral visits and other daily engagements at the commencement of his ministry, we find the following:

"December 2, 1812—Was this day examined and ordained by an ecclesiastical council from this vicinity, consisting of thirteen clergymen and twenty-one laymen. Oh, how amazing the responsibility of watching for souls. O Immanuel, may thy grace be sufficient for me, and thy strength be made perfect in weakness. Grant me, O Lord, an ardent love to thee and to the souls of men; and glorify thyself in multiplying trophies of redeeming mercy, and saving the souls of sinners in this place. May I live to glorify, and be prepared with all thy redeemed to enjoy thee for ever. O thou everlasting Jehovah, make me wise as a serpent and harmless as a dove. Teach me so to number my days that I may apply my heart unto wisdom. Guide me by thy counsel, and afterwards receive me to glory through Jesus Christ. Amen."

On the succeeding Sabbath, December 6, in the opening of the first sermon addressed to his people as their pastor, from the text, "*Preach the gospel,*" he said to them:

"The connection which God in his providence has formed between you and me by the transactions of the last week, bears a solemn and immediate relation to the welfare of the soul and to eternity. It will deeply affect our happiness, both here and hereafter. It involves consequences which will go with us through life, surround us at death, attend us to the judgment, and encircle us through eternity. Were it to affect us only in this life, or only for a thousand, or ten thousand years, it would be as nothing. But on the consequences of this connection I see inscribed, FOR EVER, FOR EVER.

"Multitudes who will outlive the sun, who are heirs of endless existence, and will spend it, rising for ever in the world of life, or sinking for ever in the world of death, are committed to the watchman's charge. How overwhelming the responsibility! To watch for souls, sound the trumpet of alarm, and beseech them to awake from the slumber of death; uncover the world of darkness; show the region of light; exhibit their danger, and point out the way and the motives to escape it; to beseech fellow-men to be reconciled unto God, when the message will be a savor of life unto life, or of death unto death, to all who hear it; to be an ambassador of God commissioned to negotiate with men about the honors of heaven and crowns of unfading glory, is a work too great for men, too great for angels; none but Christ is sufficient for it; and had He not said, 'Lo, I am with you always, even to the end of the world,' no minister would have any prospect of success. Without Christ, the strongest can do nothing; and with Christ, the weakest can do all things; for He says, 'My strength is made perfect in weakness.' Most gladly therefore will I rejoice in weakness, that the power of Christ may rest upon me. Had I the ardor of Paul, and the eloquence of Apollos; yea, more, had I the tongue of angels, and could speak in the dialect of eternity, it would accomplish nothing. In the salvation of souls, CHRIST AND HIS SPIRIT must do the work, and to Him be all the glory. Instead therefore of sinking in despair, or drawing back from the arduous work, I would rest on the arm of Jehovah, and inquire, 'Lord, what wilt thou have me to do?'"

Having shown the import of the divine command to "*preach the gospel*," the glad tidings of salvation, to men condemned to eternal death by the holy law of God: to preach "Christ the mediator of the new covenant, with all the glory of his Godhead, in the form of a servant offering himself to Justice as the meritorious ground of salvation; the Holy Spirit as the Being who creates anew in Christ Jesus and prepares the soul to enjoy this salvation; repentance, faith, and obedience as the only way to obtain it; and the glory of God and the good of men as the object for which it is given," he proceeds to say, "This exhibition of the author and finisher and subject and way and end of salvation, is all contained in THE BIBLE. This, by way of eminence, is 'the gospel,' which every minister is to 'preach.' It is the word of the Lord, to which we do well to take heed. It is a light given on purpose to shine in a dark place; and to guide all penitent believing souls through this wilderness to the heavenly rest. In the Bible the course of a minister's preaching is not only sketched, but clearly drawn by the pencil of inspiration; and the man or the angel who dares to alter it, is charged with rebellion against his Maker."

Proceeding with the discussion in successive discourses, he was guided from on high to lay down, at the outset of his ministry, the grand principle which was the key note of all his future instructions: "A MINISTER MUST PREACH THE DOCTRINES AND DUTIES OF THE BIBLE IN THEIR OWN INSPIRED CONNECTION. These doctrines and duties are all connected together, hold their proper place, and when viewed in their connection appear harmonious and consistent, divinely calculated to bring 'glory to God in the highest,' and salvation to the lost children of men. When a particular doctrine is taken out of its place, and viewed without its connection, it may appear inconsistent, and perhaps unreasonable; but in its proper place, and in its divinely inspired connection, the inconsistency is done away. The doctrines of the gospel all rest upon one foundation; they are connected together, and form one harmonious, consistent whole; but unless viewed in their connection, the consistency, harmony, fitness, and propriety which mark their divinity, cannot be seen. However much the true doctrines of the Bible may be opposed by the feelings of natural men, and however much they may hate them; yet if they were viewed in their connection, with that clearness with which all will behold them at the judgment, 'every mouth would be stopped, and the whole world become guilty before God.'"

He goes on to illustrate the principle by showing

the relations of great foundation truths of the gospel to each other—truths which, when understood by the man whose heart is opposed to God, may cause him, "without any handwriting upon the wall," to "quake like Belshazzar when weighed in the balance and found wanting;" but which to the humble, believing child of God, are a source of unspeakable joy.

He then proceeds to apply the subject by showing that every doctrine and every duty of the Bible which God has enjoined upon the minister, devolves a corresponding responsibility upon his people. If he must be a friend of God and love the truth he declares, so must they. If he must be acquainted with his own heart, so must they. If he must be constantly present to preach, so must they be to hear. If he must make the Bible, and not his own feelings, the standard of his preaching, so must they. If he must illustrate and enforce all its doctrines and duties, just as God has revealed them, because he has declared them to be "given by inspiration and profitable;" so must they for the same reason receive, love, and obey them. If he must live a life of prayer, so must they. If he must prayerfully study the Bible, and when he has learned what doctrines and precepts are contained there, must faithfully declare them; so must they "search the Scriptures," and reject no truth which God has revealed. If he must practice as well as preach, and manifest in his conduct that he has been with Christ, so must they in all things show a sacred and inviolable regard to duty. The great inquiry for pastor and people is, "What doth the Lord thy God require of thee?"

The following practical rules for the direction of his own life, which at his death were found in his handwriting in his pocket-book, and which he had evidently kept by him for a long course of years, seem to have been seriously regarded throughout the whole of his public career.

RULES OF LIFE.

"1. Act at all times as in the presence of God; and make it the great object, in all things to please him. In order to this,

"2. Seek first of all to gain clear views of his will, and with regard to all things to be perfectly conformed to it. And in doing this,

"3. Cherish no thoughts, indulge no feelings, speak no words, and do no actions, but what you really think, after all the light that you can gain, will most honor God, most benefit yourself and others, and give you the greatest joy when they come to be exhibited before the assembled universe at the judgment-day.

"4. Begin and end each day by a season of communion with God, and by a solemn and hearty commitment of yourself and all your interests, temporal and eternal, to his guidance, care, and disposal.

"5. Daily read with deep attention and fervent prayer a portion of the word of God, and for the purpose of understanding, believing, and obeying it.

"6. Never express or indulge the least degree of unkindness towards any human being, and give no needless pain to any of the human race, or any even of the animal creation.

"7. Make it your object to promote the greatest

happiness on the whole of all upon whom you may have influence, both of the present and of all future generations.

"8. Regard the hand of God in all the dispensations of his providence, and in whatsoever state he places you, therewith be content.

"9. Envy none who are above you, and despise none who are below you; but possess and manifest the utmost good will towards all men.

"10. Never speak of any, or feel towards them in a manner that you ought not to wish them, under similar circumstances, to speak or feel with regard to you.

"11. Let all statements and narrations be an exact exhibition of the real truth.

"12. Act for God, for the universe, and for eternity; and in such a manner as is adapted to promote the highest good for ever. In order to this,

"13. Look habitually to Jesus Christ; let your whole soul be imbued with his spirit, and manifest it in all your actions.

"14. Look to the Holy Ghost as the author of all good in man; seek habitually his teaching, his illuminating and purifying influences; and that he may dwell in you as his temple, and take full possession of all your powers and talents for himself.

"15. Earnestly desire that he would take of the things of Christ and more and more show them unto you; and carefully avoid every thing which tends to hinder you from becoming perfectly like him.

"16. Make it as your meat and drink to do the will of God, and perseveringly have respect to all his commandments.

"17. Feel and acknowledge that all the good that you ever have received, that you now receive, or ever will receive, is of grace through Jesus Christ; trust in him for all which you need, both for this life and the life to come; rely on his merits, imitate his example, and in view of every blessing give Him and the Father and the Holy Ghost all the glory."

Having assumed the high responsibilities of a pastoral charge embracing not far from two thousand souls, chiefly a farming community, spread over a territory about eight miles by four in extent,* with no other church organization within its bounds; the people all looking to him as the pastor, not only to sustain the public ministrations of the Lord's house, but to visit them at their own abodes, and be with them in sorrow and in joy; he entered on the fulfilment of these sacred duties with an impulse and energy doubtless kindled from on high. To every soul, whether of the rich or the poor, from the most aged trembling under the weight of years, down to the little child, he felt that he was "debtor;" and he was enabled to pursue his ministerial work with a fidelity, Christian discretion, and adaptation to the wants of all, that concentrated upon him their respect, affection, and confidence; and showed that he had been endued with preëminent qualifications to "feed the church of God which he hath purchased with his own blood."

* Andover lies twenty miles north of Boston, and nearly at the same distance from Salem and Newburyport. It is on the direct road from Boston to the capital of New Hampshire, and is now penetrated by the Boston and Maine railroad. The present population of the town is upwards of seven thousand.

Except brief memoranda of the engagements of each day for three short periods, he made no record of his abundant labors throughout his pastoral life; evidently "having respect unto the recompense of the reward," when he should give an account of his stewardship; and too intent on the duties of each passing day and hour to have time or strength to write what they were, or how they were performed. But there are enduring records in the grateful, glowing hearts of many of his surviving people, in the historic facts of divisions healed; opposition to "the truth as it is in Jesus" allayed; a slumbering people spiritually aroused; intemperance removed; the Sabbath honored; the sanctuary filled with solemn worshippers; the family altar erected; the Sabbath-schools; the Bible-classes; the organizations among male and female, old and young, for the reformation of morals and "doing good;" the pervading heavenly influence which rested on a great congregation, multitudes of whom are now, with their honored and beloved pastor, together casting their crowns before the throne of God and the Lamb.

The transient memoranda commenced on the day of his installation, December 2, 1812, were continued for three months to March 4, 1813, noticing what families he visited, and how he was employed in the morning, in the afternoon, and often in the evening of each day. These notices show a surprising amount of pastoral labor, the number of families visited being frequently ten or fifteen in a day, in many of which he "took the names of the children," who were his hope and the objects of his special care; and it was his custom throughout his ministry, in pastoral visits to read a short portion of Scripture, sometimes with explanations and singing a hymn, and to close the interview with prayer. Not one family within the limits of his congregation, however humble or obscure, or far from God, escaped his notice in his pastoral visits.

The memoranda contain repeated notices of supplying families with hymn-books, catechisms, and primers; of care for the young; of persons found anxious for their salvation; of families establishing family worship; of good seasons in the house of God; of visiting the sick; of conversing and praying in schools; of devising plans of usefulness; attending meetings for prayer, in one of which an hour of Saturday evening was set apart as a concert of private prayer for the influences of the Holy Spirit; notices of his studying particular portions of Scripture; reading the Hebrew Bible; conversing on the doctrine of the Trinity; meeting the deacons and planning for the good of souls; ejaculations to God to enable him to be faithful in visiting; of writing and preaching sermons, and similar varied and unwearied means of usefulness. To his people it seemed that he might justly say, in the language of the great apostle, "I have kept back nothing that was profitable unto you; but have showed you, and have taught you, publicly and from house to house; testifying both to the Jews, and also to the Greeks, repentance towards God and faith towards our Lord Jesus Christ."

His health soon became prostrated, and he was obliged to leave his charge for some time, and rest. It was probably of this period that he said in substance,

"My health had been so firm that I thought nothing could hurt me, and wishing to visit a young minister at C——, I started off and walked fifteen miles in a hot day. Getting very warm, I sat down in a cool place and took a cold which disabled me from preaching for months." Visiting Westhampton, his surviving elder sister, who had cared for him in childhood and youth and when pursuing classical study, remembers that he said to her, that when agitating the question of accepting the call to settle in Andover, the Rev. Dr. Austin, of Worcester, told him he would be manifestly going contrary to the will of divine Providence should he decline it; that on the morning of the installation he felt oppressed with a sense of the responsibilities he was about to assume; that often in the arduous and difficult position in which he was placed, when he looked at his own weakness and unworthiness, he felt that he should sink; but when he had the light of God's countenance and his holy, supporting presence, he hoped he did "a little good."

His deacons wrote him at Westhampton, stating the deep anxiety of his people, and that there were a number of cases of seriousness among them. The late deacon Isaac Abbot writes, "You, sir, mention that, could you see a revival of religion in Andover, and hear immortal souls inquiring, 'What must we do to be saved?' and see them fleeing from the wrath to come, and laying hold on eternal life, you should be almost well. These things, sir, you cannot see where you now are; but were you here, if only to visit and converse with the people, I have strong faith, trusting in the aid of the divine Spirit, that such a season you would behold. It was our communion last Sabbath; your address to the church and society was read, and received with great satisfaction. Our people all seem greatly rejoiced to hear from you, but would be much more so, could we see you."

While laboring for the best interests of his church and congregation, it soon became evident that God had placed him in a position where his influence was to be still more widely felt. Young men preparing for the ministry had till this time generally pursued their studies under the care of some divine who was faithfully engaged in the labors of a pastor; and those entering the walls of the Theological Seminary would fix their eyes on him, whose ministry they then attended; and the influence on them of his pastoral fidelity might extend to other churches, and even to heathen lands, to which many of them were destined.

He also, soon after his settlement, united with the Rev. Professors Porter, Woods, and Stuart, Mr. Adams, principal of the Academy, Mr. Farrar, treasurer, and Deacon Newman, a member of the board of trustees, in a weekly Monday evening meeting at Dr. Porter's study, *for devising plans of doing good and advancing the interests of the Redeemer's kingdom*, at home and abroad, in every practicable way. This meeting was continued many years. It was noiseless; but its aim was befitting the rising spirit of missions and other departments of benevolence which the great work of God at the beginning of the century had awakened; and their united prayers, counsels, and endeavors were evidently owned from on high in extensive good. Several of our excellent and cherished institutions and means of usefulness had their origin in, or were assisted and encouraged by the harmonious plans and counsels of this little meeting.

The earliest among these institutions was the "New England Tract Society," which at length was merged into the "American Tract Society," an enterprise of which Dr. Edwards, while pastor, was to have for several years the principal direction, and in which to bear high responsibilities through life. It was about the close of the year 1813, that the Rev. Dr. Porter was buying a little religious book, when it occurred to him, that a Tract Society would supply the community with better books at a far cheaper rate; and suggesting the idea to the little circle of his brethren, they took up the enterprise, made their own subscriptions, and set about obtaining collections for establishing it, which were responded to with such liberality in the principal towns in the vicinity, that they soon set presses in motion, and at the time of the public organization of the Society in Boston, May 23, 1814, no less than $3,830 had been subscribed, and $2,745 expended in issuing a series of fifty tracts, in all 297,000 copies. The printing and principal management till 1825 remained at Andover, though it had a dépôt of its publications in Boston, where its anniversaries were celebrated.

On the 20th of April, 1814, a highly efficient instrumentality, "THE ANDOVER SOUTH PARISH SOCIETY FOR THE REFORMATION OF MORALS," or "Doing Good," was organized by about seventy of the male members of the congregation: its object being to discountenance immorality, particularly Sabbath-breaking, intemperance, and profanity; and to promote industry, temperance, order, piety, and good morals. The Society met quarterly for mutual encouragement, and the pastor, who was chairman of their standing committee, gave his counsel and coöperation in all the objects before them, and for eleven successive years presented, at their annual meetings in September, an able public report or address. At their first anniversary he showed the power of associated counsels and action in discountenancing vice, and doing good; that the fathers who had united in the Society, seeing the destructive influence of the vices named, for this life and the life to come, had associated not only to benefit themselves and those around them, but to save *their children* from the corrupting influences that if not arrested must descend to them; and to do this especially by setting *a good example* themselves, and in the regulation of their own families. "As neighbors when they meet," said the address, "must have subjects of conversation, let them converse on the evils of prevailing immoralities, and the ease with which by united exertion they might be prevented." It stated that there were in the parish "*five hundred children*, whom they wished to train up in sobriety, temperance, industry, virtue, piety, and good morals, a generation for God, to be pillars in church and state when their fathers are in the grave, and who, when these heavens shall have passed away, shall through grace stand on mount Zion, crowned with immortal glory." All these children they wished to supply with suitable tracts and small books adapted to their age and wants; to throw a good moral and religious influence into all the district-schools; and by all suitable means "train them up in the nurture and admonition of the Lord."

At the next anniversary, September 13, 1815, the pastor, as chairman of the standing committee, presented a very cheering report.

At the first quarterly meeting, they had appointed their president, vice-president, and Mr. John Adams delegates to a county convention in Topsfield for preventing the profanation of the Lord's day, which the pastor attended and took part in the discussions. The object of this and similar movements in various parts of New England at this period, was especially to encourage a more faithful execution of the laws of the land, in furtherance of which Dr. Edwards wrote a petition to the legislature of the state.

At their second quarterly meeting they had appointed the Rev. Dr. Ebenezer Porter as preacher at their next anniversary, whose sermon was no other than his well-known splendid discourse, "Great Effects result from Little Causes," of which tens of thousands have been circulated by the American Tract Society as No. 74 of their series.

At their third quarterly meeting they had welcomed a new auxiliary in *one hundred and fifty females,* who had organized as the "Andover South Parish Female Charitable Society," and with their prayers and coöperation brought liberal funds to purchase books for the children.

In reviewing the year, the pastor, in behalf of the committee, stated that in reference to *profanity,* they had had little to do, for he said, "This enormous evil, which a few years ago was so prevalent, has almost ceased, except it be with a few of the most degraded, and we hope the time is approaching when this evil will be entirely done away."

"On the subject of *the Sabbath*, you need only appeal to the testimony of your own eyes, to see that the exertions of yourselves and others have been crowned with success. The alarming profanation of the Sabbath, which two years ago threatened to sweep every thing before it, and was thought to be incurable, has not only been arrested and greatly checked, partly through the coöperation given to civil officers, but apparently almost done away."

"As to *intemperance*, although some individuals are still reeling to and fro, and some families clothed in woe by this iniquity, yet the evil has been greatly lessened. A few years ago, $15,000 were expended in this town for ardent spirits in a year; $8,000 more than was paid for the support of the gospel, and of all the schools, highways, state and county taxes, and all other town expenses. The people the last year did not probably expend one third of that sum. Ardent spirits in the respectable part of the community are becoming unfashionable, and dispensed with in *social visits*. Many workmen are employed on condition of refraining from ardent spirits, and it is found that better men are secured, and that they do more business and in a better manner than before. The practice of taking wine at *funerals* is almost entirely abolished; and it begins to be understood that ardent spirits, except in special cases as a medicine, are not only entirely useless, but ruinous to the bodies and the souls of men."

"The 'Female Charitable Society' have prospered beyond their expectations. Here are one hundred and fifty females, feeling that their mercies have all been purchased by the blood of Christ, and associated to contribute annually to provide books for the children, as rewards for learning the catechism and good behavior; to furnish the destitute with Bibles and religious books, and to aid in supporting missions in this country and among the heathen. Never was there a more benevolent object than that in which they are engaged. Their benevolence begins at home, but embraces the world; not for time only, but through endless being."

He proceeds to report that small books had been procured as a circulating library for each of the seven district-schools; and that within the last four months 1,302 books, containing over 30,000 pages, had been reported as read; about two hundred children had learned one half, and one hundred and six the whole of the catechism, besides about two hundred hymns and numerous portions of Scripture. The results in each district are minutely reported; the improvement of the children in learning had been unusually great; and a gratifying progress was made towards reaching all the five hundred children whose welfare they were seeking.

"Look for a moment," he says, "at one soul, immortal and yet walking heedlessly over the bottomless pit. Like an angel of mercy, you hand him a little tract on the 'Loss of the soul.' He reads with wonder;

the eyes of his mind are enlightened; he sees himself on slippery places, and fiery billows are beneath him. Wretched, he casts himself on the blood of Jesus; and an arm of mercy from heaven snatches him as a brand from the burning, and he sings, 'Salvation, and glory, and honor to the Lord our God.' You have saved a soul from death and hid a multitude of sins. His influence, which before was leading others to destruction, is now guiding them to heaven. He comes to die. Surrounded with the light of heaven, his eye beams with hope; and his voice, though sinking in death, is raised in thanksgiving. He recommends his precious Redeemer to all around him, falls asleep in His arms, and wings his way; and a multitude which no man can number, press to the gate of heaven to shout his arrival. He ascends upon mount Zion, and joins the swelling song, 'Unto Him that loved us and gave himself for us.'"

These operations were efficiently continued from year to year; attention being gradually concentrated more and more on instructing the children in the truths of the Bible, and interesting them and others in the great benevolent movements of the age. At the anniversary in 1818, the pastor reported a new movement: it was no other than *the formation of a Sabbath-school!* in which one hundred and thirty-eight children met, in the interval of public worship, to recite portions of Scripture and receive instruction in the truths of the Bible. This event was hailed with great delight, and its benefits and promise of usefulness were dwelt upon, as showing that God was about to bless to children the truths of his word, and turn the hearts of multitudes of them to himself. In a few years more, *seven Sabbath-schools* were sustained in the several school-districts within the bounds of his large congregation, and most of the five hundred children were gathered into them.

As the donations of the charitable society and the children were distributed to almost all the principal benevolent institutions, the pastor availed himself of the annual meetings of this Society for Doing Good, to give full, and often minute and graphic information concerning the character and operations of the several institutions which they aided in our own and foreign lands; a course admirably calculated to enlarge the hearts of the little ones and others to feel for the moral wants and woes of the world.

His beloved foreign missionary brethren of the college and seminary continued to write him frequently. The Rev. Samuel J. Mills wrote from his father's, in Torringford, Connecticut, requesting him to spend the winter of 1815–16 in New Orleans, where was great need of missionary labor, and reporting a blessed revival of religion in a neighboring town; the Rev. Luther Rice wrote him both before and after sailing from Philadelphia for India; and the Rev. Gordon Hall often wrote, reporting the progress of the mission in Bombay.

In reference to *establishing in our land the monthly concert of prayer for foreign missions*, Dr. Edwards wrote the following, in the form of a circular letter.

To Rev. Dr. Ebenezer Fitch, President of Williams College.

"ANDOVER, January 13, 1815.

"REV. AND VERY DEAR SIR—While we as a nation are groaning under the judgments of heaven, and as a punishment for our iniquities appear to be sinking never again to rise, the friends of Zion in different parts of the country have expressed a wish that there might be a concert for prayer; that Christians of every age and denomination may at the same time unite in fervent supplications that the Lord would pour his Spirit upon us from on high; that he would sanctify the children and rising generation for himself, and extend the gospel with all its blessings through the world. In a word, to pray for a revival of pure and undefiled religion, the only thing which can possibly save our sinking country.

"The time proposed for the concert is the *first Monday evening of every month.* A concert for prayer on this evening has already been observed in Great Britain, Holland, Switzerland, Germany, the Christian settlements in Africa, New Holland, Asia, and other parts of the world. Could it now be extended throughout the United States, we should then unite with Christians, not only in this country but in numerous other countries, in supplicating the greatest blessings which God can bestow.

"Have we not reason to hope, sir, if such a union could be formed, that light would break forth upon us as the morning, and salvation as the noonday; that righteousness would go before us, and that the glory of the Lord would follow?

"Will you have the goodness, dear sir, to give us

your thoughts upon the subject, and also Professor Dewey, etc., as soon as may be. Should the plan meet the views of gentlemen of influence in different parts of the country, measures will be taken to extend the information as speedily and as widely as possible.

"We think of preparing a tract that may go into every family, perhaps President Edwards' work as abridged by Mr. Burder, and sending it through the United States.

"With sentiments of the highest regard,

"Most cordially yours,

"J. EDWARDS."

In October, 1815, an esteemed young lady of his church was married to the Rev. Horatio Bardwell, destined to the mission at Bombay, who sailed for India the same month, in company with Dr. Edwards' early friend Richards, and Rev. Messrs. Poor and Warren; the company receiving a solemn charge from her pastor, in the appropriate public services previous to their embarkation at Newburyport. Of her recollections of Dr. Edwards previous to her departure, she says,

"My impressions of his early ministry are still vivid. There existed at that time among the people more or less prejudice against the Theological Seminary, and many feared that the young pastor, fresh from that institution, would fail to secure the harmony of the church and society; but these fears were soon removed. He had peculiar excellences as a pastor and preacher. He was indefatigable, in season and out of season; preëminently an example of what a gospel minister may accomplish, even in an unpromising field, by diligent, persevering devotion to his work, and love for the spiritual interests of his flock. His hearers felt that he sought not theirs, but them. In the sanctuary, the prayer-meeting, the conference-room, and in more private family meetings, in which he always seemed greatly to delight, the universal impression made on the minds of his people, that he was a consistent, devoted minister of Christ, disarmed opposition. *The deep and solemn interest of one of these family meetings*, at which I was present in the early part of his labors, I can never forget.

"His prayers were peculiarly comprehensive and solemn, and in all his exercises his aim was to rivet the attention of his hearers, and fix truth upon the heart. He was both revered and loved by his people. I often heard the remark, 'Mr. Edwards can do just as he pleases.' His wishes were law, and the constraining influence of that law was love. The interest he manifested in children was great, and his labors for them abundant. All in all, perhaps there never was a more visible, happy change wrought in a church and society, than by the earnest, zealous efforts of this good man and minister."

Concurring in the above, the Rev. Mr. Bardwell further says, "As a minister of Christ, Dr. Edwards excelled, as all acknowledge, in the skilful handling of the word of God; he was 'mighty in the Scriptures.' The foundation of this eminence was laid in the early part of his ministry. I was in the seminary when he was installed, and heard most of his sermons for two years. These and all his extemporaneous performances in the pulpit, and in the conference and prayer-meeting, were strictly *biblical.* He made little display of his knowledge of the principles of technical exegesis; but honored the received version of the Bible, and encouraged his hearers to receive it as the oracles of God. He seemed to bear in mind the great truth, that the object before him was not to preach himself or any system of human device, but to explain and enforce *the gospel.* He abounded in quotations from the sacred volume, and his richest illustrations were drawn from Bible history. In the argumentative parts of his sermons, he oftener employed the language of the sacred writers, than of philosophy and of the schools; and in his appeals to the heart and conscience, he abounded in scriptural phraseology. His hearers could not fail to be impressed that the preacher honored *the Bible* as the word of God, and that it was the one great purpose of his heart to preach it.

"It was, I think, this uncommon measure of *Bible truth* in his early ministry, that gave him such power over his people. The aged felt it safe to confide in one who, though young in years, had so enriched his mind with heavenly wisdom. The children and the youth loved and reverenced him, not only because on his lips was the law of social kindness, but of scripture truth, which distilled like the gentle rain and the dew. He was eminently *a Bible man.* This, to my mind, was the secret of his power, that in which his great strength lay."

A prominent aim of the preaching to which Rev. Mr. Bardwell refers, was plainly and distinctly to show to all classes of hearers, that "except a man be *born again*, he cannot see the kingdom of God;" that "if any man have not *the Spirit of Christ*, he is none of His." Preaching from this latter text in 1814, he uttered the following heart-searching truths, in which the discerning reader will perceive many indications of the moral and religious state of things then existing.

"There is a great difference of opinion," he says, "as to what constitutes a Christian. Some suppose that being born in a Christian land, and educated under the light of the gospel, constitute a Christian. Others, that a man becomes a Christian by professing the Christian religion. Some suppose that living what is called an innocent and harmless life, and doing no hurt in the world, constitute a Christian. Others, that a man becomes a Christian by being diligent and enterprising in business, respectable in society, supporting civil and religious institutions, observing the Sabbath, and going the round of external duties. Some suppose that a mild, amiable temper, a great regard to the feelings of men, and a disposition always to please them, constitute a Christian; and others, that a man becomes a Christian by changing his outward conduct. Some suppose that believing that Jesus of Nazareth is the Christ, and that the Bible is a divine revelation, constitute a Christian; and others, that a man becomes a Christian by thinking that he is one.

"But all these are mistakes. Who, on a moment's reflection, does not know that a man may be born in a Christian land, and hear the preaching of the gospel, and yet not be a Christian? *Many* heard the preaching of Christ himself who were 'of their father the devil, and the lusts of their father they would do.' And it will be more tolerable for Tyre and Sidon, and for Sodom and Gomorrah, in the day of judgment, than for them.

"A man may profess religion; but who does not know that men are not *always* what they profess to be? Many profess Christ in words, while in works they deny him. They will say in that day, 'Have we not eaten and drunk in thy presence?' but He will say, 'I never knew you; depart from me, ye workers of iniquity.' A man may live what is called an innocent and harmless life, injure no one, and do no hurt in the world; but this does not make him a Christian. Christians do good. The man who simply does no hurt is an 'unprofitable servant.' He will be 'cast into outer darkness.' *Who gave him liberty* to hide his talent in a napkin, and simply do no hurt? A man may be diligent in business, honest in his dealings, useful to society, support civil and religious institutions, attend public worship on the Sabbath, and so far as men discover go the whole round of external duties; he may 'give his goods to feed the poor, and his body to be burned'—but *this does not constitute a Christian.* A man may do all this from supreme regard to himself. He may be diligent, to lay up for the body; be honest, because it is the best way to get rich; attend public worship, from a regard to reputation; give to the poor, to silence conscience, or purchase heaven; or sacrifice life, to be enrolled on the annals of fame. He may have a thousand motives to be moral, diligent, honest, and even draw near to God with his mouth, while his heart is far from Him; but 'the Lord looketh upon the heart;' 'he weigheth the spirits.'

"A man may believe that Jesus is the Christ, and that the Bible is a divine revelation. He may know it. But this does not make him a Christian. Multitudes of wicked men believe this. The time is coming when they will *all* believe it. They will hear the trump of the archangel; they will look up and see Jesus descending in flaming fire; thousands and tens of thousands will be round about him, and they will have no doubt of his being the Christ; but it will not make them Christians. They will 'cry to the rocks and mountains to fall on them.' A man may have all these things, and yet may still be an impenitent, unbelieving sinner.

"The Holy Ghost, as if with direct reference to this diversity of opinion, and to cut off all controversy upon the subject, declares with the plainness of eternal truth, 'If any man have not *the Spirit of Christ*, he is none of his.' A Christian is a man who has 'the Spirit of Christ.' This forms the dividing line between saints and sinners: a line which separates this assembly, and the whole human race, into two classes. Those who have the Spirit of Christ, of whatever age, profession, or name, are Christians: those who have not his Spirit, are none of his.

"The great truth revealed in the text is this: *If any man have not a temper of heart like that of Christ, he is not a Christian; and if any man have a temper of heart like that of Christ, he is a Christian.* This line separates all men into saints or sinners. My present object is, in a simple manner to show WHAT WAS THE TEMPER

OF CHRIST. Let every individual, as I pass along, compare it with his own, in order to determine whether he is a Christian or not.

"Christ had *a supreme regard to the glory of God and the good of his kingdom.* He would make any sacrifice to advance them. When necessary, he would sacrifice ease and comfort, and the respect and applause of men, houses, lands, kinsfolk, and friends; he would sacrifice his life. For this he left heaven, and came down to earth; for this he lived and toiled and mourned and wept and bled and died. While others lived and died for themselves, he lived and died for the glory of God and the good of his kingdom. Is this your object? There is some object for which you live and toil. Is it the glory of God? Does this occupy your hearts, and can you sacrifice a right hand or a right eye to promote it? Perhaps you cannot think of *standing alone* for the sake of advancing the glory of God and the good of his kingdom. If so, you have not the spirit of Christ. He was totally different. He was ready to *do something*, and to make sacrifices, whether others would or not. He stood in the gap. It was not necessary for him to go with the multitude, and have the world to support him. He had a bold independence which could stand alone. When the glory of God required, he fixed his face like a flint. He suffered trials, bore afflictions, endured hardships, encountered dangers. He was courageous. With eyes fixed on the glory of God and the good of his kingdom, he cast himself on infinite strength and broke through all opposition which stood in the path of duty, or opposed his progress in the way to heaven. He had no thought, in promoting the divine glory, that all others must do the same, or he neglect it. Whatever others did, his object was one. He lived and he died to advance it. Have you this spirit?

"Christ was guided in his feelings and conduct by *the will of God.* He came into the world not to do his own will, but the will of his Father. His meat and drink was, to 'do the will of Him that sent him, and to finish his work.' Whether he should take this course or that, was determined by the will of God. He did not inquire, Will others do it? what do men think? will it be easy, safe, or popular? but, Is it the will of God? If so, his course was fixed. Perhaps it led him through pain, and sickness, and sorrow, and tribulation, and death; but no matter for that, it led him to *eternal glory,* that was enough. Have you this spirit? What guides your conduct; is it your inclination, or is it the will of God? When you know his will, is your course fixed? Are you ready to go forward, whatever be the consequences? Christ was; and if you have not the Spirit of Christ you are none of his.

"Christ *sought his happiness in serving God and enjoying his presence.* Nothing gave him such delight as communion with God. Hence, we read of his rising 'a great while before day' for prayer. Is it so with you?

"Christ *approved the divine law;* that law which saith, 'Thou shalt love the Lord thy God with all thy heart, and with all thy soul, and with all thy mind, and thy neighbor as thyself;' and 'the soul that sinneth, it shall die.' The purity of the law, its extent, its requirements, and its penalty, every thing with respect to it, met his full approbation. He viewed it as perfectly right. He wished for no alteration. He believed that all men ought perfectly to obey it, and that if they did not they were guilty, and deserved everlasting destruction. *Do you?* Do you feel that you ought to obey the divine law perfectly, and that so far as you fall short, you are guilty and without excuse, and that you must be forgiven or perish? Do you approve the law which condemns you, and feel that you deserve the everlasting destruction which it threatens? Or do you feel that it is too strict, that it requires too much, or threatens too much? If so, you have not the spirit of Christ. He felt that the law was exactly right. He loved it, and strove constantly to obey it. You do, if you have the spirit of Christ. You approve it. It appears holy, and just, and good. You love it; you strive constantly to obey it. When you transgress you feel guilty; you condemn yourself for your sin; you loathe and abhor it; you mourn in bitterness of soul, and repent as in dust and ashes. Have you this spirit? Be honest with yourselves and with God. It will do you no hurt to learn your true character; but to be deceived will ruin you.

"Christ *was pleased with the government of God,* and ready to commit all concerns to his everlasting disposal. He was satisfied with what God does; the dispensations of his providence and his grace met his full approval. Clouds and darkness might be round about him, but he knew that justice and judgment are the habitation of his throne. Whenever he could say, 'It is the Lord,' he was ready also to say, 'It is well;' 'Not my will, but thine be done.' Have you this spirit? Christ had; and if Christians, you have.

"Christ *loved the souls of men.* Every step from the throne of God to the manger, and from the manger to the cross, was a proof of it. He was plain in his instructions, faithful in his warnings, and abundant in labors. He did not cry peace, when there was no peace. He told men their true condition, their amazing guilt and danger. He carried them on to the judgment. He opened eternal prospects, and cried with a voice of mercy, 'He that hath ears to hear, let him hear.' Have you his spirit?

"Christ *was much in prayer.* If Christians, so are you. You do not pray simply once or twice on the Sabbath, or some special occasion, but prayer is a part of your daily business. I ask every individual, do you pray in secret, in your families, in the house of God? Christ did. Have you in this respect his spirit?

"Christ *endured trials with patience.* He prayed for his enemies, and was ready to forgive. Are you? Search your hearts on this point. If Christians, you cannot pass through this world without trials. You will have enemies, and you must have tribulation. Your motives may be impeached, your actions misrepresented, and a cloud of darkness may be thrown over you. But though your enemies be ever so many, or ever so violent, *you must be an enemy to no man.* Is this your character? Do you pray for your enemies? Do you forgive them? Christ did. His friends forsake him; he is betrayed by one, denied by another, deserted by all. His enemies, who lived on his mercy, with instruments of death in their hands and the malice of hell in their hearts, come upon him. They render evil for his goodness, and hatred for his love. They bind him, and crown him with thorns, and mock and scourge him, and crucify him; yet, in the fulness of his soul he cries, 'Father, forgive them, for they know not what they do?'

"Such was Christ. Christians are like him. Are you like him? If not, your hopes of heaven will fail at the giving up of the ghost."

On the day of the annual state fast, April 4, 1816, he preached to his own people two plain and powerful sermons *on intemperance.*

The morning sermon was from the text, "Woe unto them that rise up early in the morning, that they may follow strong drink; that continue until night, till wine inflame them." One woe is *a craving appetite* which nothing can satisfy. Like the grave, it cries, "Give, give." It is a burning which seems to be kindled by the fire that never shall be quenched. They are tormented. They feel a gnawing as of the worm that never dies. Another woe is the loss of reputation. Another woe is the loss of property. Another, the loss of domestic peace and comfort. Another, the loss of health. Another, the loss of reason. Another, the loss of life. "Earthly woes pass away, but another cometh quickly—they lose *the soul.* They go away into everlasting burnings. Guilt fastens upon them and eats their souls like fire. They followed strong drink; its woes come upon them; they must drink of the fierceness of divine indignation for ever."

The afternoon sermon was from the words, "I speak as to wise men; judge ye what I say," in which he draws out at length the supposition, that an army of ten thousand men enter the United States under the garb of friendship; that they are welcomed among us; but under all forms of flattery and love, they are found to work all manner of mischief—"'Judge ye what I say,' Would it be enough to refrain from employing these men ourselves? Must we not do our utmost to have others also refrain? He then again portrays the woes brought on our country, on all classes of men, on husbands and wives, parents and children, old and young, by intoxicating liquor within thirty years—"'I speak as to wise men,' What shall be done? Shall this enemy be continued among us, or shall we declare a war of extermination, and root it out? But one says, 'It is a very useful thing.' 'It will do no hurt, if men do not take too much; they must be on their guard.' *No;* 'Be on your guard' has been the motto for thirty years; and shall we go on and perpetuate its evils on this generation, and fasten them on the necks of posterity?

"It is not drunkards nor intemperate men who control this business. It is *temperate men, useful men, honorable men.* Let them forbear to use it, and show that it is not necessary, and *the evil will die;* for they shut the door through which all intemperate men and all drunkards have entered. Those men were once where temperate men *now* are, in the temperate use of strong drink; and temperate men, if they continue this course, will many of them soon be where the intemperate now are. It is temperate using which gives the relish, prepares the way, and opens the door to intemperance. *Shut this door*, and it will not enter. Let temperate men give up the use of strong drink, and the evil will very soon be done away, for all who are now intemperate will die soon, and when they die there will be none to fill their places. Having stopped the temperate use, there is no door to intemperance. Those who are now intemperate may distress us for the present. They will frown, and corrupt, while here. But they are not to be here. He who made them has graciously decreed that if they will not reform, they shall go to their own place, and the earth be relieved of her burden.

"We are now reduced to one point, *Shall temperate men continue the temperate use of strong drink, and thus keep open the door to intemperance, idleness, dissipation, drunkenness, poverty, wretchedness, and death; or shall they forbear, and thus shut the door against those evils for ever? 'I speak as to wise men.'* Which will you approve when you come to die, and which will you approve for ever? Judge ye what I say. And may He who has all hearts in his hand lead you to form such a judgment as shall be for your own everlasting welfare, and that of your children. Amen."

It will be seen that here is the clear and distinct announcement of *the great principle* embodied ten years afterwards in the formation of the American Temperance Society, and which was the basis, under the blessing of God, of the wonderful results effected by the temperance reformation. Until the practical application of the principle of abstinence by the temperate, the efforts of philanthropists were vainly directed to the prevention of drunkenness by regulating *the moderate use.*

To the multiplied claims upon him was now added an appointment from the American Board for Foreign Missions, to act as far as practicable throughout his own county in rousing the churches to that object; but he was obliged to reply, that while he commended the board for seeking this mode of coöperation, "so numerous were his present engagements, that he must decline accepting the appointment."

His endeared friend Rev. Gordon Hall, at Bombay, having written him very earnestly for letters to strengthen and encourage him in that "dry and thirsty land where no water is," he returned the following reply:

To Rev. Gordon Hall, Bombay, India.

"ANDOVER, Jan. 20, 1817.

"DEAR BROTHER HALL—Yours of June 9, 1815, I received March 18, 1816. I have too long delayed to answer it. My only excuse is ill-health, and a vast multiplicity of avocations. I hope that I shall not be obliged to make this excuse any more.

"The letter enclosed to brother Olds, I directed and forwarded immediately to him. He was settled at Greenfield, Massachusetts, but I believe is now dismissed on account of having been appointed Professor of Chemistry in Middlebury college.

"Your class-mate Pomeroy is settled in Salisbury,

Vermont; Brunell in Vernon, New York; and Ira Olds in that vicinity. Brother Ware is settled in Ware, Massachusetts, has had two powerful revivals of religion among his people, and is doing much good.

"Brother Seward is settled in Ohio, and very useful. Griswold has been settled in Bloomfield, New York, where President Fitch is now settled. Professor Moore, formerly of Leicester, succeeds him as President. Williams College is flourishing.

"Should the Lord spare my life, and continue me in this place, I should be happy in a regular correspondence with you. If you will write one letter to me whenever you have opportunity, I will try to devote one evening every month in writing to you. This will give you twelve letters a year, and I shall receive perhaps two. If measured by numbers, you will be my debtor, but if by weight, I shall probably be yours. In your next, mention the subjects upon which you wish me to write. You have many correspondents from this country, and you do not wish me to repeat what they say.

"The great things concerning your mission I get from your communications to the board; but there are many things which will be interesting to me and useful to my people, which I do not get from any quarter. I wish you to write to me just as you would talk, if you and I could spend an hour together every month in my study. All important anecdotes, every thing which illustrates the character and condition of the heathen, and the effect which the preaching of the gospel has upon them; in short, every thing which will increase my usefulness to you, to the heathen, and to the church in this country, will be peculiarly interesting.

"I have some unusual attention among my people, several cases of deep impression, and a few of hopeful conversion.

"President Dwight, President Backus of Hamilton college, formerly of Bethlem, and Dr. Strong of Hartford, have all died within a few weeks. Thus the Lord is breaking in upon our churches; but where he is taking away one, he is raising up ten to fill their places. The American Education Society for educating pious youth for the gospel ministry, which has lately been formed, has at present fifty-three under its care. Mr. Beecher of Litchfield has just informed us that he shall shortly have fifty from that county, whom he means to send on to fit for college at our academy.

"There are various other similar societies in different parts of the United States, and there are probably four times as many persons now preparing for the ministry as at any former period. Many of them, no doubt, will be missionaries.

"Tell brother and sister Bardwell, if they are with you, that their parents are well, and their friends generally in this town.

"Between sixty and seventy students in the seminary. Professors and families well, except Dr. Porter, who has gone south for his health. A remarkable time of health the past year in all this region.

"Your affectionate brother,

"J. EDWARDS."

The systematic efforts for "Doing Good" to which we have referred, having produced a very happy influence on *the children of his congregation*, and frequent requests having been received for information as to the means which had been used, he prepared, March 1817, the following valuable communication for the Panoplist, an able monthly religious publication then conducted by Jeremiah Evarts, Esq.:

"PLAN FOR THE MORAL AND RELIGIOUS IMPROVEMENT OF CHILDREN.

"In the spring of 1814, a Society consisting of about seventy men was formed for Doing Good. In the spring of 1815, a branch Society was formed, consisting of about one hundred and fifty women. These societies have in view a number of objects, one of which is the moral and religious improvement of children. For this and other purposes, they contribute about one hundred and fifty dollars a year.

"The concerns of the society are conducted by a standing committee, consisting of twelve men, who are chosen annually. They meet once in three months to devise ways and means of accomplishing the objects of the society. The society have an annual meeting, when they unite in religious exercises, and a discourse is delivered by some person previously appointed for that purpose. The standing committee then report their proceedings during the past year, and the success which has attended them.

"In the spring of 1816, another branch Society was formed, consisting of between two and three hundred children. The exclusive object of this branch is to furnish the heathen with Bibles. Every child who daily reads the Bible himself, or if he is not old enough to read, who hears it read by others, and endeavors to understand and obey it, and who annually contributes to send it to the heathen, is a member. The particular sum to be contributed, is left entirely to the discretion of each individual.

"At the opening of the schools in 1816, each teacher was furnished with a blank-book ruled with eight columns. On the first column was to be written the name of each scholar; on the second, his age; on the third, the number of times he had been at the head of his class at the last spelling for the day; on the fourth, the number of books which he had taken from the library;* on the fifth, the number of verses of hymns and divine songs which he had learned; on the sixth, the number of answers which he had learned of the shorter catechism; on the seventh, the number of verses which he had learned of the Bible; and on the eighth, the number of cents which in the course of

* This library was established in 1815, by the Standing Committee of the Society for "Doing Good." After procuring a large quantity of books suitable for children, they divided them into as many parcels as there are schools in the place, and took one parcel enclosed in a trunk to each school. The teacher was appointed librarian. All children whose conduct and improvement met the approbation of the teacher, were allowed to take a book from the library every Saturday. The book was charged to them, and the next Saturday they were required to return it; and if their conduct during the week had been good, they were allowed to take out another. In the course of six months, the whole taken together read more than thirty thousand pages, learned more than two hundred hymns and many select portions of Scripture; and notwithstanding their unusual attention to reading, etc., their improvement in the various branches of learning was much greater than had been witnessed before.

one year he had given to the Bible Society. When any scholar had in the course of the week saved any thing for the heathen, he was allowed on Saturday, when he took a book from the library, to hand it to the teacher, and the sum was recorded against his name in the eighth column, as a donation of his to the Bible Society.

"After the scholars were made acquainted with the whole system, they were informed that the committee at the close would examine the schools, and inspect the books: when at one view they would see how many children had attended school; what was their age; how many times each scholar had been at the head of his class; how many books he had taken from the library;* how many verses of hymns and divine songs he had learned, how many answers of the catechism, how many verses of the Bible; and how many cents he had given to the Bible Society.

"The object of the Bible Society interested the children exceedingly. You might see tears of compassion trickle down many eyes as they heard of the destitute state of the heathen, and their hearts beat high with desires to send them the Bible. The great question was, *How shall we get money to give?* The committee replied, that almost every one would in the course of the year receive a few cents from his parents or friends, and that they might save one quarter or one half of these, more or less, as they saw fit; and that probably many parents would give them more,

* This would show not only how much he had read, but also what had been his behavior, as no one was allowed to take out books unless he behaved well.

when they found that they devoted it to so good an object.

"The committee then pointed out four ways in which they might earn something for this object. They informed them that each scholar who should be at the head of his class more than six times, should be considered as earning six cents, which should be paid for him out of the treasury of the Society for Doing Good, and be recorded in the eighth column against his name as a donation of his to the Bible Society; and that the scholar who should read the most books, should in the same way and for the same object receive six cents more; and each scholar who should learn such a number of hymns and chapters in the Bible, six cents more; and each scholar who should learn through the catechism, six cents more: and that in these ways they might by their diligence and good conduct greatly benefit themselves, and at the same time be constantly earning something for the heathen. Both teachers and scholars when the system was unfolded entered into it with very great ardor, and the result has surpassed the most sanguine expectations.

"At the examination, it was found that four hundred and fifteen children had attended school; that their average age was about eight years; that one hundred and eight had been at the head of their respective classes more than six times; that one hundred and twenty-seven had learned through the catechism; that two hundred and forty-one, all taken together, had learned more than seven thousand verses of hymns and divine songs, and one hundred and twenty-one, more than five thousand verses of the Bible; that two hundred and forty-two had become members of the Society, and had in addition to their contributions earned for it fifteen dollars and thirty cents.

"Their behavior at the examination was remarkably good, and it is believed that they sustained a better examination in the various branches of learning, than the committee had ever witnessed before.

"PASTOR."

The abundant labors of the pastor, and the varied means of grace to which he and his people were directed, had now been blessed in the accession to the church of more than fifty souls, who gave satisfactory evidence that they had been born again by the renewing of the Holy Spirit.

CHAPTER III.

HIS MINISTRY IN ANDOVER—CONTINUED.

FIVE YEARS, 1817-1822.

At this period of his ministry, Dr. Edwards for a short time made brief notices of the manner in which he employed each day, which we give entire for about two weeks, as illustrating the character of his pastoral life, his unwearied fidelity to the people of his charge, and the unremitting consecration of his powers to the service of Christ and the good of men.

"Monday, July 7, 1817. In order to satisfy my own mind upon a review whether I spend my time in a manner the most useful to my own soul, and the souls of my dear people, I write the following account of a part of my labors.

"O thou blessed Jehovah, who hast the hearts of all in thy hand, for the sake of Jesus Christ who died for sinners, guide me, I beseech thee; enable me in all things to glorify thee and promote the everlasting welfare of the souls of men; grant me wisdom rightly to employ my time, my talents, my influence, my property, and all which I possess; grant me thy guiding, sanctifying, and supporting presence; prepare me to meet every difficulty, support every trial, and discharge every duty. O grant me humility, repentance, faith, boldness, and perseverance in the cause of the blessed Redeemer; make me exceedingly useful, I beseech thee; guide me in my contemplations, and in my prayers, in studying the Scriptures, in selecting texts, in writing and delivering sermons. I pray that all may be done in such a manner as shall be most for the glory of God and the salvation of men; guide me in visiting and conversing with my people, and in all things. I am but a child, I need guidance, I need support, I need wisdom, sanctification, and every thing. I am a guilty, polluted, ruined sinner. O for the Redeemer's sake forgive; help me unreservedly to surrender all into his hands, and cheerfully to leave all for ever to his disposal. O be my hope, my guide, my support, my everlasting portion; make me instrumental of winning souls to Christ, and training up many among this dear people for heaven, and thine, Father, Son, and Holy Spirit, will be all the glory. Amen."

"MONDAY, July 7. In the forenoon I visited Mr. G. F., conversed with him and his family on the concerns of their souls, and on the great importance of being immediately prepared to die, and prayed with and for the family. I then visited widow Z. A., and conversed with her on eternal concerns. In the afternoon attended the *monthly concert for prayer*, and related to a large and solemn assembly the dealings of God with many churches, in pouring out his Spirit, which I learned on my late journey; also a number of instances of remarkable conversion. It was a solemn and interesting time. O Lord, for Jesus' sake, pour out thy Spirit here; call sinners to repentance; angels will rejoice, and thine be all the glory.

"TUESDAY, 8. Attended the meeting of the Andover Association at Bradford and the dedication of their meeting-house.

"WEDNESDAY, 9. Visited Mr. W. G. Conversed with him and his family on divine things, and closed with prayer. Visited the school in the Bailey district, examined, conversed, and prayed with them; and then visited the families of Messrs. S. F., and J. B.; conversed on the subject of missions, Christian experience, and the salvation of their souls.

"THURSDAY 10, A. M. I began to write from 1 Timothy, 1:8, 'The law is good,' etc. Afternoon, visited Mr. E. L. H., conversed with him and his wife on the state of their own souls and on family prayer, and prayed with them. Visited Captain J. A., conversed and prayed with him and the family.

"FRIDAY 11, A. M. Continued writing my sermon. Afternoon, visited the family of Mr. J., conversed with him and his wife on the state of their own souls, and on family prayer. Visited Mr. E. J., and conversed with his family on divine things, and some prominent traits of Christian experience. Visited Mr. J. C. and family; also Mr. H. and family, took tea, conversed, read the Scriptures, and prayed with them.

"SATURDAY 12, A. M. Finished my sermon. In the afternoon rode to Dunstable, New Hampshire, to exchange with Mr. S.

"LORD'S DAY 13, A. M. Preached from 2 Timothy, 3:15; afternoon, from 2 Corinthians, 5:17.

"MONDAY 14, A. M. Rode to Andover; stopped at Messrs. F., B., and G.'s. In the afternoon visited the school in the Holt district, and afterwards conversed and took tea with Mr. D. G.

"TUESDAY 15, A. M. Attended a little to domestic concerns, and wrote three letters to distant friends. Afternoon, visited the school in the Abbot district, and the families of J. P. and E. F.

"WEDNESDAY 16, A. M. Began to write a sermon from Acts 7:60. Afternoon, visited, examined, conversed, and prayed with the school in the Osgood district. Visited, conversed, and prayed with the family of Mrs. J.

"THURSDAY 17, A. M. Visited Deacon Newman, then continued writing the sermon above-mentioned. Afternoon, visited and conversed with Esquire K.'s family; visited Esquire A.'s family, took tea, conversed with them and several of the neighbors who were assembled, and closed with prayer. In the evening visited Mrs. W., a woman who has lately lost her husband, and is left with a family of children. May the widow's God guide and support her, and bless her children.

"FRIDAY 18, A. M. Finished my sermon. Afternoon, visited Lieutenant S. J.; conversed with him, his family, and several of the neighbors who were assembled; took tea, read a portion of Scripture, and closed with prayer.

"SATURDAY 19, A. M. Spent in reading, and attending to domestic concerns. Afternoon, visited H. R., who was sick with a fever, conversed with her and her father's family, and closed with prayer.

"LORD'S DAY 20, A. M. Preached from 1 Timothy, 1:8, 'We know that the law is good, if a man use it lawfully.' First, showed the goodness of the law; secondly, pointed out the lawful use of it; then drew some practical conclusions. Afternoon, preached from Acts 7:60, 'And he kneeled down,' etc.

"MONDAY 21, A. M. Exercised in the morning; then visited Captain J. A., and spent the rest of the morning in reading, etc. Afternoon, went to W. A. and Mr. N.'s on business; called at Mr. N. A.'s. Visited Captain B., conversed with the family, took tea, read a portion of Scripture, and closed with prayer. Visited and transacted business with A. B., Esq.

"TUESDAY 22, A. M. Spent in searching the Scriptures, reading, and writing. Afternoon, visited, conversed, and prayed with Mr. D. W., and with Mr. A. J. and family; perused the Recorder, Missionary Register, and wrote a letter to Dr. M.

"WEDNESDAY 23, A. M. Wrote part of a sermon from Numbers 14:35. Afternoon, received a visit from a parishioner; attended a meeting of the committee of the Andover South Parish Society for the Reformation of Morals, took tea, sung, conversed, and closed with prayer."

He had a quick discernment of the moral and spiritual state and wants of his people; and in his pastoral visits, as in his other labors, sought their highest temporal and eternal good. His warm heart was full of love, and they could unburden to him their sorrows; while there was in him a native dignified reserve, which, with his commanding presence, and well-weighed words, forbade what was trifling, and especially what might be said to the injury of others. "Mr. Edwards," said Major C., "will hear all you have to say, but if you speak against any body, you never get any thing back." When they sought his counsel, they received words of heavenly wisdom, often drawn directly from the inspired oracles; and the way in which he read and expounded brief portions of Scripture, and the solemnity and unction of his prayers, inspired all with love and confidence in him who was set to watch for their souls. Their difficulties, misapprehensions, or inquiries as to scripture truth or the way of salvation, often suggested to him topics for the pulpit, and frequently on a succeeding Sabbath they had an able public elucidation of the subject on which they had conversed.

His public ministrations embraced a wide range of subjects, frequently having reference to the events of Providence among his people from which he thought they should receive instruction, but mainly drawn from the exhaustless fountains of light and truth and duty in the word of God. To a young preacher who expressed his wonder that a minister could find new subjects for his stated preaching, he doubtless gave his own experience when he replied, that "to any minister who loves and prayerfully studies *the Bible*, topics rich and new will be suggested, more than he can preach from." From time to time he preached on striking passages or historic facts, as recorded in the order of the sacred records, or on some book of the New Testament; and just previous to the dates of the above memoranda, he had completed a course of able sermons on the ten commandments.

His public ministrations were always solemn, tender, impressive, as if he would rescue souls from eternal death and raise them to eternal glory. Christ and his salvation was the theme that underlay all his instructions. He preached as if what he wrote thirty years after in his comment on Christ the shepherd of the sheep had been constantly before him: "Real Christians have spiritual discernment and relish of the great truths of the gospel. No instruction, however specious or learned, which denies or omits the doctrine of *Christ crucified as a divine atoning Saviour*, satisfies them, commends itself to their conscience, if enlightened, or meets their wants as sinners." In a sermon preached about this period in several churches and in the theological seminary, (in connection with which a new church had now been organized,) from the words, "We preach CHRIST CRUCIFIED, unto the Jews a stumbling-block and unto the Greeks foolishness, but unto them who are called, both Jews and Greeks, Christ the power of God and the wisdom of God," he says,

"*The Lord Jesus Christ is the wonder of all worlds.* There is no being like him in the universe. He is the everlasting Jehovah, and the man Christ Jesus. He is 'the root,' and 'the offspring' of David, the Alpha and Omega, who liveth, who was dead, who is alive for evermore.

"The *object* of Christ is wonderful: to ransom unnumbered millions of his enemies from everlasting woe, and raise them to be kings and priests unto God.

"To accomplish this, *his work* has been wonderful. He left the bosom of the Father and the glory he had with him before the world was, took the form of a servant, and with the riches of the universe in his hand, had not where to lay his head. Although he controlled the elements and raised the dead, commanded legions of angels, and devils fell prostrate before him, 'he was led as a lamb to the slaughter, and as a sheep dumb before her shearers, he opened not his mouth.' He was the Maker of heaven and of earth; the Prince of life, yet he 'cried with a loud voice, and yielded up the ghost.'

"*The effect* was wonderful. The earth trembled, rocks rent, graves opened, and even crucifiers said he was the Son of God. The third day he arose, laid aside his grave-clothes, went out to his disciples and said, 'Behold, it is I.' He showed them his hands, his side, and said, 'Peace be unto you. All power is given unto me in heaven and in earth. As my Father hath sent me, so send I you. And he breathed on them and said, Receive the Holy Ghost. Go ye into all the world and preach the gospel to every creature. He that believeth and is baptized shall be saved; but he that believeth not shall be damned. And he led them out to Bethany, and lifted up his hands, and blessed them; and while he blessed them, was parted from them, and went up into heaven, and a cloud received him out of their sight.'

"His *present state* is wonderful. 'I beheld, and lo, in the midst of the throne and of the elders, stood a Lamb as it had been slain; and they fell down before him and sung, Thou art worthy. Thou wast slain, and hast redeemed us to God.' And angels, ten thousand times ten thousand and thousands of thousands, cried,

Worthy, to receive power, and riches, and wisdom, and strength. And every creature in heaven, on earth, and under the earth, cried, Blessing, and honor, and glory; and the four beasts said, Amen; *and all heaven bowed before him.*

"After viewing this wonderful Christ, you will not be surprised if the preaching of him should produce WONDERFUL EFFECTS. It does. 'We preach Christ crucified, *the power of God and the wisdom of God.*' The apostle Paul did not preach Seneca nor Plato, nor any of the wise men among the heathen. He did not preach St. Paul. He did not preach an angel, nor the highest created being in heaven. No; he preached CHRIST. And he did not preach Christ as a man merely, a moral teacher, an example, a pattern for imitation; but Christ CRUCIFIED, the great atoning sacrifice for sin, without the shedding of whose blood there could be no remission; who 'was wounded for our transgressions, and bruised for our iniquities.' He preached the way of salvation through faith in a crucified Redeemer, and he preached no other. Wherever he went, he 'determined not to know any thing, save Jesus Christ and him crucified.' Although he had as exalted views of Christ's personal character as any man ever had, yet he saw in him no hope for dying sinners till he beheld him on the cross—'the Lamb of God, which taketh away the sin of the world.'

"He preached 'God manifest in the flesh.' And he showed why this manifestation was necessary. Because men have 'all gone out of the way;' have altogether become filthy; because 'there is none that doeth good, no, not one;' because men naturally are carnally minded, and 'to be carnally minded is death,' for it is 'enmity against God.' He showed them, without reserve, that they had destroyed themselves, and that in God alone is their help; and held up Christ crucified, entering the holy place with his own blood, saying, 'Such a High-priest became us, who is holy, harmless, undefiled, separate from sinners, and higher than the heavens;' who was appointed of God to make atonement for the sins of the people; suffering for them, shedding his own blood, dying for them while enemies, that they might be 'reconciled,' and made the 'righteousness of God' in him. He pressed upon them their perishing need of *such* a Saviour; one who could, 'through the eternal Spirit, offer himself without spot to God,' 'a living sacrifice;' who could 'enter into the holy place with his own blood,' 'obtain eternal redemption,' and as Captain of salvation, be 'made perfect through suffering.'

"He showed them what they must *be*, and what they must *do*, in order to become interested in Christ and partakers of his blessings: that they must feel their need of him; that they must abhor sin, and look to Christ for pardon, and receive him as their hope and portion; that they must *repent, and believe on the Lord Jesus Christ.* He told them what repentance is, and pointed out the difference between that 'godly sorrow' which worketh repentance unto life, and that 'sorrow of the world' which worketh death; and the difference between that faith which 'worketh by love,' and the faith of devils. He showed them, that repentance and faith are evidences of love to God; and that they must be created anew in Christ Jesus unto good works. He showed the author of this change: that Christians are born of the *Spirit*, 'not of blood, nor of the will of the flesh, nor of the will of man, but of God;' that it was 'not by works of righteousness which they had done, but according to his mercy he saved them, by the washing of regeneration and renewing of the Holy Ghost,' 'that they should be holy and without blame before him in love.'"

On the 17th of September, 1817, Dr. Edwards was married to Miss Lydia Bigelow, daughter of Asa Bigelow, Esquire, of Colchester, Connecticut, and till the close of his earthly life, she was his firm, consistent, devoted "helper in Christ Jesus." It gives us pleasure to state, that for more than three years from the time of his ordination, the venerated widow of Samuel Abbot, Esq., welcomed Dr. Edwards as a guest in her own mansion, not neglecting the noble animal that bore him over the hills and plains in his abundant pastoral labors, until her death, February 12, 1816, at the advanced age of eighty-nine. Not far from the time of her death, a commodious house, in a favorable location for the pastor, having been offered for sale, with characteristic forethought, economy, and discretion in the management of his worldly concerns, to which he had been trained in early life, he purchased it; applying in payment what could be saved from his salary before his family became large and expensive; and this, except at intervals, was the home of his family till his death. He scrupulously refrained from all unnecessary business engagements, or speculations, from buying or selling for purposes of gain, and from incurring unnecessary debts, as inconsistent with the duties and responsibilities of his sacred calling. He was careful, accurate, and noiseless in his pecuniary transactions, always husbanding his resources, though giving liberally to the poor and to charitable objects. What from time to time was saved, he committed chiefly to a responsible business relative, who took charge of it. Few ministers ever had so little hinderance in their work from pecuniary perplexity; and as his life was long preserved, under the smiles of Providence, the small savings of years enabled him to leave his widow and the children remaining with her in comfortable circumstances, in the pleasant home endeared to them by the memory of the husband and father.

In January, 1818, he was acting with the Rev. Drs. Jedidiah Morse of Charlestown, and Samuel Worcester of Salem, as a committee of the General Association of Massachusetts to adopt proper means for establishing a Domestic Missionary Society, for supplying needy parishes and the waste places of the state, which resulted in the formation of the "Massachusetts Missionary Society." He was frequently engaged in consultations and plans for the society then recently formed to Educate Pious Youth for the Ministry, into which the Rev. Professor Porter threw all his energies. He was also examining and acting on important publications for the Tract Society; and in behalf of the Board of Foreign Missions wrote the following letter to the "Church Missionary Society," in London.

To the Rev. Josiah Pratt, Secretary of the Church Missionary Society.

"ANDOVER, April 28, 1818.

"REV. AND DEAR SIR—A few days ago I received from the hand of the Rev. Dr. Morse, of Charlestown, a copy of your truly excellent Missionary Register. I have perused it with the greatest satisfaction. Its spirit is catholic and evangelical, and the facts which it records transcendently glorious. It must, I think, be extensively useful not only in this country, but wherever it circulates throughout the Christian world.

"The friends of Zion will rejoice to see the church of England rising in her strength, or rather the strength of her Redeemer, and scattering the light of his salvation over the world. Her example will awaken a holy emulation in the breasts of millions, and the record of her achievements be a lasting monument of her glory. She in a peculiar manner is a city set upon a hill. May her light so shine, that even the ends of the earth shall see and glorify her Father who is in heaven.

"Let all portions of the Christian church follow her noble example; let them forget minor, unessential distinctions, fix their eyes on the great interests of the Redeemer's kingdom, and with one heart and soul steadily pursue them, and He shall soon have 'the heathen for his inheritance, and the uttermost parts of the earth for his possession.' He shall reign from sea to sea, and earth be indeed an emblem of heaven.

"One powerful means of hastening this day of glory, would be the circulation of your Missionary

Register. I trust that it will circulate extensively; that your labors, and those of your associates, with all of every kindred and name, will be abundantly blessed, and receive at last a gracious and eternal reward.

"I remain with respect and affectionate salutation,

"Your brother in the gospel,

"J. EDWARDS."

The next month he preached a sermon on "How is it that ye do not discern this time?" which shows how deeply his heart was enlisted for the conversion of the world; and at the same time how interesting and hopeful was the period in which he was then acting. His object was to show some of the then existing indications that Christ was about to appear in the glorious enlargement of his kingdom.

One sign was, "*The kingdom of Christ has become exceedingly dear to the hearts of his people,* and they are now ardently wishing and fervently praying to have it extended through the world."

Another sign was, "*The widely extended concert for prayer.*" He says, that about twenty years before, a few Christians met in a private room in Great Britain and agreed to spend a part of the first Monday evening in every month in prayer for the conversion of the world; that it was now observed by Christians in almost every part of the earth, and probably by as many as fifteen hundred churches in the United States. "When such multitudes 'agree touching the thing they shall ask,' is it not a sign that 'it shall be done for them by their Father who is in heaven?'"

Another sign is, "*The many answers to prayer which*

God has already given. While Christians have been praying, the Lord has been pouring out his Spirit. There have been more revivals of religion during a few years past, than for many years before; and a far greater proportion of the subjects of grace are *young men*, and a great portion of them are preparing for the ministry—while the fields are white to the harvest, and a cry is heard from six hundred millions, 'Come over and help us.'"

Another sign is, "*The exertions which have been made to supply the destitute millions.* More than three hundred missionaries have already gone forth; and old men and maidens, young men and children, are giving for their support. Who would have thought, twenty years ago, that *more than three thousand dollars in a month* would have been contributed in this country for this purpose?"

Another sign is, "*The circulation of the Bible.* It has already been circulated in more than *sixty* languages, and is read by thousands, and even millions, where till lately Christ never was known. This shows that the work is of God. It is not the work of Satan, nor of the pride of man. If these would translate and distribute Bibles, it would have been the work of every generation since the fall. Wicked men and devils may oppose this work; but it will go onward, borne by millions of hearts and millions of hands, and on the arm which is almighty, till it scatters light and life on every land."

The last sign is, "*The great attention which is paid to children.* They are beginning to be viewed as they actually are, as the rising hope of the church. Often has God poured out his Spirit; children have been born again, and 'out of the mouths of babes and sucklings has he perfected praise.' God will raise up new generations to fill the places of their fathers, and do vastly more than they, till the 'kingdoms of this world become the kingdom of our Lord and of his Christ.'"

The preservation of the following gem from his distinguished, self-sacrificing friend in Burmah, will not be unacceptable to many readers.

"RANGOON, October 1, 1818.

"MY DEAR BROTHER—As I do not know any person in Andover connected with the Society of Mission Inquiry in the Theological institution but yourself, I take the liberty of sending you by the hands of Dr. Baldwin one hundred and twenty-seven dollars, which *I consider due* from myself to that society, desiring that you will have the goodness to pay it to the treasurer or proper officer; and you will greatly oblige,

"Your friend and brother,

"A. JUDSON.

"Rev. J. EDWARDS."

To a dear and intimate friend, under different dates, he writes more respecting his work and the relations he sustained to the people of his charge, than he has before expressed.

"I wish to place *myself* 'behind,' with those things which the apostle says must be forgotten; and before me to place *Jesus Christ.* It is good to look much on him. The sight is transforming. The more we love, admire, and copy his excellences, the more we shall be like him; He is the source of all good, and other things will be the *means*, just in proportion as they lead us to him.

"I have a great work to do: the spiritual care of three hundred and fifty families, and perhaps twenty that I have promised to visit *now*, as soon as I can. The schools are now opening, and I must visit them. I must prepare the constitution of their Bible Society and a catalogue of their members. My good women are helping me in this as much as they can."

Again he says, "I do think that my enjoyment consists less and less in worldly things, and that I am happy just in proportion as I enjoy the guiding, supporting, sanctifying, comforting presence of the Spirit of God. His favor is life; his loving-kindness better than life. How blessed would it be to be able to say at all times, 'Whom have I in heaven but thee?'

"A young woman called upon me on Saturday in a state of great anxiety for her soul. She could say but little, appeared to be burdened with a sense of sin, and by her looks and many tears expressed the anguish of her soul. I hope God will grant her, and many others, repentance unto life. How important that ministers should preach faithfully, walk humbly, pray fervently, and suffer patiently the whole will of God."

Again he says, "It is good to receive all our mercies as from the hand of God, to feel that He gives them, and that they come as the purchase of Immanuel's blood. A number are anxiously inquiring what they must do to be saved; and a few are entertaining the hope that they have lately passed from death unto life. But there is the same opposition to the truth as it is in Jesus here, as in all other places. How we ought to rejoice that the Lord has all hearts in his hands. I hope that he will yet here subdue multitudes to himself. Next Sabbath is our communion. Pray that the Lord will manifest his saving power in the midst of us."

At another date he says, "Several persons are most deeply impressed. I need wisdom, I need grace, I need every thing. Precious promise, 'Whatsoever ye shall ask in my name, that will I do.' I hope the Lord will prepare us to see a great revival here. It is a great honor, as well as a source of rich comfort, to be permitted to labor for God in promoting the kingdom of his Son. How much we are indebted to Jesus Christ. We owe him *all*, ALL.

"That minister is exceedingly unwise who says, or even thinks much about his trials; for however great, they are but light and momentary, not worthy to be compared with the glory that shall be revealed. Trials do not destroy a Christian's happiness; nay, sometimes the greater the trial the greater the joy. If I could always feel as I think Paul and Silas felt in prison, when they sang at midnight so that the prisoners heard them, I should not envy the mightiest monarch that ever graced a throne. If when we do well we suffer for it, happy are we. If called to suffer with Christ, may we not hope to reign with him? this is enough; and what a wonder of wonders, that guilty rebels may hope for it. Our happiness must not be expected from the world; nor in what the world calls exemption from trials; nor from the praises of men;

but from communion with God, enjoying his presence, doing his will, and striving by his grace to prepare ourselves and all around us for his glory. I preached yesterday from 1 Tim. 6:17; a large and solemn audience. Some, I trust, are mourning in bitterness over their sins."

Again he writes, "Last Monday I attended a wedding at H., with Rev. Mr. W. the pastor. A great collection of people assembled. After the marriage was solemnized, they were earnest in their requests that I should speak to them. After speaking of the marriage union, I attempted to describe the union between Christ and believers; and to show that it is a *vital* union, an *endearing* union, and an *everlasting* union; that those who possess it have the pardon of sin, justification, a growing conformity to Christ, support in trials, consolation in death, a part in the first resurrection, triumph at the judgment, and everlasting glory with Christ in his kingdom. It was a very solemn, interesting time."

Again, "There is more than usual attention in one part of the town to 'the one thing needful,' and several have hopefully obtained it."

To Mrs. Edwards' brother, then in a desponding state of mind.

"MY DEAR BROTHER—I learn by a letter from A. E., which Mrs. Edwards received yesterday, that although you have at times enjoyed some hope that you are born of God, yet you were, when she wrote, in darkness, borne down by the apprehension that you remain still impenitent. And should you continue, my dear brother, to look only at yourself and ruminate on the state of your own heart, you might never obtain relief. For the heart is at best a sink of iniquity, which none but the eye of God can fathom; it is full of pollution and black with guilt; and so long as you continue to look only at that, you may see nothing but darkness and despair.

"But 'the chief end of man,' is not to continue looking at *himself*. It is to glorify God, in whom there is light and no darkness at all; who is the centre and source of blessedness, and the sum of all perfection. Make it, then, the single object of your soul, in all things to honor and glorify Him, to live not unto yourself, but unto Him that died for sinners and rose again.

"So long as you continue to look at yourself, you can see nothing but darkness; but look to God, act for *Him*, labor for *Him*, and live for *Him*, trusting alone in Jesus to enable you to do it and to be accepted in it, and you may have light. Or if you do *not* have light, you may do that which is infinitely more important, you may glorify God, you may do good, you may be instrumental in the salvation of souls who will bless God for ever, and a revenue of everlasting glory will redound to his great and holy name."

To an afflicted woman.

"Dear Mrs. W.—Yours of the 2d inst. to Mrs. Edwards was received and read with the interest which she takes in all cases of sorrow, especially in every thing which relates to her dear Mrs. W. As she has not been well for a few days, she requested me to acknowledge the receipt of your letter.

"We rejoice that you have been so far favored by the Lord, and hope that his mercies will still be continued to you. We sympathize with you in your afflictions, and hope that the Lord will sanctify them to you. We know that they must be great, very great, but *how* great none can tell till they feel them. Yet such afflictions do not rise from the dust, nor spring from the ground; they are ordered by a wise and good God, and they go where he sends them, and like all other trials, will work out an exceeding and eternal weight of glory to those who love Him. We hope that they will be the means of leading you to see the evil of sin, to loathe and abhor it, to be humble under the chastising hand of God; to choose Jesus Christ for your portion, and find great satisfaction in committing yourself, your dear children, your husband, and all your interests and concerns to his infinitely wise and good disposal.

"The Lord has all hearts in his hands, and he can turn them as the rivers of water are turned. He can overrule all your concerns, and bring them to such a result as will be most for his glory, for your good, and the good of your children. We know not what is best for us. It is good to have all our concerns in the hands of God, and commit them all for time and eternity to his disposal. Dear Mrs. W., we hope that you will give him your own heart, your children, your husband, and rejoice to have him do with and for you all, as seemeth good in his sight. If your trials should be the means of leading you to Jesus Christ, and teaching you to lay up your treasure, not on earth, but in heaven, you will number them in eternity as among your choicest mercies. They will be light afflictions, but for a moment, and you will say, Blessed afflictions, which weaned me from the world, led me to seek God as my portion, and lay up treasure where sins, and of course sorrows, never enter, where the Lamb leads his people to fountains of living water, and wipes away all tears from their eyes.

"Praying that you may have the guidance and blessing of God; that he will direct all your concerns in mercy, and hereafter bring you, your dear children and husband, with all the redeemed, to his heavenly kingdom, we remain, with tender sympathy and affection,

"Your unworthy

"FRIENDS."

To his sister, Mrs. C., on the birth of her first child.

"BELOVED SISTER—When I have seen a smiling babe in a mother's arms, I have often thought that God might be considered as speaking to her as the daughter of Pharaoh spoke to the mother of Moses, 'Take this child, and nurse it for me.' Mothers are generally the means of forming the character of their children, and often of their children's children, for many generations; and the effects of their pious example, judicious government, and salutary instructions, are not confined to this life, but will run on through eternity. As often as the fond mother views her smiling babe, or clasps it in her arms, so often should she bear it in the arms of faith and prayer to the throne of divine grace, commending it to the mercy of Him who made it; beseeching him to wash it from its native pollution, create it anew in Christ Jesus, adopt it into his chosen family, and train it up for usefulness in this world, and for immortal glory in the world to come.

"That little one now in your arms has a soul worth more than a thousand worlds; having begun an existence which is never to end, after continuing here its appointed time, and forming a character which shall fit it for happiness or misery, it will burst from its little prison, and like an angel for ever rise higher and higher in a world of light, or be for ever sinking deeper and deeper in a world of woe. Although it now appears innocent and lovely, yet it belongs to a sinful race of beings, and it must be born again, or it cannot be happy here, or meet the smiles of God hereafter. How important that parents should have hearts to pray. And how wonderful the love which has opened a way in which parents and children may be adopted into the chosen family of Christ, and through riches of free grace be prepared to meet each other in the world of glory, to part no more for ever.

"That this, after a useful and happy life, may be the case with you and yours, is the earnest desire and daily prayer of your affectionate brother,

"J. EDWARDS."

Under another date he says, "To the little girl whose arm I once hurt, I mean to write a letter and send a little book. Her name, I am sorry to say, I have forgotten; but you will not think it strange, when you recollect that I have five hundred little girls and boys to think of here. Perhaps, however, I shall think of her name before I begin to write. If I do not, I shall call her *the dear little girl;* for I love her much, and hope that the Lord will bless her. I was pleased to hear that you were going to Plainfield, because you would have such a good minister. Father Hallock is one of the excellent of the earth. Give my love to him and Mrs. Hallock, to dear brother C. and all friends."

To a friend who had written him in reference to some impending difficulty, he gave, in his reply, the following maxims of peace:

"In speaking about others, never say any thing but what you are willing they should hear, and what if they should hear would appear to be the fruit of love, and be adapted to be the means of doing good to their souls. If others speak against us, it is good to imitate Him who, 'when reviled, reviled not again, but committed himself to him that judgeth righteously;' and if they urge us to come down and meet them in disputation in some one of the villages on the plains of Ono, to say in actions as did Nehemiah, 'I am doing a great work, and cannot come down.' 'Out-preach them, out-pray them, and out-*live* them,' and as you ought to wish that they, under a change of circumstances, should speak of you, so speak you of them. 'If any man offend not in word, the same is a perfect man, and able also to bridle the whole body.'"

Note accompanying the presentation of Baxter's Saints' Rest.

"DEAR E.—Perhaps in your weak and feeble state you may be able to read some. This book was written by Mr. Baxter when in near prospect of heaven, and it has hopefully been the means of preparing many for that blessed abode. You now have a good time to secure your salvation. Be careful diligently to improve it.

"That you may feel your need of Jesus Christ, give him your heart, and devote all that you have to his service, is the prayer of your affectionate pastor,

"J. EDWARDS."

"P. S. Read this book attentively, and pray that God will bless it to the good of your soul."

When this work was distributed to every family in Andover, from the proceeds of a fund left by Lieut.-Governor Samuel Phillips, Dr. Edwards said its influence was like that of a gentle revival of religion throughout his parish.

A sister of Mrs. Edwards, who, at the age of about ten, in the years 1818 and 1819, was an inmate of Dr. Edwards' family, has kindly communicated some recollections of him, which fill a chasm in our narrative that otherwise could hardly be supplied.

"It was in 1816, in the days of my childhood, that I first saw this man of God, and learned to love him. Though he was not at that time much accustomed to amuse or interest children, and the movements of his giant frame were not the most graceful, yet I soon felt myself strongly attracted towards him, and I remember finding myself more than once seated on his knee, supported by his strong arm, and listening with delight to the deep, rich tones of his voice as he poured forth the 'Pilgrim's Farewell,' and 'Guide me, O thou great Jehovah,' in the tune of Hotham.

These at that time were his favorite tunes, and they became mine also. For years afterwards he often indulged me in the singing of them, and I shall never forget the peculiar emphasis with which he rolled out the lines, 'I 'll take my staff and travel on, till I a better world can view.' I remember well the love and veneration with which I then regarded him, and in the many days and weeks and years which I have since spent in the bosom of his family, they have not been diminished. Always kind, open, and affable in his deportment, he was ever ready, when not too much engrossed with the deep workings of his own mind, to attend to the veriest want even of a child, and the answer he would give to each childish inquiry would be so simple and plain that I at once understood its meaning.

"The first sermon I ever remember hearing with any interest was from his lips; and the reason why I felt interested at that early age was, that he made every part of it so simple and so clear, that the little child could not fail to understand it. The subject was the six cities of refuge to which the manslayer must flee for safety; and so plain and simple did he make every part of his discourse, and so impressive was his manner, that no other sermon which I heard in early life is still so vividly before my mind. Beautiful simplicity was the grand characteristic of his preaching, all the way through his ministry; and this, combined with the purity and strength of his elocution, together with the peculiar solemnity of his manner, and the richness of Bible truth which he uttered, formed the great attraction of his sermons, which, when he was in the prime of life, were considered by most of his hearers as remarkably impressive.

"For two years after his marriage, at an age when a child is noticing every thing that occurs, and trifles make an impression, I was a constant inmate of his family. At the fireside, at the social board, at the hour of prayer, at the parochial visit, everywhere, except in the study, I was daily in his society, and witnessed the meek and quiet spirit, the consistent walk and conversation, he uniformly exhibited. Indeed, vivid as are my recollections of those days, as well as of after-years, when his children were growing up around him, and every parent has much to perplex and harass, I do not remember ever seeing the slightest variation of temper. Let what might occur, he always preserved his equanimity and remained unruffled. 'Let patience have its perfect work,' was his motto for himself, and he often recommended it to others.

"In his parochial visits he was free and communicative, inquiring with kindness about the things most likely to interest those whom he was visiting, and expressing an interest in all that concerned them. His conversation on religious subjects was much like his preaching, a familiar discussion and illustration of the subject, rather than a direct and personal address to those that heard him; and yet it had so much point, that it could not fail to have its effect. These visits among his people were always closed with reading the Scriptures and prayer."

The joy occasioned by the election of Rev. Dr. Edwards on the Board of Trustees of the Theological

Seminary and Academy, September 28, 1820, is well remembered. Such was the influence of gentlemen of high standing who were connections of the early founders of the academy, that it was feared they would succeed in perpetuating in the Board of Trustees men unfriendly to evangelical truth. The late venerable William Phillips, Lieutenant-governor of Massachusetts, a man of great integrity and single-hearted piety, in the consultations of the board, entreated his honored relatives even with tears, that they would withdraw their opposition to the election of Dr. Edwards, and let the seminary be what its founders designed, a distinctly evangelical institution; and when the result of the election was announced to the Hon. William Bartlet, the largest donor to the seminary, and one of its board of visitors, it is stated that he also wept for joy.

To Mrs. Edwards.

"PORTLAND, Maine, May 20, 1822.

"MY VERY DEAR WIFE—On Thursday we [the late Rev. Dr. Woods and himself] dined in Exeter, arrived in Dover before night, and lodged at Dr. W.'s, a brother of Mrs. Woods. On Friday dined in Kennebunk, and arrived before night at Saco, distant from Andover about eighty-five miles, and Saturday morning rode to Portland. We both preached all day on the Sabbath, and Dr. Woods preached in the evening.

"This forenoon we went out twenty miles to sea with Dr. Payson and a few other friends; then returned and dined with Dr. Payson. This afternoon expect to take tea at Mr. C.'s, the father of one of our Andover students. There is more than usual attention to religion in this place, and there are a great many most excellent Christians.

"To-morrow morning we expect to go to North Yarmouth. We hope to be able to leave there on Thursday, and with the leave of Providence, to arrive in Dover on Friday, and in Andover on Saturday. God has been very kind to us, and our journey so far has been pleasant, and I trust in some measure useful.

"I hope it gives me some comfort to commit you and the dear family to Jesus Christ, and hope that you will find Him to be a very present helper in all times of need; that He will grant us his holy presence, use us as instruments of doing good, provide for us all needful blessings while on earth, and prepare us with all his redeemed people for the everlasting enjoyment of himself in glory.

"I have been rather unusually interested with the first nine verses of the Thirty-fourth Psalm. That we and all our friends, with the whole Israel of God, may experience the blessedness there described, is the prayer of

"Your affectionate husband,

"J. EDWARDS."

The occasion of the visit described in the above letter, appears to have been a call to sit in an ecclesiastical council, on a question of great difficulty and perplexity; and though such occasions, in which his counsel, or mediation, was sought from time to time, laid heavy claims upon his heart, his sound judgment, and bodily strength, in the midst of his other pressing public responsibilities, few men had such qualifications for reaching a wise and harmonious result, which in this case was drawn up by him, and is preserved on file. In such deliberations he was calm and peaceful, as if the presence of God were with him. His single aim was evidently the glory of God and the best interests of his kingdom. He gave the energies of his mind to the subject, but said little, or if any thing, only words of love; and when the whole subject was understood, he often showed uncommon discernment and singleness of purpose in suggesting a course by which the great interests at stake might be secured, and yet in which the parties could acquiesce.

In the progress of the "New England Tract Society"—which in 1819 and 1820 received a vigorous impulse from a year's agency of the late Rev. Louis Dwight—the management of its concerns fell gradually into the hands of Dr. Edwards; Mr. Blanchard its treasurer, and Messrs. Flagg and Gould its printers and business agents, being all members of his congregation. From 1817 he had acted on its Executive Committee, and in 1821 was elected Corresponding Secretary, by which the labor and responsibility of superintending the press and directly managing its concerns were officially devolved upon him, though he was still fulfilling all his arduous duties as pastor. In May, 1821, he wrote the able and soul-stirring Seventh Annual Report of that Society, the spirit of which appears in the following summary of its contents in the closing paragraphs:

"If two of our tracts have been connected with the hopeful conversion of twelve persons, which have come to our knowledge, what may we not hope, with the blessing of heaven, from the four hundred thousand which have issued from our depository the past year; and from the millions which have issued in seven years; and from the millions and millions which will continue to issue to all future generations?

"Who can contemplate *these six considerations* connected with this Society, namely, the ease and effect with which it may speak at the same time to millions; the immense call for tracts; the great amount of good which may be done by small means; the ease and effect with which it may assist all other benevolent societies; its permanency, its adaptedness with present means for perpetual operation; and above all, who can witness the approbation of God which it has already received; see one tract instrumental in the hopeful conversion of four persons, and more indirectly in the conversion of forty, another in the conversion of eight, another of twelve, another of thirteen, and many of these out of the way of other means of grace—who can see a tract put in operation all the Bible Societies in Russia, Sweden, and the neighboring countries, and not expect, when he stands on mount Zion, to see the multitude which no man can number, vastly augmented through the instrumentality of tracts?

"And who, with a conviction that he had been instrumental in their salvation, would not join with ineffable delight in their anthems of glory 'unto Him that loved us, and washed us from our sins in his own blood, and hath made us kings and priests unto God and his Father; to whom be glory and dominion for ever and ever?'"

In June, 1821, he received from his friend Rev. Gordon Hall, at Bombay, the well-known eloquent appeal, "The Conversion of the World, or the Claims of Six Hundred Millions," which was then published by the Tract Society as No. 138 of their series.

Under such a pressure of public duty, and the impossibility of performing the superadded labors involved in his official relations to the Tract Society, as he was riding on horseback to visit some of his people, July 26, 1822, he called at the room of the compiler of this memoir, who was near the close of his course in the seminary and contemplating labors at the West, and said in substance, "The New England Tract Society is in a very low state, and we think we must have one from the Senior class to engage for a time in its agency. We have been looking over the class, and according to the best light we have, we think it may be your duty to labor for a time in this department. We wish you would think of it, and hope you will have light and direction from above. My duties are at this time very pressing. Good-morning, sir." The result was that the young man thus addressed, the day after closing his studies, commenced the agency, in which he had the benefit of Dr. Edwards' wise and disinterested counsels and affectionate sympathy for two and a half years in Andover; and when, in 1825, the Society united with other societies in forming the American Tract Society located in New York, of which he was elected Corresponding Secretary, the kind and effective coöperation of Dr. Edwards, as a member of the Publishing Committee of the national Society, and in various ways, was still faithfully continued throughout the further period of twenty-eight years, till God called him to rest from his earthly labors.

On the 12th of June, 1822, Dr. Edwards preached his sermon on "*Christian Communion*," at the installation, in Gorham, Maine, of the Rev. Thaddeus Pomeroy, his class-mate in the Theological Seminary, which was published in three editions at the Andover press, and also in an able magazine edited by a man of kindred spirit, the Rev. Dr. John H. Rice, of Richmond, Virginia. The discourse is founded on the words, "Receive ye one another, as Christ also received us, to the glory of God," and shows that "the communion of all real Christians is an object dear to Christ. He bore it upon his heart, in his dying prayer, 'that they all may be one.' To open the way for this, he laid down his life. To accomplish it, he now intercedes in heaven. The union for which he prayed, is *a union in God*, the only real, permanent union that can ever be formed—a union of souls that truly receive Christ, with Christ—founded on no merely external distinction whatever; but they receive him as their prophet to teach them the will of God, their priest to atone for their sins, their king to rule in their hearts and to receive their choicest affections and govern their lives." *All such Christ receives;* and they are bound by the divine command, and the most sacred and inspiring motives, *to receive one another.*

In the autumn of 1822,* (or more probably two years later,) a man partially intoxicated, passing through Andover on a wagon loaded with apples, fell under its wheels within a few rods of Dr. Edwards' church, and was crushed to death. This, and another death occasioned by intemperance, led to his preaching two more, powerful sermons, probably from the texts, "The way of transgressors is hard," and, "At the last it biteth like a serpent, and stingeth like an adder;" showing, as he did in 1816, the woes of the intemperate, and the duty of doing all in our power to *induce the temperate to abstain* from the use of intoxicating drinks, that when the existing race of the intemperate should be removed, the land might be free from the curse of drunkenness. We were not present to hear these sermons, but well remember that the report of them filled the region around; and that the main idea was seized by all, and passed from mouth to mouth, "Keep the temperate people temperate; the drunkards will soon die, and the land be free;" a happy illustration of the power God had given him, to seize on a great, simple, practical idea, that all could understand and put in practice, and which yet was the germ of an all-pervading moral influence and good which the mind of man cannot estimate.

Early in 1823, it appears that Dr. Edwards, learning the distinguished usefulness of a humble and aged

* This date, from a printed paper, may be an error of the press. The death here described is recorded as occurring Oct. 18, 1824. The man was seen to reel as he passed, seated on the tongue of his wagon; and as he descended a hill near the residence of the late Deacon Poor, he fell and met his untimely end.

pastor at Boscawen, New Hampshire, who had trained many youth for public usefulness, and among them the late Hon. Daniel Webster—whose name the pastor in his modesty does not mention—requested of him some of the results of his labors, which might be discreetly used for the advancement of the Redeemer's kingdom. The questions proposed appear in the pastor's meek reply, which we gladly insert as a testimony to the usefulness of many ministers of Christ who serve Him faithfully, and receive a glorious reward, though far removed from the pomp and splendor of this world.

"BOSCAWEN, Jan. 23, 1823.

"REV. AND DEAR SIR—I received yours of Jan. 15th but yesterday. On reading, I found some questions hard, if not too delicate, for me to answer: hard, as I have not sufficient guides to direct me; delicate, as pride may insensibly tempt me to exaggerate; or on the other hand, an affected humility may lead me to keep some things back which the Lord has done for us. But if I can gratify and encourage a Christian brother in the ministry, and directly or indirectly do something to promote the cause of religion by relating, as far as I am able, what God has done by me for his people, I ought to suppress my own feelings, and to suggest a few things in reply to your questions, as far as my memory shall serve, with what helps records may afford.

"Ques. 1. 'How many scholars have you fitted for college?' Perhaps I have offered to college or fitted between ninety and a hundred, of whom thirty-seven have entered upon the ministry, and some others are in progress.

"Ques. 2. 'How many of them became hopefully pious in your family?' As many as sixteen or more.

"Ques. 3. 'How many of those who became hopefully pious in your family have entered the ministry?' Ten at least.

"Ques. 4. 'How many have made a profession of religion under your ministry, and about how many of those do you suppose have been or now are heads of families?' The church that acted in my ordination consisted of twenty members in all, male and female, all of whom were heads of families, and now all but one have been removed by death. Since my settlement, about four hundred and thirty have been added, and I should suppose that three hundred of those have been or now are heads of families.

"Ques. 5. 'About how many souls are there in your congregation, and how many in your church?' My congregation contains about one hundred families, and I think our assemblies are from two to four hundred; the regular members of the church are some short of three hundred.

"Ques. 6. 'About how much is done in your society in a year for benevolent objects?' There are various societies, ways, and means, by which these objects have been promoted, and no annual estimation has been made that has come to my knowledge, except one year, when it amounted to about five hundred dollars. More has been done some years than others, perhaps some years not more than three hundred.

"Ques. 7. 'To the conversion of how many souls do you suppose there is reason to hope, that with the divine blessing, your labors have been instrumental;

and how many of those have been members of your family?' To the first part of your question I have no direct answer prepared, for I have never attempted to make any such estimate. When I entered on the ministry, I reflected with myself, that if I should labor all my days and be instrumental of the salvation of *one soul*, that would be more than an ample reward. But now more than forty-three years have passed since I commenced preaching, and I may say that goodness and mercy have attended me. I experienced one special season of the outpouring of the Holy Spirit before I came to this town, at which season twenty or thirty were hopeful subjects, and a respectable church was established. And since I came here I have been favored with seven or eight; the two first and two last were very powerful. In the former part of my ministry, special revivals were far less frequent than in later years.

"In this region, when I entered on my ministry in this town, *the state of religion wore a very gloomy aspect;* a revival of religion had hardly been known. And in consequence of our first revival, forty years since, I was abundantly called upon to labor in the neighboring towns; and as the doctrines of grace had been but little inculcated, the churches were in a very low and formal state. In a number of instances I witnessed a revolution in sentiment, and a revival of the spirit of religion, which the work that the Lord had wrought among my people served greatly to strengthen and increase, till nearly the whole vicinity became revolutionized.

"But in answer to your question, what shall I say?

If I have been instrumental of good to one soul, to ten, to a hundred, or to a thousand, the glory is all due to God our Saviour; to him be the praise. A Paul may plant and an Apollos water, but God only can give the increase. As to how many of those hopeful subjects of grace have been members of my family, nearly thirty have professed a hope while connected with my family, and a number of others have received impressions, and obtained a hope after they left.

"My dear brother, the work of the ministry appears to me greater and greater as I advance in life. When I look back, I have to mourn my unfaithfulness before Him who weighs the actions of men. I rely on your candor in the freedom which I have used in this hasty epistle. That our Lord Jesus Christ, the great Head of the church, may direct and prosper you in your labors in his vineyard, is the prayer of your friend and brother in the faith and fellowship of the gospel,

"SAMUEL WOOD."

In the silence of the subject of our narrative as to his own labors and usefulness in the five years of his pastoral life at which we have now glanced, we gratefully acknowledge the aid of another sister of Mrs. Edwards, in kindly sketching reminiscences of events which occurred more than thirty years ago, but are still fresh as yesterday, and some of which, we are sure, will lose none of their interest when suns and systems shall have perished.

"On a Sabbath morning when I was about fourteen," she says, "our pastor in Colchester introduced to the pulpit a stranger whose solemn and awakening sermon produced no small stir among the people, with many inquiries as to who he could be, and why they had not before heard of him. My father, who was a man of strong and decided character, and opposed to the doctrines of grace, remarked, that as his erect athletic figure rose before the audience, and he heard his deep-toned impressive voice, he wondered 'what sort of a preacher we had got now,' but soon said to himself, 'that man knows what he is about.' Little did he imagine that this stranger was to become a member of his own family, to exert a powerful influence over his household, and reach even his own mind, which had already so yielded itself to error, that it appeared invulnerable to the truth.

"The impression I received from that sermon was abiding as eternity. The solemnity of his manner when for the first time my eye rested upon his countenance, the expression of awe and reverence with which he opened the Bible and cast his eye around the house, as if to say, 'God is here,' I shall never forget. His text was, '*If any man be in Christ, he is a new creature.*' His voice was powerful and commanding, and every eye was fastened upon him. That sermon opened my eyes to the nature of the new birth. It was evident that the speaker knew by experience what it was. I saw that it was to give God the supreme place in the heart, and to do every thing with reference to pleasing him. There was a reverence, solemnity, humility, and majesty, such as I had never observed in any preacher. He seemed to me to have seen God as Isaiah saw him in the temple, 'on a throne high and lifted up,' and to bow down like Job in the dust before his awful presence. Yet, as I afterwards discovered, it was God *in Christ* that he knew. There was no gloom, no terror, but the most simple confidence, mingled with the profoundest reverence.

"When Mr. Edwards became a visitor in our family, he seldom addressed me directly on the subject of personal religion; and yet he inspired me with deeper convictions of my own ungodliness and selfishness, and of the vanity of all worldly pursuits, than any other man. I give one incident by way of example. At sixteen years of age, returning from my boarding-school with an Album, I waited with much interest for an expected visit from him, to request of him a contribution to its pages. Instead of meeting the wishes of a worldly young girl, he wrote a familiar verse of a hymn. I was at first almost disposed to resent it, and wished to tear it out. But I read it and reread it. Every time I took up the book, that verse seemed to stand out more prominent than any thing else in it—

"'God is my all-sufficient good,
My portion, and my choice;
In Him my vast desires are filled,
And all my powers rejoice.'

"It had the effect upon me that he intended; to reprove me for giving my mind and heart to the vanities of this world. It concentrated in a few words what every thing else he had done and said had before signified to my conscience. I saw that always and everywhere he was supremely desirous to turn my heart from the world to God. I pondered the stanza, displeased, yet impressed. The first line told me the secret of his piety. I saw myself in contrast with him, and he was my human model. For two years I had earnestly studied his character, and now I endeavored to put it to a practical use. I saw that he sat down before the word of God to be taught his will, *that he might do it;* that he resorted thither for instruction and guidance in every thing; and that its truths were incorporated into his very being.

"When he heard that I was hopefully converted, he wrote me an instructive and affecting letter. It was the first I had ever received from him; and I had no doubt what was the nature of its contents. I took it into the attic to read it alone and with prayer. This letter was burned up with the house of my father more than twenty years ago, but I well recollect the first sentence in it: 'And has God, my dear E——, given you a heart to love Him? If so, he has done more for you than if he had bestowed upon you all the wealth of this world.' Every word I esteemed as very precious. The power of his example made it so. I burst into tears on reading this sentence, and after reading the remainder, continued on my knees weeping, and praying that I might be enabled to follow the instructions it contained, and this reading of it was for some time repeated daily in the same way and the same place.

"At the time of Mr. Edwards' early visits at my father's, our household consisted of fifteen or twenty persons. My parents had nine children, all making their home with them. The other persons were house-servants, and laborers on the farm. The colored servant-woman we called Amy. She was a slave, purchased by my father before the emancipation act, but so old that this act did not reach her. There was also in the family a man-servant named Thell, an Irishman of very limited mental capacity. We could not teach him to read, and he could retain scarcely any portions of the Bible. Several of the other laborers had been taken young, and trained by my father on the farm, and so were permanent members of the family. This was the circle to which Mr. Edwards was introduced on his first coming to our house, and on which he was to exert a great and beneficial influence. He was a man of few words, but of gentle and kind manners. On entering the house at first, and ever afterwards, he noticed and addressed every one, taking especial care not to overlook Amy and Thell. Nor was his kindness lost upon them. This stupid man would watch every opportunity to render a service to Mr. Edwards, in return for his kind manner. His remark was, 'I would do any thing for Mr. Edwards; he is the politest man I ever knew.' Gentleness, kindness, and courtesy marked his intercourse with all the members of our family.

"In reviewing his whole connection with us, God's faithfulness in fulfilling the desire of them that fear him is manifest. It must be regarded as a striking instance of answer to prayer. Our mother was descended from a very godly ancestry. Her grandparents had left their home and all their possessions on account of the great profligacy and wickedness prevailing around them, and had settled in Colchester when it was a wilderness, for the sake of enjoying unmolested their religious sentiments, and training up their children in the fear of God. My mother believed that she was converted when about six years old. My earliest recollections are of her faithfulness in inculcating religious truth, and other endeavors for the spiritual good of her household. For a long series of years, she bore the burden of their souls' welfare on her heart alone, feeling that she was the only one of this large household who sought communion with God. At the time of Mr. Edwards' introduction to the family, two only of her children had been given her in answer to her prayers. Long had she wrestled with God in secret for the conversion of my father, being much afflicted by his opposition to true piety, but yet sweetly and patiently waiting upon the Lord, trusting in that word of promise in which he had led her to hope. Our house was always open to visitors, and clergymen were so often entertained there, that it came to be called the 'ministers' home.' But although ministers were always most hospitably welcomed by my father, yet no one of them ever addressed him on the subject of personal religion; nor did my mother ever venture to pray in his presence, or often speak to him on the subject. But here was a young man who at once commanded his respect, and brought to his view a specimen of elevated piety, combined with courtesy and good sense. Whenever he knew that Mr. Edwards was coming, he arranged his business so as to be at home; and during his stay with us, the whole family would be daily assembled to have him lead us in worship.

"I love to recall that large family group, as they

were seated on these occasions in the long family-room, which was almost large enough for a chapel. We often wished it might be used as such, for it would have accommodated all the neighbors, and we lived four miles from any church; but no other religious meetings were ever allowed in the house by my father. This rendered these seasons peculiarly interesting to the pious members of the household. Mr. Edwards would be seated at one end of the room, my father beside him in his arm-chair in the attitude of an attentive listener; my mother next him, in her easy-chair, with such a look of delight and gratitude as could not be mistaken. Then came the children, ranging from the man of thirty-five, down to the child of ten years; then the blacksmith, the cooper, and perhaps a shoemaker, with the other laboring men, and boys and servants. Mr. Edwards would take the large family Bible, which had been in use nearly forty years, and open it with an impressive manner, which seemed to say, now God is about to speak, and we must listen; then closing his eyes with great humility and simplicity, he would ask the aid of the Holy Spirit in reading it. When reading, he would pause on passages that might not be understood, and explain them to the comprehension of the most unlettered of the company. It was evident to all, that he came to the Scriptures as a learner to be taught; and what he might know more than others, he wished to communicate for their benefit.

"One winter, my father having more than usual leisure, had taken up and read several authors on his favorite subjects in theology. They confirmed him in his erroneous views, professing as they did to prove all their teachings by the Scriptures. The time was approaching for Mr. Edwards' visit at the mansion; and the books were read and carefully laid up, to await his visit. 'Now I intend,' said my father, 'to have a thorough talk with Mr. Edwards, and I shall ask him to examine these volumes thoroughly. I 'm sure he will not object to give the time to it, and I do not believe he will be able to answer these powerful arguments.' His interest increased as the time drew near, and upon Mr. Edwards' arrival, my father could scarcely wait for the usual salutations, before saying, 'I wish, Mr. Edwards, that you would take these volumes and look them over carefully, and tell me, if you can, why I should not believe as they teach.' Their principal and favorite doctrine was that of universal salvation. My father's manner of proposing the subject convinced Mr. Edwards that the request was very serious, and he evidently felt himself urgently called to devote time and thought to the subject. He replied that he would do so. The next morning he requested to have a fire in a room by himself. He took the Bible, with the books in question, and spent the whole day alone; probably much of it in prayer. After tea, he informed my father that he was ready. They sat down, surrounded by such of the family as felt interested in the discussion.

"His manner in answering all my father's questions and arguments was kind, respectful, and amiable. He did not aim to show any superior learning or power, and thus to confound him; but in the most patient manner listened to every thing he had to say. He then showed him the fallacies of his favorite authors, their misuse of Scripture in proving their doctrines; and at the same time quoted passage after passage to prove the contrary. He closed by stating facts from his own experience at the death-beds of those who had professed to hold these sentiments, none of which had been peaceful and happy. He then contrasted the life, character, and general influence of this class of men with that of those who had yielded their hearts implicitly to the guidance of the Holy Spirit in reading the Bible. With what interest the discussion was listened to by those members of the family who, in concert with others, had for many years been praying that his eyes might be opened, and his heart prepared for the reception of the truth, you can well imagine. His countenance and manner gradually changed, as Mr. Edwards proceeded to undermine his confidence, and as he was obliged to yield one point after another, until the whole fabric upon which his hopes had been built for eternity, was shaken to its foundation. As he leaned upon the arms of his chair, his whole frame was agitated, and he sat in perfect silence, and listened to an earnest and affectionate appeal to make the Lord Jesus Christ his refuge and trust. In the most solemn manner our friend assured him that none other would be sufficient for him in life, in death, and the judgment; that all other dependences would, at the last, prove refuges of lies, and be swept away like the spider's web.

"After this the books were returned to their owner. Those gentlemen of my father's acquaintance who professed these doctrines, and who had been accustomed, much to the grief of my mother, to visit the house and continually converse upon them, came no more. Never, after this interview to the day of his death, do I recollect hearing my father allude to these doctrines in any way. He read his Bible more, and with deep attention. He was changed in many respects; whether he was savingly converted is not for us to say, but no such effect was produced on him by any other means. No act of Mr. Edwards' life endeared him to us so much as this. We remembered it with gratitude to God, as we looked for the last time upon the lifeless remains of one of the kindest of fathers, whose death was instantaneous.

"I always recur with interest to a residence of six months in Dr. Edwards' family in the year 1821, during which time I had ample opportunity to become acquainted with him as a Christian and a minister. I had not been long in his family before I began to desire that the work of grace should become more deep and thorough in my own heart. His preaching created in me a taste for such works as Bellamy's, Baxter's, Edwards', and Chalmers'. It led me to read the Scriptures with more diligence, and with earnest prayer for the teachings of the Holy Spirit. It brought Christ to my view as I had never previously conceived of him, and inspired me with strong desires not only to know and to love him better, but to be more like him. Mr. Edwards appeared to me to have been favored with unusual views of the preciousness of the Saviour. I inferred this, not merely from the tenor of his preaching, but of his life from day to day, and his prayers both in public and in his family. The latter were always short, comprehending much in a few words. It was a favorite petition, 'that the light of the knowledge of the glory of God might shine into our hearts as it shines in the face of Jesus Christ.' His whole life, as I saw it in the family and elsewhere, led me to believe that this constant desire of his heart was granted him. Just before I left Andover, Mrs. Edwards told me one day, confidentially, that Mr. Edwards had lain awake the last part of the preceding night. She said that she spoke to him, but he did not incline to converse, and on rising in the morning, he remarked to her that he had enjoyed during the last few hours some very precious views of the Saviour. I do not recollect the words, but he described them as such as to fill his soul with inexpressible delight. This was the only time that I ever knew of his speaking of his own religious exercises to any one. He *never* talked about himself; but as I once heard him preach from the text, 'I shall be satisfied, when I awake, with thy likeness,' I felt sure that he drew from his own rich experiences of the presence and power of Christ.

"In this visit I became acquainted with his pastoral character. He seemed to know every one of his large flock, not only by name, but their past history and present condition. I often rode with him to different parts of his extensive parish when he went to preach his weekly lectures. It was very common for him when we passed a house to give me the name of the family residing in it, and its history for several generations. He was peculiarly fond of tracing the dealings of Providence with individuals and families. Pastoral visitation was attended to by him most faithfully. In his visits in the latter part of the day, he usually took tea with the family. This enabled him generally to see and speak with them all. After tea, he always proposed to pray with the family before leaving. If all the members were not present, the absent ones were called. The Bible was brought and placed before him. He would say, 'We will unite in singing a hymn.' He would repeat the first line of one familiar to himself, and if it was not familiar to the family, he would continue to repeat two lines at a time. His favorite hymns for such occasions were,

"'Guide me, O thou great Jehovah.'
'Jesus, lover of my soul.'
'Lord, thou wilt hear me when I pray.'
'While thee I seek, protecting power,' etc.

After this he would open the Bible, close his eyes and audibly ask the teachings of the Holy Spirit to accompany the reading of it. Sometimes he would explain the passage or make other pertinent remarks. It was so evident that he yielded his own understanding implicitly to the teachings he sought, that when he explained a verse the conviction was deeply felt that he had expressed the very mind of God. 'Open thou mine eyes, that I may behold wondrous things out of thy law,' was constantly on his lips. How often would he say, 'We should always listen to the Bible as to God speaking to us: be still—listen when God speaks.' 'Some complain that they do not feel enough. If they want feeling, this is the way to get it. Go away alone with the Bible and let God speak to you, and always that you may *obey* him; learn his will, that you may *do* it.'

"During this winter he had familiar conferences for the families in his own neighborhood. They met at different houses, as if for a visit. He would sometimes commence them with reading a hymn, and expressing the thoughts it suggested. Once he took the 119th Psalm, 9th part, by Watts. The Psalmist, he said, seemed suddenly to awake to a sense of God's goodness, and he exclaims,

"'Thy mercies *fill the earth*, O Lord!'

Then he sees his goodness in his works,

"'How *good* thy *works* appear;'

and quickly his word comes to mind, and this calls forth a prayer, 'Open mine eyes'—not because he was physically blind, but his understanding was darkened by sin—

"'Open mine eyes to read thy *word*,
And see thy wonders there.'

Then he looks at himself, and is reminded of God and acknowledges him as the author of his frame:

"'My heart was fashioned by thy hand;'

and what inference does he draw from this? Why, the most natural in the world,

"'My service is *thy due*.'

Who else can have such claims to it? Then follows another prayer, because he feels his dependence even to think a good thought:

"'O make thy servant understand
The *duties* he must do.'

Then,

"'Since I'm a stranger here below,
Let not thy path be hid.'

Here he described a man wandering in a wilderness without guide or compass, when one competent to lead him safely through appears, and offers to become his guide. Such an one the Psalmist found; he trusted him, yielded himself to him, and he prays,

"'Mark the road my feet should go,
And be my constant guide.'

'God is in his word; it is a light, a lamp to our feet,' etc. Thus he went through the whole of the eight verses of that Psalm. I remember with what interest and delight those families would listen to these familiar instructions, and hope I have not yet lost their influence. His aim seemed to be not merely to bring truth before the mind, but to help his people to digest it, to revolve it over and over until it became a part of themselves, and they were transformed by it.

"I well remember the visits the pious, praying women used to make at his house with their knitting-work. Some of the time would be spent by them in prayer; and he would always come into the parlor, either before or after tea, and give them an opportunity for some conversation with him. This would often be introduced by questions from them on some point of practical religion, or about some passage of Scripture. Such visits from his people were always closed by singing a hymn, reading the Scriptures, and prayer.

"When individuals came to ask his counsel, or to state difficulties in their religious experience, I never knew him appear to consider it an intrusion, or wish them to leave, but he gave himself up to do them all the good he could. I think it was his intimate acquaintance with his people that gave to his preaching such weight. He knew what they needed, and it was evident that he aimed to meet their necessities, and feed them with the bread of life.

"I shall never forget a series of familiar lectures he delivered on the 119th Psalm. The effect was to make me feel that there were treasures in the Bible which I had not yet found, and to make me resolve that I would never give over till I could say with the Psalmist, that I had found them 'sweeter than honey and the honey-comb.'

"There were uncommon Bible readers under his ministry. The Bible was the great book. Some of the aged women might answer well to the description of Anna, so familiar were they with its pages, and so constant at the place of prayer.

"It was not merely Mr. Edwards' sermons which attracted his people in such numbers to the sanctuary Sabbath after Sabbath, and led them to sit there with profit and delight. The aged people being unusually numerous, many of them were seated according to an old custom just in front of the pulpit. Their punctuality was very noticeable, as if they were glad when it was said unto them, 'Let us go into the house of the Lord.' Order and stillness were observable both in and about the house. The people were early in their places. His very manner when he entered the sanctuary, seemed to indicate that he had come there communing with God. He seemed never to forget the directions, 'Be not rash with thy mouth, and let not thy heart be hasty to utter any thing before God; for God is in heaven, and thou upon earth: therefore let thy words be few.' While he was a pastor, he gave himself eminently to a pastor's work. He made it his study how he could do his people the most good, and best fit them for heaven. He did indeed take a deep interest in the objects of the Tract and Foreign Mission Societies, and his labors for them at this time were abundant; but he allowed nothing to interfere with his duty to the souls for whom he was thus personally responsible. His addresses before missionary meetings were not usually written, but flowed spontaneously from his heart. In a few moments, he would often present some grand and sublime view, that would deeply affect and elevate the audience. His comprehensive mind seemed to embrace the present world and the coming eternity. He believed that this earth belongs to Christ, and that he is to possess it; and the glory of the Saviour in the success of his gospel, seemed to be the great inspiring motive which led him to spend and be spent in laboring to bring the world into subjection to him.

"Surely never had a pastor more constant and unremitted proof of the confidence and affection of his people. When he married, it was enough that they received among them the companion of his choice; and there was no scene of which my father seemed to take more delight in speaking, in the latter years of his life, than that of the cordiality and kindness with which a great company assembled to welcome to her new home one who was to share the pastor's sorrows and joys; and their love and esteem were neither withheld nor diminished. Of the mothers in Israel, whose sympathy in sickness or trials was ever manifested, I well remember one. Her deeply furrowed cheek and withered hand seemed to indicate that she had already served her appointed time, but she lived many years a comfort and support to her pastor by her fervent prayers and unwearied devotion to himself and his family. It is sad to think that such relations of a pastor and his flock must be sundered, and joyful to think that after the earthly tie that binds them is broken, there is one above that shall endure."

CHAPTER IV.

HIS MINISTRY IN ANDOVER—CONTINUED.

BIBLE VIEWS OF THE MINISTRY AND CHURCH OF CHRIST. 1823, 1824.

On the 12th of February, 1823, he preached in Boston his published sermon, "I am doing a great work, so that I cannot come down," before the Young Men's Education Society. Nehemiah was building an earthly city; but these young men are raising up instruments to build the city of the Redeemed in heaven. "Their object is to increase the number of pious, able, and faithful ministers of the gospel, who shall spend their days in preaching the unsearchable riches of Christ to their fellow-men—ministers who in temper and conduct shall resemble Paul, and all who in every generation have followed his example; who have themselves been born of the Spirit; who glory in the cross, and by it are crucified to the world, and the world crucified to them; who determine not to know any thing among their hearers, save Jesus Christ, and him crucified; and who count all things but loss for the excellency of the knowledge of Jesus—ministers who will be able to teach others with the same teaching which they receive from God; who will not shun to declare all his counsel; will keep the faith; not count even life dear unto them; and, as the Lord shall open the way, will go forth 'into all the world, and preach the gospel to every creature.'"

He proceeds to show that "the labors of such ministers are the grand means which God has appointed for the salvation of men;" that "of these means a vast portion of men are destitute;" and that "by these means God accomplishes great ends." Men are in a state of apostasy, sin, and ruin. They need salvation. A great salvation has been provided in Christ; and the preaching of his gospel is the grand means of turning them from sin to God.

"What nation, or body of men, have ever been led to turn from idolatry to the service of the living God, without the preaching of the gospel? What church has ever been gathered, even in Christian lands, without the preaching of the gospel? What body of men have ever been led to remember the Sabbath-day and keep it holy, to assemble statedly for the worship of God, daily to search the Scriptures, to pray in their families, to train up their children in the nurture and admonition of the Lord, and walk before them in all his ordinances, except those who have heard the *preaching* of the gospel?

"What body of men have ever been led to feel that they 'are not their own,' but 'are bought with a price;' and been persuaded by this to 'glorify God in body and spirit, which are his?' What body of men have ever learned to imitate Him who 'maketh his sun to rise on the evil, and on the good; and sendeth rain on the just, and on the unjust?' Who has ever seen a company of Howards, or a single 'Howard Benevolent Society,' among all the generations and tribes of men who have never heard the gospel? What extensive plan of charity ever was known of any kind, calculated to convey substantial good to men, in any, I might say, even of the concerns of *this* life? But these I shall omit—for while I speak it, I see the heavens passing away, and the elements melting down; the earth and the things of it burnt up, and all its concerns swallowed up in an opening and boundless eternity.

"Who has ever engaged in the benevolent plan of making known Jehovah in that wondrous exhibition of himself, which drew forth from the lips of angels, 'Glory to God in the highest, and on earth peace, good will towards men?' Who has ever engaged in making known God as a *Saviour*, coming down from heaven 'to seek and to save that which was lost,' and in opening upon the dying nations the infinite riches of his grace, except those who have heard the gospel?

"Would our Mayhews and Eliots have gone from island to island, and spent the daytime in traversing the desert, and the night in translating the Bible, if they had never heard the preaching of the gospel?

"Would Brainerd have poured out his thousands of supplications in the wilderness, and spent the vigor of his days in bringing wandering pagans back to God, if he had never heard the preaching of the gospel?

"Would Swartz or Carey, Vanderkemp or Buchanan have broken into the empire of darkness, and held up to the perishing nations the light of the glorious gospel, if they had never themselves heard the gospel? Would the gospel itself ever have passed the limits of Judea, or its glad tidings been published to a single gentile nation on earth, if it had not been done by those who had heard the gospel? Search the records of all ages, and you will find that such works of mercy have never been done, except by those who have heard the preaching of the gospel. Search the Scriptures; examine the economy of divine grace; look at the promises of God, and see their fulfilment in his providence; and you will find that such works of mercy never will be done, except by those who hear the gospel.

"Nor is this all. Extinguish the light of a living ministry, and let it not be revived, and all Christendom will sink into pagan darkness. Bibles, and the writings of pious men, they may continue to have; but if these do not produce influence enough to raise up among them a living ministry, all will soon be locked up in the slumbers of moral death.

"This is not because the Bible does not reveal every principle of holy action which is or can be exhibited by living preachers, and every principle too which is needed in order to arouse the whole world, and pour the tide of benevolence over all its population; but it is because, without living preachers, men have not the grand means which God has appointed for causing the principles of holy action which are revealed in the Bible, to take possession of the heart, and to govern the life.

"The Bible may be sent to every family in the world, yet if they never hear the preaching of the gospel, it will not by the great mass of people ever be daily read. Its holy principles will not be received, and its holy commands will not be obeyed. If its principles are examined enough to be understood, they will lodge in the understanding, and not take possession of the heart. They will be viewed as matters of speculation, rather than *felt* as principles of holy practice.

"How is it with those parts of our own country which once had the light of a living ministry, but in which *that light has been extinguished only for half a century?* Is there not a great increase of moral darkness? Is not the Sabbath almost universally profaned; the worship and ordinances of God neglected? Do not idleness, dissipation, and iniquity prevail? And even with the sober part of the community, is it not the great inquiry, 'What shall we eat, what shall we drink, and wherewithal shall we be clothed?' Who will show us *earthly* good? And do not the great interests of vital godliness visibly and rapidly decline?

"In one part of our country, there were *sixteen towns* which were all supplied with settled ministers. Churches were gathered in every town, and many of them were in a flourishing condition. In the mysterious providence of God, they have within half a century all been left destitute.* They retained the Bible and the writings of pious men in every town; but the great interests of vital religion visibly and rapidly declined. Ten years ago there were not, upon an average, nine members of the church in a town, although

* We have reason to believe that these towns were within about fifty miles of Boston; another illustration of the low state into which the churches had fallen in the latter part of the last century.

the towns contained, upon an average, nearly a thousand people. In four towns the churches had become extinct. In one of those towns, when they had a settled minister, there was a church of forty members; and in another, there was a church of more than sixty members; but those members were not suffered to continue by reason of death. And none arose to fill their places. At length the grave closed upon the very last member, and the light even of a Christian profession was extinguished. One church not extinct had had no communion for five years. Two other churches had had none for twenty years. Is it not plain that they had not the grand means which God has appointed for awakening men from the slumber of moral death, and leading them out of darkness into the light and liberty of his children? Even the passing traveller, in view of the footsteps of depravity which he everywhere witnessed, could not but feel that the glory had departed. So would it be without the preaching of the gospel in every town in our country, and throughout the world. * * *

"SALVATION! who can measure its mighty import? Who can tell the greatness of that deliverance, when a soul is born of God? Who can tell what it is for an immortal soul, which must exist as long as God shall exist, to be delivered from inheriting everlasting burnings, changed into the image of God, and raised to dwell with Christ, to see him as he is, and be *like* him for ever? Oh, salvation, even to *one* soul, is *a great thing*. And every faithful minister that you raise up, may, with the blessing of God, be the means of salvation to great numbers.

"When Richard Baxter began to preach the gospel at Kidderminster, there was but about one praying family in a street. The Sabbath was openly profaned; immorality of almost every kind prevailed; and the whole town was a scene of moral desolation. Before he had preached there fourteen years, in passing the streets on the Sabbath, one might hear a hundred families engaged in family devotion, and in some streets there were not more than two families that neglected it. The number of communicants at the Lord's table was more than six hundred; and among them all were not twelve persons who did not give reason to hope that they were born of God. At the same time, he was hopefully the means of salvation to numbers in Worcester, Cleobury, Dudley, Sheffield, and many other places where he occasionally preached the gospel. Several of these were afterwards distinguished ministers of Christ.

"Almost every week he received letters, mentioning instances of hopeful conversion by means of his 'Call to the Unconverted.' More than twenty thousand copies of this work were printed in a year. It was published not only in England, but in Scotland, Ireland, France, Germany, Holland, and America. And yet it was believed by himself and by others, that his 'Saints' Rest' had been the means of salvation to still greater numbers. Portions of his works have been read in nearly all the Protestant countries of Christendom, down to this day. And it is not too much to suppose, that there has not been a year since Baxter died, in which his works have not, to some, been the means of salvation. And this, should the

Lord so order it, may continue to be the case to the end of the world. Go forward into eternity, and by its everlasting light look at the greatness of what God accomplished by means of Richard Baxter.

"Do you say that Baxter was a rare example? I grant it. And in this day, when the children of Zion are taking pleasure in her stones, and favoring her dust, you may expect *other* rare examples; and that they will be multiplied until they shall become *common* examples.

"Henry Martyn, before he reached the age of thirty-one, besides preaching the gospel to great numbers, in demonstration of the Spirit and of power, had translated the whole of the New Testament for the millions of Hindoostan; and also for the millions of Persia.

"By the labors of another minister, God has prepared the whole Bible for the hundreds of millions of China.

"And our own countryman, Samuel J. Mills, although he died a young man, lived long enough to be a leading instrument in the formation of a Bible Society in Pennsylvania, and in Ohio, Indiana, Illinois, Tennessee, Mississippi, and Louisiana. And he was also a leading instrument in the formation of the American Board of Commissioners for Foreign Missions, the United Foreign Missionary Society, the African School, and the American Bible Society; institutions which are extending the word of life to hundreds of thousands of our fellow-men.

"But you say, these were *missionaries*. Missionaries? So, I trust, will be many whom you are raising up, and missionaries who will explore every dark region under heaven, and spread the light of holiness 'from sea to sea, and from the river to the ends of the earth.'"

A few months afterwards, Dr. Edwards was called to advocate, at a public meeting in Boston, the resolution, "That *the influence of education societies upon our literary institutions* ought to be acknowledged with gratitude to God." He begins by showing that the pilgrim fathers, in establishing *common-schools*, sought that their children should become "wise unto salvation, through faith in Christ Jesus," and hence regarded piety an essential requisite in a teacher. "Those men who left the delights of their native country, braved the dangers of the ocean, and settled in a waste howling wilderness, that they might educate their children for God, would not commit them to one who knew not God. 'How,' said they, 'can he teach others what he does not himself know? Besides, if he is not a pious man, his example, instead of leading them to God, will tend to lead them away from him. And what advantage will it be to our children to become wise for this world, and yet be fools for the world to come; to become great and distinguished here, and yet be outcasts from the presence and favor of God hereafter? Nor had they much confidence that, without pious instruction and example, their children would ever become wise or happy for this world. They had learnt the lesson which ought to be written upon every man's heart, that godliness is that alone which is profitable unto all things, 'having promise of the life that now is, and that which is to come.'

"It was the promotion of this also which was their object in the establishment of *academies*. This also was their object in the establishment of *colleges*. They were founded for the purpose, primarily, of raising up ministers of the gospel. Our fathers, in making this the object in establishing our literary institutions, were *wise* men, and if we do not make it our object in supporting them, we shall be as far from wisdom as they were from folly. Whatever tends to promote this object in our literary institutions, tends to promote their prosperity.

"Education societies tend strongly to promote this object. Since their formation they have assisted more than seven hundred and fifty young men, of hopeful piety, in their preparation for the gospel ministry. About two-thirds of these, it is supposed, have been instructors of schools. Education societies then have furnished five hundred instructors of common-schools. Suppose that each one has had the care, upon an average, of forty children; this has brought two thousand children under their daily instruction. To them they have read the Bible; with them united in morning and evening supplication. And often, after showing them their sins, have they pointed them to 'the Lamb of God, that taketh away the sin of the world;' and that too at the most interesting period of their existence, when they were forming and fixing their character for eternity. Who that knows the worth of the soul, or views it on a state of trial, and bound to eternity, does not here see cause for gratitude to Almighty God for the influence of education societies? I have known a single teacher, a charity scholar too, in a single season, hopefully the means, under God, of leading no less than ten of his pupils to that knowledge of Christ which is life eternal. Eight of these are now members of the church, and have for years adorned the doctrine of God our Saviour by their lives and conversation.

"Probably more than four hundred of the beneficiaries of education societies have been members of academies. Here they have come into contact, as daily companions, with not less than one thousand youth who are preparing for public life. And as 'he that walketh with wise men shall be wise,' their influence on them in promoting diligence, sobriety, and the fear of the Lord, has been eminently salutary.

"Several hundred of these beneficiaries have been members of colleges. In thirteen different colleges there have been, within seven years, revivals of religion. In seven of them, in the course of two years, one hundred and eighty students were added to the church. And it is the united opinion of the officers of these colleges, that no inconsiderable part of these efforts must be ascribed, under God, to the influence of beneficiaries.

"We hear of a revival of religion in a college, and rejoice in it as a great event. But when we look at it only in general, we have but a very inadequate idea of its importance. Fix your eyes upon a single individual. He has distinguished talents, and has come to college for the purpose of preparing to make a distinguished figure in the world. He has no religion, has in view no higher object than himself, and never casts a look beyond the limits of time. Upon the members of that college God pours out his Spirit. Numbers are convicted of sin, and anxiously inquiring what they shall do to be saved. He remains unmoved. He looks down with scorn and contempt upon those who are anxious for eternity.

"But He who inhabiteth eternity has made him for a different purpose, and an arrow from his quiver pierces his heart. He too is distressed, and finds no rest. In the class of which he is a member, there is one charity student. No sooner is this young man distressed on account of his sins, than he attaches himself to that charity student. Often they are seen in the lonely walk engaged in ardent counsel, one anxious to know who can 'take away the heart of stone,' and the other anxious to tell him. On a certain day they retire to a mountain, in imitation, I trust, of Him who 'went up into a mountain to pray,' and there unite in supplication to the God of heaven for the blessings of his grace. Impressions are made by the power of the Holy Ghost upon the mind of that young man which will *never* be effaced. He becomes an ardent disciple of the Lord Jesus Christ, and devotes his time, talents, and influence to the promotion of His glory and the salvation of His people.

"Much is done by him before he leaves college. Then he enters the ministry, and his labors are blessed. Numerous churches and congregations, who have heard him with delight, are anxious to obtain him for their minister, to go in and out before them, break to them the bread of life, and guide them and their children in the way to heaven.

"But God has opened a fountain in that man's soul, from which flows a current of benevolence too strong to be confined within the limits of Christendom. He crosses the Atlantic, passes round the Cape of Good Hope, and up through the Indian Ocean, and for years proclaims the glad tidings of salvation on the islands and continent of Asia. From that land of moral death, he cries with a voice that is heard half round the globe, 'O ye blood-bought churches of Christ, let the cry among you be, Whom shall we send, and who will go for us as messengers to the heathen? And O, ye pious youth, let the echo among you be, Here are we, send us.' Nor does he speak only to those in Christian lands; no, he daily tells the wandering pagans of a Saviour who has bought them with his blood. With one hand he points them to the cross, and with the other gives them the New Testament which he and his associates have translated and printed in the language of ten millions of people. More than two thousand children are collected together in missionary schools, to read in their own tongue the wonderful works of Jehovah. Hundreds of thousands of religious tracts are put in circulation, and a system of Christian means opened, which, like streams from the fountain of life, are uniting in one great and mighty river to carry the blessings of salvation through that extended and desolate part of the world.

"At some future day, I see a Hindoo traveller crossing that mighty desert. Weary and thirsty, his soul faints within him; but directed by a hand unseen, he meets this current of mercy, and it is to him 'as a river of water in a dry place,' and its banks are 'as the shadow of a great rock in a weary land.' He drinks of this water, and never thirsts. It is 'in him a well of water springing up into everlasting life.' And as he rises and goes onward 'from strength to strength,' his heart kindles with holy desire to know the source of this celestial river. With an enthusiasm more ardent than ever sought the source of the Niger or the Nile, he traces it through a course of eighteen thousand miles, and finds that it comes from America. Not content with this, he traces it among our hills and dales, till he comes to a *literary institution.* Not content with this, but wishing to see the very crevice from which it sprung, he enters the interior, and after searching, finds that he who was honored of God as an instrument of opening this fountain with all its blessings upon the world, was *a charity student.* And uniting with all pious charity students, and all pious benefactors of charity students, all who have been or shall be saved from eternal death by their labors, he gives the glory to God for ever."

HIS ADDRESS ON SACRED ELOQUENCE.

The "Porter Rhetorical Society of the Theological Seminary" having appointed him to deliver an address before the officers and members of the seminary, and the body of clergymen and others to assemble at the anniversary of the institution, September 26, 1824, he chose the great theme of *a minister's preaching the gospel as it is given by inspiration in the Old and New*

Testaments, in which he gives by far the best testimony and record within our reach of his own aims, and how he fulfilled them in his public ministrations.

The editors of the Boston Recorder doubtless echoed the impressions of the community of evangelical Christians at the time, when they said, "Who would not expect on such an occasion, and before such an audience as annually collects at Andover, that an address of this kind would contain fine specimens of writing, labored periods, rich selections of imagery, sublimity of description, and a powerful combination of language? But no; here is no display, no dazzle, no apparent effort. Mr. Edwards was to speak to an audience whose sympathies and consciences were awake, and his is the eloquence of the heart. It is not boisterous, not vehement, no swell, no dashing, but you are borne on a stream so clear, that the very foundations over which it rolls are laid bare, and so deep and so strong, that resistance is mocked. We never recollect hearing or reading an appeal so simple in its plan and execution, and yet so powerful in its effect. The plan is, to answer three questions: 'What was the object of God in appointing the ordinance of public speaking on sacred subjects? What kind of speaking most strongly tends to accomplish that object? And how may men of competent talents and learning attain to that kind of speaking?' We give some extracts, to show how *an inimitable simplicity* can be united with true eloquence. We consider this style as the true style for a sermon. A child can understand every sentence, and a philosopher kindle at the energy of its deep-toned eloquence.

One thing more. The writer derives his eloquence and power from the Bible. The language of inspiration is inseparably interwoven with his style, and the profound infidel of France would, we think, have extolled the Bible with a double enthusiasm, could he have often seen its eloquence embodied in such writing as the discourse before us. When Mr. Edwards takes up the second point of discussion, he lays down what we consider a very important position, and no less ably supported than clearly laid down. It makes sacred eloquence spring from a heart burning with love to God and the souls of men; and all attempts at sacred eloquence without these, are like the splendor of snow in the moonlight of December—it shines and sparkles, but the more it does so, the more it freezes. Preachers may talk about eloquence, they may write prettily, they may speak charmingly, but unless they feel the everlasting truths which they utter, they are not and cannot be eloquent."

Having premised that sacred eloquence is the art of *speaking well on sacred subjects,* he says, "These are subjects which relate to God, to Jesus Christ, to the Holy Ghost, to the souls of men, and to eternity. They relate especially to the wondrous manifestation of the Godhead for the deliverance of unnumbered millions of our race from the ruins of the apostasy, and their exaltation to the holiness and bliss of heaven. The character of God; the creation and fall of man; the way opened for his recovery by the incarnation, obedience, and death of Christ; the transformation of those who believe, by the power of the Holy Ghost, into the divine image; the dissolution of the world; and the eternal destinies of the righteous and the wicked, are all appropriately subjects of sacred eloquence."

"What, then, was *the object of God in appointing the ordinance of public speaking on sacred subjects?*

"It was the promotion of his glory in the salvation of men. This salvation consists in deliverance from a state of eternal sinning and suffering, and in exaltation to a state of eternal holiness and bliss. It includes a change of character from a state of enmity to a state of friendship with God. This change is manifested by repentance of sin, faith in Jesus Christ, and obedience to his commands. The grand means of effecting it is, by divine appointment, public speaking. This then is the object of sacred eloquence, *to reconcile men to God, for the purpose of promoting his glory in their salvation.*

"This is stated to be the object by the highest authority. Said one of the most eloquent men that ever lived, who was taught this divine art from heaven, and who spoke as he was moved by the Holy Ghost, 'Knowing the terror of the Lord, we persuade men.' To what did he persuade them? 'Be ye reconciled to God.' 'We pray you in Christ's stead, be ye reconciled to God.' 'Believe on the Lord Jesus Christ.' And 'whether ye eat or drink, or whatsoever ye do, do all to the glory of God.' Why did he wish to persuade them to this? 'Knowing the terror of the Lord:' 'Other foundation can no man lay than is laid, which is Jesus Christ.' 'Neither is there salvation in any other; for there is none other name under heaven given among men, whereby we must be saved.' 'And he that believeth not the Son shall not see life, but the wrath of God abideth on him.' 'The Lord shall be revealed from heaven with his mighty angels in flaming fire, taking vengeance on them that know not God, and that obey not the gospel of our Lord Jesus Christ, who shall be punished with everlasting destruction from the presence of the Lord, and from the glory of his power.' To save men from this overwhelming and endless destruction, and to raise them to that 'exceeding and eternal weight of glory,' is the object of sacred eloquence. This was the object of Paul. It was the object of Him who spake as never man spake. It is the object of all who are like him, and who, with his spirit, engage in this employment. This *ought* to be the object of every minister of the gospel; and of every individual who unites with this society for the purpose of improvement in sacred eloquence. And on this occasion, brethren, I shall take it for granted that this is *your* object. I shall take it for granted that your object is the same with that of Paul, from the memorable period when light shone around about him from heaven, and it was said of him, 'Behold, he prayeth;' and when he was borne onward by the love of Christ, through perils of waters, perils of robbers, perils by his own countrymen, by the heathen, in the city, in the wilderness, in the sea, among false brethren, in weariness and painfulness, hunger, cold, thirst, and nakedness, not counting life dear to him, till he broke out in triumphant strains, 'I have fought a good fight, I have finished my course, I have kept the faith. Henceforth there is laid up for me a crown of righteousness, which the Lord, the righteous Judge, shall give me at that day; and not to me only, but unto all them also that love his appearing.' Yes, I hear your hearts echo, this is the object.

"*What kind of speaking* then most strongly tends to accomplish this object? It is not every kind of speaking, nor is it every kind of speaking on sacred subjects. 'What is the chaff to the wheat, saith the Lord?' 'If I say unto a wicked man, Thou shalt surely die, and thou dost not *warn* that wicked man, he shall die.'"

A WORLD-WIDE OBJECTION CONSIDERED.

"What kind of speaking then will save men? I hear it whispered, 'No kind of speaking whatever. To save men is the work of God. Repentance of sin, and faith in Jesus Christ, are his gifts. It is not of him that willeth, nor of him that runneth, but of God that showeth mercy.' I know it. Every man who understands and believes the Bible, knows it. Paul may plant, and Apollos may water, but God giveth the increase. But *how* does he give it? Without the planting of Paul and the watering of Apollos, or with them? After he has appointed means, and commanded men to use them, does he give his blessing without the use of those means, or with it? And does the fact that *he* gives the blessing, render the means which he has appointed useless? Does it give the least hope, or furnish the least excuse to those that neglect them? Let God answer. 'He that is idle in seed-time, shall beg in harvest, and have nothing.' Although neither is he that planteth any thing, neither he that watereth, as to being the *author* of blessings, yet he that planteth and he that watereth are both as instruments essential, because God has appointed them. And working all things after the counsel of his own will, he gives blessings in the way of his own appointment. Hence, it is a principle in his administration, settled as the ordinances of heaven, that 'as a man soweth, so shall he reap.' And this is as true in spiritual things, as in temporal. He of whom are all things, and by whom are all things, ordinarily apportions the harvest in kind and quantity to the seed sown, the ground cultivated, and the labor bestowed upon it. Hence the foundation for that which is the *glory* of creatures on a state of probation, *an abiding conviction of absolute dependence on God, and of obligation perfectly to obey him;* leading to deep humility, fervent gratitude, untiring perseverance in duty, a disposition to view all blessings as the gifts of God and render to him for ever all the glory. And this, instead of palsying the powers of the human soul, will raise them to the highest pitch of exertion. It will give to men a boldness and an energy, a vigor and perseverance, both in willing and in doing, which nothing but a conviction that God is working in them both to will and to do, will ever accomplish. Hence when He, in whom dwelt the fulness of the Godhead bodily, would lead those who were not sufficient of themselves even to *think* any thing as of themselves, to undertake, and to accomplish the most difficult and glorious work ever thought of by mortals, he told them, 'Without me ye can do nothing.' Having fastened the conviction of this truth in their minds, he commanded, 'Go ye into all the world, and preach the gospel to every creature.' And to sweep away every objection which the ignorance, sloth, pride, or malice of men could raise, he said, 'He that believeth and is baptized, shall be saved; and he that believeth not, shall be damned.' 'And lo, I am with you alway, even unto the end of the world.'

"Believing his declaration, and relying on his promise, as workers together with him, they went forth, in the plenitude of their weakness and his strength, conquering and to conquer. Satan and his legions, driven out from strong-holds which they had fortified for ages, surrendered their captives, and retired in dismay before this band of martyrs, as they waved in holy triumph from continent to continent, the banner of the cross. Songs of deliverance even from eternal death, broke from a thousand tongues, and ten thousand hearts poured forth their choicest strains to God their deliverer. But in doing this, they lost sight neither of the instruments, nor of him who used them. With one breath they cried, 'How beautiful upon the mountains are the feet of them that bring good tidings, and that publish the gospel of peace.' With the next they cried, 'Unto Him that loved us, and washed us from our sins in his own blood, and hath made us kings and priests unto God and his Father, to him be glory and dominion for ever and ever.'

"So it has been in every generation. So we learn from the Bible it will be. I heard a voice saying, Who are these, and whence came they? I looked, and lo, a multitude which no man could number, of all nations, and kindreds, and people, and tongues, stood before the throne of God and the Lamb, clothed with white robes and palms in their hands, and cried with a loud voice, saying, Salvation to our God that sitteth upon the throne, and unto the Lamb. Such, by divine appointment, are to be the trophies of sacred eloquence. Attended by the power of the Holy Ghost, it is destined to be the means of peopling heaven—preparing multitudes which no man can number to shine before the throne of God in the lustre of his image, and reflect the brightness of his glory through the universe.

"The question then returns, and with augmented interest, What kind of speaking most strongly tends to accomplish this? How must a man speak, in order to promote to the greatest extent the salvation of men?"

THE TRUTHS OF THE BIBLE IN THEIR OWN DIVINELY INSPIRED CONNECTION.

"*He must declare all the truths which God reveals, in the connections in which he reveals them. And he must declare them with those* FEELINGS *which these truths, clearly apprehended, cordially embraced, and faithfully obeyed, will inspire.* The only reason why preaching of any kind is ever effectual to the salvation of men is, God has appointed it, and attends it with his blessing. And he has appointed not only that men should preach, but has told them *what* to preach. 'Preach the preaching that I bid thee.' 'Hear the word at my mouth, and give them warning from me.' 'He that hath my word, let him speak my word *faithfully.*'

This requires him to preach *whatever* God reveals, and *as* he reveals it. A preacher has nothing to do to invent new truths, to preach those which God does not reveal, or those which he does in any different manner and connection from what he reveals them. To the law and the testimony—if preachers speak not according to these, there is no light in them. The law of the Lord, as he reveals it, is perfect, converting the soul. It needs only to be understood and obeyed to prepare men for heaven. The testimony of the Lord, as he gives it, is sure, making wise the simple. All that a preacher has to do is, in the clearest and kindest manner, to exhibit this; illustrate it to the understanding, and impress it upon the heart. 'Go ye into all the world, and preach *the Gospel* to every creature.' This gospel is that revelation which is made to men in the Bible; all of which is given by inspiration of God, and is profitable for doctrine, reproof, correction, and instruction in righteousness, that the man of God may be perfect, thoroughly furnished unto every good work. The whole of this revelation, would you be instrumental to the greatest extent in saving souls, you must preach, and nothing more. The Bible must be to you what the pillar of fire and of cloud was to Moses. Where that goes, *you* must go. If you stop, God moves on without you. You are left behind in a wilderness, without a guide, without a helper. Your safety and your success both depend upon following him. Where he stops, *you* must stop. If you move, go which way you will, you go without God. Fight as you may, you only beat the air. Instead of conquering, you are conquered. Or if you *seem* to yourselves to gain a temporary triumph, and begin to scowl upon less adventurous spirits, who dare not move without God, it is only a feint of the enemy to draw you into thicker ambush, and sink you into deeper ruin. You may imagine that you have hosts strong and mighty, who can overcome in battle; but like the Egyptians in the sea, the more numerous your hosts and the heavier your artillery, the deeper you sink. In a warfare like this, nothing can be done without God. And he will accompany none but those who follow him.

"Would you rise in sacred eloquence to the highest possible pitch, your eloquence as to matter, must be the echo of the eloquence of God. That, like its author, is perfect. The perfection of human eloquence is to be like it. That is the pattern which you must always follow. And those who honor me, saith God, I will honor; but those who despise me, shall be lightly esteemed. In the battle with flesh and blood, principalities and powers, and the rulers of the darkness of this world, and spiritual wickedness in high places, *you,* without God, are nothing; less than nothing and vanity; as the chaff which the whirlwind driveth away. You cannot for a moment sustain yourself; how can you conquer others?

"In illustration of the principle under consideration, look a moment at the grand topic of revelation: that which as a means in saving sinners is the principal instrument of doing all that revelation can do, namely, *the character of God.* Who understands it, and who can understand it but himself? Who else can reveal it? And after he has revealed it, who can add to that revelation, or take from it, or in any respect essentially alter it, without making it *essentially* imperfect? No matter how great a man's talents, or extensive his learning; had he a mind surpassing a thousand-fold the mind of Gabriel, and stored with all the wisdom and knowledge that has ever existed, or that ever will exist out of the mind of God, he could add nothing and take away nothing from divine revelation without rendering it, so far as he altered it, imperfect; and tending to prevent its proper effect on minds. Would you produce the right effect on minds, and raise this effect to the highest pitch of intensity, and give it the greatest extent, show them the character of God just as he reveals it. If you fail *essentially* here, you may expect to fail everywhere. You may speak with the tongue of men and of angels, but without exhibiting the character of God, in the work of saving sinners you will be nothing; and you will do nothing but hinder it. Should your voice be music itself, and reach the ear of every being in creation, it will fall powerless upon the heart which is at enmity with God, and produce in it no reconciliation to him.

"You will not make men feel that while they live in known sin they are enemies to God. You will not make them feel that on account of this, they deserve to perish. You will not make them feel that except they be 'born again,' they *will* perish. And you will not reconcile them to Him, who, if they do not repent, believe on Jesus Christ, and serve him, will punish them with everlasting destruction from the presence of the Lord, and the glory of his power. How can you reconcile men to God, unless they feel their need of reconciliation? When he offers them deliverance from destruction, all of grace, how can they accept it, as all of grace, if they feel that they do not deserve that destruction? And if they feel that they do not deserve it, how can you reconcile them to Him who threatens it, and who, if they are not reconciled to him, will bring it upon them? The thing is impossible. Hence I say again, if you fail essentially here, you may expect in the work of saving sinners to fail everywhere. Their hearts will remain cased in impenetrable adamant, and not the voice even of an angel would reach them. This adamant must be broken, and the heart within pierced. And there is but one instrument that will do this, THE WORD OF GOD. This *will* do it. 'Is not my word like as a fire, saith the Lord; and like a hammer, that breaketh the rock in pieces?' Would you assail hearts of stone and turn them to hearts of flesh, use this. 'And as the rain cometh down and the snow from heaven, and watereth the earth, and maketh it to bring forth and bud, that it may give seed to the sower, and bread to the eater, so shall my word be that goeth forth out of my mouth. It shall not return unto me void; it shall accomplish that which I please, and prosper in the things whereto I sent it.' Mark the instrument of which this promise is made, *my word that goeth forth out of my mouth.* Use this. And attended by the omnipotence of Him who speaks, it will be quick and powerful, sharper than a twoedged sword, piercing to the dividing asunder of the soul and spirit, the joints and marrow, a discerner of the thoughts and intents of the heart. It will stain the pride of human glory, bring down high looks, and lead him who said, I am rich, and increased in goods, and have need of nothing, to cry, Woe is me; I am undone. From the crown of the head to the sole of the foot there is no soundness. Against thee, and thee only have I sinned, and done evil in thy sight.

"And strange as it may seem, the same instrument, the word of God which goeth forth out of his mouth, that wounds, will also heal. It will bind up the broken heart, and heal the wounded spirit. It will give deliverance to captives, and the opening of the prison to them that are bound. It will even open blind eyes, and let in the light of the knowledge of the glory of God, and lead the heart that was dead, to cry, 'Whom have I in heaven but thee? and there is none upon the earth that I desire beside thee.' 'The Lord is my portion.' 'Though he slay me, I will trust in him.'

"Nothing but the *word of God* will do this. Nothing else is the sword of the Spirit. Other weapons are carnal; formed by the pride and ignorance of men. Be furnished with them as abundantly as you will, and use them as dexterously, in the day of battle you will fall. Every man who uses them will fall, and the army of the aliens move on in triumph. The god of this world is never conquered, he never retreats, and never yields a captive, but at the point of the 'sword of the Spirit.' To cope with him you must use this weapon. And you must use it naked in all its brightness. Then it will be mighty through God, to the pulling down of strong-holds, casting down imaginations and every high thing that exalteth itself against the knowledge of God, and bringing every thing into captivity to the obedience of Christ. However numerous or powerful your foes, you have nothing to fear; for the Lord will consume them with the breath of his mouth, and destroy them with the brightness of his coming.

"Show to every sinner Jehovah, as he shows himself, a 'just God, and a Saviour.' Call, in his name, upon every one to love him with all the heart and soul and strength and mind; and whether they eat or drink, or whatever they do, to do *all* to his glory. Tell them from him, that it is a reasonable service for them to be holy as he is holy, and perfect as he is perfect; but that they have all gone out of the way, have together become filthy, that there is none righteous among them, no, not one. Tell them from him, that into heaven can enter nothing that defileth, and that except a man be born again he cannot see the kingdom of God; that the wicked will be driven away in their wickedness—be turned into hell—go away into everlasting punishment—and the smoke of their torment ascend up for ever and ever. And if while you lodge his testimony on the ear, he carries it to the heart, and fastens there the conviction that not one jot or tittle of what he has said will fail till it all comes to pass, you will not need to add *your* demonstration. They will *feel* its truth. And think it not strange if some set their faces against the heavens, and are almost ready to curse their God and King, and look upward; while others, with clearer views of their own guilt, and a deeper conviction of God's justice, close their lips in silence, and are ready to sink into eternal despair. As they cast a lingering anxious look to you, show them God as a Saviour; although infinitely rich, for *their* sakes becoming poor, that they through his poverty might be rich. Go with them to the manger, and thence through prayers and tears and sufferings to Calvary. Follow him by the blood of his footsteps, till he bears their sins in his own body on the tree; and let them hear him as he groans, 'My God, my God, why hast thou forsaken me?' Tell them from him, that he is wounded for their transgressions, and bruised for their iniquities; that the chastisement of their peace is on him; that the Lord hath laid upon him the iniquities of us all. And as he struggles under the amazing load, and the sun shrinks away, the rocks break asunder, and the dead start from their graves, ask them, If these things are done in the green tree, what will be done in the dry? And as they sink under the unutterable answer, he cries in agony, 'Father, forgive them.' And if they are not dead, they will feel that God has no pleasure in the death of the wicked, but that the wicked turn from his way and live. They will hear from the cross the voice of infinite *kindness*, saying, 'Turn ye, turn ye, for why will ye die?' And if they are not *twice* dead, they will feel that if they turn not, there will remain no more sacrifice for sin, but a certain fearful looking for of judgment and fiery indignation, which shall for ever devour them.

"But supposing they are dead, twice dead, consumed, and their bones bleaching under the winds of heaven, be not discouraged. If you are surrounded on every side with dry bones, even if they are *very* dry, and you are asked by God, Can these dry bones live? never answer, No; but prepare to preach the preaching that he bids you. Stand before the cross, and in view of 'earth's sole hope,' cry, 'Come, O breath, and breathe upon these slain.' 'Awake, thou that sleepest; arise from the dead, and Christ shall give thee light.' And there will be a shaking among the dry bones; they will come together, bone to its bone; flesh and sinews will come upon them, and skin cover them above, and the Spirit of the Lord breathe into them the breath of life. And as soon as they open their eyes, show them 'the Lamb of God, which taketh away the sin of the world.' Invite all to look unto him and be saved. Tell them that He who spared not his own Son, but freely gave him up for them all, will, with him also, to those who embrace him, freely give all things; that neither death nor life, nor angels, nor principalities, nor powers, nor things present, nor things to come, nor height, nor depth, nor any other creature, shall be able to separate them from the love of God in Christ Jesus. And that they may have strong consolation, tell them that he hath confirmed it by an oath, that by two immutable things, in which it is impossible for God to lie, they may have strong consolation who flee for refuge to the hope set before them.

"But tell them too, that other foundation of hope for the guilty can no man lay, than that is laid, which is Jesus Christ; that if he who despised Moses' law died without mercy, of vastly sorer punishment will he be thought worthy who treads under foot the blood of the Son of God; that whosoever believeth not on him shall not see life, but the wrath of God abideth on him.

"And that they may have no doubt of it, carry them forward, till he comes in his glory and the glory of his Father, with the holy angels; the dead small and great stand before him, and he divides them one from another as a shepherd divideth his sheep from the goats. Let them *hear*, 'Come, ye blessed of my Father, inherit the kingdom prepared for you from the foundation of the world;' and, 'Depart from me, ye cursed, into everlasting fire, prepared for the devil and his angels.' Let them see the wicked going away into eternal punishment, and the righteous into eternal life. Yes, my brethren, let them *see* it. And that they may, see it yourselves. Stand, when you preach, on the ruins of the world; see the heavens passing away with a great noise, and the elements melting with fervent heat; the earth also and all things in it burnt up; your hearers going away, some into everlasting punishment, and others into life eternal—and this to depend as a means upon you; and you cannot but be eloquent. With the groans of the damned and the songs of the blessed mingling on your ear, and the love of Christ in your heart, you cannot but be eloquent. Every look, every action, every word, and every tear will be eloquent. And it will be the eloquence of the *heart*, which is the means of God's appointment to reach the heart. This is the eloquence which he delights to bless, the eloquence of the heart, in view of an eternal heaven, and an eternal hell, to one of which each individual of the human family is hastening; constrained by love to pour out its emo tions to save immortal souls from sinking eternally in the one, and raise them to dwell eternally in the other. And though this eloquence has none of the trappings of human oratory, and is nothing but faith in Christ, and love to souls uttering itself in the strong unaffected language of the heart, it will, with the blessing of God, impress the heart and subdue it; for it pleases God, by the foolishness of such preaching, to save them that believe.

"Preach, my brethren, the truth of God in this manner, for the purpose of glorifying him in the salvation of men, and you may hope, through grace, to turn many to righteousness; and afterwards to shine as the brightness of the firmament, and as the stars for ever and ever."

THIS KIND OF SPEAKING TAUGHT BY THE HOLY SPIRIT.

"*How then can you attain to this kind of speaking?* You, I mean, who have competent talents, learning, and powers of utterance; who have all needful human instruction, and are willing to make the sacrifices and efforts which such an attainment requires. *You must be taught it by the Spirit of God.* Human teaching is needful to show you how, in the best manner, to express your feelings; but you must have *divine* teaching, in order to *possess* those feelings, which are essential to sacred eloquence. No one but God can teach you rightly to apprehend his truth, cordially to embrace it, and powerfully to feel its efficacy on your own hearts; or with those feelings which truth inspires, communicate it to others. On these points, each of which is essential to sacred eloquence, you must be taught of God. To receive his teaching, you must feel deeply your need of it. God does not communicate his instruction where it is not desired. To receive it you must desire it, ardently desire it. You must daily ask for it, and be ready, with the meekness and docility of children, implicitly to receive it. For this purpose you must daily listen to what he declares in the Bible; and with that fixed attention which you would, should you hear him declare it from the throne of his excellent glory. And you must feel, deeply feel, that it is *all* true, and *all* important; that the Bible is all given by inspiration of God, and is all profitable. And as such you must receive it, and obey it. Love the same things that God loves, hate the same things that He hates, and seek in all your efforts the same great end. In doing this, let his will made known in the Bible be your guide. When you understand, always follow it. Do nothing, even in thought, which he forbids. Neglect nothing, even in feeling, which he requires. Form no plans, engage in no business, do no actions, speak no words, cherish no thoughts, exercise no desires, and indulge no feelings but what you really believe, after all the light that you can gain, God approves. In every place, and at all times, let, 'Thou God seest me,' be written upon your hearts; and underneath this inscription, 'Thy favor is life, and thy loving-kindness is better than life.' Act continually under this conviction, and let it be your grand object to please God, and be like him. Those books, those studies, those conversations, those amusements, and those desires which draw you away from God, and render you unlike him, abhor, renounce. Have nothing to do with any thing which you cannot, in some way, make subservient to the glory of God, in the salvation of men. Would you rise to the highest pitch of sacred eloquence, keep your eye and your heart fixed on this grand point, and towards it direct, without ceasing, your highest efforts. Let the same mind be in you which was also in Christ Jesus. Let no trials, no sacrifices, no temptations turn you from the path of duty. Walk with God. Live by faith. Reside at the throne of grace, and habitually commune with Him who sits upon it. One hour's communion with God daily, amidst the realities of eternity, will do more to make a man excel in sacred eloquence, than a whole life of laborious study without it. Select your text, prepare your sermon, and preach for *eternity*. This will make you truly eloquent. This was the grand secret in the eloquence of Baxter, when there was scarce a family, through an immense congregation, which was not a family of daily prayer; and which did not become such through his instrumentality. It was because the fire was kindled from heaven, which glows on the pages of his 'Saints' Rest,' that it has lighted its thousands to glory. It is because it was thus kindled, that it continues to burn, and will continue with increasing brightness and glory till the last conflagration.

"This was the grand secret in the eloquence of Brainerd: as it echoed through the trees of the forest, the savage dropped his tomahawk, and with streaming eyes cried, *Guttummaukalummeh, guttummaukalum-meh*—Have mercy upon me, have mercy upon me.

"This was the very soul of the eloquence of Paul, as kings on their thrones trembled, and beggars leaped for joy. It made songs of triumph echo in the dungeon, and carried transports of joy to the rack, and the flames.

"Nor has it lost the least degree of its power in eighteen hundred years. No, even now, it melts icy hearts on the cliffs of Greenland, lights with celestial brightness the plains of Hindostan; it removes blackness even from the Hottentot, and opens upon the Otaheitan the 'light of the world.'

"Excel, my brethren, in this kind of eloquence, and extend it through the world; and the light of the moon will be like the light of the sun; the light of the sun will be *sevenfold*—and the LIGHT OF ZION will eclipse them. Kings will come to her light, and princes to the brightness of her rising. Her sun will not go down by day, her moon not withdraw itself; the LORD will be her everlasting light, and the Lamb her glory. A voice will be heard, 'The kingdoms of the world are become the kingdom of our Lord, and his Christ.' And the whole earth will be full of his glory, as the waters fill the seas."

THE CHURCH THE PILLAR AND GROUND OF THE TRUTH.

He was now called to another public occasion: an installation in one of those numerous, and often small, self-sacrificing evangelical churches in eastern Massachusetts, who, for the sake of Christ and the gospel, separated themselves from the sanctuary of their fathers, in the midst of obloquy and opposition. It was at *the rock of Plymouth*, the very landing-place of the Puritan fathers, November 3, 1824. The responsibility boldly and faithfully to proclaim the truth of God, he felt to be great; and his subject and manner of treating it give the intelligent Christian reader no little insight into his own character as a minister of Christ, and the perilous state of the churches when he was called into public life.

His theme was, "That thou mayest know how thou oughtest to behave thyself in the house of God, which is *the church of the living God, the pillar and ground of the truth;*" from which he undertook to show, "in a plain scriptural manner," "What is the church? What is the truth which the church supports? How does the church support it; and for what reasons?"

"The word CHURCH is sometimes used in the New Testament for all persons who have been, or shall be, born of God; and who will stand at the last day on the right hand of Christ. Thus it is used in the fifth chapter to the Ephesians: 'As Christ also loved the church, and gave himself for it, that he might sanctify and cleanse it, with the washing of water by the word; that he might present it to himself a glorious church, not having spot, or wrinkle, or any such thing; but that it should be holy and without blemish.'

"But the word *church* is more often used for only a part of these persons; who are at the same time on earth, and so near as to unite with such as profess to be like them, in supporting the worship, observing the ordinances, and obeying the commands of God.

Thus we read of 'the church of God which is at Corinth;' 'the churches of Asia;' 'the church of the Thessalonians, in God our Father, and the Lord Jesus Christ.'

"But what was the character of these persons, such of them as were in reality what they professed to be? *They were born of God.* They all professed to receive Jesus Christ. And 'as many as received him, to them gave he power to become the sons of God; who were born, not of blood, nor of the will of man, but of God.' To be *born of God,* is a phrase used in the Bible for that change without which a man cannot see the kingdom of heaven.

"That the members of the church, in the days of Paul, if they were what they professed to be, had experienced this change, is evident from the manner in which the Holy Ghost speaks of them. 'The Lord added to the church such as should be *saved.*' Paul said to members of the church, 'According to his mercy he saved us, by the washing of regeneration, and the renewing of the Holy Ghost.' The preaching of the cross is foolishness to them that perish; but unto us that are saved, it is the power of God. 'Who hath saved us, and called us with a holy calling, not according to our works, but according to his purpose and grace.' Speaking of openly immoral persons, he says to members of the church, 'Such were some of you; but ye are washed, ye are sanctified, ye are justified in the name of the Lord Jesus, and by the Spirit of our God.' 'You hath he quickened, who were dead in trespasses and sins.' 'God, who is rich in mercy, for his great love wherewith he loved us, even when we were dead in sins, hath quickened us together with Christ.' 'We are his workmanship, created in Christ Jesus unto good works.'

"Such were members of the church in the days of Paul. They were the 'household of faith.' They were 'built upon the foundation Jesus Christ;' 'in him fitly framed together, and growing up unto a holy temple in the Lord.' 'They were builded together for a habitation of God, through the Spirit.' 'The Holy Ghost dwelt in them.' 'They were members of Christ's body, of his flesh, and of his bones;' and were so joined to the Lord as to be 'one spirit.' These persons repenting of their sins, believing with the heart on the Lord Jesus Christ, and to whom he was 'the end of the law for righteousness,' united together with such as professed to be like them, to support the worship, observe the ordinances, and obey the commands of God. In this united character they were the 'church of the living God, the pillar and ground of the truth.' And such has been 'the church of the living God' in every generation, down to the present day. *They are persons who*, if they are what they profess to be, *are born of God, repent of all their sins, believe on the Lord Jesus Christ, and have passed from death unto life.*

"What is THE TRUTH WHICH THE CHURCH SUPPORTS? What truth did it support in the days of Paul? The truth which Paul preached, when he 'determined to know nothing among them, save Jesus Christ and him crucified;' and 'delivered unto them, *first of all*, that Jesus Christ died for our sins, according to the Scriptures; and rose again for our justification, according to the Scriptures:' when he said, 'God forbid that I should glory, save in the cross of our Lord Jesus Christ, by whom the world is crucified to me, and I to the world; for in Christ Jesus neither circumcision availeth any thing, nor uncircumcision, but a new creature.' 'And if any man be in Christ, he is a new creature; old things are passed away; behold, all things are become new.' That the church supported this truth, is evident from the fact, that it is the truth of God, and they were converted by it. 'I neither received it of man,' said he, 'neither was I taught it, but by the revelation of Jesus Christ.' And 'I have begotten you through the gospel;' 'which ye have received, wherein ye stand, and by which ye are saved, unless ye have believed in vain.'

"This will not be denied. All will admit, that the church of the living God, when faithful to him, did, in the days of Paul, support the truth which he preached. But the great question is, What is the truth which Paul preached? About this, there is a great difference of opinion; and there was, even in the days of Paul. Some said, that he preached what he said that he did *not* preach. Others said, that he did not preach what he said that he *did*. Yet Paul was one of the plainest preachers, as well as one of the best, that ever lived. And had there been but one feeling about his preaching, and that of cordial approbation, there would have been but one opinion as to what it was. And it would have been to all, 'the wisdom and the power of God.'

"But as there was a difference of *feeling* about his preaching, there was a great difference of opinion as to what it was. A similar difference of feeling, has made a similar difference of opinion ever since. After all the light which has been thrown upon it by the dispensations of Providence, and the manifestations of grace, for more than seventeen hundred years, there is now a great difference of opinion about the preaching of Paul. The Holy Ghost, seeing the end from the beginning, knew that this would be the case. He therefore directed Paul, in the next verse to the text, to tell what the truth is which he did preach; and which the church of the living God does support. This he has done, in words which the Holy Ghost taught him. '*God was manifest in the flesh, justified in the Spirit, seen of angels, preached unto the Gentiles, believed on in the world, received up into glory.*'

"This is the truth which Paul preached, and which the church of the living God supports: 'God was manifest in the flesh.' 'He who in the beginning was with God, and who *was* God, was made flesh, and dwelt among us.' 'He took not on him the nature of angels, but the seed of Abraham;' 'of whom, concerning the flesh, Christ came, who is over all, God blessed for ever;' 'the Wonderful, Counsellor, the Mighty God, the Everlasting Father, the Prince of Peace;' 'the Alpha and Omega; the beginning and ending; which is, and was, and is to come, the Almighty;' 'by whom all things were created, that are in heaven, and that are in earth; visible, and invisible; whether they be thrones, or dominions, or principalities, or powers;' 'all things were created by him and for him;' 'and without him was not any thing made that was made.' Yet though he was so rich, 'for *our* sakes he became poor, that *we*, through his poverty, might be rich.' Though he was God, for our sakes he took upon him the form of a servant, and was made in the likeness of men. Let it be told to every being in creation; let it be echoed by every tongue in the universe, and felt by every heart to eternity, '*God was manifest in the flesh.*'

"This is the truth which the 'church of the living God' supports. By this is not meant, however, merely the single fact that he became a man; but this fact taken in connection with other facts as God has revealed them. Hence said Paul not only, 'God was manifest in the flesh,' but 'justified in the Spirit, seen of angels, preached to the Gentiles, believed on in the world, received up into glory.' 'Being found in fashion as a man, he humbled himself,' and for the sake of accomplishing his work as a Saviour, 'became obedient unto death, even the death of the cross.' But death could not hold *him*. He was never its prisoner, but only a voluntary captive. And having accomplished his object in dying, he arose, with all power in heaven, and on earth. Then he was 'justified in the Spirit.' The truth of his declarations was demonstrated, and his claims as Messiah established for ever. In this condition, as conqueror of earth and hell, he was 'seen of angels.' Multitudes beheld him. Chosen witnesses were sent to declare his resurrection, and preach the unsearchable riches of his grace, not to Jews only, but to Gentiles—to all nations. And although they did not see him, and had no ocular demonstration of his resurrection, yet he was 'believed on;' and by vast multitudes, even after he was 'received up into glory.' And although 'not seen,' he was '*loved.*' To all that believed on him he was 'precious,' the 'chief among ten thousand,' 'altogether lovely.' And this has been the case with all who have believed on him, down to the present day. They have been ready to cry, with Thomas, 'My Lord, and my God;' with Paul, to 'count all things but loss for the excellency of the knowledge of Jesus;' and with Stephen, full of the Holy Ghost, to cry, 'Lord Jesus, receive my spirit.'

"These persons, wherever found, have united together; that, not as individuals only, but churches, they might 'serve the Lord Christ;' and thus support the truth, that 'God was manifest in the flesh.'

"In view of this truth, thinking men have always been disposed to ask, *Why* was he manifest in the flesh? The church has answered, in the language of the Holy Ghost, 'That he might be a merciful and faithful high-priest in things pertaining to God, to make reconciliation for the sins of the people;' and 'such a high-priest,' say they, 'became us.' 'He was wounded for our transgressions, he was bruised for our iniquities; the chastisement of our peace was upon him, and with his stripes we are healed. All we like sheep have gone astray; and the Lord hath laid on him the iniquity of us all.' 'Christ hath redeemed us from the curse of the law, being made a curse for us.' 'And he is the propitiation for our sins; and not for ours only, but for the sins of the whole world.'

"The moment this is believed, another question arises, Why was he the propitiation for our sins, and for the sins of the whole world? And the answer of the church is, 'That God might be just, and the justifier of him that believeth.' 'He hath made him, who knew no sin, to be sin,' (a sin-offering,) 'for us, that we might be made the righteousness of God in him.' And 'there is now no condemnation to them that are in Christ Jesus, who walk not after the flesh, but after the Spirit.' 'The law of the Spirit of life in Christ Jesus hath made them free from the law of sin and death.' 'For Christ is the end of the law for righteousness to every one that believeth.' And 'he that believeth on the Son hath everlasting life.' No sooner is this heard as the declaration of God, and believed, than the question arises, What will be the condition of those that believe not? And the church answers in the language of God, 'They shall not see life, but the wrath of God abideth on them.' 'He shall send forth his angels, and gather out of his kingdom all that offend, and them that do iniquity, and shall cast them into a furnace of fire, and there shall be wailing and gnashing of teeth.' 'They shall go away into everlasting punishment;' 'and the smoke of their torment ascendeth for ever and ever.'

"Such is the truth which, on the declaration of God, and in the connection in which he has revealed it, the church of the living God supports."

He proceeds to show that the church SUPPORTS THIS TRUTH—by believing it—by openly professing it—by the preaching and ordinances of the gospel—by teaching it to her children, under which head he says,

"The wisdom that is from *beneath* says, Give to children no religious instruction; and exert upon them no moral influence in favor of the gospel, lest they receive an improper bias; let them alone to choose for themselves, and when they come to years of understanding they will choose right.

"But the wisdom that is from *above* saith, 'Train up a child in the way he should go.' 'Teach these things diligently to thy children, when thou sittest in the house, and when thou walkest by the way; when thou liest down, and when thou risest up.' 'Suffer *little* children to come unto me.' 'Train them up in the nurture and admonition of the Lord.'

"In yonder distant country was a little feeble band inspired with love to Christ, who covenanted to educate their children for him. Not able to do it according to his word and the dictates of their consciences in their own land, they escape under the cover of night, with their little ones, to a foreign clime. But their children still exposed, they embark upon the ocean with no protector but their covenant God. And though the very elements seem to join with earth and hell to oppose them, borne in his arms, I see them approaching, till they enter yonder haven, and stand upon a *rock*.* And though winter and famine and pestilence attack them, and cut down half their numbers, around them I see the arms of the everlasting covenant, within them the Shekinah, and hear a voice saying, 'Leave your fatherless children, and let your widows trust in me.' 'I will never leave nor forsake thee;' and 'they that seek the Lord shall not want any good thing.' They hearken, and lo, they 'break forth on the right hand, and extend themselves on the

* At Plymouth, where the sermon was preached.

left;' 'a little one becomes a thousand, and a small one a strong nation.' They spread from sea to sea, and 'he is a God to them, and their children after them, from generation to generation;' 'keeping covenant and mercy to thousands of them that love him, and obey his commandments.'

"The church of the living God supports this truth, by *extending it to the destitute.* Ever since Jesus Christ gave the command, 'Go ye into all the world, and preach the gospel to every creature,' the church has acknowledged her obligations to obey. And she has prayed that she might fulfil them. For a time her efforts, in some measure, corresponded with her prayers. Her missionaries were found in various lands. Trophies of grace were multiplied; churches were gathered from among the heathen; and the gospel seemed ready to be extended through the world.

"But the church, which was to be the instrument of this, elated by prosperity, became corrupt in doctrine. The consequence was, she became corrupt in practice. Her prayers grew formal, her efforts were palsied, and the progress of truth ceased. The darkness which she had rolled back, now began to return; the smoke, and the locusts from the bottomless pit overshadowed; the beast and the false prophet came upon her; and she had to struggle even for existence, a thousand years. Some, however, among her children sighed over her abominations, and bewailed her calamities. With the souls under the altar, they cried without ceasing, 'Lord, how long?' And he who had promised that the gates of hell should not prevail, heard. He arose, light broke in, and Zion 'looked forth as the morning, beautiful as Tirzah, and comely as Jerusalem.' But she again slumbered; and, for two hundred years, did little more than maintain the truth within her own borders. Yet all that time she acknowledged her obligations to extend it to every creature. She constantly prayed, that 'the heathen might be given to Christ for his inheritance, and the uttermost parts of the earth for his possession.' But, shameful to relate, with the exception of her Eliots, her Brainerds, and a few kindred spirits, she did next to nothing, that her own prayers might be answered. The consequence was, the truth which she supported, and which is destined in its progress to enlighten and renovate the world, was confined within the limits of Christendom. Five hundred millions of the human family, eighteen hundred years after Christ died to redeem them, had never heard of it. Fifty generations of immortal souls in danger of eternal death, were suffered to go down in unbroken succession to the grave, and never even to hear that 'God was manifest in the flesh,' till their probation was closed, and their accounts sealed up to the judgment.

"O, had not her Saviour been God, long ere this the church had been consumed! She had been swept away, and her name blotted out. But 'glory to God in the highest,' her Maker is 'her husband, the Lord of hosts is his name.' 'The Holy One is her Redeemer, the God of the whole earth shall he be called.'

"By a convulsion which shook half the globe, he awoke her from her slumbers—by the finger of his providence pointed her to her duty. By his Spirit he impressed upon her heart that she must not only pray that the heathen may be converted, but give them the Bible, and the preaching of the gospel, that her prayers may be answered.

"She arose not only to pray, but to *act;* and from that time she has 'lengthened her cords, and strengthened her stakes.' More than four hundred of her missionaries are now among the heathen; and more than two hundred churches has she gathered in pagan lands. More than fifty thousand children are now in her missionary schools; and more than fifty of her ministers, who, thirty years ago, were abominable idolaters, are now preaching 'the unsearchable riches of Christ.' Ministers born in pagan lands, and ministers born in Christian lands, are now telling the wandering idolaters of a Saviour, 'God manifest in the flesh.' And the Holy Ghost sent down from heaven is leading them to embrace him. You may hear his praises in the western wilderness; in the islands of the southern sea; for a thousand miles on the continent of Africa; in Ceylon, and India; in Astrachan, and Greenland. Hearken, my brethren, and you hear the Cherokee and Choctaw, the Hottentot and Hindoo, the Greenlander and Otaheitan, all mingling their praises 'unto Him that loved us, and washed us from our sins in his blood, and hath made us kings and priests unto God and his Father; to Him be glory and dominion, for ever and ever.'

"And every real convert to Christ from among the heathen, is a new accession to the 'pillar and ground of the truth.' From the heart they embrace the 'great mystery of godliness,' and unite their prayers and efforts to support it.

"By sending the gospel to the destitute, the church also supports the truth in another way. She lets the light of holiness shine on those at home, and thus leads *them* to glorify her Father. While she waters others, God waters *her*. For every measure which she gives, she *receives* 'good measure, pressed down, and running over.' The more she scatters, the more she *increases*.

"As soon as she began to send the blessings of salvation beyond her own borders, God began to increase her numbers, multiply her resources, and augment her strength. And these have been steadily advancing, with every new effort which she has made, until, without lessening their increase, she can stretch out her arms, with the blessings of life, half round the globe. And what she has done, is only the beginning of what she will do. 'For brass she will bring gold; for iron, silver; for wood, brass; and for stones, iron.' The bells of her horses shall be holiness; her very walls be salvation, and her gates praise. Then shall God, who was manifest in the flesh, be known, from the rising to the setting sun, and the whole earth be filled with his glory, as the waters fill the seas. Hence, we are prepared to see

"The REASONS why the church supports this truth. It is the truth of God. By an unction from him, she knows it. Upon it she builds her immortal hopes, and it is the only foundation of hope for a dying world. In its support, are involved the glory of God, and the salvation of men. His manifestation in the flesh was the grand effort of infinite grace, for bringing out to view the glories of the Godhead. It was made in behalf of the *church.* And should she refuse to support it, the very stones would cry out against her. To it she owes all her hopes of deliverance from hell, and of exaltation to the light and bliss of heaven.

"Reject universally the great mystery of godliness, and godliness will take its last flight from the world. No shaking after that will ever be witnessed throughout all this valley of dry bones—no voice cry, O breath, breathe upon these slain; and no heart desire it.

"But let the great mystery of godliness be supported, let it be extended, accompanied by the Holy Ghost, and cordially embraced, tears of repentance, in view of the Crucified, will drop from a thousand eyes, and ten thousand hearts will bow in contrition before the cross. The love of Him who bled upon it, shed abroad in their hearts by the Holy Ghost, will constrain them, and will purify them, even as God is pure. From this will arise a hope which will not make ashamed, but which will be an anchor to the soul, sure and steadfast. It will support them even in death. Thousands have tried it, and not one has found it to fail them. As they go down the dark valley, I hear them sing, 'O death, where is thy sting? O grave, where is thy victory?' and shout, 'Thanks be to God, who giveth us the victory through our Lord Jesus Christ.' 'We shall see him as he is, and be *like* him.' Ah, that last, 'be like *him*,' swallows up death—and they mount upward, shining in the glory of his image, and break forth with ten thousand voices, 'Thou art worthy, for thou wast slain, and hast redeemed us to God by thy blood, out of every nation, and kindred, and people, and tongue;' while angels, ten thousand times ten thousand, and thousands of thousands, cry, 'Worthy, to receive power, and riches, and wisdom, and strength, and honor, and glory, and blessing.' And every creature in heaven, on earth, and under the earth, hear I saying, 'Blessing, and honor, and glory, and power, be unto Him that sitteth upon the throne, and unto the Lamb, for ever and ever.' And their song never wears out, never grows dull, no heart is languid, not a voice falters, not a tongue tires; but with increasing ardor, and increasing powers, and ever-growing views of God manifest in the flesh, their accents of glory rise higher and higher, and to every heart grow sweeter and sweeter, to endless ages."

CHAPTER V.

HIS MINISTRY IN ANDOVER—CONTINUED.

LAST THREE YEARS, 1824-1827.

In addition to the efficient system of Sabbath-school instruction, and the other various means employed for the spiritual welfare of his people, he established, in October, 1823, *a female Bible-class*, which at length had no less than *one hundred and sixty* members, and which, though it added to his labors, proved to be one of the most efficient means of his usefulness. This had become so apparent that, in November, 1824, he was induced also to form a *Bible-class of males*, in which his instructions awakened so deep an interest, that about *one hundred and fifty* men, from youth to advanced years, became stated attendants.

No part of his ministerial labors seems to have been more evidently productive of spiritual good, than these two Bible-classes. He here witnessed the power of the simple truth of God's word, prayerfully studied and understood, and made effectual by the accompanying influences of the Holy Spirit, to the salvation of many souls. Some of his preparations for successive meetings of these classes, in the Gospels and the Acts, remain; their general character resembling that of his more condensed notes and instructions in his valuable comment. We find also a little hand-book, containing alphabetical lists of both classes, and what is more interesting, a list of those who from time to time *had called on him for personal conversation on the state of their souls*, the number of whom is no less than *one hundred and six;* and also a list of persons who had commenced family worship, to the number of *thirty-one.*

To a brother of Mrs. Edwards.

"ANDOVER, July 6, 1824.

"MY DEAR BROTHER—Yours, enclosing $20, I received yesterday. I have directed the agent to put you up a box of Tracts, and send them to the depository in Hartford, directed to you.

"I am glad that you have formed an Auxiliary Society. All that is worth living for is to glorify God, and to do good to all as we have opportunity, and especially to the household of faith. I hope that you will make it your single object to inquire, 'Lord, what wilt thou have me to do?' And to answer this question, you have only to ascertain what He commands; and when you know this, let it be the single object of your heart to do it. Be not afraid or ashamed to be openly for God in all places, and at all times, and you will find that as your day is, so your strength will be. It is perfectly safe to trust in God, and go forward in the path of duty. And there is no other way to enjoy the light of his countenance, and experience the blessings of his salvation. God meets men and manifests himself to them when striving in all things to obey him, and not while they are letting a sense of unworthiness, or any thing else, hinder them from doing this."

To the same.

"ANDOVER, Aug. 18, 1824.

"MY DEAR BROTHER—Things are in an encouraging state in Reading, and also in this place. A number will probably make a profession here at the next communion.

"All who have determined to make it the great object of living to serve Christ, and to do good, ought to acknowledge him before men. They ought to let neither their own unworthiness, nor the fear that they shall not live as they ought, nor any thing else, hinder them from doing this in remembrance of Christ. The reason is, Christ has commanded them to do it; and the only course of duty, or of safety, is in all things to obey him. God does not manifest his presence much, even to his own children, while they continue to neglect any of his known commands; but when they make it their great object, in all things, to do them. 'Then shall I not be ashamed, when I have respect to *all* thy commandments.'

"It appears to me that if you should acknowledge Christ before men, pray daily with your family, (unless your father is willing to pray in it,) and take a part occasionally in conference-meetings, *if God seems to call you to it*, it would be greatly for the benefit of your soul, pleasing to God, and useful to the souls of others. We know not how long we shall be permitted to act in this world, and we ought, without delay, to be setting such an example as will testify for Christ when we are in the grave. God has done a great deal for you and your father's house, and he ought daily, not only in secret, but in the family, to be worshipped in that house. It might, nay, there is great reason to hope that it would be, the means of salvation to all the members of the family.

"My brother, it is high time for us to live in earnest for eternity. Great things are depending. Let us strive in all things to be faithful, and great will be our reward. 'Be thou faithful unto death, and I will give thee a crown of life.' That we may know what this means by experience, is the prayer of

"Your unworthy brother,

"J. EDWARDS."

To a sister of Mrs. Edwards.

"ANDOVER, Aug. 18, 1824.

"MY DEAR SISTER ANN—I learn from your letter to Mrs. E., that brother G. and some of the family go up stairs frequently and unite in prayer. Why, my dear sister, go up stairs? God has done wonders of grace for your father's family, and why not worship him daily in the family below? I think that if your father, or if he is not willing to lead, if brother G. should daily pray with as many of the family as are disposed to attend, it would be pleasing to God, and highly useful to men. In a family to which God has been so kind as he has to that of your beloved father, how suitable, how strong the obligation, for the whole family daily, and unitedly, to acknowledge it. It might be the means of the conversion of all who are now unconverted.

"It is always safe openly to acknowledge God, and it is a peculiar duty thus to acknowledge him daily in every family. More than twenty families have set up the daily worship of God in this place, since the beginning of the year; and in several cases there is reason to hope that it has had an influence in the salvation of souls.

"In a town in ———, a few years ago, the Lord sent down his Spirit, and led a number of persons to embrace the Saviour. Among them was one young man whose father had never prayed in his family. After the son became pious, he said to his father in the field one day, 'Father, we ought to have prayer in the family.' Said the father, 'I know it.' 'Well,' said the son, 'why do you not pray?' 'Ah,' said the father, 'I have no *heart* to pray.' 'Well,' said the son, 'are you willing that I should pray? We ought to have prayer in the family.' And said the father, 'Yes, with all my heart.' So the next night they had, for the first time, family prayer. And they continued, morning and evening, reading the Bible and uniting as a family in prayer, until, in the course of a little time, the father hoped that through wonders of grace in Christ Jesus, he had obtained that inestimable blessing, a *heart to pray;* and then the father used to pray in the morning, and the son at night. Thus they were mutual helpers of each other in the road to heaven. And when they arrive there, may not that son say, 'Here, Lord, am I, and the father whom thou hast given me?'"

At a later date, he writes, "Tell brother G—— to 'trust in the Lord, and do good, and verily he shall be fed.' Who ever trusted in him, and was disappointed? 'They that wait upon the Lord, shall renew their strength.' It is wise, and safe, to leave all things to his infinitely wise guidance and disposal.

He can give us, and preserve to us as much character and ability for usefulness, as he sees it best for us to have; and when precious interests *seem* to be in danger, he can easily shield them. He says to us, 'You do those things which are plain, and see how easily, how wisely, and how benevolently I can direct those that are difficult, and to you impossible.' 'Cast thy burden on the Lord, and he will sustain thee.' He loves the church better than we do, and his way to promote her welfare is better than ours. It is good both to hope and to wait for the salvation of the Lord. Never say, 'All these things are against me;' because, if you love God and serve him, it is not true. 'In all thy ways acknowledge him, and he shall direct thy paths.'"

The doubts and darkness in this dear brother's mind were ere long succeeded by an humble trust in Christ. He was enabled to erect the family altar, the fire of which, for a long course of years, has not ceased to burn.

In the autumn of 1824, negotiations were entered into between the "New England Tract Society," which had already changed its name to the "American Tract Society," of which Dr. Edwards was Corresponding Secretary, and the "Religious Tract Society in New York," for forming a more truly national institution, to unite the principal Tract Societies of the country and Christians of various evangelical denominations, and to be located in Boston, or New York, as a suitable commercial centre. The raising in New York of $20,000, which was soon increased to $25,000, to erect a house for the new Society, with other considerations, after many conferences and much deliberation, led to a harmonious union in the American Tract Society, formed in that city, May 11, 1825, as the principal publishing institution. The American Tract Society at Boston, whose business had been mainly conducted at Andover, became a Branch of the national Society; but still retained its name and distinct organization, and greatly enlarged its operations. Its stereotype plates and engravings were transferred to New York; and as *a bond of union*, Dr. Edwards, who had had the primary responsibility of the issues at Boston, was unanimously elected on the Publishing Committee at New York, and all the publications continued to be issued with his sanction, in which for some time he had the concurrence of the Rev. Dr. Woods, of the Committee at Andover, who had taken a kind and active part in the negotiations, and was, from the formation of the Society in New York, till his death, one of its honored Vice-presidents. The Rev. Dr. Edwards, at the time of his decease, was a member of the Publishing Committee of the Society in New York; and the two institutions have continued the most harmonious coöperation; the Rev. Dr. Nehemiah Adams of the Committee of the Society in Boston, succeeding Dr. Edwards as a member of the Publishing Committee in New York.

In the two years following the formation of the American Tract Society in New York, Dr. Edwards performed an invaluable service in revising and adjusting the new series of tracts, in connection with the members elected in that city, the object of all the members having been found to be one and the same, to preach "Christ crucified" for the salvation of a perishing world.

The Publishing Committee, July 1825, requested Dr. Edwards to prepare a tract "On the Divinity of our Lord and Saviour Jesus Christ," which they believed might be eminently useful among the first publications issued; but the multitude of his engagements did not allow him to prepare it.

To his sister, Mrs. Cook, in Ohio.

"ANDOVER, July 12, 1825.

"DEAR BROTHER AND SISTER COOK—I hope that sister Cook is better, and may yet be restored if it is the Lord's will. Trials, in this world, we must expect; and it should be our daily fervent prayer, that they may lead our hearts to God. Our great business should be, to serve him, in the places in which he has put us, and then we shall not, in the end, want any good thing. In no other way can we ever be happy in this life, or in the life to come. His favor is life, and his loving-kindness is better than life. Jesus Christ is able and willing to be a very present help in all times of trouble, to those that put their trust in him. I hope that you find him to be a very present helper to *you*, and to yours, in all your wants.

"Though we are separated by a long distance, and may never see each other in this world, it is but a short time that we shall any of us live here, and if we love God, trust in Jesus Christ, and delight to do his will, we shall shortly meet in heaven, to part no more for ever; but O, how dreadful would it be, if we should there be separated, to meet no more. Lord, search us, and try us; see, and show us, if there be any wicked way in us, and lead us in the way everlasting.

"It is with us a very fruitful season, and some drops of spiritual rain are descending; about *eighty* have been added to our church, since the beginning of last year. I send you ten dollars, with my best wishes for your present and future welfare, and remain

"Your affectionate brother,

"J. EDWARDS."

To Rev. Wm. A. Hallock, Secretary American Tract Society, New York.

"ANDOVER, June 22, 1825.

"MY DEAR BROTHER—Yours of the eleventh instant was duly received. I have read the address of the Committee with high satisfaction. I would not suggest any alteration. So far as I can judge, the indications of Providence with regard to the Tract cause are highly encouraging; and seem to call upon all connected with it, especially upon those intrusted with its management, to walk softly, uprightly, briskly, and *perseveringly*. I have no doubt that then, if they continue to look *upward*, they will walk *safely*.

"Would it not be well for you to suggest to Connecticut the expediency of their becoming a branch of the national institution. They would receive their tracts and their magazine much more economically from New York, than from Boston.

"Would it not be well, to have a first-rate agent stationed at New Orleans; to spend the winter there, with an overflowing depository, and the summer in traversing the country west of the Alleghanies, to open the way for tracts to come into every village and family, and to keep them in brisk circulation. Such an agent might circulate an immense number of bound volumes, obtain life members, etc. I have mentioned this to one or two gentlemen from the West, who were delighted with it. Said one from Kentucky to me the other day, 'Your Tract system, if carried forward with energy, will be the salvation of the western country.'

"I hope that the Lord will give wisdom to you and to the dear brethren with whom you are associated, and strength according to your day; and if from love to him, you meet the openings of His providence, and persevere in following it to the end, I have no doubt that, for all your anxieties and labors, you will receive a reward as great as you can desire. With Christian salutations to all the brethren,

"I remain most affectionately yours,

"J. EDWARDS."

To the same.

"ANDOVER, July 23, 1825.

"MY DEAR SIR—Yours of the eighteenth instant containing the proposed alterations in the first fifteen tracts, came to hand yesterday. I make no objections to the proposed alterations. Dr. Woods makes none. I have communicated to him all that you wished concerning the stereotype plates, etc.

"On the subject of an agent, Mr. G—— is doing, I believe, what he can. I will also do what I can. Two or three are considering the subject, but no one is engaged. It is not easy to find the men and persuade them to engage. We must look to God to furnish us with *men*, with *money*, with *tracts*, and with every good and perfect gift, while we must neglect no means in our power to obtain them; and if our plans are essential to the prosperity of his kingdom, or will promote it, they will no doubt succeed, and in such a way as to make it manifest that to God belongs *all* the glory.

"With my best wishes that the blessing of the Lord may rest upon you, and upon the gentlemen of the Committee, and all with whom you and they are associated,

"I remain, very affectionately, yours,

"J. EDWARDS."

In the examination of tracts and books, Dr. Edwards felt a sacred responsibility that all instructions as to the sinner's salvation should be in strict accordance with the word of God, that no soul might be misled, and perhaps perish, through erroneous or defective teachings going forth with the Society's sanction. He well knew the lurking places of error, and how ready the human heart is to seize upon something short of a living faith in Christ, through the sanctifying influences of the Spirit, as acceptable to God. He had been accustomed to weigh and guard his own instructions as to the way of life, and show that no mere external observances whatever, without genuine repentance, humility, faith, and love, can be acceptable to God. He writes, "I think we ought to be exceedingly cautious about saying that the characters described *are* pious, unless the evidence is very decisive; and then some qualifying word, such as, we trust, or hopefully, or apparently, might be thrown in, with safety and to advantage." In his report on a long manuscript from a worthy writer, submitted for a tract, he shows his high estimate of the merit which every tract should possess, and his fidelity in declining to sanction what he did not judge to be of true permanent value. "The thoughts," he says, "are not sufficiently *dense* to be either heavy, or hot; and the language is not sufficiently definite, concise, or select. The figures could not all be painted without exhibiting some incongruities. Yet the subject is important, and the spirit excellent." Again he says of a tract on gaming, "The facts are the best part of it. The rest of it wants the unction of the gospel. Had it been written by Baxter, it would have been a truly valuable tract."

All the influence exerted by Dr. Edwards, from first to last, to give the American Tract Society its present, and we hope permanent, evangelical character will doubtless be fully known and revealed in the final day.

To Rev. Wm. A. Hallock, Secretary, New York.

"ANDOVER, August 28, 1825.

"MY DEAR SIR—I rejoice to hear of the movement in the United and Foreign Missionary Society towards a union with the American Board for Foreign Missions. There is scarcely any thing which I more ardently wish, than *Christian union among all good men.* It was an object so dear to Jesus Christ, that he bore it on his heart in prospect of his own death, and earnestly prayed for it. And it would no doubt greatly promote his cause, to have them all receive one another as he receives them. Then, union in effort will vastly increase their strength.

"Would it not be well to have the American Sunday-school Union become the American Sabbath-school and Bible-class Union? Then all the state auxiliaries might become Sabbath-school and Bible-class auxiliaries, which would probably increase the number and usefulness of both. These two most important branches of benevolent operation are too closely allied to form two separate systems; one being in fact only a continuation of the other.

"Our benevolent operations should combine and consolidate as much as possible, and yet be *simple;* and then, if they are impelled by *love* and guided by *prayer* and continued by *faith*, they will be easily managed and become *mightily efficacious*.

"Very affectionately, yours,

"J. EDWARDS."

September 22, 1825, he presented to his people the annual report of the organization among them for "Doing Good," as he had done annually since 1814; not only presenting the results among themselves, but spreading before them the wide-reaching influence of the various benevolent institutions they aided, in our own land and the world. In this report he gives a summary view of what, in eleven years, they had been enabled to accomplish.

In the same month the Boston Recorder reports a brief, glowing address, which he delivered at a Foreign Missionary meeting, in which he takes the most cheering views of the results which had then been witnessed in heathen lands, and especially at the Sandwich Islands.

"We *are* permitted," he said, "to witness *success*—and success so glorious, that it has already been celebrated with ecstasy of joy by every being in the universe that has heard of it, and rejoices over him that repenteth.

"It is but a few years since the present system of missionary efforts began. Many who are now present can remember the first missionary meeting, the first monthly concert, and the first contribution, in the present system of efforts to send the gospel to the heathen.

"Now you may witness, on the first Monday of every month, members of thousands of churches, in countries which extend half round the globe, assembled at the throne of mercy, having agreed together touching the thing that they should ask, and uniting in supplication that it may be done for them. And He who hath said, 'Ask, and it shall be given,' is manifesting his faithfulness.

"Even now you may witness set up in heathen countries more than forty printing-presses, furnishing Bibles, school-books, religious tracts, and various other productions for the literary, moral, and religious improvement of the heathen world.

"On distant shores, where forty years ago the name of Jesus was not known, I can show you every Sabbath numerous congregations, averaging more than four thousand souls each, all bowing before Jehovah, and rendering united thanks for his 'unspeakable gift.' In that small portion of the world, you may count not less than fourteen thousand persons who can in their own tongue read the Bible; and more than seven thousand who can with the pen transact the ordinary business of life.

"You may go to their Sabbath-school, and there at an annual meeting witness thousands of children. And as they sing, 'Hosanna to the Son of David,' you may see the tear drop down the cheek of a hundred parents, as their hearts swell with emotions too big for utterance in view of what the gospel has done for their children. And as you hear the deep groan break through the assembly, and ask, What is the matter? with streaming eyes one will tell you, 'O, if the missionaries had only come here a little sooner, I too should have had children to attend the Sabbath-school; but before they came, when Satan reigned and we were all in darkness, I killed them.'

"You may see parents around the communion-table, melting in contrition at the dying love of Jesus; and parents too who have with their own hands, before they had the gospel, killed two, three, and in some cases, four of their own children. Now, were they living, most joyfully would they lead them to Him who took little children in his arms and blessed them, and said, 'Of such is the kingdom of heaven.' You may go, in that country, to a missionary meeting and find collected together seven thousand people, bearing their offerings to the Lord of hosts. You may see the fond parent move with rapid step, at the birth of his infant, to enroll his name as a member of the Missionary Society. 'You,' he says, as he looks on his offspring, with feelings which no parent born in Christendom ever knew, 'if it had not been for the gospel, might have been killed. And as the gospel saves you, it is no more than right that you should do something that it may save others.' And very careful is he to pay the child's missionary tax every year, until the child is old enough to earn and pay it himself.

"In short, sir, there is throughout that country a moral renovation. The wilderness and solitary places are glad; the desert rejoices, and blossoms as the rose. The eyes of the blind are opened, and the ears of the deaf unstopped; the lame man leaps as a hart, and the tongue of the dumb sings. A highway is there, 'the way of holiness;' and the ransomed of the Lord are already returning, and coming home to Zion with singing. Joy and gladness are found among them; while sorrow and sighing flee away.

"Is not here encouragement to go forward, to persevere with increasing diligence to the end? And is there not encouragement enough to persuade every individual to do this? If not, I can show you three thousand pupils in missionary schools among our North American Indians, three thousand in the Sandwich Islands, and twelve thousand in islands farther south. I can show you three thousand in West Africa, and four thousand in South Africa; fifty thousand in the East Indies, and not a smaller number in the West Indies. Among them are thousands of females, of whom Paganism has said, and repeated the lie a thousand times, that for them to learn to read is impossible, because they have no souls. Now they are by thousands in missionary schools; and making as rapid improvement, considering their condition, as any individuals on the globe.

"Here, then, are thousands of persons who are to be mothers, and tens of thousands who are to be fathers, in a course of Christian instruction; four hundred and fifty ministers of the gospel, more than fifty of whom were born in Pagan lands, now proclaiming the unsearchable riches of Christ; two hundred and fifty missionary stations, at most of which are Christian churches; and tens of thousands who have renounced their idolatry and acknowledged Jehovah as the only living and true God.

"And what sacrifices have been made, by the inhabitants of Christendom, to produce this mighty change? Have farmers generally given their farms, and merchants their merchandise, to replenish the treasury of the Lord? No. Have men generally given their income, above the needful expenses of their families? No. Have they given half, or even one tenth part? No. What have they done? If all that has been done to send the gospel to the heathen, should be averaged upon the individuals in Christendom, it would amount to about one half cent in a year."

December 18, 1825, he preached before the Penitent Females' Refuge Society in Boston the sermon which was then published, and the substance of which was soon after issued at New York as tract No. 178, "Joy in Heaven over the Penitent."

About this time, as the happy results of the introduction of the principle of total abstinence from ardent spirits in a large farming establishment, (that of S. V. S. Wilder, Esq., at Bolton, Massachusetts,) came to his knowledge, he encouraged the careful collection of the facts, and embodied them in the valuable tract, "The Well-conducted Farm," No. 176 of the series.

In January and February, 1826, after much consultation with the worthy friends around him, he united with the Rev. Dr. Woods and fourteen others, ministers and laymen, in forming, in Boston, "The American Society for the Promotion of Temperance," more fully noticed hereafter. At first it proceeded noiselessly, employing no agent till the succeeding year, printing no report till December, 1829, and electing no corresponding secretary till May, 1831, when Dr. Edwards was appointed to that office.

Mr. T——, a respected merchant of Boston, states that when Dr. Edwards and Dr. Woods visited Boston to propose this new organization, Mr. T—— replied, that "he had been laboring fifteen years to effect a temperance reformation by the moderate use; but he did not see that it did any good, and he was tired of the whole thing." "But," said the gentlemen who called on him, "we have *a new idea.* Our main object is, not to reform inebriates, but to induce *all temperate people to continue temperate* by practising total abstinence: the drunkards, if not reformed, will die, and the land be free." "I confess," said the merchant, "that is a new view of the subject, and worth thinking of. If you see best to call a meeting, I will attend it." He did so, and from that meeting proceeded the American Temperance Society.

To Rev. Wm. A. Hallock, Secretary, New York.

"ANDOVER, February 10, 1826.

"MY DEAR BROTHER—We are at present fast hold of a project for making all people in this country, and in all other countries, temperate; or rather, a plan to induce *those that are now temperate to continue so.* Then, as all who are *intemperate* will soon be dead, the earth will be eased of an amazing evil. This, you will see at once, is a *great* plan, and to execute it thoroughly will require great wisdom and strength. And though we are so destitute, the Lord has enough of both. 'Of his fulness' may we all receive.

"I hope all hearts and all hands in New York will aid in forming the Domestic Missionary Society. I believe it is a plan that meets the approbation, and will receive the blessing of the Lord Jesus Christ.

"The pressure to attend meeting in my parish has become so great, and the number of people who wish for this privilege so much larger than can be accommodated in our house, that the parish last Monday 'voted to erect *another house on the west side of the river;* to be dedicated to the worship of the one only living and true God, the Father, the Son, and the Holy Ghost.' They are next Monday to consider, and with the leave of Providence, decide on the spot, appoint their building committee, etc. I ask your prayers and the prayers of all good people that this subject, which is so apt to cause roots of bitterness to spring up among a people, may here promote brotherly harmony and love, and be the means of preparing the multitudes who are here to spend their day of grace, for the kingdom of God. We greatly need the divine presence and blessing. Without it we cannot succeed; no, not in any good thing. How delightful that Jehovah has all hearts in his hands, and can turn them as the rivers of water are turned. And how inexcusable will every man under his government be, if he is not a man of prayer, of faith, of deep humility, holy boldness, and of vigorous, untiring devotion to his service. And how inexcusable will every man be if he does not have *great wisdom*, since whenever he lacks he may ask of God, who giveth liberally and upbraideth not."

He adds, March 3, "A Society *is formed, not for the suppression of intemperance*, but for *the promotion of temperance.* It is on the plan of the American Board of Commissioners, and is designed to be national. It will meet, a week from next Monday, for the election of members in the different states. The Executive Committee directed me to request you, in connection with Dr. Spring and such other brethren as you may think proper to consult, to inform us what gentlemen in New York and vicinity, or in the state, we can elect to advantage as members. We want holy men, who do not use intoxicating liquors, unless prescribed by a physician as a medicine; and who will be willing to make sacrifices, and perform labors, or give money to induce all others who are now temperate, *for ever to continue so.* If all temperate men can be induced to *continue* temperate, all drunkards will soon die, and the land be eased of an overwhelming burden. The constitution of the Society we shall give you shortly; till then we wish nothing published.

The plan is, to raise a fund to support a *strong* man, who shall be permanently and wholly devoted to this object. Will you please inform me, as soon as possible, of a few *good* men and *true*, who may to advantage be elected at the next meeting.

"Affectionately, yours,

"J. EDWARDS."

Dr. Edwards' two BIBLE-CLASSES, of about one hundred and fifty men and one hundred and sixty women, were still continued with most cheering evidences of good. Within about two years he had admitted to the church *ninety-two*, as giving evidence of faith in Christ and the renewing of the Holy Spirit, *fifty-nine* of whom were heads of families, and *thirty-seven* were members of these Bible-classes, the solemnity and interest of which are still remembered by many, as occasions when they stood on the very heights of Zion. On the invitation to those who wished to converse with him, to meet him at his study on specified evenings, the room was sometimes crowded with those who, conscious of their sin and ruin, sought his prayers and counsel and guidance in the way of life.

As intelligence of these Bible-classes was widely diffused by students of the seminary and others, Dr. Edwards received many requests, from various directions, for information as to the best methods of conducting such instructions, which led him to preach to the students of the seminary, March 12, 1826, a discourse, from the text, "Search the Scriptures," "*on the manner of forming and conducting Bible-classes*," which, at their request, was published. He says:

The first prerequisite is in the qualifications of the minister. "Let him be a good man, and ardently devoted to the service of the Lord Jesus Christ. Let him daily search the Scriptures, feeling that they are the voice of God speaking to him and communicating the divine will. Let him search them with a real and earnest desire to understand their whole meaning; seeking heartily, as he reads, for the illuminating and purifying influences of the Holy Spirit, that he may have spiritual discernment, understand spiritual things in a spiritual manner, and find the word of God to be spirit and life to his soul. The declarations of the Bible let him heartily believe, on the testimony of Jehovah; and the directions of the Bible, as to feelings, thoughts, words, and actions, immediately and perseveringly follow. He will then understand its doctrines and precepts, and will know that both are of God. He will know God himself, and Jesus Christ whom he has sent, which is life eternal. He will also earnestly desire that others may have the same knowledge; and be willing, if God calls, to perform labors and make sacrifices to impart it to them. If it shall appear that he can do this most effectually by means of a Bible-class—although pressed with business, as every faithful minister must be—he will not shrink from the additional labor of establishing and conducting one."

With prayer for divine direction, he may then show from the pulpit that "all Scripture is given by inspiration of God," and present the evidences, external and internal, of its divinity; "such, for instance, as the agreement of all its writers. Although they were men of different education, occupation, and habits; lived at different times, through a period of more than fifteen hundred years; wrote upon a vast variety of subjects, some of them that which no mortal eye had ever seen, or ear heard, and of which no human mind, uninstructed by what they wrote, ever thought; yet they all agree. They give the same views of God, of Jesus Christ, and of the Holy Spirit; of heaven, and of hell; of time, and eternity; of the character of men, and what they must do to escape destruction, and inherit eternal life. Although each writer does not speak to the same extent, or with the same clearness on all these subjects, yet what he does say is in accordance with what the others say. *A unity of design and execution runs through the Bible, which stamps upon it the impress of God.*" And such are its effects, that "if all men should perfectly believe and obey it, it would transform this lost, guilty world into the likeness of heaven; every son and daughter of Adam on earth, it would change into the image of the God of heaven; it would fill the world, as the waters fill the seas, with the bliss of heaven. Would a book, which professes to be from God, if it were not so, make all who believe and obey it like unto God? Would it, simply by being followed, transform this world into the likeness, and fill it with the joys of heaven? Let a man believe the Bible and obey it, and he will *know* that it is from God."

"Having made an impression upon the audience, vivid and strong, that the Bible is the word of God, as really as if they heard him declare what it contains directly out of heaven, let the minister show them how they ought to treat it—that they ought to read it *daily*, *attentively*, *devoutly*, and *perseveringly*, and that when they understand its directions, without delay and without ceasing, they must follow them. He may then show the benefits, for time and eternity, of thus studying the Bible; and may offer to assist all among his beloved people who wish to enter upon the study of it, in a Bible-class."

Suggestions are then given as to forming the class; various ways in which the minister may assist them to a right understanding of the Scriptures; with specimens of proper questions and answers on select portions of the Bible, and explanations of the topics suggested, which the minister may give. "And let the members of the class commence with a fixed purpose, trusting in Jesus Christ alone, to ask of God daily to teach them his will; and daily to listen to his voice speaking to them in his word, that they may understand it. And when they do understand it, let nothing hinder them from doing it, for the purpose of glorifying God, becoming in temper like him, and performing his will. They will then find that the Bible is perfect, converting the soul; sure, making wise the simple; right, rejoicing the heart; pure, enlightening the eyes; true and righteous altogether; more to be desired than gold, yea, than much fine gold; and that in obeying it there is indeed a great reward."

March 19, 1826, he preached to his own people a most effective sermon, which was then printed, and immediately after embodied in the series of the American Tract Society at New York as tract No. 179, "THE WAY TO BE SAVED." It is one of the best tracts that have been written, and has been specially blessed of the Spirit in bringing souls to Christ. It has been translated into modern Greek, Armeno-Turkish, and other foreign languages. Two or three paragraphs may show the character and aim of this precious tract.

"'I am a great sinner,' says one. 'I have sinned against great light and great love. I have sinned a long time. My heart is very hard, and I sometimes think that for me there is no hope. I fear I have sinned away my day of grace. I deserve to perish; and unless God have mercy, I must perish. I know that Jesus Christ died, 'the just for the unjust;' that 'he was wounded for our transgressions,' and 'bruised for our iniquities;' that 'he bore our sins in his own body on the tree;' and that 'the Lord hath laid on him the iniquity of us all.' I know this, because God has declared it, and I believe what he says. I know also, because he has declared it, that the wicked will go away into eternal punishment. I feel that I am wicked, exceedingly wicked, and should I for ever perish, I know that it would be just. But I cannot dwell with devouring fire, I cannot inhabit everlasting burnings! I wish to escape, and I know that if I do, it must be quickly. WHAT MUST I DO?'"

As a reply to this anxious inquiry, the four questions are then seriously asked, and considered in their order, "*What have you done?*" "*What are you willing to do?*" "*When are you willing to begin?*" "*How long are you willing to continue?*"

"Give, without delay, yourself and all that you have to Jesus Christ, resolving in his strength, that, by the assistance of the Holy Spirit, you will 'live not unto yourself, but unto Him that died for you, and rose again.' Break off, without delay, whatever you know to be sin, because it is offensive to God, and ruinous to you. Engage in whatever you know to be duty, for the sake of glorifying God, and doing good. For the sake of becoming like him, let it be henceforward your grand object to learn his whole will, and to do it, *trusting wholly in Jesus Christ* for whatever you need, both to do this, and to be accepted in it. Continue this course to the end of life, and you shall be saved with an everlasting salvation. God will be your portion, and you shall not want any good thing. He will guide you by his counsel, and afterward receive you to glory. You shall see him as he is, and be like him, to everlasting ages. I will tell you why.

"This breaking off of all known sin, because it is offensive to God, and ruinous to you, is *repentance*. This engaging heartily in what you know to be duty, for the sake of glorifying God and doing good, is *obedience*. And surrendering yourself, and all that you have, to Jesus Christ, trusting alone in him for whatever you need, is *faith*—that faith which has subdued kingdoms, wrought righteousness, and obtained promises; stopped the mouths of lions, quenched the violence of fire, escaped the edge of the sword, out of weakness been made strong, waxed valiant in fight, and will, wherever it is exercised, overcome the world, the flesh, and the devil, and come off conqueror, and more than conqueror, through Him that loved us, and gave himself for us."

To Rev. William A. Hallock, Secretary, New York.

"ANDOVER, March 24, 1826.

"DEAR BROTHER—We conclude to have you print the Christian Almanac for the whole country. I have written two tracts, (Joy in Heaven over the Penitent, and the Way to be Saved,) and am examining two more to fill out the eighth volume. Although I am not now of the Committee here, yet, as usual, I have to do the work. Of course it moves slowly. The other gentlemen are by no means negligent, but are full of other work.

"I exceedingly wish to see a man of the right stamp at New Orleans, with a full depository, to defend the mouth of the Mississippi and secure that world of back country. I think that we ought to pray much that the Lord would open the way for it speedily. A man at New Orleans with arms long enough to reach from Pittsburgh to Mexico, and strong enough to scatter the good seed all the way between, might expect, through grace, an *abundant* harvest. Would it not be well for you to print the *Christian Almanac in German*, for the back settlements of Pennsylvania; and in Spanish for Mexico and South America?

"The Society for the promotion of Temperance, although it costs much labor, promises well. The first conversation which a few had about funds, led one man to say, 'I will give a thousand dollars.' We want twenty other men to do the same, and hope that we shall then be able, through grace, to save thousands of lives and millions of dollars a year; or lead others to save them. Then, should the amount saved be, as a thank-offering, put into the Lord's treasury, we should have new cause to bless him and double our diligence in his service. But so much good can probably never be effected without much prayer and fasting.

"Dr. Beecher's installation, (in the new Hanover-street church, Boston,) was on Wednesday. The occasion was very interesting, and the cause of truth in Boston is evidently rising. Let us pray much for Zion, and prefer her prosperity above every earthly joy.

"Affectionately yours,

"J. EDWARDS."

On May 10, 1826, he attended the first anniversary of the American Tract Society in New York, of whose Publishing Committee he was a member, and delivered an address worthy of the man who had nursed the Tract enterprise from its beginning in this country, and perhaps done more than any other man to give it the high evangelical and spiritual character which, by the grace of God, we believe it yet possesses. This address struck the key-note of the institution; it was made the basis of action and of public appeals, and is perpetuated in one of the series of tracts, No. 104. He began by saying,

"The object of this Society is to deliver immortal souls from a course of eternal sinning and eternal suffering; to transform them into the perfect image of God, and raise them to a state of eternal holiness and bliss in heaven.

"The means by which we are to accomplish this, is the dissemination of the truths which God has revealed, in the form of interesting and impressive religious tracts. I say, *the truths which God has revealed,* for no other truths will accomplish this glorious end: such truths as the utterly lost condition of sinners, and their indispensable duty, without delay, to love God with all their heart, and soul, and strength, and mind; the necessity of being born again, not of blood, nor of the will of the flesh, nor of the will of man, but of God; the infinite dignity, divine beauty, excellence, and glory of Him on whom their help is laid; his amazing condescension in becoming a servant, and having not where to lay his head; his unparalleled kindness in bearing their sins in his own body on the tree, and having laid on him the iniquity of them all; the necessity of believing on him in order to be interested in the blessings of his salvation; that every person to whom he is made known is under immediate obligation to embrace him, repent of sin, and live not unto himself, but unto him that died for sinners and rose again; that a day is coming when 'all that are in their graves shall hear his voice, and shall come forth; they that have done good unto the resurrection of life, and they that have done evil unto the resurrection of damnation;' that the wicked will go away into eternal punishment, and the righteous into eternal life. These are the truths, with kindred truths, in their divinely inspired aspect and connection, stamped in bold relief on the face of religious tracts, and extended to every city and town and village and family and soul, by which this Society is to aid in renovating a world, and preparing a 'multitude that no man can number,' to shine in the beauty of holiness, and shout the triumphs of grace to everlasting ages.

"These are the truths which were proclaimed on the hills and in the vales of Judea; by which the fishermen of Galilee, and men of like spirit, went out, and unarmed, in the face of an opposing world, planted the standard of the cross on the throne of the Cæsars. These are the truths which blazed at the Reformation, scattered the darkness of papal midnight, and kindled a light that will 'grow brighter and brighter, even to the perfect day.' These truths, as they go forth, 'proclaiming deliverance to captives, the opening of the prison to them that are bound,' and pointing them to 'the Lamb of God, which taketh away the sin of the world,' will cause tears of contrition to drop down from ten thousand eyes, and ten thousand hearts to pour forth their strains of gratitude in hallelujahs to the Redeemer.

"These truths it is our duty to extend, not merely because we have associated for this purpose, but because God has revealed them, and commanded us to extend them to every creature. And, if I do not mistake, sir, there are some peculiar reasons why we, in this country, should extend them by means of religious tracts.

"We are a great people, and, if not blasted by our sins, shall become greater and greater, till the light of revealed truth and the light of human science, the light of true religion, and the light of civil and religious freedom, shall blaze from one end of this continent to the other, and with a brightness that shall illumine the world. We are called by the God of heaven to make an experiment, and one of the most momentous that was ever intrusted to mortals.

"Blessed with a country of almost unparalleled extent; settled by a people of invincible energy, of ceaseless action, and untiring perseverance; enjoying civil and religious liberty to a greater extent than any other people on the globe; holding property of every description, and to any amount, in pure fee-simple, with the strongest motives bearing upon the mass of minds to the highest possible effort, we must make a development of character such as creation never witnessed, and rise to a height of goodness and greatness, from which we shall be the benefactors of the world, and instruments in bearing its millions to glory—or from which we shall sink, under a load of guilt such as earth never bore, to endless perdition. Ah, then there would be shouting through all the world of darkness, and among all the sons of darkness, through the universe; ages of darkness, which the gospel has heaved away, would roll backward, and cover millions and millions in deep and everlasting gloom.

"And are we in no danger of this? We are a republic, with no government but that which rests on the will of the people, and which cannot be perpetuated without holiness among the people. Some may say, it cannot without *public virtue.* But public virtue never did exist, sufficient to perpetuate a republican government over such an extent of country as ours, without holiness, and it never will. This holiness is not the natural growth of a single heart in the land. No means will produce it, but the means of God's appointment. Of these means a vast portion of our countrymen are now destitute. Millions and millions, increasing every day, are destitute of that influence which is so essential to the preservation of all our social, civil, and religious blessings. Nor is this all: but each individual of these millions has a soul worth a thousand worlds. And without holiness they had better have had no existence; for they will spend it in weeping and wailing and gnashing of teeth. While I speak it, I see them borne onward towards the close of their probation, destitute of that holiness without which no one can see the Lord, and destitute of the means of holiness which God has appointed.

"What then shall be done? Send them living preachers? You have not got them. Thousands, with the ardor of Paul, with the eloquence and might in the Scriptures of Apollos, are needed to-day, in order fully to supply this country. Do you say, 'Encourage Education Societies, and train up pious young men for the ministry?' By all means. Let these efforts be vastly increased, and prosecuted with all possible vigor, and generation after generation will pass away before they can all have the regular and stated ministrations of the gospel. Do you say, 'Send them the Bible?' By all means. Let efforts to extend it be increased and increased, till there shall not be a family, from one end of the land to the other, that has not the sacred volume. But then multitudes will not read it; and multitudes more will act directly against its holy dictates.

"What then shall be done? Take the truths of the Bible, and in 'thoughts that breathe, and words that burn,' stamp them on the pages of religious tracts; multiply these tracts by thousands and millions; send them forth, attended, in answer to prayer, by the Holy Ghost sent down from heaven, to every city and town and neighborhood and family, till all shall see Him who was rich, for their sakes becoming poor, that they, through his poverty, might be rich. And as they see him 'bearing their sins in his own body on the tree,' and hear him cry, 'My God, my God, why hast thou forsaken me?' and the sun shrinks away, the rocks break asunder, and the dead start from their graves, there will be mourning; yes, there will be a *very great* mourning, and there will be a great turning unto the Lord our God."

He proceeds to give some very striking and cheering facts, showing that God had made this means of grace effectual in the salvation of many; then takes a view of the wants of our country, at that time containing about twelve millions of souls; then considers the means required, and shows that the churches are most abundantly able and doubtless willing to supply them; and then turns to the Canadas, Mexico, South America, Africa, and all our foreign missionary stations among the heathen as embraced in the Society's field of labor.

"Thousands and thousands are now perishing, for the want of tracts, on the island of Ceylon. 'We visit,' said a missionary, 'from two to eight families in a day; sometimes we take long journeys, and are out six or eight days. At such times we take a number of boys from the schools, and we exceedingly need tracts. As we pass from village to village, where the gospel was never preached, we find hundreds who can, and would read, had we Bibles or tracts to give them; but, alas, we have none: no Bible, no tract to show the poor heathen how to flee from the wrath to come. Oh, that we could get a supply printed. Into how many villages might the gospel be sent by means of tracts; and how many souls, by a single tract, might be saved from endless misery.'

"And shall the missionary who has left his father's house, his native land, and gone thirteen thousand miles to tell the dying pagans of a Saviour, cry in the ears of a thousand churches abounding in wealth, 'Oh, that we could get a supply of tracts printed. Into how many villages might the gospel be sent by means of tracts, and how many souls might be saved by a single tract from endless misery'—and yet cry in vain? Let those churches answer.

"At Bombay is a printing-press, in the midst of a population, speaking the same tongue, of eleven millions of people; nearly all of whom are destitute of the gospel, and among whom tracts might be circulated to the utmost advantage. A strong feeling of doubt and uncertainty exists in the minds of multitudes throughout that country with regard to their own religion. Numbers have come to the conclusion that it is false. Multitudes are halting between two opinions, and all are becoming impressed with the expectation that a great change is approaching. In this state, they greatly need tracts, and many strongly desire them. Individuals have come twenty miles, and in some cases thirty and forty miles, to obtain a tract. And writes a missionary, 'Tracts may be printed at Bombay as cheap as in America; and in no part of the world can they be distributed to greater advantage. Many of the people would be likely to receive more instruction from a little tract, which they could read in five minutes, than from the whole of the New Testament, because they would be so much more likely to read it.'

"Writes another missionary, 'The distribution of tracts is the only possible way in which we can exhibit any portion of the gospel to *vast multitudes of the present generation* of India. Ministers enough to go and preach to them the gospel, cannot be obtained. We must print and circulate tracts, or millions and millions of the present and future generations must go down without the gospel, in unbroken succession, to the grave.'

"And these millions, Mr. President, exceedingly need tracts; for they are exceedingly wretched, even for this life. A man who has resided among them twenty years, for the purpose of investigating their spiritual condition, told me that he knew of a numerous class with whom it was an article of religion not to suffer a single female child to live. One of them, however, on the birth of a daughter, being overcome by natural affection, resolved to preserve her life. He secreted her, and intended, unknown to his countrymen, to preserve her to mature years. He succeeded without its being known, till she was, I think, seven years old. Then it became known that he had in his house a daughter. And being abroad one day, he was so overcome with the scoffs of his countrymen, and with the obloquy which they cast upon him, that he returned, and with an axe hewed her in pieces.

"And not only are they miserable in this life, but in death. A Hindoo of a thoughtful, reflecting turn of mind, but devoted to idolatry, lay on his death-bed. As he saw himself about to plunge into that boundless unknown, he cried out, 'What will become of me?' 'O,' said a Brahmin who stood by, 'you will inhabit another body.' 'And where,' said he, 'shall I go then?' 'Into another.' 'And where then?' 'Into another, and so on, through thousands of millions.' Darting across this whole period, as though it were but an instant, he cried, 'Where shall I go then?' And paganism could not answer. And he died, agonizing under the inquiry, 'Where shall I go, last of all?'

"Another Hindoo lay on his death-bed; he, however, had seen a religious tract, and had read it. It had led him to religious teachers, and to Christ. His friend, hearing of his sickness, came to see him, and found him in the last stage of disease; and as he bore up his languishing head, watching to see him breathe his last, the dying man broke out in ecstasy, 'Sing, brother, sing.' 'What,' said he, 'shall I sing?' 'Salvation,' said he; 'salvation, by the death of Jesus'— and winged his way to bow with ransomed millions before the throne.

"Let us send tracts to those sinners, and all other sinners on the globe—tracts blazing with the effulgence of the *truths which God has revealed, in the aspect and connection in which he has revealed them*, and attended, in answer to the prayers of God's people, by the Holy Ghost sent down from heaven; and multitudes out of every nation, and kindred, and people, and tongue, will assemble on mount Zion, and open an everlasting anthem 'unto Him that loved us, and washed us from our sins in his blood;' and every holy creature in the universe will cry, 'Unto him be glory, for ever and ever.'"

To Mrs. Edwards.

"PHILADELPHIA, Monday Morning, May 15, 1826.

"MY VERY DEAR WIFE—The longer I am absent from you, the more I learn how much I love you and the dear little children, and the more, I trust, I feel my obligations to God for such precious blessings. The more I see of the condition of others, and contrast it with our condition, the more I feel that we are under obligations of special gratitude to God for his kindness. I hope it may lead us to himself, and excite us to greater activity in his service.

"Last Monday I left Colchester, and took the steamboat at East Haddam. On board I found a large number of ministers, and among others, Mr. Vail from the Osage Indians. He came and told me that he had a letter for you from one of the Osage girls at the missionary station. He wished, however, to keep it, for the sake of reading it at New York and Philadelphia, after which he said that he would hand it to me. In the evening he gave an account of the Indians, and the exercises were closed by singing a hymn, and a prayer. In the morning we found ourselves at New York. I attended the meetings of the American Home Mission Society, the American Tract

Society, the Bible Society, and the Education Society. On Friday I took the steamboat, with Rev. Dr. Porter, for New Brunswick; then the stage to Princeton. There we attended the examination of the Theological Seminary, and spent the night with the professors; then took the stage to Trenton, then the steamboat to Philadelphia. Yesterday I preached in the morning, and in the evening. To-night the Sabbath-school Union have a meeting in this city. Other meetings will come along from day to day till Thursday, when the General Assembly meet, and will hold their session two weeks. I have concluded not to go any farther south. The weather is as hot here now, as it is with us in the midst of summer. Apple-trees and peach-trees were in bloom more than a week ago. Rye is almost as high as the top of the fences, and grass almost high enough to mow. I shall stay here a few days, and then, with the leave of Providence, shall return. Love to all.

"Your affectionate husband,

"J. EDWARDS."

As above intimated, the large edifice in which Dr. Edwards preached could no longer accommodate the thronging audiences, and a portion of the congregation were set off as the West-church in Andover. On June 15, 1826, he was called to lay "the corner-stone" of the new edifice, on which occasion he recounted the way in which they had been graciously and harmoniously led, and set before them the high spiritual aims by which he hoped all who took part in the enterprise had been and would be governed.

"But little more than two hundred years ago," he

said, "New England was a waste, howling wilderness; inhabited only by savage beasts, and savage men. No altar for Jehovah, and no house dedicated to his worship, was to be seen from one end of it to the other.

"A little band of pilgrims under the guidance of Abraham's God came across the Atlantic, and on the 22d of December, 1620, planted their feet on these western shores. At the opening of a long and dreary winter, on a bleak, frozen coast, without a house to shelter them, or any human arm for their protection, they commenced a settlement; resolving, in the strength of the Lord, here to spend their days, and here to leave their children. Before the opening of spring, sickness swept off half their number; trials gathered, thickened, and pressed upon them, enough to break down and overcome any common purpose; but they persevered, through dangers seen and dangers unseen, resolving, with increasing firmness, here to spend their days, and here to leave their children.

"What was their object? The glory of God in the salvation of their posterity. What supported them in their privations and dangers and toils and sufferings? 'Christ in them the hope of glory.' Faith in him which overcomes the world, and love to him stronger than death, bore them up in their trials, gave them an elevation of feeling, an extent of vision, a boldness of design, a vigor of execution, and an inflexibility of perseverance, the effects of which have been felt by millions and millions down to this day; and will continue to be felt by greater and greater numbers, to the end of the world.

"Let it be distinctly stated, let it be universally understood, and by the children of the pilgrims always remembered: The grand object of our fathers in coming to this land, was the glory of God in the salvation of their posterity; not their salvation merely from civil and ecclesiastical oppression, or their exaltation to the privileges and enjoyments of freedom, but their salvation from the power and pollution of sin, their restoration to the image of God, and their exaltation to the holiness and bliss of heaven. It was, that the Son of God might make them free, that they might be free indeed. They sought for their posterity, principally, not an earthly, but a *heavenly* country; a city that hath foundations, whose builder and maker is God. Hence, among their first acts after their arrival, was a dedication of themselves and their children anew to him. Among the first buildings which they erected, after obtaining for themselves a shelter, was a house for his worship. The foundation was laid in prayer, the structure reared in faith, and the head-stone brought forth with shouting, Grace, grace unto it.

"Whenever, on account of their increasing numbers, they settled a new town, one of their first objects was a meeting-house; and another, a minister. In selecting him, they sought for one who believed that men are lost, and that all their hope must be in Him who came down from heaven to seek and to save; that when he died for all, all were dead; and that without being born, not of blood, nor of the will of the flesh, nor of the will of man, but of God, they cannot see his kingdom; that it is their duty, when he is revealed, without delay to love him with all the heart, and soul, and strength, and mind; and live, not unto themselves, but unto Him that died for them and rose again; that the Word, who was in the beginning with God, *was* God; that when he took upon him our nature, and in this nature died on the cross, he was wounded for *our* transgressions, and bruised for *our* iniquities, that the chastisement of *our* peace was on him, and that by his stripes we are healed; that the Lord laid on him the iniquity of us all, and that whosoever believeth on him, with that faith which works by love, hath everlasting life, shall not come into condemnation, but is passed from death unto life; while he that believeth not, shall not see life, but the wrath of God abideth on him. They sought a man for their minister, who believed that all that are in their graves shall one day hear his voice, and come forth, they that have done good, to the resurrection of life, and they that have done evil, to the resurrection of damnation; that he will separate them one from another, as a shepherd divideth his sheep from the goats, and that the wicked will go away into everlasting punishment, when the righteous go into eternal life.

"These great truths which God has revealed, with kindred truths, in their divinely inspired aspect and connection, they had been taught by the Holy Ghost to *feel;* and they had found them to be the wisdom and the power of God to salvation. They wished their ministers to *feel* them, and to preach them, not only because they are revealed, but that they might be the wisdom and power of God to the salvation of their children and children's children. And their ministers *did* preach them. 'Christ and him crucified' was then the grand theme in every pulpit; and it came not in word only, but in power, in the Holy Ghost, and in much assurance. As they took the truth of God as he reveals it, he was not ashamed to be their God. He enlarged the borders of their tents, and stretched forth the curtains of their habitations. He drove out the heathen from one place and another, and planted them. In about twenty years after the first landing of the fathers, Christian families were settled in this town. A meeting-house was erected, and a minister ordained; who, says the historian, 'abounded in devotions, of serious, devout, heavenly, experimental Christianity.' The same gospel that sounded on the shores of Plymouth, was from Sabbath to Sabbath preached in Andover; and under the influences of the Holy Spirit, it produced its appropriate effects.

"Between sixty and seventy years after this, the first house was erected for public worship in this parish. A minister was settled, a descendant of the Puritans, and partaking of their spirit. Of his grandfather it is said, 'His love of the Bible was so great, that he was in the habit of reading it through six times in every year.' His grandson loved the Bible, and was cordially attached to the doctrines of grace, as embraced by the fathers of New England; for more than sixty years he earnestly preached them, persuaded, says the historian, and as his own works abundantly testify, that 'they are the faith which was once delivered to the saints.'

"This gospel, through the kindness of God, has

been preached in this parish down to the present day. And to many, there is reason to believe, it has been the wisdom of God and the power of God to salvation. Numbers now on earth, and numbers now in heaven, will testify for ever that it is *the glorious gospel of the blessed God*. May it ever be preached here in simplicity and godly sincerity, be attended by the Holy Ghost sent down from heaven, and be the means of salvation to all future generations, down to the end of the world.

"Hitherto you, and your fathers, have worshipped in one house; and it has, I trust, been to many the house of God and the gate of heaven. Peace be within its walls, and the God of peace with all who meet in it to worship him.

"In the course of divine Providence, under the smiles of heaven, you have now become too numerous any longer to be accommodated in one assembly. In consequence of this, you have been led to unite your prayers, your counsels, and your efforts, for the erection of another place of worship. Through the goodness of God, you have selected a spot, provided the means, and made arrangements for the erection of the building. You have prepared the foundation, and now, after united supplication to the Father of lights for his presence and blessing, have laid the *corner-stone*. May you have wisdom, grace, and strength from on high, speedily to complete the edifice; and then, as an offering of gratitude, to dedicate it with all its appurtenances to God, the Father, the Son, and the Holy Ghost, your God, and your father's God, *which is your reasonable service*. In his own good time, may he send you a minister after his own heart; a man of faith and prayer; of wisdom and a sound mind; of humility and zeal; boldness, energy, and perseverance; who shall determine not to know any thing among you, save Jesus Christ, and him crucified; who shall open to you with great clearness his unsearchable riches, and count all things but loss for the excellency of the knowledge of *Him;* who shall go in and out before you, and break unto you the bread of life; bear you and your children daily to the throne of mercy, and be honored by the Holy Ghost as an instrument of leading you and them to that knowledge of God and his Son Jesus Christ, which is life eternal. That this may be the case, let all your efforts spring from love to God, and love to men; let all profaneness, intemperance, and immorality of every description, be banished from among you; let the voice of humble, believing supplication ascend from every one of you daily in secret, Jehovah be acknowledged by every one of you daily in your families, his fear reign in your hearts, and his revealed will govern your lives. Then may you hope speedily to hear the gospel, to meet the presence and enjoy the blessing of the Lord Jesus Christ, in this house of prayer. And after worshipping God in spirit and in truth, in this temple made with hands, you may hope to meet in a temple made without hands—a temple large enough to hold all the redeemed, from every nation, and kindred, and people, and tongue; into which they shall all enter, a multitude that no man can number; and he shall open to their admiring vision the infinite glories of his character, with greater and greater brightness for ever and ever."

Not long after the laying of the corner-stone of the new church, Dr. Edwards, in a sermon to his people, recounted to them the various proceedings which had been happily consummated in the erection of the new edifice and the dismission of fifty-six members for the new organization. He calls upon his remaining people to give thanks to God for the harmony with which the whole proceeding had been conducted; still to regard those who had united in the new enterprise as their brethren beloved; to pray daily for his presence and blessing to be with them, and especially upon the young, of whom there were many within the bounds of the new congregation; that he would send them a pastor who should be a man after his own heart; and that brotherly love between the two churches might ever continue.

A few months afterwards, June 6, 1827, the Rev. Samuel C. Jackson, with the cordial welcome of Dr. Edwards, was installed pastor of the West church, where a blessing attended his labors; and the two churches have long preserved "the unity of the Spirit in the bond of peace."

While fulfilling all these responsibilities in his own more immediate field of labor, public calls and claims multiplied upon him. The more faithful and successful were his labors at home, the more was he appreciated abroad, and the more the hallowed influence of his services was sought in other portions of the Lord's vineyard.

At the time of his visit to New York in May 1826, the "American Home Missionary Society" was organized; he was elected a Director; and, July 1, an urgent application was made to him to give, for as long a time as he could be spared from his people, his "efficient exertions and personal influence" in labors in the principal towns in Connecticut, and in the cities of New York and Albany, to establish the Society in the affections of the people, and lay the foundations for its future success.

September 14, he was elected a member of the "American Board of Commissioners for Foreign Missions;" and at the same time was acting on a Committee of the Board of Trustees of the Theological Seminary as to proper arrangements in the department of Ecclesiastical History, on which he obtained valuable letters from the Rev. Drs. Miller and Perrine, professors at Princeton and Auburn, and from other sources. He was invited to deliver the *concio ad clerum* at Williams College, and to preach on other public occasions; was requested to assist a pastor where the influences of the Spirit were manifest, and who wished "warm-hearted preaching" by those "not afraid nor ashamed to preach the gospel in its purity;" and by another pastor of a very important church, at N——, was requested to tell him how so to preach to his great congregation, that the truth might reach the hearts of his people, how best to conduct Sabbath-schools and Bible-classes, and how so to perform pastoral duties as to win his people to Christ.

On July 20, 1826, he received a call from the

Park-street church, Boston, as he had not long before been informally requested to consent to overtures for his settlement in the new church established in Hanover-street in that city, where the Rev. Dr. Lyman Beecher was soon after installed. The Committee to present the call to Park-street comprised the Hon. Samuel Hubbard, Hon. George Odiorne, Jeremiah Evarts, and Henry Hill, Esqrs., Deacons Bumstead and Proctor, Mr. Henry Homes, and other citizens of distinguished worth, all personal friends of Dr. Edwards; and it was prosecuted with a zeal and ability that prompted to all discreet and proper measures to accomplish an object dear to their hearts, and in which they believed that the interests of evangelical truth, not only in Boston, but throughout the country and the world, were deeply involved. The call was enclosed in the following note from the Hon. Mr. Hubbard, chairman of the Committee, and was urged upon Dr. Edwards by the most powerful motives which some of the ablest members of the Committee could personally present, not the least of which was the influence he might there exert in behalf of his and their favorite object, the American Board of Foreign Missions.

"Boston, July 21, 1826.

"Rev. and dear Sir—These lines announce to you, that the members of Park-street church, after solemn deliberation and many prayers for the divine guidance, have, with most desirable unanimity and with feelings of cordial respect and attachment, elected you to become their pastor. The church are not unmindful that you sustain endearing and highly important relations, in the place where your divine Master has made use of your talents and services. But they wish to lay before you the reasons which have induced them to offer the present invitation; and which, unless they are mistaken, will make it your duty to accept it.

"The accompanying copy of the proceedings of the church will sufficiently explain the principal facts relating to this important transaction. It may be proper, however, for the Committee who wait upon you with this document, to make such verbal statements as shall seem to them likely to cast any light upon the path of duty.

"Praying that you may experience the divine guidance with reference to this great concern, and that the Lord would cause the hearts of all who are interested in the result of this application, humbly to acquiesce in that course which shall be most for his glory, we are, reverend sir, with sentiments of sincere friendship and Christian affection,

"Yours in the gospel.

"By order of the Committee appointed by the church to present their call,

"SAMUEL HUBBARD, CHAIRMAN."

As a means of learning the will of divine Providence on the momentous question submitted to him, Dr. Edwards addressed a large number of distinguished clergymen and laymen, inquiring, "Is it in your view probable that I can on the whole be more useful to the kingdom of our Lord Jesus Christ, by becoming pastor of the Park-street church, than by continuing where I am?" To this inquiry more than thirty who were addressed returned him faithful, well-considered replies, all implying a deep conviction that the best interests of religion were involved in the question of the station he should occupy. At a meeting also of several esteemed pastors and laymen, the whole subject was patiently and seriously discussed: the powerful reasons for his removing to Park-street, and the powerful reasons for his remaining at Andover, being fully presented and weighed. Students of the Theological Seminary put in their plea that he should remain, for the sake of his influence on that institution; and on the whole, especially as the enterprise of establishing the new church in Andover remained to be consummated, the path of duty did not appear to him so clear as to warrant the sundering of all the sacred existing ties, and he declined the call as follows:

"ANDOVER, August 28, 1826.

"To the Church in Park-street, Boston:

"DEAR BRETHREN—The invitation which you have been pleased to give me to become your pastor, I received through the hands of your Committee, on the 22d ult. The subject is immensely important, and I have given it an attentive and prayerful consideration. I have endeavored, by all suitable means, to ascertain the will of God, and, if I know my own heart, for the purpose of doing it. So far as I can judge from the indications of his providence, it does not appear to be his will that I should accept the invitation; I therefore decline it. In doing this, I am not insensible of the peculiarly interesting manner in which it was presented, nor of the vast importance of your situation as a church, being called to shine with the light of holiness not merely on a city, or a country, but on the world. That the Lord will guide and bless you, and in his own way and time send you a pastor after his own heart, who shall be instrumental in your salvation and that of your children, in extending the kingdom of our Lord Jesus Christ throughout your city, throughout our country, and throughout the whole earth, is the prayer of your affectionate and unworthy servant in the gospel,

"J. EDWARDS."

The Hon. Mr. Hubbard, in a letter a few weeks later, having expressed a desire that some of his children might visit the family of Dr. Edwards, says, "I feel solicitous concerning them, and I have an increased desire that their minds may be early impressed with a sense of divine truth, and that they may act from an habitual regard to the fear and favor of God." He adds,

"I will not indulge my feelings on the subject of your answer to our church. I hope I endeavored, with much mixture of infirmity and sin however, to commit the subject to God, after using all proper and upright means to place the case in the light which appeared to me correct; and it is my duty to say, The will of the Lord be done. In looking at my dear family, I feel the want of a pastor, and I thought I saw those wants supplied far better than I deserve; but I am brought back again, or ought to be, to more simple and direct dependence upon God, and I pray Him to strengthen our faith, and to provide for us in his good time a true servant who shall feed his sheep and his lambs, and be a faithful laborer in his Master's sheepfold."

"You stand," wrote an esteemed pastor near Boston, when the question of his removal to Park-street was pending, "in the full view of one hundred and fifty young men who are to be pastors, and move around in your parish, with so many eyes out on you as a living example in a work in which no small part of their usefulness must consist. God has enabled you, in an important sense, to say to them in *this work*, 'Be ye followers of me;' at least, they, as I know, have felt this. If you leave Andover, will your place in this respect be filled? And will your relations as a member of the Board of Trustees be as well sustained?

"Your meetings with the professors for devising good—what have they done? You know, sir, better than I; but, if I am not mistaken, they have been at the foundation of some of the richest blessings to the world. One man of mighty power to pray and plan there, is Archimedes with his lever. I am always glad to feel that you are in those counsels, in which I have sometimes had the privilege to mingle."

In October, 1826, Mr. Homan Hallock, who, on September 5, 1824, had united with Dr. Edwards' church on the profession of his faith, sailed as a missionary printer for the Mediterranean; claiming the pastor's counsel, sympathy, and prayers; and writing back to him from time to time cheering missionary intelligence.

In November he received a request from the American Sunday-school Union, to prepare a *Manual for conducting Bible-classes, both of youth and of adults,* founded on his own experience of what is "best fitted to answer the important ends of the social study of the word of God."

In January, 1827, he preached his published sermon on "the Inspiration of the Scriptures" at installations in Henniker, N. H., and Conway, Mass.; a sermon which was translated by the Rev. Dr. Goodell, and printed in Italian, and afterwards in Modern Greek, and still later in Armeno-Turkish.

In this month he visited Boston, and with the counsel and coöperation of active ministers and laymen, raised in that city $5,400, to which he soon added $2,000, from Andover, Salem, Newburyport, and Northampton, towards the support of an agent or secretary to devote himself permanently to the pro motion of the cause of temperance.

March 22, 1827, he wrote to the Secretary of the Tract Society, New York, "The indications for good, in all this region, are more numerous and decisive than I have ever known before. There is rather a growing attention among my people. Pray for us."

A few weeks later he says, "The unusual anxiety among my people, and the increasing numbers who are inquiring what they shall do to be saved, leaves me not a moment's time to try to supply the defects of this manuscript."

At the close of May, he again writes from Boston: "We have, I think, had more evident tokens, during the celebration of our anniversaries this year, that the Lord is among us by his Spirit, than ever before.

There is a remarkable tenderness of spirit manifested by the ministers, and an earnest desire for the salvation of men. It was suggested to my mind in passing the new theatre, which is rapidly going up there, whether it is not the will of God that his people should agree together to pray that the building may be, as soon as the designs of infinite benevolence shall permit, consecrated as a temple for the worship of the living God; and that instead of its being, as it must be if appropriated according to the present designs, a place in which multitudes, perhaps some of our own relatives, will be ripened for perdition, it may be a place in which multitudes, in answer to prayer, shall be prepared for glory. Will you think of it, ask counsel of the Lord, and let me know your thoughts upon it. Is it too much for the Lord, in the course of no long period, to take possession of that theatre,* of Harvard College, of all Boston, and this whole commonwealth; and of the four millions of the destitute west of the Alleghanies; and of the five hundred millions equally precious, from the rising of the sun to the going down of the same? Our brethren from New York have done us much good; and I hope have not been injured themselves.

"P. S. I have been wishing for some time to save twenty dollars from the expenses of my family to transmit to your Society. I now have it, and send it to you, lest, if I should delay, it should slip some other way. It will make me a life member."

* This theatre, the Tremont, was, about fifteen years afterwards, purchased and converted into a free evangelical church in the Baptist connection, where the gospel is statedly preached.

In this month he was invited to deliver anniversary addresses before the American Bible Society in New York, the American Sunday-school Union in Philadelphia, and the American Tract Society at Boston; but the pressure of other duties compelled him to decline the invitations.

In the number of the National Preacher for this month appeared his evangelical and excellent sermon, "The Great Change," from the text, "If any man be in Christ, he is *a new creature.*"

The gracious influences of the Holy Spirit having been manifested in many churches, and serious questions having arisen as to the measures employed by some for the promotion of the work, a convention of several prominent clergymen from the New England states and New York, met, July 18, 1827, at Lebanon Springs, and spent several days in a serious consideration and discussion of the proper principles and measures to be observed in labors in revivals. A report of the discussion, published in the New York Observer of August 4, 1827, and signed by Rev. Heman Humphrey, D. D., Moderator, gives the following propositions relating to evils supposed to exist, which were submitted by Dr. Edwards, and unanimously adopted:

"That revivals of true religion are the work of God's Spirit, by which, in a comparatively short period of time, many persons are convinced of sin, and brought to the exercise of repentance towards God and faith in our Lord Jesus Christ."

"That the preservation and extension of true religion in our land have been much promoted by these revivals."

"That according to the Bible and the indications of Providence, greater and more glorious revivals are to be expected, than have ever yet existed."

"That though revivals of religion are the work of God's Spirit, they are produced by means of divine truth and human instrumentality, and are liable to be advanced or hindered by measures which are adopted in conducting them. The idea that God ordinarily works independently of human instrumentality, or without any reference to the adaptation of means to ends, is unscriptural."

"There may be some variety in the mode of conducting revivals according to local customs; and there may be relative imperfections attending them, which do not destroy the purity of the work, and its permanent and general good influence upon the church and the world; and in such cases, good men, while they lament these imperfections, may rejoice in the revival as the work of God."

"There may be so much human infirmity, and indiscretion and wickedness of man, in conducting a revival of religion, as to render the general evils which flow from this infirmity, indiscretion, and wickedness of man, greater than the local and temporary advantages of the revival; that is, this infirmity, indiscretion, and wickedness of man, may be the means of preventing the conversion of more souls than may have been converted during the revival.

"In view of these considerations, we regard it as

eminently important that there should be a general understanding among ministers and churches, in respect to those things which are of a dangerous tendency and are not to be countenanced."

"Those meetings for social religious worship, in which all speak according to their own inclinations, are improper; and all meetings for religious worship ought to be under the presiding influence of some person or persons."

"The existence in the churches of evangelists in such numbers as to constitute an influence in the community separate from that of the settled pastors, and the introduction by evangelists of measures without consulting the pastors, or contrary to their judgment and wishes, by an excitement of popular feeling which may seem to render acquiescence unavoidable, is to be carefully guarded against, as an evil which is calculated, or at least liable, to destroy the institution of a settled ministry, and fill the churches with confusion and disorder."

"All irreverent familiarity with God, such as men use towards their equals, or which would not be proper for an affectionate child to use towards a worthy parent, is to be avoided."

"From the temporary success of uneducated and ardent young men, to make invidious comparisons between them and settled pastors, to depreciate the value of education, or introduce young men as preachers without the usual qualifications, is incorrect and unsafe."

"To state things which are not true, or not supported by evidence, for the purpose of awakening sinners, or to represent their case as more hopeless than it really is, is wrong."

"Unkindness and disrespect to superiors in age or station, is to be carefully avoided."

"In promoting and conducting revivals of religion, it is unsafe, and of dangerous tendency, to connive at acknowledged errors, through fear that enemies will take advantage from our attempt to correct them."

"The immediate success of any measure, without regard to its scriptural character, or its future and permanent consequences, does not justify that measure, or prove it to be right."

"Great care should be taken to discriminate between holy and unholy affections, and to exhibit with clearness the scriptural evidences of true religion."

"No measures are to be adopted in promoting and conducting revivals of religion, which those who adopt them are unwilling to have published, or which are not proper to be published to the world."

In August, he was requested to prepare for an able quarterly a review of the subject of "Revivals," in which it was hoped that all the friends of genuine revivals might cordially unite.

In September, he received a kind note from the Rev. President Day, informing him that the Corporation of Yale College had conferred on him the degree of Doctor of Divinity, and expressing the hope that, though "these academical titles are of small account with one who elevates his aims above the transient distinctions of earth," he would not refuse their "tribute of respect."

Dr. Edwards had now ministered to a beloved and confiding people for nearly fifteen years, with a cheering and constant accession to the church, on the profession of their faith, of those who gave evidence of true and saving conversion to God. In 1813, seven were thus admitted; in 1814, twenty-three; in 1815, fourteen; in 1816, six; in 1817, fourteen; in 1818, twenty-one; in 1819, sixteen; in 1820, eleven; in 1821, eight; in 1822, ten; in 1823, ten; in 1824, when the Bible-classes were greatly blessed, fifty-five, of whom forty were heads of families, and twenty-seven members of the Bible-classes; in 1825, twenty; in 1826, eight; in 1827, sixteen; being, in fifteen years, two hundred and thirty-nine admitted on profession of their faith, making, with twenty-seven received from other churches, two hundred and sixty-six. But this was far from the measure of all the good effected. The steady influence of his ministry for fifteen years was as the gentle descent of the Holy Spirit on the congregation. Every visit he made to a school or family, to the sick, suffering, or sorrowing, every personal interview, every smile and word of counsel to the child, every funeral attended, every marriage celebrated, every pastoral or social visit, every prayer he offered, every brief portion of scripture he expounded, all the variety of circumstances in which the people, old or young, came in contact with the man of God, impressed on their minds the fact that true, vital religion is a blessed reality, and that they must be born again by the washing of regeneration and renewing of the Spirit. His efficient influence in Sabbath-schools and Bible-classes was a pattern for imitation, and awakened interest and encouragement extensively in other churches. His devotional services and expositions of the Scriptures, in the social prayer-meeting, or the parochial family visit, were a feast to the hungry soul. He not only loved and venerated the Bible, but he himself fed upon it, and drew refreshment from it for others. It afforded exhaustless supplies, and the more he drew from it, the richer were its remaining treasures.

Well do we remember the spiritual refreshment imparted by his official labors in the sanctuary. When, under the chilling influence too often felt in studying the Scriptures in the originals, perhaps with learned but unsanctified helps, or investigating theological truth as a science, the soul seemed to be famishing, it was as a visit from on high to be permitted to join in his prayers, which seemed to breathe "an unction from the Holy One," and listen to the great life-giving truths of salvation by the once crucified, but risen, exalted, and interceding Redeemer. His deep-toned voice, often tremulous from the swelling emotions of his heart; his tender beaming eye; the whole expression of his countenance and demeanor, as if he lived in sight of the holiness and bliss of heaven, and of the misery of the lost, and would pluck sinners as brands from the burning; his sense of the fulness of Christ, of the power of the Spirit, of the prevalence of prayer, and the worth of the soul; his hiding himself in the riches of divine grace; his moving entreaties—still live before us, as "the glorious gospel of the blessed God."

Yet the time had come when the bond that had united him to his people without a jar, must be sundered. From an early period, as has already appeared, his soul had been stirred within him by the sad influence of intemperance in steeling the heart against the gospel. Again and again he had presented the subject to his people, and seen the beneficent results. The American Temperance Society had been formed in a great degree through his influence; it needed some master-spirit to carry it forward; and there was "*no man like-minded, naturally to care for it.*" A work wide as the world, and requiring more than human power, was to be done; his brethren enlisted with him in that Society, urged that work on him; the eyes of the community were fixed on him for this service; and he felt that the great Master called him to enter it, with all its sacrifices and self-denials. Besides, he felt that his multiplied and growing public engagements must diminish his usefulness as a pastor; and in addition to this, he perceived that his firm native strength and vigor could not long sustain the constant pressure that had rested upon him. He consulted the Ministerial Association with which he stood connected, and able and faithful Christian friends, who examined the subject with prayerful deliberation. The path of duty seemed plain. He laid the subject before his deacons, and then submitted it to his congregation in the following terms:

"To the South Church and Society in Andover:

"DEAR BRETHREN AND FRIENDS—In the course of divine Providence, I have received from the Executive Committee of the American Society for the Promotion of Temperance,' the following communication: [a commission appointing him Agent of that Society for three months, with a view to his being elected its permanent Secretary.]

"The above appointment, so far as it relates to engaging for a time, in order, with the leave of Providence, to lay a foundation for the permanent support of a man who shall devote his life to the promotion of Temperance, I feel it to be my duty, after having received the opinion of many Christian friends, to accept; provided you shall be willing to grant me a dismission for this purpose. And I hereby request that I may be dismissed from my pastoral and ministerial connection with you, in order that I may accept the above-mentioned temporary appointment; and then be in a situation, should any other appointment be made, to act with regard to it as Providence shall seem to call.

"This request, dear brethren and friends, is not made on account of any diminution of affection for you, or regard for your welfare, and that of your children, but on account of a conviction that the good of the kingdom of Jesus Christ will be promoted by my dismission, and that it will be better for you and your children to have a good minister whose whole time can be devoted to your service, than to have one who is called to be absent as much as I am for the promotion of public benevolent objects.

"Wishing you the divine guidance and blessing, and praying that the Lord will ever dwell among you by his Spirit, and bring all in this place to that knowledge of himself and of his Son which is life eternal,

"I am, with tender affection,

"Most cordially, your much obliged pastor,

"J. EDWARDS.

"ANDOVER, Sept. 8, 1827."

A meeting of the church having been appointed for September 14, on the preceding day Dr. Edwards received a call from the church which had then been formed in Salem-street, Boston, to become their pastor, which call he also laid before the church in connection with the above communication. His church and congregation, seeing the determined purpose with which he had resolved to yield to what he believed to be the call of God, though at great apparent sacrifice both to themselves and to him, acquiesced in his decision, and the pastoral relation was dissolved, October 1, 1827.

Such a sundering of the tender and sacred relations which God has established between an endeared pastor and his flock, whom he is leading by the still waters, and training for usefulness on earth and for glory in heaven, is among the most trying and inscrutable events in the dispensations of a holy and unerring Providence. It was a bitter stroke to his unanimously confiding people, who had come to feel that all he did and proposed was for their highest and eternal good. An honored officer of the church recently said, "We had but one thing against him, and that was his leaving us."

Could all the history of this pastoral life for fifteen years be recorded as seen by the omniscient Eye, it would be full of interest and encouragement to the ministry, and to all who love the welfare of the Redeemer's kingdom. Thanks for the seed sown and fruits reaped for eternity, in which the subject, the writer, and the reader of this memoir may rejoice for ever before the throne of God. Would that we had a record from the pastor's own pen of the emotions of his heart, and of what God was doing in and by him; but in this most laborious, active, and useful portion of his life, when his public services were most abundant, when calls were pressing on him from every direction, and his powers were tasked to the utmost in fulfilling his weighty responsibilities, he kept no written memorial even of the most important events, as if he had then been guided by what he wrote twenty or thirty years later in life in his comment on Paul's words, "Would to God ye could bear with me a little in my folly:" "A judicious and modest Christian *will not speak of himself and his labors*, unless the public good evidently requires it; and then he will do it, not to exalt himself, but to magnify the grace of God."

Those who know most of the influence and results of this happy period of Dr. Edwards' life, of which the writer, from the years 1819 to 1825, was not a distant or indifferent spectator, appreciate them the most highly; but they will never be fully recorded here on earth.

A few worthy servants of Christ, still adorning the gospel, who recall, with overflowing gratitude, his public ministrations, his Bible-classes, Sabbath-schools, pastoral visits, and godly life, must not be denied the privilege of uttering their testimony to the grace of God manifested through him.

The venerable Mr. John Adams, long Preceptor of the Phillips Academy at Andover, and yet active in the Master's service at the advanced age of more than fourscore years, says of Dr. Edwards as a pastor:

"I was intimately acquainted with him, from the time he entered the Theological Seminary till I left Andover in 1833. On my first acquaintance, I often met him at the prayer-meeting, and in the conference-room, especially at the central school-house. It was here, at these solemn and interesting meetings, that Mr. Edwards, then a student in the seminary, so won the affections of the people in the parish, that they fixed their eyes upon him as their future pastor. And so intent and eager were they, that before he had completed the regular course in the seminary, he, with the full consent of the professors, was installed pastor. Here he labored with great success, highly esteemed, and greatly beloved. And his labors were richly blessed in the conversion of sinners, and the increase and purity of the church. When the church for the seminary and academy was organized, my family of course changed our place of worship; but Betsey Cleaveland, long an interesting member of the family, was so strongly attached to her minister, loved him, his instructions and counsels, so much, and had such confidence in him, that nothing could separate her from Dr. Edwards. If her wish, and the wishes of many others, could have been gratified, he would never have left Andover.

"Dr. Edwards, no doubt, had his faults, but I do not remember them. He was remarkably cautious and prudent; a safe counsellor, and a peacemaker. He did not indulge in polemics or metaphysics. He did not attempt things too high for him, nor 'to be wise above what is written.' He was very solemn in his public prayers. His manner of preaching was so plain and simple, that those of common attainments could not fail to understand him. He was sound in doctrine; his delivery good, earnest, solemn, and calculated to make the impression on the audience, that he did really believe what he said."

An aged lady, Mrs. C——, recalls with the deepest interest "his faithful labors, his wise counsel, and judicious explanations of Scripture, by which many were made wise unto salvation. The instruction I received from his public discourses," she says, "I shall never forget. Even now, I recollect distinctly with what eager and delightful anticipation I looked forward from Sabbath to Sabbath, knowing I should be fed with the sincere milk of the word, and hoping thereby to grow in knowledge and in grace."

Others recall the *first Sabbath-school;* the anniversary occasions, when *three hundred* children each received from the hand of the pastor a little book, with kind words of counsel and incentives to study the word of God; the visits and instructions of the pastor in the day-schools; and the plainness and solemnity with which, in the Bible-classes, divine truth was brought down to the comprehension of all.

An aged member of the church says, "The silent but pervading descent of the Holy Spirit in 1823–24 greatly enlarged the church, and endeared the pastor to his people. The work was still and solemn. No extraordinary measures were resorted to, but a divine influence manifestly attended the common means of grace. The prayer-meeting and room for religious inquiry were places of deep solemnity. The appeals of our pastor were direct and pungent. It was the time of God's gracious visitation. There seemed a steady, uniform growth of piety, which was the legitimate result of the faithful preaching of the gospel. The house of God then answered well to the sentiment which for so many years was inscribed on its venerable walls, '*Holiness* becometh thy house, O Lord, for ever.' His pastoral visits were highly prized. They were strictly religious, always closed with prayer, and suited to make a deep impression on every member of the family. If any subject of interest to the family, any passage of Scripture, or religious topic was brought up in the course of the conversation, which needed light, it was not unusual to hear more about it the next Sabbath. His charities were kind, unobtrusive, but eminently judicious. His basket was always at hand, and filled for the supply of the poor and needy."

Two letters, written more than thirty years ago, by H. F., a lady who spent some years in Andover, are still preserved, which report to distant friends the religious privileges she was enjoying under the ministry of Dr. Edwards. In one she describes a lecture at a school-house, from Revelation 20, on the resurrection and general judgment, when the books shall be opened, and all, small and great, appear before

God. In the other, she first describes a Bible-class when the subject was the Lord's opening the heart of Lydia, and the conversion of the jailer; and then an evening lecture on Faith, as illustrated in Hebrews 11. "He was in his element," she says, "and you may judge how he appeared. He seemed to soar on the wings of faith, and to take us all with him. He told us what faith is, the necessity of having it, and the happiness of those who live by faith. He said we must always follow the way that God leads; there may be difficulties and trials, but we must surmount them, take up the cross, and never regard the sneers and scoffs of the world. He described Noah's faith, who went on building the ark a hundred and twenty years, as if he could see the clouds gathering, and the rain descending. This is true faith: to live in the belief of things not seen. O, it was good to be there, though I know that all these precious privileges, if misimproved, will rise against me in the day of trial."

Another member of his church says, "I well remember the hold he had on the hearts of his people, and how strong a tie was sundered when, in the providence of God, he was called to labor elsewhere. He often visited his people in regular course by neighborhoods, holding in each a neighborhood meeting. These meetings awakened a deep interest, and it was esteemed a rich privilege to attend them. He gave such clear and distinct views of the truths explained, and enforced them in such a familiar and practical manner, that it seemed to carry conviction to every heart of the importance of becoming personally interested in religion. The amount of labor he performed in this way is truly surprising, considering the great extent of his parish. But this constant and familiar intercourse with his people was, under God, one of the grand secrets of the success of his labors, and aided him to prepare a word in season for all.

"The cause of missions lay near his heart, and he labored to impress its importance upon his people, that they might aid it by their prayers and efforts and contributions. He made the monthly concert of prayer an occasion of deep interest; and the first Monday in January he wished to have observed by the church as a day of fasting and prayer. These were precious seasons, not soon forgotten by those who enjoyed them.

"He sought out and visited the abodes of want and sorrow. Of the good he thus did, and the charities he bestowed, the record is on high, and the final day will declare it. Many facts illustrating this I learned of my father, whose calling, as a physician, led him to witness much suffering, and of whom Dr. Edwards frequently inquired as to cases he had met. One such case shows with what energy and perseverance he would overcome obstacles, to accomplish a good object. My father had been called, on a very cold and stormy day, to visit a poor sick woman in a family consisting only of three females, who lived on a cross street a mile from the public road. He found them almost perishing with cold. The heavy snow, which was still falling and piling in drifts, rendered the roads almost impassable; yet Dr. Edwards made his way through it all no less than three times during the day, with wood from his own wood-pile, and other articles for their relief."

Another, who resided in a distant part of the congregation, says, "A few years after he was settled, he established a meeting in the most westerly part of the parish, on the first Tuesday of every month, when the house was generally crowded with attentive hearers, many coming from the neighboring towns. Among the happy results of this meeting was the hopeful conversion of a number of persons, some of them mothers of families, who seldom had the privilege of attending church. Many remember these meetings as among their choicest privileges, the texts from which he preached, and the deep earnestness and solemnity with which he spoke, seldom going through a sermon without his eye being moistened with a tear. Though his congregation was very large, he did not neglect the most remote corners, but sought out the sick and afflicted, and in his visits administered not only to their spiritual, but also to their temporal wants. The memory of that revered man is enshrined in many hearts."

Another, in a distant part of the congregation, says, "In our district-school he took a deep interest, not only visiting it at the opening and at the close, but often during the term, and encouraging us not only in our regular school-studies, but to commit passages of Scripture and the catechism, for which he presented us tracts which were highly esteemed, and some of which are still preserved in remembrance of the giver. He also established among us a neighborhood Bible-class, which was attended in the afternoon; and in the evening, prayer-meetings were held in the neighboring houses, as the result of which a large number were added to his church, and many who have since professed faith in Christ, have dated their first religious impressions from those interesting seasons."

A lady says, "In his family, where I was often privileged to be, I was struck with many traits of his character. One was, the entire absence of any thing like detraction, fault-finding, or unkindness. Returning from public worship on the Sabbath, as he found two of his children engaged in something like play, he mildly said, 'Is this the way to keep the Sabbath-day holy?' and related how careful *his mother* was that he should keep the Sabbath; which had the desired effect. Usually his words were few, and he was especially reserved in speaking of himself. I suppose the person is not living who ever heard him speak of his own good deeds. What he said was instructive and edifying; and he seemed to speak only what he would be willing all his people should hear. There was a kindness and benignity in the expression of his countenance and his manner which inspired confidence and love, and you always wished to hear more from his lips."

Another says, "He never talked for the sake of talking. It seems to me no one will have so few idle words to answer for at the judgment. He frequently repeated the passages, 'In the multitude of words there wanteth not sin.' 'A fool uttereth all his mind, but a wise man keepeth it in till afterwards.' He was probably never accused of slander, or of speaking unadvisedly with his lips. He seemed to be fully aware that 'the tongue is a fire, a world of iniquity.' His words were often 'like apples of gold in pictures of silver.' Many of his short pithy sayings are laid up as treasures by his friends: 'It always requires more light to move, than it does to stand still.' 'In order to know what a man's judgment is worth, you must know his circumstances in relation to the matter about which he is consulted.' 'No man of sense and right feeling will be lifted up or made vain by human honors, much less by flattery. To this every man of talent, learning, and accomplishments of any kind will be exposed, and the weak will often bestow it upon him, but none but the weak will be lifted up by it.' It was common for him, when asked about any thing he was thinking of doing, to say, 'If Providence opens the way.' When asked about his health, even if unwell, his usual reply was, 'comfortable.' This doubtless arose from an aversion to making himself the topic of remark."

The trait frequently alluded to above, of watchfulness over the tongue, was one not easily portrayed for imitation; yet it marked his character, and doubtless increased his usefulness. He acted as if the inspired injunction had been well considered, "By thy words shalt thou be justified, and by thy words shalt thou be condemned." In this trait we have doubtless one reason why there were *so few drawbacks* in his character and influence. The respected gentleman who was in the profession of law in Dr. Edwards' parish throughout his ministry, said, at its close, that he did not remember hearing any man, in any grade of society, or in any circumstances, speak disrespectfully of Dr. Edwards. No man found an evil report started concerning himself, through the indiscretion of his pastor; and though hundreds unbosomed to him their trials, perplexities, and sorrows, they rested in his own bosom till the judgment; and by this means he had sometimes a wisdom in counselling a man as to what he believed would be most for his usefulness and the welfare of the Redeemer's kingdom, which he could not otherwise have possessed. There were no *personalities* in his conversation or preaching, though many a man found the truths he uttered rankling like barbed arrows in his conscience.

At a monthly concert for prayer, interesting statements as to the success of foreign missions had been made, and the usual contributions were about to be received, when an aged gentleman asked leave to state his views, and proceeded to urge an array of objections against all foreign missions. As he sat down, many looked for an able reply from the pastor; but he simply said, with great calmness—"The collection may be taken up."

On one occasion he and a member of his church heard the first sermon of a student in divinity, who boldly undertook to *eclaircise* the subject of God's hardening Pharaoh's heart; but with little regard to the principle that every part of Scripture is to be interpreted "in its own divinely inspired connection." As they were retiring, his parishioner said to him with some enthusiasm, "That was very fine, was n't it?" "I thought they had *very good singing*," was the only reply.

When the young pastor of the new church in Andover was entering on his labors, Dr. Edwards intimated to him, that if, in intercourse with his people, remarks should be made as to the *location* of the church, it would always be safe to say that it is important that a church should be located in the right place ; and that it is well for a minister to remember, that God has given him two ears, and but one tongue. That pastor has said, "I took my people directly from Dr. Edwards, and there was but one testimony as to the acceptableness and usefulness of his ministry. Their confidence in his wisdom and judgment was unbounded. While I was a student in the Seminary, he was regarded by us all as an admirable illustration of what a pastor should be. We learned the theory on the hill, and our eyes turned to the village for the example."

On the sundering of Dr. Edwards' pastoral relations to the church in Andover, he was so happy as to be the means of introducing to the pulpit the Rev. Dr. Milton Badger, in whom the people united, and under whose labors rich harvests of souls were gathered. The retiring pastor, (whose permanent residence continued among them till his death,) with a discretion not always exemplified, withdrew himself as much as practicable from the affairs of the church, that, though he loved them as one who had "begotten them through the gospel," they might speedily transfer their affections to his worthy successor.

CHAPTER VI.

HIS MINISTRY IN BOSTON.

NEARLY TWO YEARS—1828, 1829.

DR. EDWARDS, having resigned his pastoral charge at Andover, October 1, 1827, entered immediately on the agency he had accepted for the American Temperance Society. But Christians, both in the city of Boston and in the city of New York, had aroused to the duty of forming new churches for the supply of the destitute thousands congregating in those commercial centres; and the well-known character of his pastoral labors at Andover, and the happy and constantly accumulating results with which God had crowned them, had fastened their eyes on him to give a controlling influence to evangelical plans and enterprises in those cities; while the fact that his pastoral relations had been sundered, seems to have given new confidence, in each city, of success in securing his services. At the same time his brethren, whom he had himself encouraged to form the Temperance Society, felt it to be indispensable that he should prosecute that enterprise.

WHAT SHALL HE DO? In 1805, he had given himself to Christ. In 1806, he had consecrated all his powers to the ministry and the upbuilding of his kingdom. In College and in the Theological Seminary, he had united with Mills and Richards, and other pioneers of foreign missions, in looking at the claims of the world, and regarding it as an individual duty to labor wherever God should call, and seek, by prayer and unreserved devotion to his service, to learn and to do *His will.* It had been clearly the divine will that he should settle in the ministry at Andover, and to that work he had given the vigor of his early manhood: threatening dangers had been removed; and the one church had become two, both firmly established in the faith. He believed that God had called him to resign the pastoral charge, especially as the constant tension and excitement of mind, in his unceasing public labors and responsibilities, had produced a chronic bilious state which gave indications of utter prostration, without some change of life like that he was now pursuing in the Temperance agency. Yet the call from each of the two cities was urgently renewed: he had full confidence in those engaged in founding the new churches in both cities; and in each of the three enterprises before him he saw a field of boundless usefulness. He must definitively decide among these momentous interests; and he had learned, in his own words, "that a man's wisdom and safety, happiness, duty, and usefulness, consist in looking distinctly, in all events, at the face of God, and watching the indications of his will as manifested by his providence, *for the simple purpose of following it.*"

The call from Boston had been in his hands some weeks, when he convened a council of brethren in whom he had confidence, and laid the whole subject before them; having expressed to leading men engaged in that enterprise, "a willingness, if Providence should permit, to follow the advice of that council, provided it should be unanimous." The council, on deliberation, came to the result unanimously that he ought to accept the call from Boston; and after further delay, and receiving also applications that he would consent to be elected as Secretary of the American Home Missionary Society, and as Professor of Divinity in Hamilton College; and after holding another serious consultation with esteemed brethren, he accepted the call from Boston, and negatived that from New York, as follows:

"To Messrs. J. C. PROCTOR, L. P. GROSVENOR, D. GREEN, D. SAFFORD, S. TENNEY, E. PALMER, Committee of Salem Church, Boston.

"ANDOVER, Dec. 3, 1827.

"DEAR BRETHREN—The invitation which you gave me to become your pastor, I have made the subject of attentive and prayerful consideration. I have endeavored by all suitable means to learn the will of God; and in accordance with the advice of friends, and what appear to be the indications of Providence, I now accept your invitation, and consent, with the divine leave, to take the oversight of you in the Lord.

"In doing this, I am not insensible of my amazing responsibility, and of the momentous consequences which may result, both to you and to me. I ask an interest in all your prayers, that I may come to you in the fulness of the blessings of the gospel, determined to know nothing among you, save Jesus Christ and him crucified; that my labors may spring from love to Him, and love to you, be attended by the Holy Ghost sent down from heaven, and be the wisdom and the power of God to your salvation, and that of your children.

"Commending you, and myself, unto Him who is able to do exceeding abundantly for us, above all that we ask or think, according to the riches of grace in Christ Jesus,

"I am, dear brethren, most cordially,

"Yours in the Lord,

"J. EDWARDS."

"To Messrs. A. TAPPAN, E. LORD, J. WHEELWRIGHT, JAMES BROWN, and MOSES ALLEN, Committee, etc., for building a new Church in the city of New York:

"BOSTON, Dec. 13, 1827.

"DEAR BRETHREN—Yours of the 3d inst. came to hand on the 7th, the very day on which my answer in the affirmative, which had already been sent, was communicated to the Salem church, Boston. The object in which you are engaged has a magnitude, and I view it with an intensity of interest, which no language can describe. A church such as you propose, if properly manned, and under the divine guidance and blessing, must in its effects be felt not only through your city, and through our country, *but through the world.*

"The reason why I cannot comply with your request is, not any doubt as to the importance and practicability of the object, nor any doubt but that my temporal wants and that of my family would in New York meet a ready and an abundant supply; nor is it any want of interest in your object, or of desire to render you all the assistance in my power, consistently with following the will of God; but it is the fact, that in my view, and in the view of those with whom I take counsel, he assigns me other labors. I should feel as if I were going *before* Providence, and also endangering many precious interests which seem to be committed to my hands, were I, in my present situation, to comply with your request. * * *

"I have looked at the whole subject, as carefully as my limited time and great pressure of business would permit; have asked counsel of our wisest and best men, and have endeavored to carry the whole subject, and every thing pertaining to it, to the Lord; to lay all at his feet, and follow his direction. And I have come to the result which I have communicated.

"But it grieves me, my brethren, while it almost overwhelms me with a conviction of responsibility, that such an object, so noble in its origin, so heavenly in its nature, and so boundless in its results, should for a moment seem, even to you, to be suspended on *my* decision, or the decision of any one man. Is it not the Lord's work; and as he has in his providence rendered it unsuitable for me, in my present situation, to comply with your request, *can* it not, *ought* it not, *must* it not go forward in humble dependence on Him and with a single eye to his glory, without me? Ought you not, as they have done in Boston, to commence the work without delay, and prosecute it with untiring vigor and perseverance, for the sake of glorifying God; putting your trust in Him, and expecting, when the house is completed, that God will provide a minister, open the way for him to come among you in the fulness of the blessings of the gospel of Christ, and make him an instrument of your salvation and that of your children, and of multitudes in your great and growing city, throughout our whole country, and throughout the world?

"Brethren, I commend you to God, who is able and willing to *guide* and to *bless;* and to do exceeding abundantly for you, above all that you ask or think, according to the riches of grace and glory in Christ Jesus.

"That you may have much of the divine presence, and be led forth in the right way, is the fervent and habitual prayer of your unworthy, but most cordial brother in Christ,

"J EDWARDS."

On Tuesday, January 1, 1828, he was installed first pastor of the "Salem church," just erected in Salem-street, in the north and more destitute part of Boston. In entering on his labors in this new field, he again gave special attention to pastoral visitation; and as he did on his settlement in Andover, began brief memoranda of the families visited, with a notice of the manner in which he employed each day. These memoranda were continued about two months, and show with what self-denying, unwearied fidelity, and Christian hope, he devoted himself to the fulfilment of the high responsibilities he had assumed. He begins by committing himself to God in Jesus Christ.

"In the great and momentous work which is before me, I would go in the strength of the Lord God; and in humble reliance on Him who is the propitiation for my sins and the sins of the world, who is my advocate with the Father, Jesus Christ the righteous, would I commit myself and all my interests, mortal and immortal, to his infinitely wise and good disposal.

"Prepare me, O Lord, for whatever is before me in thy providence. Grant me thy holy presence at all times. In thy light may I see light; by thy wisdom be wise; in thy strength be strong, and with thy consolations be greatly comforted. Grant me at all times supreme devotion to thyself, holy confidence in thy Son, and an ardent desire for the indwelling and the teaching, guidance, and blessing of the Holy Spirit. Grant me ardent love to souls, a deep and abiding conviction of their ruin by sin, and a willingness to spend and be spent for their salvation.

"In reading thy holy word, open thou mine eyes to behold the wondrous things contained in thy law. Illuminate my understanding, purify my affections, subdue my will, and grant that all my powers of body and of soul may be brought into sweet and humble subjection to thee. Make me mighty in the Scriptures; may I love them more than thousands of gold and silver; and find in keeping thy commands great reward.

"In preparing to preach, guide me, I beseech thee, as to subjects, and the manner of treating them; and enable me to bring forth from the treasures of revelation things new and old. May I determine to know nothing among this people, 'save Jesus Christ and him crucified.' Give me, I entreat thee, for his sake, enlarged views of his infinite excellence, loveliness, and glory, and enable me to open with great clearness his unsearchable riches; and O, grant that the Holy Ghost may take of the things of Jesus Christ and show them to men; that my labors may be attended with an influence from on high, and be 'the wisdom of God, and the power of God,' to the salvation of many.

"Remember the prayers which have been offered

on this spot by those who through faith and patience now inherit the promises, and answer them in rich and abundant blessings on their descendants. Hear the prayers which may be offered by those whose hearts' desire is, that sinners may be saved; and show them that every one that asketh receiveth, that he that seeketh findeth, and that to him that knocketh the door is opened; and may our eyes see thy salvation, and our hearts rejoice in thy love.

"Guide me, O God, in conversation with all to whom I may be called to speak; and may I speak at all times according to the lively oracles, and my words be with grace, that they may be to the salvation of the hearers. Guide me in visiting the sick, the sorrowful, and dying; and grant me thy presence, that I may know how I ought to address every man. Guide me in all my conduct, and in every thing may I act for eternity, glorify God, and be honored as a chosen instrument in thy hand of honoring the Saviour. In consultation with my brethren in the ministry, make me wise; may I discern with great clearness the 'signs of the times,' and the will of God, and be a helper of their faith, activity, and joy. In every action and situation, O God, be with me. I am weak, ignorant, and guilty; leave me not, and suffer me not to trust to my own understanding, but to the living God; and may I find by blessed experience that such as trust in thee are 'as mount Zion, which cannot be moved, but abideth for ever;' that thou dost keep those in perfect peace whose minds are stayed on thee, and that such as seek thee do not in fact want any good thing.

"Bless him who has been called in thy providence to take the oversight of my former people. Be with him and grant him all the blessings which I can ask for my own. Give him, I beseech thee, all their souls as seals of his ministry, and their children as jewels in his crown of future joy.

"Pour out thy Spirit in rich effusions upon all this city, the city of our solemnities, the place of our fathers' sepulchres. 'O Lord, revive thy work,' and cause that all this people may come to the knowledge of thee, and of Jesus Christ, which is life eternal. Cause the truth as it is in Jesus to triumph in every place throughout our land, that this land may in every part be Immanuel's, a mountain of holiness, and a habitation of righteousness; that the triumphs of his cross may be extended to every land, and that all flesh may speedily see his salvation. O God, fill my heart with thy love, and my mouth shall declare thy praise."

On the day of the installation he attended a meeting at Hon. Samuel Hubbard's, "to consult concerning Pine-street church, and the church in Cambridgeport," and in the evening addressed his people from, "Brethren, pray for us."

The next day he went to Andover, where he says, "I attended the examination and ordination of Rev. Milton Badger, who was installed pastor of my former church and people. May the Lord grant him his holy presence, and make him the means of salvation to them and their children; and make me truly grateful that he has kept them united in such a wonderful manner, and so kindly sent them a man who appears to be a man of prayer and supreme devotion to Christ.

May the Lord make him wise, faithful, and abundantly successful. The day was most interesting to me. Had enlarged views of the all-sufficiency, glory, and love of Christ; and was encouraged, in view of my great work, to trust in him, and to expect to see his salvation. O let me never lose sight of his infinite glory, but always trust in him, and find that his grace is sufficient for me." Returning from the installation, he says, "Had on the way an unusual sense of the goodness of God, especially as a prayer-hearing God, and of the great importance of praying for destitute churches, that he would send them pastors after his own heart."

On the next day, he says, "Preached in the evening, preparatory to the communion; subject, 'A just God, and a Saviour,' as illustrated in the Bible, the dealings of God, and especially in the death of Christ. A full meeting, and interesting. O Lord, follow it with thy blessing. Grant that it may be found that some souls received impressions which will never be effaced, and which shall, through grace, be connected with their salvation."

The next day he says, "Attended a meeting at the missionary rooms for consultation as to the monthly concert of prayer, and it was agreed to have three meetings in the city, instead of one as heretofore: one at Park-street church, one at Pine-street, and one at Salem church. The Lord grant his presence in those meetings, and make them the means of salvation to those who attend, and to the heathen."

The next day, the first Sabbath after his installation, he says, "Preached morning and afternoon; the house full to overflowing. At the close, the three deacons were consecrated to their office, and the Lord's supper was administered. Preached in the evening; house crowded. O Lord, follow the truths spoken with the illuminating and purifying influences of the Holy Spirit, and make them 'the wisdom of God and the power of God' to the salvation of many souls, and the glory shall be thine."

The next day, "Attended a meeting with ministers of Boston and others for prayer and consultation, and the monthly concert in Salem church in the evening. O Lord, follow these services with thy blessing; grant me at all times thy holy presence, and furnish me for thy whole will."

On January 9, his memorandum is, "In the morning, preparing sermon. Attended the installation of Rev. Howard Malcom at the Federal-street Baptist church; and a meeting of the Committee of the Massachusetts Missionary Society. In the evening, a meeting of boys for religious inquiry at Mr. G.'s. O Lord, increase, I beseech thee, the number of those youth who shall seek thee with the whole heart, and find thee as their hope and portion for ever."

The next day, he "attended a meeting of the Executive Committee of the American Temperance Society at Mr. Odiorne's," and the following day "a meeting at Mr. John Tappan's, for consultation on the subject of publishing a *religious magazine*," which was not long after commenced under the title, "The Spirit of the Pilgrims," Dr. Edwards being one of the Publishing Committee.

On Sabbath, January 13, he preached morning

and afternoon, and says, "In the evening attended an inquiring meeting. About *sixty* attended. O may they all be saved, and greater and greater numbers attend, and obtain eternal life."

The daily memoranda proceed: noticing pastoral visits; supplying children with books and tracts; conversation with persons on the state of their souls, and with particular individuals in affliction, or in spiritual perplexity and darkness; meeting the members of the church for special prayer; meeting the pastors for prayer and conference; the preparation of sermons; consultations as to the new magazine; the concert of prayer for colleges; the interests of religion in places around Boston, and other evangelical enterprises; and kindred labors, interspersed with ejaculations for the divine presence and blessing.

"Dwell, O Lord, I beseech thee, in the midst of this church for good, and bestow upon them and around them the rich blessings of thy grace."

"Great God, forgive, I beseech thee, all my sins, and follow with thy blessing my labors this afternoon; lead —— to thyself, and make him an instrument of eternal good to many souls; sanctify the afflictions of S——, and make them the means of her salvation." "Lord, remember that young woman, and lead her to repentance and faith in Christ."

"O Lord, bless each of those persons with whom I have conversed, and to whom I have distributed tracts. Let thy Spirit, I beseech thee, impress thy truth upon their hearts."

"O Lord, incline many to assemble and hear the gospel, 'the glorious gospel of the blessed God.' Prepare me to address them 'in demonstration of the Spirit, and with power.' Assist me, O God, with thy presence."

"O Lord, let thy Spirit descend on B——," (a neighboring village where he had gone out to preach on a Friday evening,) "take of the things of Jesus Christ and show them to that people, and work a mighty work of grace among them."

"Follow with thy blessing, O God, I beseech thee, the labors of this day, and guide me at all times by wisdom from above; forgive all my sins, and assist me, through Jesus Christ. Multiply convictions and conversions abundantly, and the glory shall be thine."

Among the powerful, heart-searching sermons to which Dr. Edwards' congregation in Boston listened with deep interest, was that from the text, "Ye have AN UNCTION FROM THE HOLY ONE, and ye know all things," which was published in the National Preacher for June, 1830. Its aim is to show that those who are savingly taught by the anointing of the Holy Spirit, *have a spiritual understanding of the great truths of the gospel, of which all other men, however moral, or learned, or refined, are ignorant;* and "this teaching consists in leading them rightly to apprehend and suitably to feel the force of the truths revealed in the Bible." Those thus taught, see that God has revealed that "the heart is deceitful above all things, and desperately wicked"—that this is a state of sin and death—that without a great change, called in Scripture being "born again," no man can be saved—that in God is their "help"—that "other foundation can no man lay, than that is laid, which is Jesus Christ"—that "whosoever believeth on Him shall not perish, but have everlasting life"—they feel that unto them "that believe, He is precious," and their hearts respond to his words, "Ye are not your own, ye are bought with a price; therefore glorify God in your body and in your spirit, which are God's."

"Hence you see them, in seasons of trial, not counting even life dear to them; but counting all things but loss, that they might win Christ, and be found of Him in peace. In short, the whole Bible becomes to such persons the testimony of God; which is therefore believed; and to a great extent is illustrated and confirmed in their own experience. And when these truths are known by experience, they have a reality, a fulness, and a power, of which before they had no conception.

"The man who feels the heat of fire, has a very different conception from the man who only hears about it, or reads concerning it, or only stands at a distance and looks at it. His conceptions are cold; and when shivering under the blasts of winter, they do him no good. He may have read about fire, he may have seen it, may have disputed about its properties, and may have thought, perhaps, that he was acquainted with it; but when he comes near and receives its genial warmth, and still nearer, and feels its penetrating heat, it has a reality, it has a pungency, of which before he had no conception. My word, saith God, is a fire, and a hammer; it breaketh the rock in pieces. The man who feels it has a totally different conception from the man who only hears about it, or reads concerning it, or reasons and disputes about it. The conceptions of the latter are cold and heartless, and leave him dead in sin. The momentous truths of the Bible may appear to him like fables; may pass by him unheeded, and leave upon his heart no permanent impression; while, to the real Christian, who has been taught them by 'an unction from the Holy One,' and who receives them in love, they have a reality, and they have a fulness and power, which stamp upon the Bible, and upon his heart, the impress of God.

"True religion begins with *experience*. The knowledge which real Christians have is taught them, not merely by men, but by the Holy Ghost, and attended with a permanent conviction that this knowledge is from God. Hence they will not, for any opposite errors, renounce it.

"These things cannot be said of the opposite sentiments. Real Christians cannot find them in the Bible. They do not describe their true condition as *sinners;* they do not meet their wants. To remove this difficulty, you may try to show them that they have no such wants as they suppose—that they have been among the enthusiastic, and are deluded. And upon this subject you may reason with great learning and acuteness; but their wants are not matters of mere speculation, but of *feeling*.

"A man before you is starving, and you feed him on the east wind. He tells you that it does not satisfy him—that he wants food. You try to show him that he has no such want—that he has been among hungry men, and is deluded. You reason with great learning and acuteness; and if he is not a learned man, he may not find it easy to answer you. But his wants are matters, not of reasoning, though there is good reason for them: they are matters of feeling, and when a man feels pain, you cannot convince him that he has none. What he wants is *ease*, not proof that he has no pain; on that point he has proof enough, and proof which will for ever convince him, all your reasoning and efforts to the contrary notwithstanding.

"A man is in agony under the pangs of *conscious guilt* in not having believed on the Saviour. What he needs is pardon, not proof that he has no guilt; on that point he has proof enough, and proof which will carry overwhelming and eternal conviction to his mind, though all the rest of creation should doubt it.

"Suppose you undertake to prove to real Christians, that they have never had *a carnal mind*, or that the carnal mind is not enmity against God; how can you make them believe it? What revelation has God given to men but the Bible? and where in the Bible is it written, that when God looked down from heaven to see if there were any that did understand and seek him, he found that there were some that *had not* the carnal mind, or that the carnal mind is *not* enmity against God? And how can you make this accord with their experience? They were ten, twenty, perhaps fifty years, supremely devoted to themselves and the world. How can you show them that they were all this time not at enmity with God? Not from the Bible; this declares, 'They have rebelled against me.'

Not from their own feelings; these cry, 'Pardon mine iniquity, for it is great.' Now, if all other men should declare that they never had carnal minds, or that the carnal mind is not enmity to God, Christians will not believe it; they know it to be false.

"Try, if you will, to make them believe that they *do not deserve* to perish; and that if they should perish with everlasting destruction from the presence of the Lord and the glory of his power, God would be unjust; and in their view you contradict the Bible; and you contradict also their own feelings, and that knowledge of themselves which the Holy Ghost hath given them.

"Try to make them believe that they do not *need* the special influences of the Holy Ghost; and when they are quaking in fearful apprehension under conscious guilt, crying, Who will take away the heart of stone, and give a heart of flesh? or who shall deliver us from the body of this death? direct them to themselves, or to creatures, as their only hope, and you only mock their anguish. 'Miserable comforters are ye all.' But when they hear a voice from the throne, saying, '*I* will take away the heart of stone, and give a heart of flesh; and from all your filthiness, and from all your idols, will I cleanse you;' and experience the truth of these declarations, they cry, 'Thanks be to God, who giveth us the victory through our Lord Jesus Christ.'

"This inflexible firmness, this persevering adherence to sacred truth, which real Christians manifest, notwithstanding all the improvements which men imagine they have made, is thought by some to result from *ignorance*. They hold, it is said, to that old way, because they do not know any better. And it is a fact that *they do not know any better;* and so long as they continue to have 'an unction from the Holy One,' they never will. But though they trust to the wisdom of another, yet they know something; and something too, which is 'hid from many wise and prudent, and revealed unto babes.' Others, however, do not think that they hold to this old way because they are ignorant, but because they are *bigoted*. They have, say some, been taught it, and they never will renounce what they have been taught. *They have* been taught it. This is what the apostle declares; but who was their teacher? Let the apostle answer, 'Ye have an unction from the Holy One.' He was their teacher, and they will not give up what he has taught them.

"Two things are peculiar to the Holy Ghost as a teacher: his disciples will *believe him;* and what he teaches they will *never renounce:* though they should be tempted, or sawn asunder, or slain with the sword, or have to wander about in sheep-skins, and goat-skins, destitute, afflicted, and tormented, on account of their faith, yet they will not renounce it.

"It is not strange that different men, with the same external means, have very different views about the gospel, and very different feelings towards it. Take, for instance, the doctrine of *human depravity*. If one man feels it, and when he looks into himself, finds that he is actually poor and wretched, miserable, blind, and naked, in want of all things; and another man, when he looks into himself, imagines that he is rich, and increased in goods, and has need of nothing; it is not strange that the one believes the doctrine of human depravity, and the other rejects it. Just give to that man the same kind of evidence which the other has; let him look again into himself, his mind being enlightened by the Holy Ghost to 'discern spiritual things,' in a spiritual manner; and let him find, as thousands have found, that instead of being, as he supposed, rich, and increased in goods, and in need of nothing, he is actually poor and wretched, miserable, blind, and naked, and in want of all things; and he too will believe the doctrine of human depravity. He will feel it, and thus *know* that it is true. What the man needs may be neither learning, nor talents, nor opportunities, but an humble spirit, receiving the truth as God has revealed it. He needs *faith*—that faith which is 'the substance of things hoped for, and the evidence of things not seen.' If one man has this, and another has not, it is not strange that they should differ in their views about the truths of the Bible; and in their feelings towards them. It would be unaccountable if it were not so.

"Hence we see the reason why *children* and poor persons, persons of little learning and small abilities, sometimes embrace the gospel, appear clearly to understand it, and deeply to feel its truths. It is because the Holy Ghost can and does teach them as really as others. The truths of the gospel are adapted to their condition, and exactly meet their wants. They can understand them.

"The little child, when weeping over the wickedness of his own heart, in godly sorrow and true penitence, understands the doctrine of depravity as really as a man; and more so, unless the man has been taught it in the same way, by *feeling* it. And that child may pray as sincerely, 'Create in me a clean heart, O God, and renew a right spirit within me,' as any man on earth. And he may turn from sin, look to the Lord Jesus, and believe on him, love him, and obey him; Christ may be formed in him the hope of glory, be all his salvation and all his desire, and be the end of the law for righteousness to him, as truly as if he were the greatest philosopher on earth. The reason is, the gospel, the glorious gospel of God our Saviour, is adapted, not merely to adult sinners, or to learned sinners, or sinners of great talents, but to sinners of every class. 'Come unto me, all ye that labor and are heavy laden, and I will give you rest. Learn of me, for I am meek and lowly in heart, and ye shall find rest to your souls.'

"We see also the reason why some men, with the Bible in their hands, are 'ever learning, and yet never come to the knowledge of the truth.' They do not feel their *need* of the teaching of the Holy Ghost. They perhaps do not believe 'that there is any Holy Ghost.' They do not seek his teaching. They do not obtain it; and the truths which he has revealed, they do not believe. Hence, they grope in darkness at noonday, and stumble as in the night.

"If Christians, to whom the gospel has come, not in word only, but in power, in the Holy Ghost, and in much assurance, would have others embrace it, and in such a manner that they will never renounce it, but be sanctified and saved with an eternal salvation;

while they use all suitable means to convey divine truth to their minds, they must depend for success upon 'an unction from the Holy One.' And for this he 'will be *inquired of;*' he will be sought unto. Hence Christians, while they make all possible efforts to convey divine truth to the minds of men, should at the same time *abound in prayer.* 'Paul may plant and Apollos water, but God giveth the increase.' Nor is this the least discouragement either to effort or to prayer; it is rather the grand encouragement to both: for would any of you, being a father, should a famishing child ask bread, give him a stone? or should he ask a fish, would you give him a serpent? 'If ye then, being evil, know how to give good gifts to your children, how much more shall your Father in heaven give the Holy Spirit to them that ask him?'

"Let then Christians, who have 'an unction from the Holy One,' of every denomination and of every name, use the means of God's appointment, and there is no insuperable difficulty in the way of the conversion of sinners, or of a revival of true religion, which shall not stop till it has extended to every district and state and kingdom, and has reached every family and every individual on the globe. Give each a Bible; let him daily read it, and listen to it as the voice of Jehovah; let the gospel, 'the glorious gospel of the blessed God,' be preached, in purity and with power, to every creature; let prayer, believing, effectual, fervent prayer, ascend without ceasing; and in answer, let there be given to all people 'an unction from the Holy One,' and there would be a mourning for sin all over the earth; and then, let the Lord

Jesus Christ be proclaimed as the only hope of glory, and every heart would embrace him, the song of salvation would echo from sea to sea, and the whole earth join the blessed anthem, 'To the Lamb that was slain, and hath redeemed us to God by his blood.'"

We well remember, as do many others, hearing this sermon on the "Unction from the Holy One," as he preached it before the New Hampshire General Association of Clergymen, at their meeting in the east parish of Londonderry, now Derry, September 7, 1824. The clergymen assembled, in their harmony, and fervent prayers that their meeting might be blessed to their own increased spirituality and usefulness in the ministry, and especially to the reviving of the work of the Lord in the congregation among whom they met, set an example worthy of imitation by clerical bodies throughout the world. The godly and lamented Rev. Samuel Green, of Boston, was also present, and preached as if endued with power from on high, from the text, "Restore unto me the joy of thy salvation, and uphold me with thy free Spirit; then will I teach transgressors thy ways, and sinners shall be converted unto thee." Here were two preachers from the sister state, magnifying THE WORK OF THE SPIRIT in man's salvation. The meetings were crowded. They were silent and solemn, but the unbidden tear and the suppressed sob showed the presence of the Father, and of the Son, and of the Holy Ghost. The hands of the pastor, the Rev. Edward L. Parker, were strengthened, and his heart made glad. A work of grace commenced immediately, the blessed results of which the pastor, in his History of Londonderry, records in these words: "This year the General Association of New Hampshire held its anniversary in the east parish of Londonderry. A divine blessing attended its deeply interesting and solemn services. *Sixty-two* were, in consequence, added to the church."

Under such preaching, and the abundant labors of faith and love indicated in the above brief memoranda, rich spiritual blessings were evidently descending. The memoranda contain the following cheering items: January 17, "twelve persons were examined for admission to the church." January 27, "about forty attended the inquiry-meeting." February 10, "more than fifty inquirers." February 24, "a meeting for inquirers in the evening, at which between thirty and forty attended." Under date of February 21, there is also this item: "Seventy-six pews in the Salem church were sold for about $18,700. O Lord, fill this house with thy presence."

We gather other indications of the spirit and success with which he was laboring, from letters to his family, who remained at Andover for a time after his installation in Boston.

To his eldest son, then about the age of nine, he wrote January 8, 1828, "You must pray for your dear papa every day, that the Lord would enable him to do much good; that his life and health may be preserved, and that he may be the means of saving very many souls. Pray also every day, for yourself, that the Lord would teach you to love and serve him. Remember, that unless you love God, and keep his commandments, you can never go to heaven. I hope you daily read the Bible. Some little boys in Boston, not much older than you, have this winter become pious, and have meetings to read the Bible, and to pray together. God says that he loves those that love him, and that those who seek him early shall find him; and it is better to have God for your friend, than to have every thing else.

"There were, the last Sabbath evening, more than a hundred at Dr. Beecher's inquiry-meeting; more than a hundred at Rev. Mr. Wisner's; sixty or seventy at Park-street, and about the same number at Rev. Mr. Green's, besides others in other places. Many are inquiring what they shall do to be saved, and we hope that many will repent of their sins, believe on Jesus Christ, and by keeping his commands, be prepared for heaven."

To Mrs. Edwards.

"BOSTON, Jan. 14, 1828.

"MY VERY DEAR WIFE—Through the kindness of our heavenly Father, I am continued to the present time, and though somewhat hoarse through a slight cold, I preached twice yesterday; in the afternoon, to a large assembly. In the evening, I had an inquiry-meeting; about sixty attended; some of them persons who belonged to churches in the country, but have not joined any in this city; some of them persons who have hope, but have not made a profession; and some of all stages of religious impression, from a little seriousness up to deep conviction. Several persons, of various ages, had their minds deeply impressed at the lecture last Tuesday evening; among them was Mr. ——, the merchant in Market-street. He called to converse with me on Saturday evening. Some at the inquiry-meeting were from Roman-catholic families, and some from Universalists. Our friends are encouraged to hope that they shall see the salvation of God. I hope you pray much for us that the work of God may revive and spread over all this city.

"I generally retire about 11 P. M., rise about six, and find as much as I can do. I hope you pray daily for me, that I may be wise, humble, bold, faithful, and win many souls to Christ. I preached yesterday all day from, 'Not by might, nor by power, but by my Spirit, saith the Lord.' I hope it made a good impression, and will be followed by the divine blessing. Pray much for Mr. Badger and the people at Andover. Give my love to him and to all.

"Your affectionate husband,

"J. EDWARDS."

To the same.

"BOSTON, Feb. 25, 1828.

"MY VERY DEAR WIFE—My health after you left was very poor; and I became so bilious, that I felt more like giving up, than I have for years. On Saturday I rode out to see Dr. Chaplin, at Cambridgeport. On the Sabbath I preached twice. In the afternoon felt better, and spoke with freedom on the nature of repentance, the reasons why angels rejoice over the repenting sinner, and the instructions which this fact affords us. In the evening very stormy; had between thirty and forty at the inquiry-meeting, one head of a family, whose mind was deeply impressed in the course of the day. Between seventy and eighty pews were sold last week for about $19,000; about

$1,500 more than they were prized as worth. About twenty pews were also leased. Our meeting, the last Sabbath, about as full as when the pews were all free.

"My health to-day is much better; and though I have been in consultation with the ministers and others all day, I feel this evening quite comfortable. I never felt so much the need of your prayers, and the prayers of all God's people, that I may be sustained, strengthened in the inner and outer man, be guided by wisdom from on high, and have the constant presence and blessing of God. I find that without him I can do nothing; and hope I sometimes feel, that through his strengthening me, I can do all things. My preaching seems to me, and I presume often to others, to be very poor; but the Lord can bless the weakness of means, and that gives me some hope. I rejoice that they have so good a minister at Andover; and hope I am thankful that he may probably be instrumental in saving many more souls among them than I should.

"Give my best love to the dear boys; and tell them my earnest hopes that they every day pray to God, and strive to obey him; that they are very attentive and obedient to their mother, and are very thankful for the many things which she does for them. Kiss the dear little girls: tell them that papa thinks of them, and tries to pray for them and all the people at Andover every day. Tell Sarah that she does not know what a precious time she now has to secure the salvation of her soul; and I fear, if she does not obtain an interest in Jesus Christ, by believing on him soon, that she never will. She may die suddenly, and go unprepared to the judgment. And Fanny too should remember God, and seek the salvation of her soul now, while she is young; for she does not know but she may die before she grows up.

"I hope God will dwell with you, and give you and sister A. J., to whom I feel under many obligations, wisdom and grace to serve him, and do much good. I hope to come up and see you at no distant time; but when, is at present uncertain. I lecture to-morrow evening. Prayer for colleges on Thursday, A. M. United meeting of all the churches, in Park-street in the evening. Preparatory lecture, Friday evening. Communion on the Sabbath; lecture, or inquiry-meeting in the evening, and so on.

"Your affectionate husband,

"J. EDWARDS."

February 29, he writes, "Our little band of praying people met yesterday afternoon to pray for the youth in our colleges; and in the evening we had a meeting of all the churches in Park-street, full, and very interesting, rather more so than any united meeting that we have had since I have been here. Pray much, my dear wife, for me your unworthy husband, and for the dear ministers in this city, that we may all be men full of the Holy Ghost and of power; be clothed with humility, be strong in the grace that is in Christ Jesus, and be furnished by him for every good word and work; that by well-doing we may put to silence foolish and wicked men, and prevail against every foe, 'for we wrestle not with flesh and blood' merely, 'but with principalities and powers, with the rulers of the darkness of this world, and with spiritual wickedness in high places.'

March 4, he says, "Our little band of praying ones are, I think, growing in grace, as well as in numbers, and feel that we have a great work before us. Boston appears to be more full of God than I have ever before known it, and I think that the manifestations of his presence are increasing. I preached three times on the Sabbath, administered the communion, admitted eighteen to the church, wrote all Monday forenoon, consulted in the afternoon with the brethren, and spoke and prayed at the concert in the evening, and am this morning remarkably well for me. But my strength, you know, is only weakness, and I am well only as long as I am held up; and wise only by wisdom from above.

"Brother Wisner has gone to Philadelphia for Dr. Skinner."

About the same time that the Salem-street church was erected in the north part of Boston, the Pine-street church was erected in the south part, in which the services of the Rev. Dr. Thomas H. Skinner were secured as pastor.

To Rev. Wm. A. Hallock, Secretary, New York.

"BOSTON, March 5, 1828.

"DEAR BROTHER—I believe that some time ago the printing of my sermon on the 'Inspiration of the Scriptures,' as a tract, was spoken of. I am now placed where, for thirty years, error has reigned over multitudes. The consequence is, infidelity is extensively exerting its deadly influence over their souls. I now propose, if the Lord gives me wisdom, strength, grace, and opportunity, to rewrite on the subject of inspiration, more at length, and I hope in a better manner. My first Bible lecture will probably be delivered in about two weeks.

"God seems to be in the midst of us of a truth. Pray for us, especially those of us who are appointed to be watchmen in these perilous and difficult times, and on this perilous and difficult spot: that we may be humble, united, bold, active, and strong in the grace that is in Christ Jesus, giving glory, all the glory of every good that is done in us and by us, to God to whom it belongs; that we may also in all our movements look at the world, the whole world, and bear upon those points and in that manner in which we shall most rapidly and permanently promote its renovation and salvation from sin and death, and its restoration to the image and favor of God.

"I would thank you again to read my sermon, and let me know what alterations and additions it wants in order to produce the most extensive and deep impression, that *the Bible is the word of God, and as such ought to be daily listened to by every son and daughter of Adam, and to be believed and obeyed wherever known, from the rising of the sun to the going down of the same.*

"I have a project also for reaching the consciences of all professors of religion in the land, so that they cannot come into contact with distilled liquors, either in the use, the making, or the sale of them, without an apprehension and a foretaste of the certainty, if they continue to aid in their distribution, that they will ere long kindle around them and all who follow them a fire, the fierceness of which they never can mitigate, and the raging and consuming power of which no man can quench.

"Yours in the best bonds,

"J. EDWARDS."

Such were the unceasing labors, such the faith and prayer, such the love to souls, the dependence on Christ and humble trust in him, with which Dr. Edwards was pressing on in his career of usefulness, with his eye fixed on the advancement of evangelical truth, not only in his own congregation, but throughout the city, and the land, and the world. The hearts of Christians far and wide were made glad by the descent of the Holy Spirit on the New England capital, where moral dearth had so long prevailed; and the most pleasing anticipations of future good were indulged—when his vigorous bodily powers yielded to the pressure of mental labor and excitement, and he was compelled to suspend all active exertions. This was but a renewal of what he had experienced before resigning his charge in Andover. In a letter written April 18, 1828, to a relative in Colchester, he says, "In the month of September last, I had a severe turn of bilious obstruction, occasioned, I suppose, by a spasmodic contraction of the biliary duct, and accompanied with great pain; and I have not been well since. Almost every effort of mind has occasioned threatening symptoms of the same disease, and five weeks ago it became so violent that I was obliged entirely to desist from preaching and all kinds of mental effort. For ten or twelve days I was confined to my chamber in Boston." Of the hazards, in respect to the state of his health, of assuming the responsibilities of the new charge in Boston, he was probably more fully aware than the counsellors who unanimously advised him to assume them; and the relief he had experienced by the change in prosecuting for several weeks the Temperance agency, may have given him hope that his bodily powers were radically restored. But the very sundering of the tender and sacred ties that bound him to his former charge, and the meeting and adjusting of the claims so soon and so urgently pressed upon him from important churches and institutions, in which his own usefulness and the dearest interests of the kingdom of the Redeemer seemed to be involved, renewed and increased that long-continued mental excitement, which was as an internal flame burning at the seat of life.

About the first of April he left Boston, on horseback, for some weeks of recreation and rest among his relatives and friends on the Connecticut river—passing the Sabbath, on his way, at Hardwick, where he "worshipped with a little company of orthodox Christians in an upper chamber." Proceeding to Hatfield, he engaged Rev. Mr. Waterbury to supply his pulpit for four weeks; and spent a few days at Hadley, with his esteemed friends Dr. and Mrs. Porter. He then visited his relatives in Westhampton, where he found "an unusual attention to religion;" and was also cheered by a letter from Dea. Proctor, informing him that nine or ten were to be received to his own church in Boston on the profession of their faith. He then "rested a while" among his friends in Northampton, where he wrote to Mrs. Edwards, "I hope the Lord is teaching me and you and our dear people, that *to be where he puts us* is to be in the best place; that with his presence and blessing, we can be happy anywhere and in any condition, and that without it, all else is vanity."

On May 20, he is at Cambridgeport, where he had been consulting Dr. Chaplin, and writes to Mrs. Edwards, "Dr. Chaplin has decided that I must not go into Boston at present. As soon as our deacons learned his decision, they invited Hon. Mr. Hubbard, Mr. Tappan, Mr. Evarts, and others, to a meeting for consultation, and it was forthwith decided to obtain a house for us, for the summer, a few miles out of Boston. This was an instance of kindness and prompt generosity which my unbelieving, ungrateful heart did not expect. It was manifestly the Lord's doing, and I hope he will bind us all in everlasting gratitude to himself. It appears to me that he is leading us, and all his people, in the right way, that we may 'go to a city of habitation.'

"I had a most delightful walk this morning about Cambridge University, while all were asleep, and it was a good time to pray that God would come down there by his Spirit. Will you, my dear, pray daily for a revival of religion in that university. It is a delightful spot, and the Lord is owner of it, and doubtless designs to make it subservient to the interests of his church. Dr. Skinner appears to be getting on finely" in the Pine-street church.

In accordance with a suggestion above, a house was provided for Dr. Edwards' family in Dorchester, six miles from Boston, where they resided during the summer months.

To a brother of Mrs. Edwards, in New York.

"NORTHAMPTON, April 21, 1828.

"MY DEAR BROTHER—Since I experienced your kindness in Boston, I have thought of you with peculiar interest almost daily; and with special desire that the vigorous and active powers with which the Lord has graciously blessed you, might all be devoted to his service. I do not wish you to change your business, or leave your employment as a merchant, for that is the calling in which you are called. But what I desire is, that you may engage in it, and prosecute it daily, not supremely for yourself, but for the Lord Jesus Christ, of whom, and through whom, and to whom are all things.

"If a man is active in business and acquires property, but all supremely for himself, and for this world merely, his activity stands in the way of his salvation; and his acquisition of property, if this course is continued, will engross his whole heart, and drown him in destruction and perdition. But if he is active and acquires property for the sake of honoring God, and doing good, his very activity will tend to promote his salvation, and while diligent in business he will be fervent in spirit, serving the Lord. He will also enjoy vastly greater comfort in the acquisition of property itself, because he will be acquiring it for a nobler purpose; and it will have a more elevating, purifying, and benevolent influence upon his whole character.

"Be careful, my dear brother, every day to set apart a season for meditation, reading the Scriptures, and prayer, to look backward and forward, to examine yourself and see whether the course that you are now pursuing, should you continue it, will lead you to heaven. If not, make no delay to change, and set out in that way which if continued will end in glory. Give your heart to God, and make it your constant object to render unto him the things that are his; trusting wholly for what you need in the Lord Jesus Christ, and seeking daily the teaching and guidance of his blessed Spirit. Act in all things for eternity, and strive to do good, as you have opportunity, to all, and especially to those that love him.

"Your affectionate brother,

"J. EDWARDS."

A renewed attack still prevented Dr. Edwards from resuming labors among his people, when he received the following brotherly communication from a highly respected pastor in a sister city.

"NEW YORK, July 3, 1828.

"REV. AND DEAR SIR—I write because I know that what I am about to say is of importance. Men will praise you, my brother, after you are dead; and when you have labored and toiled, *and died*, they will greatly commend your disinterestedness—and until then, they will urge and goad you to labors which no human mind or frame can sustain. I do not know but it is too late to save your shattered constitution; but if it is saved, you must not leave it to the sympathy even of the best of men.

"I write to say, not this only, but that you have no chance for permanent recovery while at home. My own experience tells me, there is nothing like a long sea-voyage. The perfect repose—the novelty—the atmosphere—the regimen—the storms—the sleep—the exercise—the tumbling about—these are what the jaded mind and body of a minister require. I beg of you to try the experiment—not coastwise, but across the western ocean. Your people must furnish you means and society: both are necessary. Be absent a year; and go, not to labor, but to rest. Seven or eight hundred dollars will cover the expense. Do not lose a month, but go. Do not say, your usefulness is not worth the effort. One minister, well trained to the service of the sanctuary and to the labors of the church, is worth ten years' preparatory service, and surely one of repose. I rejoice in all that is good at Boston.

"Your affectionate brother,

"GARDINER SPRING."

August 21, 1828, he writes a letter, from the neighborhood of Saratoga Springs, to the Rev. Dr. Wisner of Boston, stating that he had attended a highly interesting meeting of the Albany Presbytery, when the subject of missions in our own country was taken up, and its immense magnitude and importance most seriously considered. "It would have done your heart good," he says, "to see worthy fathers in the ministry weep like children while this subject was under discussion, and the tender, strong emotion which pervaded the whole assembly. It was indeed a time of refreshing, I trust, from the presence of the Lord. They hope to raise within their bounds $4,000 for this object, in one year. A delightful spirit now pervades the Presbytery, and one which seems to promise much, not only for the destitute, but for themselves and their children.

"Rev. Mr. Yale is a noble spirit. I wish the world was full of such men, as manifestations of the lovely, transforming, and mighty power of grace. I rejoice exceedingly to see such men in health, and able, in the strength of the Lord, to move on the holy and life-giving projects of his kingdom.

"I am much interested in Dr. Nott, and we lodge at the same house. We have talked much on the subject of the sanctification of the Sabbath. May the Lord give us wisdom equal to the importance of the crisis to which we have come, and the magnitude of the interests which may be affected by our conduct.

"On the subject of Sabbath-schools this Presbytery are preparing to do nobly. And on the whole the work of the Lord, if his people shall continue humble, prayerful, and active, is evidently advancing towards a glorious consummation; and the laying aside of one man, or a dozen men, cannot stop its progress.

"With love to the brethren, and asking an interest in your prayers, that I may honor God, and be prepared, in his own way, time, and place, to be eminently instrumental in bringing our world into subjection to the Saviour, and spreading the honor of his precious name through the universe, I am cordially yours," etc.

"To the Members of Salem church, Boston:

"SARATOGA SPRINGS, Aug. 26, 1828.

"DEAR BRETHREN AND FRIENDS—The ways of the Lord are wonderful, sought out of all them that have pleasure therein. When the Lord disappoints the expectations of his people, it is not because he does not love them—not because he does not design to promote their highest good in the best way, or the highest good of his holy kingdom. He does design to do both, yet he often takes a course and uses means for this purpose directly the reverse of what we should.

"Who would have thought of sending Israel into Egypt as the best way of leading them to Canaan; of sending Moses for forty years into obscurity as the best way of preparing him to do the greatest good to the world? Who of us would have kept the children of Israel for so long a time in the wilderness, and led them in such a circuitous route to the land of promise? And yet God did it; and who will say that it was not the best way—the way to glorify himself, and most effectually bless his people? How many benefits have already resulted to his church from his taking that course, and how many will yet result through eternal ages, above what would have resulted had he taken the course which we should have taken, none but God can determine.

"Who but God would have thought, in a time of such abounding wickedness, when the labors of the Lord's prophets were so much needed, of sending away Elijah the ablest of them to a solitary place alone, and feeding him there for so long a time by ravens? Yet the Lord did it; and who will say that Elijah was not during that time more useful to the kingdom of Jehovah, viewed in its connection with eternity, than he could have been anywhere else?

"Had Jehovah become in any measure indifferent to the interests of Zion, or did he mistake the best way to promote his own cause? No; he takes ways different from what we should, and often from what we desire and pray for, not because he loves Zion less than we, but infinitely more. He is infinitely more wise, more benevolent. In prayer, we look perhaps supremely to this or that particular church, or to the course which the Lord shall take in the disposal of his servants, and regard principally the present time, or at most the time in which we shall live; but God regards supremely *himself*, and the holy interests of his whole kingdom for endless ages. And though we, in the bitterness of disappointed hopes, cry, 'All these things are against me'; and perhaps feel, if we do not say, that they are against the cause of Zion too; yet how foolish and how ungrateful it is for us to think so. Has 'He who spared not his own Son, but freely gave him up for us all,' forgotten his people, or mistaken the best way to promote their interests? They desire perhaps earthly prosperity, especially in their religious concerns. He desires their sanctification and salvation, and he leads them in the right way, that they may go to a city of habitation.

"Who of us, after Saul of Tarsus was converted, with his immense learning and talents, and when there was so much need of his labors in Damascus, Jerusalem, and many other places, would have sent him into the deserts of Arabia; or, when all his strength was so much needed, have caused him even at the first, in the populous region of Galatia, to preach the gospel through severe bodily infirmity, even such as to make his speech, in the view of many, contemptible. Who of us, had we the power to prevent it, would have suffered him, in the metropolis of the world, when thousands were perishing for lack of knowledge, to be bound and imprisoned? Yet God did it; and contrary to all human expectation, it turned out, *as the ways of the Lord always do*, to the furtherance of the gospel. 'Wherefore lift up the hands that hang down, and confirm the feeble knees; say unto them that are of a fearful heart, *Be strong; fear not.*' Zion is placed as a seal upon the Lord's arm, and bound as a signet upon his heart; he will never leave, never forsake her. Though for a little time he afflicts her in some of her branches or members, yet with everlasting loving-kindness will he have mercy upon her. He afflicts her for her profit, to show all her members what is in their hearts, and that he may do them good in the latter end. Though he tarry long, wait for him; in due time he shall come, and will not tarry. Who ever trusted in him and sought him with the whole heart, and was disappointed? No one; and no one ever will. He will give them the desires of their heart, or he will give them what is *infinitely better;* and while the youth, and the most strong, vigorous, and powerful, who seek supremely their *own*, shall faint and be weary, and all who trust to themselves and creatures shall utterly fall, they that wait upon the Lord shall renew their strength; they shall mount up on wings as eagles, shall run and not be weary, walk and not faint.

"Who of us would have permitted that Preacher of righteousness who spake as never man spake, to be apprehended, bound, and buffeted, spit upon, and crucified between two malefactors? And should we not all, had we beheld it, like the weeping disciples, have trembled for the rising prospects of his infant kingdom? Yet God, who seeth the end from the beginning, permitted this; and what amazing benefits have flowed from it to his church, and what brighter glories will continue to encircle it, in consequence of this, to everlasting ages. How will those very disciples, who when their Leader was taken from them were ready to say, 'All these things are against us,' be filled in view of that event with celestial ardor, and sing in more exalted strains, Oh the length and the breadth, the height and depth of the wisdom and the love of God, it passeth knowledge.

"Let us then, my brethren and sisters, choose to have the Lord govern in his own way, not only in the armies of heaven, but in the habitations of the earth, and dispose of us and ours as seemeth good in his sight; and let the language of each of our hearts be, at all times, in all places, and under all circumstances, 'Not my will, but thine be done;' and let us inquire each one for himself habitually, 'Lord, what wilt thou have *me* to do?' and leaning upon God go forward in duty, living not unto ourselves, but unto Him that died for us, and rose again; and then we may rest assured that all things shall work together, not only for the good of Zion, but for our good, as they do for the good of them that love God, and who are the called according to his purpose; and by and by, from the heights of heavenly glory we shall look back on the way through which Jehovah has led us, and see that every step was ordered by infinite wisdom and goodness and love, and shall with one heart and one voice adore the riches of divine grace with the millions of the redeemed for ever.

"Through the kindness of our heavenly Father, I arrived here safely about three weeks ago, and have since been here for the benefit of the waters. My health is slowly, but I believe daily improving, and I am not without expectation of being restored to perfect health. If the Lord has any thing for me to do among you, I shall rejoice, in his own way and time, to be restored to you, to minister as of the ability which he shall give, and to spend and be spent in promoting his glory in the salvation of men. Praying daily that he would dwell among you by his Spirit, and grant you at all times his presence; make you wise by his wisdom, strong in his strength, and comfort you by his consolation; that he will increase you with the increase of God, build you up, and give you an inheritance among all them that are sanctified,

"I am, with tender regard,

"Your affectionate pastor,

"J. EDWARDS."

Soon after writing the above, he was enabled to return to his people and resume his labors; and his family, in the course of the autumn, removed from Dorchester into the city.

To Miss P. C——, a niece in Ohio, he wrote, Sept. 9, 1828, "I send you $10, with which, and with what your father may assist you, I hope you will be able to accomplish your object. I approve entirely of your fitting yourself to keep school, and if you improve all the time and opportunities that you can get, I have no doubt that you will be able to do it. It is an important and useful employment; and to prepare you for it, I hope you will give your heart to God, and daily seek the teaching and guidance of his Spirit, and make it your great object, should you have the care of children, to train them up 'in the nurture and admonition of the Lord,' and to fit them, not only for usefulness on earth, but for glory in heaven. If you serve God, and in all your ways acknowledge him, he will be your guide, will lead you in the right way, will provide for you, and train you up for heaven.

"If you have the tracts of the American Tract Society, the one entitled, '*The Way to be Saved*,' and another, '*Joy in Heaven over the Penitent*,' may assist you in the way to heaven. I hope you will read them with attention and with prayer; they were both written by your affectionate uncle, as was also another, entitled, '*The Well-conducted Farm*.' This, you may hand to your father.

"Seek, my dear, first of all, to serve God, and to do good; live for Jesus Christ, and then you shall not want any good thing, he will guide you by his counsel, and afterwards receive you to glory. Seek him with your whole heart, and you shall find him.

"Your affectionate uncle,

"J. EDWARDS."

To Mrs. Edwards' brother in New York, who had requested religious counsel:

"BOSTON, Jan. 17, 1829.

"MY DEAR BROTHER—If you would be saved from the power and dominion of sin, be changed into the image of God, and prepared for the joys of his kingdom, you must *feel* that this is the most important subject in the world, and you must make it *at present* your *chief* concern. It must appear more important to you than wealth, reputation, ease, health, friends, or even life itself. Without this view of its importance, you will never give it the attention which it requires, and which it must have, or the soul be lost, for ever lost. Come then to a fixed decision, before God, and for eternity on this point, namely, Are you willing to make your deliverance from *sin*, and your restoration to holiness and the image and favor of God, your chief present concern? If so, let me say,

"Recollect, fix it in your mind indelibly, that all you have you receive from God, and it is your reasonable service to employ it according to his will. *Common honesty* requires this. Without it you do not render to God his own, and cannot, in his estimation, be at heart an honest man; for honesty is rendering to all their dues, and it applies to God no less than to men. Merchants who would be esteemed honest, often overlook this. And so do other men. But, my brother, be honest at *heart*, and really attempt without delay to render to God *all* his due. And that you may,

"Set apart a portion of each day, morning and evening, to see how your account stands with him, and ask him to teach you by his Spirit how much you are indebted to him. And at the same time listen to his voice speaking to you in his word, the Bible, that you may learn his views on the subject, and you will find his demand to have been every day, since you first knew his character and your relation to him, 'all the heart, and soul, and strength, and mind.' Now have you, my dear brother, ever for one day rendered this? Have you ever, as the *chief* present concern, attempted it? Have you done what you could? Have you devoted the time, talents, influence, and property which he has given you, to *him?* that is, have you attempted to use it according to his will, and for the purpose of promoting his glory, and the spiritual and eternal good of your fellow-men? If not, you must be greatly in debt. He has given you *many* talents, and those with which you might do immense good to his kingdom, and if you have not used them for him, you have all your days been robbing him of what was his own; and to defraud God is a sin as much greater than to defraud men, as he is more worthy than they. If you will daily examine your account with God, with an honest heart, really desiring to know the whole amount, you will find that you owe him ten thousand talents, and that you really have nothing to pay. For, should you henceforward render to him for ever all his due, and never run into debt for any thing more, it would only be rendering to him what you will be constantly receiving from him, and thus merely acting honestly in time to come, without cancelling or even lessening one iota of the debt which is past.

"But such is his *amazing kindness*, that he offers freely to forgive *all*, and receive you and treat you as if you had never offended, on the simple condition of trusting in his Son, and devoting yourself henceforward to *the doing of his will.* And that he might do this without dishonoring himself, or injuring his kingdom, he gave up that Son, whom he loved with infinite love, to bear your sins in his own body on the tree, to feel the effects of them himself, to be *wounded* for your transgressions, and bruised for your iniquities, that you, by believing on him, that is, trusting in him for all that you need, both to do the will of God, and to be accepted in it, might through his stripes, that is, his suffering unto death, be healed, and saved with an everlasting salvation.

"Of course you can have no excuse if you do not immediately and for ever devote yourself, with all your powers, faculties, and talents, to his service. He has given up his Son to buy you off from the curse of the law, that is, from the penalty of your past transgressions, by being himself made a curse for you, or bearing the effects of your sins in your stead. And by trusting in him you may receive *all* that you need, both to do his will, and to be accepted in it.

"If you do not under these circumstances immediately commence his service, you will incur tremendous guilt. You will be continually increasing the debt which you already owe to God. You will show an awful indifference to the wishes of God concerning you; and also to his interests, and the interests of his kingdom. You will reject the provision which he has made for your pardon, sanctification, and salvation. You will cut yourself off from all the benefits of Christ's death. You will be farther than ever before, treasuring up wrath against the day of wrath. You will provoke God to say, Cut him down; why should he cumber the ground? And you will show that you are not willing even to attempt to be honest towards God. In short, you fail of deliverance from sin. You will lose eternal life; and after a few days of toil and disappointment on earth, during your vain life, (which will flee away as a shadow,) you will sink down to the pit, and under the awful guilt of being for ever a *self-destroyer*.

"But on the other hand, if you will without delay make it your chief concern to learn the whole will of God, and as you learn it, the chief object *without delay to do it*, trusting in Christ for all that you need; and henceforward live supremely, not for yourself, or the world, but for God and heaven, that you may glorify him and become in temper like him, and set an example by doing the highest good to men in your power, that all may safely follow, you will,

"1. For Christ's sake, and out of regard to what he has done, be freely forgiven all your past sins. And,

"2. You will through him receive the Holy Ghost to enlighten your mind, purify your heart, and change you into his own image. And,

"3. You will have peace of conscience and peace with God. And,

"4. You will experience more or less of joy in believing his declarations, and keeping his commands.

"5. You will ardently desire that all others may take the same course, and you will pray and make efforts that they may. And,

"6. You will have good hope through grace, that when absent from the body you will be present with the Lord, see him as he is, and be like him. And,

"7. This hope will tend strongly now to make you more humble, more prayerful, more weaned in your affections and expectations from this world, and more anxious to be prepared for the business and joys of the world above. And,

"8. While it will not deprive you of one excellence of character, or innocent enjoyment in this world, or in the least hinder your success in any lawful concern, it will give you excellence, and that of the highest kind, such as is esteemed by angels and the spirits of just men made perfect; and it will give you joy compared with which all that you have yet experienced, or ever could experience, should you have the whole world, and live here a thousand years without religion, would be like a dream when one awaketh.

"Halt then no longer, my dear brother, between two opinions. Decide *without delay*, and remember that you do it for *endless* being. Life and death *eternal* are both before you. Choose life, and walk in the way that leads to it, and it shall be yours, *eternally* yours, which is the ardent desire and daily prayer of

"Your unworthy, but affectionate brother,

"J. EDWARDS."

After some years, this beloved brother, who was made the subject of prayer by his mother, sisters and friends, was enabled to rejoice in the great salvation, and publicly joined himself to the people of God.

To an older brother of Mrs. Edwards', on the death of a son.

"BOSTON, June 12, 1829.

"MY DEARLY BELOVED BROTHER AND SISTER—It seems to be one of the great objects of God, in all his dealings with his people, to make them feel that they are not at home in this world, and that there is nothing on which they can, with safety or comfort, place their hearts, but *himself*. Though in great kindness, when they are panting under the burden and heat of the day, he will often grant them a gourd to shelter them, or when they are hungry, a little manna from above; yet soon a worm at the root will cause the gourd to wither, and that on which they expected at some future time to feast, will be found to have spoiled. And as they find themselves again exposed, hungry and thirsty, they will feel, and every time more and more deeply, that there is no tree under whose shadow they can safely and permanently repose, but that whose leaves are for the healing of the nations; and no bread which will permanently satisfy their hunger, but that which cometh down from heaven and giveth life to the world; and no stream which will quench their thirst, but that which flows from the throne of God and the Lamb. He gives life, health, reason, friends, property, and all other blessings, as seemeth to him good, and he continues them as long as will consist with his infinite glory, and the highest good of his kingdom, and the personal benefit of those that love him; and when these require, he wisely and kindly removes them. And blessed are they who can say from the heart, and who do say by their lives, Even so, Father, for so it hath seemed good in thy sight. Not my will, but thine be done, by me and mine and all. Let the Lord do as seemeth good in his sight; he doeth all things well.

"*He* had a Son, a dearly beloved, an only begotten Son, in whom he delighted with infinite delight; yet when our good required it, he gave him freely, and to all the agonies of the cross, even under the excruciating tortures of bearing our sins in his own body on the tree; and shall not we, when his glory and the good of his kingdom require it, give up and be willing that he should take what he will of his own? Shall we not rather have all our concerns governed by infinite wisdom and goodness, by One who sees the end from the beginning, and who does all things well, than to govern them ourselves? What has he ever done, what will he ever do, which could on the whole be altered for the better? Trust in the Lord with all thy heart, and lean not to thine own understanding; in all thy ways acknowledge him, and he shall direct thy paths. They that trust in him shall be as mount Zion; they that seek him shall not want any good thing; they that do his will shall abide for ever; they shall find it good for them to draw near to him, that in his presence is fulness of joy, and at his right hand are pleasures for evermore.

"My health is better much than last year, though moderate enough for comfort or usefulness. Mrs. Edwards thinks, if Providence should favor it, of taking the children and visiting Colchester during the months of July and August, while I go to the Springs, and perhaps take a journey on horseback. Things here are much as usual. All send love.

"Your affectionate brother,

"J. EDWARDS."

In this month, June, 1829, was published in the National Preacher his persuasive and awakening discourse, "Preparation for Eternity," from the text, "The end of all things is at hand; be ye therefore sober, and watch unto prayer."

His family having left the city to spend the warm season with Mrs. Edwards' relatives in Colchester, he wrote a pleasing letter to the five younger children, with special messages to each of the little ones; having previously prepared the following counsels for the eldest, on his leaving home to reside there for a longer period.*

"Directions to my dear son, Justin Asa Edwards, when he shall go to Connecticut.

"1. Remember God, and not forget that he is always looking upon you; that he sees every thing that you do, hears every thing that you say, and knows every thing that you think and feel.

"2. Every morning, and every evening, pray to Him in spirit and in truth, that he would pardon all your sins, and teach you to love and serve him.

"3. Every day read one chapter in the Bible, because it is the word of God, and able to make you wise unto salvation. Believe what it says, and follow its directions.

"4. Strive, in every thing you do, to please God; trust for all that you need in Jesus Christ, and seek the teaching and guidance of the Holy Spirit.

"5. Never do any thing that you know to be wrong.

"6. If you have done wrong, never deny it; but always in all things speak the truth.

"7. Never be angry; and never differ with other boys.

* Dr. Edwards had three sons, Justin Asa, Jonathan, and Newton; and three younger daughters, Elizabeth, Lydia, and Ann Eliza, all of whom survived their father.

"8. Remember the Sabbath-day, and keep it holy. When you go to meeting attend to the preaching, remember the text, and as much of the sermon as you can, and repeat it to your uncle and aunt when you get home.

"9. Do not forget that you may die while you are young, and not live to grow up.

"10. Read Janeway's Token for Children and other good books which tell you about good boys, and strive to be like them.

"11. Think much about Jesus Christ, and try to be like him. Love and serve him with all your heart, and then when you die you will go and dwell with him and all good people in heaven.

"Remember that these directions were written by your affectionate father, who loves you, thinks much about you, and ardently wishes that you may love God, and do much good.

"Pray for your affectionate father,

"J. EDWARDS."

To the members of Salem church, Boston.

"BOSTON, July 15, 1829.

"DEAR BRETHREN AND FRIENDS—On Monday of this week, I received an appointment from the American Society for the Promotion of Temperance, to act as agent for that Society for the space of one year. I have also received an appointment as agent of the General Union for promoting the observance of the Christian Sabbath.

"As my health has required me to be absent from you much in time past, and, I fear, will require me in future to be absent more than is consistent with the highest usefulness of a pastor; and as the journeyings to which the acceptance of either of the above-mentioned appointments would call me, would probably be more conducive to a sound and vigorous state of health, than the labors of a city pastor, I am led seriously to inquire whether your good, and that of the kingdom of our Lord Jesus Christ, might not probably be promoted by a dissolution of my pastoral connection, that I may be at liberty, should it appear to be the divine will, to accept for a time one of the above-mentioned appointments, or any other to which Providence may appear to call me.

"I shall endeavor to ascertain the will of God, and with his leave will, in two or three weeks, communicate to you the result of my contemplations on the subject. In the mean time, I ask an interest in your prayers, that I may be guided in all things by wisdom from above, be led in that way which will conduce most to the divine glory, to our mutual spiritual advantage, and to the good of the kingdom of Jehovah.

"Wishing you, and all connected with you, the guidance and blessing of the Lord; praying that He will dwell among you by his Spirit, and communicate to you richly the blessings of his grace, I am

"Your much obliged and grateful pastor,

"J. EDWARDS."

To Mrs. Edwards.

"SARATOGA SPRINGS, July 25, 1829.

"MY DEAR WIFE—Loving-kindness and tender mercy have followed me continually since I left Colchester. The first night I lodged in Springfield. The next day at eleven o'clock I was on the summit of mount Tom, from which I had one of the most delightful prospects in the world; dined at Westhampton, found all well, and all send much love. The next day, Wednesday, I went to Williamstown; and saw it for the first time for nineteen years. I slept in the house where I dined on Commencement-day, and the next morning had some very impressive views of the shortness of human life—to think that it was nineteen years since I was there, and yet it looked like yesterday. I recollect the countenances and the conversation of that day with perfect distinctness. Nineteen years more, should I live in this world, will make me sixty-one years old. Surely life is a vapor; but if spent for God, it will be just long enough, and filled with just mercies enough, and trials enough, and every thing enough, to fit the soul for heaven and for the everlasting enjoyment of God. In the morning I visited the grave of my classmate; saw the place where Mills, Richards, and other good men used to pray; and then called upon, and spent the forenoon with Dr. Griffin.

"Your affectionate husband,

"J. EDWARDS."

To the members of Salem church, Boston.

"SARATOGA SPRINGS, Aug. 1, 1829.

"DEAR BRETHREN AND FRIENDS—On the subject of my last communication to you, I would observe, that so far as I at present understand the indications of Providence, it appears to be the divine will, that I should request that my pastoral connection with you may be dissolved. I do therefore hereby request, that my pastoral and ministerial connection with Salem church and congregation, Boston, may be dissolved; provided it shall appear, to an ecclesiastical council called for that purpose, to be the divine will.

"I have been led to make the above request from the following considerations:

"1. It appears to me that it will be more for your good, and that of your children, to have a pastor who can spend his whole time with you, than to have one who is required to be absent from you as much as I have been, and probably must be in future, should my pastoral connection with you be continued.

"2. To engage, at least for a time, in some employment, that will call for habitual and vigorous bodily exercise, will, I believe, be more conducive to my health, than to continue the labors of a city pastor.

"3. Should the Lord, by a course of active employment, give me health, it is probable that I can be more useful to the church of God and the world in some other situation, than I can with my present health, or the health that I can expect to enjoy, as pastor of Salem church.

"And if, dear brethren and friends, in view of the above considerations, it shall appear to you to be in accordance with the divine will, I would invite you, and I do hereby invite you to unite with me in calling an ecclesiastical council to consider, and if they think proper, to comply with the above request. * * *

"Praying and expecting that the Lord will dwell among you by his Spirit, build you up as a church, and give you and your children an inheritance among all them that are sanctified,

"I am your grateful and affectionate pastor,

"J. EDWARDS.

"To SAMUEL TENNEY, Clerk of Salem church, Boston."

With this request the church felt it to be their duty to comply, and on the 20th of August, 1829, his relations as pastor of a confiding, united people were again dissolved.

His last year's labor as pastor had been a constant struggle to fulfil his high responsibilities, while every exciting effort he made but disabled him the more. His heart was intent on the work upon his hands. He wished to see the house of God filled with spiritual worshippers, rescued from the highways of sin and the labyrinths of destructive and prevailing error. He wished to see Boston redeemed, and her energies consecrated to Christ and the salvation of men. The prospects in his early labors there had been bright as the rising dawn; the gift of gifts, the power of the Holy Spirit, was richly descending; God was with him; every thing indicated that the most sanguine hopes would be realized; and when he sunk under the pressure of labor, he still hoped that his vigorous physical powers would rally. But the working of the moral machinery within, the fire burning in him as he put forth his impassioned appeals to rouse men from the slumber of death, and wake them, through the power of the Spirit, to life eternal; the bearing of others' burdens in the Christian counsel he was continually called to give; and his keen sense of responsibility to God and men, had deranged some of those delicate organs on which the healthy action of the physical frame depends. He sought rest and recreation; he and his people hoped against hope; till it became clear to all, including the best medical advisers, that he must resign his charge, leave the city, and seek a more active out-door life; or his cenotaph and his precious memory would ere long be all that his devoted people could retain of him.

This was the turning-point of his history. He had been "watching providence," and by a discipline, doubtless as kind as it was trying, God had been deciding the point that he must close his labors as pastor, and enter on plans of benevolent effort wide as the world, which were to mark the age in which he lived.

Being dismissed, as above stated, on the 20th of August, and regarding the claims of the Temperance Society, which he had left for the charge in Boston, as taking precedence of others then laid before him, he, on the 27th of the same month, resumed his labors in that department of benevolence which must ever be associated with his name.

Among the calls made at this time for his public services, were an invitation to a professorship in a New England college; overtures for the professorship of sacred rhetoric in the Theological seminary at Auburn; besides his appointment, above referred to, as agent of the General Union for promoting the observance of the Christian Sabbath, formed in the city of New York. In declining the last-mentioned appointment, he says, "Sabbath-breakers are generally rum-drinkers; and while they continue the use of distilled liquors, it will not be possible to lead them duly to observe the Christian Sabbath. In order, therefore, to accomplish the great object of the General Sabbath Union, as well as that of the Bible Society, the Home and Foreign Missionary societies, and every other benevolent institution, I think it proper for me at present to labor to banish the use of distilled liquors from the earth."

Without rebelling against the decisions of a wise and unerring Providence, who had purposed that Dr. Edwards should yet be employed successively in four great public enterprises and institutions of the age, we yet record with a degree of sadness the termination of his labors as pastor of a church of Christ, for which God had given him such distinguished qualifications; while it must be acknowledged, that by his experience in the pastoral office, he was trained and fitted for the eminent usefulness he attained in other spheres of action. On the whole, the indications of Providence have perhaps rarely been more clear, than that, in his existing state of health, he was now called to resign the pastoral charge; and at the same time, that he must throw himself again into the great temperance movement, which God had made him so prominent an instrument in originating; its journeyings and active labors, however toilsome and self-denying, being precisely what was necessary to restore his health and prolong his usefulness.

In his successful labors as pastor at Andover and Boston, he reached an eminence which few servants of God in the ministry have attained, and the sweet savor of that period of his life must ever remain, ascending like incense, acceptable to God. He was the man whom such parents as the lamented Hon. Samuel Hubbard, as he has said in the extract quoted above, the praying members of the church at Andover, the church in Salem-street, the church in Park-street, the First Presbyterian church in Philadelphia, and those single-hearted Christians who united for the new enterprise in the city of New York, wished as their pastor, to stand between a sin-offended God and their own souls and the souls of their children; to draw eternal truth from the inspired oracles by which the famishing soul might be fed; to guide them to Christ the only Redeemer, and to the Holy Spirit the only Sanctifier; to preach "the glorious gospel of the blessed God;" to throw his heavenly influence into the family circle, in prosperity and joy, in sickness and in sorrow, and on the bed of death; the pastor to whom they were to unbosom the burdens of their hearts, who would betray no confidence reposed in him, would counsel them in difficulties, promote their peace with God and one another, and guide them in all the way of life. They insisted not on classical elegance, refined human speculations, the polished gesture, or the beautiful trope; but loved the man of God, "mighty in the Scriptures," set for the defence of the gospel, and intent on guiding men to "the Lamb of God which taketh away the sin of the world." Such a pastor they wished to labor with them through life, and at last to present them faultless before the throne of God with exceeding joy.

We find a pleasing letter referring to his character as pastor, from the late excellent Rev. Dr. Ebenezer Porter, professor in the Theological Seminary, to whom Dr. Edwards had written before the close of his first year in Boston, for counsel as to accepting the presidency of a college at the West.

"ANDOVER, Nov. 25, 1828.

"MY DEAR SIR—My only reason for not writing sooner is, that I deferred the subject one week for a meeting of the faculty, it being difficult in the multitude of our engagements to get any consultation earlier. The result is just as heretofore, that in our opinion God made you for pastoral action and influence. We have no doubt that a great work in the West is to be done, and that you have many eminent qualifications to do it. But as that work will require immense mental effort and responsibility, probably it would be more unfavorable to your health, (lungs being sound in your case,) than the ministry, for which you have so much stock of furniture on hand.

"With your present prospect of health, it seems that Boston at present is your field. To this opinion I am inclined by other considerations which render your influence specially important there in the present posture of its ministerial organization. Dr. Church, whom I saw the day I received your letter, spontaneously expressed an opinion similar to the foregoing.

"The Lord guide and bless you.

"Your brother,

"E. PORTER.

"P. S. It may gratify you to know that our ship is again before the wind, with a fine breeze. Our chapel, at prayers, is so full that a part of the Senior class are seated on the platform by the desk. The Junior class is forty-eight or fifty, probably some more coming; Middle class, about forty; Senior class, thirty-five. Not more than two or three members of the seminary absent; the two old classes were all here, with few exceptions, the first day of the term; four new members of the Senior class, two from Princeton, and two more in the Middle class. Pray that we may be guided from above in our great work."

The Rev. Dr. William Goodell, the veteran missionary on the Mediterranean, in his recent visit to this country, poured out the fervor of his warm heart, as he spoke of the solemn, glowing, resistless power with which Dr. Edwards proclaimed "the terror of the Lord," and salvation only by Jesus Christ and the renewing of the Holy Ghost, when he sat under his preaching while a student at the academy in Andover, fitting for college; and then afterwards, when he had returned to the Theological Seminary, and was one of many students who, as often as propriety admitted, repaired to his church, and refreshed their spirits by waiting on his public ministrations.

Dr. Edwards' sermon on the Inspiration of the Scriptures, and his tract, the Way to be Saved, had been translated by Rev. Dr. Goodell, and circulated in several languages, concerning which he writes to his esteemed and beloved friend the author.

"MALTA, July 25, 1829.

"REV. AND DEAR SIR—Your sermon on 'the Inspiration of the Holy Scriptures,' in *Armeno-Turkish*, I forwarded to you on the 27th ult.; and, lest it should not have been previously sent you in *Italian* and *Modern-Greek*, I now forward you a copy in each of these languages. I forward also at this time your sermon on 'the Way to be Saved' in *Modern-Greek* and *Armeno-Turkish*. The text under the cut in the latter is, 'For it is not possible, that the blood of bulls and of goats should take away sins.' The poetry at the close and on the cover is on salvation by grace through the blood of Christ, by Wortabet.

"Many copies of it in Modern-Greek have already been sent forth to 'show the way of salvation' to perishing men. And many others will soon follow in both of the above-mentioned languages, and will probably go 'throughout all Judea, and Galilee, and Samaria;' will 'travel as far as Phenice, and Cyprus, and Antioch;' will 'come to Perga in Pamphylia,' and 'to Antioch in Pisidia,' and 'to Lystra, and Derbe, cities of Lycaonia,' and 'to Philippi, the chief city of Macedonia,' and 'to the seven churches that are in Asia;' and will be read 'in the midst of Mars' hill,' and 'in the isle of Patmos,' and at Corinth and Colosse and Thessalonica, at Scio and Samos and Rhodes and Miletus, and by 'the strangers scattered throughout Pontus, Galatia, Cappadocia, Asia, and Bithynia.' May it, like 'the grace of God, that bringeth salvation, appear to all' these and many others, 'teaching them, that denying ungodliness and worldly lusts, they should live soberly, righteously, and godly in this present world!' And may many of the sermons which you shall hereafter preach, be not only like a lamp, giving light to a circumscribed spot, but like the sun, emitting its rays to the poles, and enlightening now *this*, now *that* entire half of the globe.

"You will accept, dear sir, our kind regards for yourself and yours, and our best wishes for your success in the work of the ministry; and will remember us and ours, and our important work, in your prayers.

"Yours affectionately,

"W. GOODELL."

CHAPTER VII.

HIS LABORS IN THE TEMPERANCE REFORMATION.

FIRST TWO YEARS—1830, 1831.

On the 27th August, 1829, Dr. Edwards, at the distinct call of divine Providence, turned aside from the labors of the pastoral office, and concentrated the powerful energies of his mind and heart on the enterprise he had already done so much to originate and establish, the promotion of TOTAL ABSTINENCE FROM INTOXICATING DRINKS, and thus *the removal of one of the most terrific obstacles to the spread of the gospel*—a novel idea, majestic in its simplicity, for which millions bless God, and which, if universally put in practice, would rid this sin-ruined world of one of the heaviest curses under which it groans.

The intelligent Christian reader will mark with interest, in the preceding pages, that long train of providential events by which Dr. Edwards was prepared for and brought into this service as General Agent and Secretary of the American Temperance Society:—his early training—his consecration to the universal spread of the gospel—his being led to feel, as a pastor, the influence of intemperance palsying the truth from his own lips and spreading desolation among those he loved—the particular providences which concentrated his attention upon this subject—the success of endeavors among his own people—the strong hold the subject took upon the minds of the ablest and best of men with whom he was accustomed to act—the feeling that the responsibility of rousing and directing the public mind on this subject *rested much upon himself*—and that state of his physical system which compelled him to relinquish the labors of a pastor and a sedentary life.

The history of THE ORIGIN AND PROGRESS of this wonderful movement, to the period when he commenced his seven years of labor, which form so prominent an era in his life and in the benevolent enterprises of the age, we are permitted to give mainly in the terse, well-weighed, and glowing language of his own pen in a public document, though recorded with such characteristic delicacy, that most of the allusions to his own efficient endeavors are perceptible only to those otherwise cognizant of the facts.

Having stated that the fatal error, that ardent spirit is useful as an article of diet, or as an aid to labor, began to prevail in Great Britain less than three hundred years ago, and did not prevail generally among the mass of the people in our own country until after the war of the Revolution; that "the cause of this error was the deceptive feelings of those who use it: being in its nature a mocker, it deceived them; by disturbing healthy action and inducing disease, it created an unnatural thirst, the gratification of which, like the gratification of the desire of sinning in the man who sins, causes it to increase, and the end is death;" and having presented a summary view of the wide-spread ravages of intemperance upon property, health, reason, life, morals, and religion, at which the intelligent, on both sides of the Atlantic, had become appalled, and were uttering their loud notes of woe and of alarm, while yet *governments and churches, ministers and people, philanthropists and Christians, still favored the making, vending, and moderate use!*—he thus proceeds:

"But a great change has been commenced; and one which, in the rapidity and extent of its progress, has no parallel in the history of man. Already it is spoken of, by the wise and the good in this and other countries, as one of the wonders of the world.

"'The great discovery,' says a European writer, 'has at length come forth like the light of a new day, that the *temperate* members of society are the chief agents in promoting and perpetuating drunkenness. On whose mind this great truth first rose, is not known. Whoever he was, whether humble or great, peace to his memory. He has done more for the world than he who enriched it with the knowledge of a new continent; and posterity, to the remotest generation, shall walk in the light which he has thrown around them. Had it not been for him, Americans and Europeans might have continued to countenance *the moderate ordinary use* of a substance, whose most moderate ordinary use is temptation and danger; and amidst a flood of prejudice and temptation urged onward by themselves, they would have made rules against drunkenness, like ropes of sand, to be burst and buried by the coming wave.'

"About seventeen years ago, a communication was made by a member of this committee," (Dr. Edwards himself, in 1815, two or three years after he was settled at Andover,) "on the evils of using intoxicating liquors at *funerals;* and reasons were presented, why this practice, which had become common in some parts of the country, should be done away. Not long after, he made another communication on the evils of furnishing ardent spirit as an article of *entertainment,* especially to ministers of the gospel; a practice which was also common, and was thought by many to be a suitable expression of respect and kindness towards the ministerial office. The effects were strongly marked; and some persons from that time adopted the plan of not using ardent spirit on any occasion. The benefits of abstinence were striking; facts were collected, and arrangements made for a more extended exhibition of this subject. Men were found who had been led by their own reflection, in view of the evil which it occasions, to renounce the use of this poison; and others, who had never used it; yet, as a body, they enjoyed better health than those who continued to use it, were more uniform and consistent in their deportment, and more ready for every good word and work.

"In 1822, (1824?) a teamster, partially intoxicated, by using what some persons, for less, probably, than twenty-five cents, had given him, fell under the wheels of his wagon, and was crushed to death. Another man, tending a coalpit, became partially intoxicated, fell asleep on some straw, and was burnt to death. These events occasioned the delivery of two discourses, (by Dr. Edwards,) one on the wretchedness of intemperate men, and another on the duty of *preventing sober men from becoming intemperate; that when the present race of drunkards should be removed, the whole land might be free.* The means of doing this, the sure means, and the only means, were shown to be, *abstinence from the use of intoxicating liquors.* This was shown, by facts, to be both practicable and expedient, and was urged as the indispensable duty of all men; a duty which they owed to God, to themselves, their children, their country, and the world.

"This doctrine appeared to many to be strange; excited great attention, occasioned much conversation, and through the blessing of the Lord, produced great results. It was again and again enforced. A conviction of the duty of abstinence was fastened on many consciences; and it became evident from facts, that this doctrine is adapted to commend itself to every man's conscience in the sight of God.

"And the question arose, Who knows, should the subject be presented kindly and plainly throughout the United States—be illustrated by facts, and pressed on the conscience—but that it may, through the divine blessing, change the habits of the nation? Who knows, but that our children, and children's children, may be raised up free from this abomination, to be instrumental in perpetuating the blessings of free institutions—to be themselves made free by the Son of God—and to spread the light and glory of *that* freedom round the globe?

"In 1825, the present Corresponding Secretary wrote the tract No. 176 of the American Tract Society's series, entitled, 'THE WELL-CONDUCTED FARM,' exhibiting the happy results of an experiment made by an original member of this committee, in the introduction of the principle of total abstinence upon an extensive farming establishment in the county of Worcester, Mass. This tract was the same year printed, and circulated extensively through the country.

"The evils of using, and the benefits of abstaining from ardent spirit, became more and more conspicuous; and also the necessity, as well as the encouragement, to make more systematic, general, and persevering efforts on the subject. Individuals not only abstained, but in some cases agreed together, that they would not use or furnish to others that destructive poison. But there was no system, no plan of operation, to cause such a union to become universal; and it was evident, that unless something more universal, efficacious, and persevering should be done, our country would be ruined; the gospel would never have its legitimate influence over the human mind, and the reign of darkness and sin would be perpetuated to the end of time. Past efforts, though they had on some spots and in some cases done good, had not struck at the root of the evil. Their object was, to *regulate* the use of ardent spirit, not to *abolish* it. Those who made it admitted, and most of them practised, the fundamental error, that men in health might, without injury, and of course without sin, use the poison, *if they did not use too much.* This was the case with members of societies for the suppression of intemperance. Thus, while they only retarded the growth, or clipped off a few of the top twigs of this poisonous tree, the roots were constantly nourished, and daily struck deeper and deeper. While the friends of temperance were reforming one old drunkard, their own habits, if followed, would make a hundred new ones. They were indeed sounding the alarm, but were treading in the footsteps of the lost; denouncing intemperance, and encouraging the use of strong drink; bewailing the effect, and perpetuating the cause; warning men not to be drunken, and urging them to drink. Many were enraged, almost to madness, at those who represented the use of ardent spirit to be a sin; and though they had followed a promising son to the drunkard's grave, and were expecting soon to follow another, and another, they would denounce as enthusiasts and treat as enemies, those who urged them not to drink. The husband who had lost his wife by intemperance, would, for the sake of money, furnish that which killed her to all who would purchase, and even give it, as a token of kindness, to his nearest friends. The wife who had seen her husband die by this poison, would use it herself, and give it daily to her only son. And it was perfectly evident, that unless a new movement could be started on a new plan, and one which should be commensurate, in place and time, with the evil—one which should *strike it at the root and exterminate it*—drunkenness could never be done away; the people would never become 'all righteous,' nor the day of millennial glory ever break on the world.

"A meeting of a few individuals was therefore called," (near the close of 1825,) "to consider the question, '*What shall be done to banish intemperance from the United States?*'

"After prayer for divine guidance, and consultation on the subject, the result was a determination to attempt the formation of an AMERICAN TEMPERANCE

SOCIETY, whose grand principle should be, *abstinence from strong drink;* and its object, *by light and love, to change the habits of the nation* with regard to the use of intoxicating liquors.

"A correspondence was therefore opened, and a meeting of gentlemen, of various Christian denominations, holden in Boston, January 10, 1826, when a committee was appointed to prepare a constitution, and the meeting was adjourned to February 13, 1826.

"At the adjourned meeting, a constitution was presented and adopted, and the following persons were chosen by the members of the meeting at the commencement, to compose the Society: namely, Rev. Leonard Woods, D. D.; Rev. William Jenks, D. D.; Rev. Justin Edwards; Rev. Warren Fay; Rev. Benjamin B. Wisner; Rev. Francis Wayland; Rev. Timothy Merritt; Hon. Marcus Morton; Hon. Samuel Hubbard; Hon. William Reed; Hon. George Odiorne; John Tappan, Esq.; William Ropes, Esq.; James P. Chaplin, M. D.; S. V. S. Wilder, Esq.; and Enoch Hale, M. D. The Society was then organized by choosing the Hon. Marcus Morton, President; Hon. Samuel Hubbard, Vice-president; William Ropes, Esq., Treasurer. Executive Committee: Rev. Leonard Woods, D. D.; Rev. Justin Edwards; John Tappan, Esq.; Hon. George Odiorne, and S. V. S. Wilder, Esq.

"On the sixteenth of January, Rev. Calvin Chapin, D. D., of Wethersfield, Conn., commenced the publication of a series of thirty-three numbers, in the Connecticut Observer, entitled, 'THE INFALLIBLE ANTIDOTE.' His motto was, '*Entire abstinence from ardent spirits is the only certain preventive of intemperance.* This was strikingly illustrated in the various numbers, and strongly urged upon all as an indispensable duty. He had himself, as had a number of others, practised it for many years, and urged it as the duty of all men.

"In April, 1826, the National Philanthropist, a weekly paper, devoted to the cause of temperance, was established in Boston by the Rev. William Collier. Its motto was, '*Temperate drinking is the downhill road to intemperance.*'

"In January, 1827, the present Corresponding Secretary visited Boston, and commenced an effort to obtain means for the support of a permanent agent. At the first meeting, although the evening was exceedingly stormy, the amount subscribed was more than \$3,500. At the second meeting, the amount subscribed was more than \$1,200; and at the third meeting, more than \$700. In Salem, Newburyport, Andover, and Northampton, were obtained upwards of \$2,000 more.

"As the pastoral duties of the Secretary did not permit of his continuing his agency, the Committee appointed the Rev. Nathaniel Hewit, of Fairfield, Conn., who was known to have preached and acted successfully on this subject, who spent twenty weeks in the service of the Society. He visited various places in Massachusetts, Rhode Island, Connecticut, New York, and Pennsylvania; preached on the subject, addressed public bodies, and in various ways promoted successfully the great and good cause.

"In September of the same year, the present Secretary was again appointed to an agency of three months, and visited various places in Maine, New Hampshire, Massachusetts, and Connecticut.

"In the course of the year, were published Kittredge's First Address, Dr. Mussey's Address before the Medical Convention of New Hampshire, Mr. Palfrey's Sermons, and Dr. Beecher's Sermons on the Nature, Signs, Evils, and Remedy of Intemperance; and they were all powerful auxiliaries to the cause."

On January 1, 1828, when Dr. Edwards was called from his temperance labors to the church in Boston, the Rev. Dr. Hewit resumed his agency; the Rev. Joshua Leavitt, Mr. Daniel C. Axtell in Western New York, Rev. Dr. John Woodbridge, and many others, rendered important services in the enterprise, and at the close of that year more than two hundred Temperance Societies had been formed. See First Permanent Temperance Document, 1831.

The following "Hints" indicate the spirit with which Dr. Edwards prosecuted his labors in the cause of temperance; and those who knew him best, best knew how consistently, faithfully, and conscientiously he put them in practice.

"HINTS FOR MYSELF, AND FOR EVERY MAN WHO ENGAGES IN THE PROMOTION OF TEMPERANCE.

"1. Let your object be, the glory of God in the salvation of men.

"2. Feel deeply your dependence on him; in all your ways acknowledge him, and let every step of your course be sanctified by the word of God and prayer.

"3. Make yourself thoroughly acquainted with the nature of intoxicating liquors, and with their effects upon the body and the mind; upon the property, health, reputation, reason, life, and salvation of those who use them.

"4. Exhibit these effects in a kind, affectionate, lucid, humble, and powerful manner, as illustrated, not by philosophy, but by facts; remembering that but few understand philosophy, and that all understand and feel facts.

"5. Never dispute with any one; and never converse, on this subject, with a man who is intoxicated.

"6. When a man does not believe what you say, never be angry, or try to force him to believe; but remember that once you did not believe: treat him kindly; ask questions, relate anecdotes, and state facts to meet his objections, and facts too which no one can gainsay or resist.

"7. Never try to force people forward any farther than, from the light which you have thrown before them, they choose to go.

"8. Try, if possible, to have every one that you address give you something; and if they do it, this will tend to secure the influence of their example.

"9. Never be uncivil or impolite towards those who will give you nothing, or even abuse you. Overcome evil with good.

"10. Say nothing and do nothing but what you are willing should be told through the world.

"11. Use no intoxicating liquors yourself. Abstain entirely from tobacco, snuff, and all needless things.

"12. Be temperate in the use of tea, coffee, and every kind of food and of drink.

"13. Say nothing concerning any one behind his back, but what you would be willing to say to his face; and what, if you should say it, would tend to illuminate and purify his mind.

"14. Strive to leave such an impression everywhere, that all will wish to see and hear and assist you again.

"15. Be yourself a pattern of temperance in all things; and strive ever to enforce all that you say by the irresistible eloquence of your own example. For this end be timely, regular, and temperate as to diet, sleep, exercise, and every thing to which you are called.

"16. Never exaggerate, or state any thing more than the simple truth.

"17. Show how the use of intoxicating liquor mightily obstructs the progress of the gospel, and all the means of grace; hinders every effort for the improvement, and especially for the salvation of men; and in this way actually ruins for eternity many souls.

"18. Never be discouraged; and never self-confident. Go forward in duty from love to God and love to men; humble in prosperity, calm in adversity, committing yourself, the cause in which you are engaged, and all your interests, mortal and immortal, to the divine guidance and disposal; and in due time you shall reap, to your perfect satisfaction, if you faint not."

After successfully prosecuting his labors in the cause of temperance for a few months in New England, he proceeded to New York, where, January 2, 1830, he wrote to relatives in Colchester, who had charge of two of his children, giving a cheering view of the work in which he was engaged.

"The millennium," he says, "will never come so long as sober men continue the use of ardent spirit, nor will the gospel and the means of grace have their legitimate effects on the minds of men. And as the Lord is pleased to make me instrumental in leading many in every place where I go to break off the use of it, I am encouraged to proceed. If I have ever been instrumental in doing any good in the world, perhaps I was never more so than at present.

"Since my arrival in this city, I have had a bad attack of biliary obstruction, which has disabled me from making much effort for the present. Thus when it appeared to me that the great interests of the world might be promoted by my being enabled to make a great effort, the Lord sees it to be best that I should be able to make next to none at all. I preached once last Sabbath, and expect, if the Lord will, to preach once to-morrow. But unless I should be better, it probably will not be safe for me to continue long in the city. Pray for me, my dear brother and sister, that I may be enabled to know and do the whole will of God; and that the language of my feelings and actions may ever be, 'Not my will, but thine be done.'

"I desire to be thankful, that while I am called to be absent from my dear wife and six dear children, seven as strong reasons to bind me to my home as a man can well have, the Lord has graciously provided so kindly that two of them can be in your family, and one of them with our dear sister M——."

Two weeks later he writes to Mrs. Edwards from Washington city, stating that he was that evening to form a Temperance Society among the colored people, and adds, "I have been much struck lately with President Edwards' 47th resolution:

"'Resolved, to endeavor to my utmost to deny whatever is not most agreeable to a good and universally sweet and benevolent, quiet, peaceable, contented and easy, compassionate and generous, humble and meek, submissive and obliging, diligent and industrious, charitable and even, patient, moderate, forgiving, and sincere temper; and to do at all times what such a temper would lead to; and to examine strictly at the end of every week whether I have so done. Should all act upon this plan, what a delightful world this would be.'"

To his eldest Son.

"NEW YORK, Jan. 18, 1830.

"MY DEAR SON—It would give me a great deal of pleasure to be at home with your dear mother, and to see all my six dear children around me. I should like to see Justin Asa, and Jonathan, and Newton, and Elizabeth, and Lydia, and Ann Eliza, all sitting around the table, or around the fire at the time of reading the Bible in the morning. I should like to live with them all the time, and give them that instruction and those counsels which, if followed, would make them wise and good—would prepare them to be very useful in this world, and happy in the world to come.

"But perhaps you ask, Papa, why do you not live

at home, and take care of us? It is because there are so many parents who, by drinking rum, destroy their reason, and thus unfit themselves to take care of their children. There are now 200,000 children, whose parents are so wicked in consequence of drinking rum, that they will not provide food, or clothing, or schools for their children; so that these poor children, whose condition is as bad as if they had no fathers, are often hungry and almost naked, and grow up in ignorance and sin. Now I am absent from my dear family, and go to Boston, to New York, and other places, to teach the people that it is *wicked* for men to make distilled liquors, to *sell* them, and to *use* them, because they do nothing but mischief. And if the use of them should be continued for thirty years to come, as it has been for thirty years past, it would cause a loss to the people who should use these liquors, of more than $3,000,000,000; and would kill 900,000 people, and would ruin for eternity very many of the souls of men.

"And while I am absent for the sake of doing good to other children, I am exceedingly anxious that my own children should not suffer for want of a father to take care of them. And I hope that you, my dear son, will every day seek to your Father in heaven, that he would bless you, and teach you to love and serve him."

Two days later, he wrote from New York to Mrs. Edwards, "Since I last wrote, I have preached every Sabbath, and attended two or three meetings during the week. Several associations have been formed in congregations, and the cause of *entire abstinence* is fast gaining ground. And if it were not for the woful fact, that many of the professors of religion in evangelical churches in this city are still making and selling the poison, it would gain much faster. If the man who uses so much as to kill himself, is a self-murderer, what, in the sight of the Lord, must be the man who, for the sake of getting money, is furnishing the means of killing hundreds and thousands, when he knows the use which they will make of it? I hope that whoever lives a few years will see the time when not a professor of religion in the country will be found in this destructive traffic.

"I cannot but hope that in some way the Lord will provide means to extend and perpetuate this work of mercy, till there is not a drunkard on the globe, and not a sober man to make the drunkard's drink. Mr. A. T——, at the monthly concert, put in $1,000 for foreign missions; and soon after, at a missionary meeting, subscribed $4,000, about three times as much as all the rest of the people. I expect that he will give me something for temperance."

January 26, he writes to relatives in Boston, "When I came to this city, I did not intend to stop till this time; but as a wide and effectual door seemed by divine Providence to be opened into many churches, into which no temperance agent has before been admitted, I thought it the will of Providence that I should. Promoting temperance here is promoting it west and south, through the whole country.

"I hope and trust that the Lord has some one, whom he is preparing for you," (as pastor of the Salem-street church,) "and whom he will, in his time, which is always the best time, by the use of suitable means on your part, send to you. He loves his church infinitely better than we can, and knows infinitely better how to promote her highest good. If we love him, and do his will, we may safely commit ourselves, our friends, the interests of Zion, and all our concerns, mortal and immortal, to his infinitely wise, holy, and benevolent disposal."

A week later he says, "The gentlemen who attended the meeting at the Medical College, on Saturday evening, were exceedingly anxious that the statement which I made to them should be made to a larger assembly, both of gentlemen and ladies. Several of the physicians and others have invited a meeting this evening, at Masonic Hall. There seems to be an impression, which increases daily upon the minds of reflecting men, that the object is a momentous one, which will deeply affect the welfare of our country to all future generations.

"As every man is bound to pursue such business, and such only, as is on the whole useful to men, it is impossible to see on what principles any man can pursue, consistently with duty, the business of making or vending distilled liquor. I am confident that if sober men saw this thing as they will soon see it in the light of eternity, they would not be guilty of conniving at it, or assisting in it, for all the wealth of creation."

February 20, he is at Boston, and says, "The meeting here, Wednesday evening, was full, and appears to have had a good influence. The subject was, the folly and wickedness of selling distilled liquors.

The legislature were nearly all present. The lieutenant-governor the next morning, by the payment of $30, made himself an honorary life-member of the Society."

To a friend in trying circumstances, he wrote March 11, "I have generally found that it is best to do little or nothing in vindication of our character; but to mind our own business, seek in all things to please God, and trust in him in due time to set all things right. By this, I do not mean that it is not best, if things have been wrongly stated, when Providence gives opportunity, to state the truth. But I would not press for an opportunity to do this; would do it only when Providence opens the way, and then do it simply, and rather that the truth may be known, and others be saved from error, than to vindicate ourselves. If we please the Lord, feel kind and forgiving, and strive in all things to do good, never rendering evil for evil, but contrariwise blessing, God will take care of us and ours, and direct all things to the right result.

"It is sometimes necessary, however, to let patience have her perfect work, in order to be perfect and entire, wanting nothing; and 'if any man offend not in word, the same is a perfect man.' I recollect one who, when they laid many grievous things to his charge, answered *nothing*. And if when ye do well and suffer for it, ye take it patiently, happy are ye. The spirit of grace and of glory resteth upon you. On the part of others Jesus may be dishonored, but on your part he is glorified. And if we suffer with him, and for his sake, we shall also reign with him."

About the same date he says, "I have ten times as many applications as I can comply with. The temperance cause is gaining, and I hope that God designs to work a change which shall be of unspeakable benefit to all future generations of men."

"FLEMINGTON, N. J., May 5, 1830.

"MY DEARLY BELOVED WIFE—I left New York on Monday morning, and arrived here yesterday. In the afternoon I addressed the people in the meeting-house, and in the evening the gentlemen of the court and others in the court-house, on the subject of temperance. Immediately after, the Hon. Samuel L. Southard, late Secretary of the Navy, and now Attorney-general of the state of New Jersey, made a speech, and a county society was formed under very favorable circumstances. Some, I learn to-day, came for the purpose of opposing; but when they had heard, they concluded to hold their peace."

He proceeds to say, "I have had my mind too much filled with men, and not enough with God. I have not spent time enough in communing with him, and listening to his voice, and *feasting, as with marrow and fatness, upon his word* revealed in the Bible. I often resolve, and I hope, sometimes strive, to do better; but our strength is weakness, and our wisdom folly, and our righteousness rags. Let us come daily and habitually, and freely and humbly and boldly, to the throne of grace, that we may obtain mercy, and find grace to help in all times of need, according to all our wants; and I verily believe that we shall then receive of his fulness grace for grace.

"I have often tried to decide things to-day, which

the Lord, should I live, would not call me to decide till next week or month; and been more anxious as to what will be the condition of things next year, than I have to please God and enjoy his presence, and be prepared to *die* to-day, or to-morrow; and so I shall do again and again, if the Lord does not prevent. How much better it would be to say and to feel, that 'if the Lord will, we shall live and do this or that.'"

Of the Hon. Mr. Southard's address above alluded to, he wrote to his little son, "Mr. Southard said that he had not drank any ardent spirits for more than twenty years; while many younger than he, who have used it, have gone down to the drunkard's grave. He said, I have two sons, and if they might each of them have one hundred thousand dollars, provided they would begin to drink rum, and if they did not they should not have a farthing, I should rather they would not have a farthing. So poisonous are ardent spirits, that they kill thousands and thousands of people every year, and render very wicked and very wretched thousands of others that use them."

About the same time he says, "I hope to obtain means to employ an agent over the whole state of Pennsylvania, in which are a million and a half of people."

On the 4th of May, 1830, he was appointed Associate Secretary of the American Home Missionary Society at New York, and on the same day the gentlemen in that city who had previously chosen him as pastor of the new church they were about to organize, presented a renewed call from the congregation, that he would become their pastor. To both these appointments he felt constrained to give a negative reply, assigning in his answer to the new congregation "two reasons:"

"1. From the testimony of physicians, and from past experience, I am led to conclude that a longer continuance in my present employment will be more conducive to a speedy and complete restoration to health, than an immediate engagement in the duties of a city pastor.

"2. The great interests of our country and the world seem to me to require that a more permanent foundation should be laid for a united and ever-growing effort to abolish, as an article of luxury or living, the traffic in distilled liquors, throughout the globe. And as Providence has, for the present, committed the instrumental superintendence of this concern to me, the time seems not yet to have arrived when it is proper for me to leave it."

To Mrs. Edwards, announcing the death of her father.

"BOSTON, August 1, 1830.

"MY DEAR WIFE—God is very kind, and we should make it our simple business, in mercies and in trials, to please him. Let us, at all times, lean upon him. Let us be satisfied with all that he does, remembering that he could not in any thing do better. Hence the reason why we should say, 'Not my will, but thine be done;' and ask, with regard to every thing, 'Lord, what wilt thou have me to do?' and make it our simple business in all things to do it, trusting in him for all that we need, and striving to glorify him in body and in spirit.

"I intend this afternoon to write to your mother,

and the friends at Colchester. I found on my return from Reading, that Mary had received a letter from Ann Eliza, mentioning that your father had been unwell for three weeks; and more so for a week past—that on Wednesday he died, and was buried yesterday. He had a dropsy of the heart; was sitting on the side of the bed in the middle room, and talking with George while the family were taking tea. They observed a change, and in a minute or two he was dead. He had spoken, within a day or two, a few times about dying suddenly, but had said little."

From Eastport, Maine, he writes, August 13, "I preached on Sabbath morning and evening at Calais, on Monday evening at Milltown, on Tuesday, 10 o'clock, A. M., at St. Stephens in New Brunswick, on Tuesday evening at St. Andrews, on Wednesday at Robbinstown, on Thursday evening at Perry, and on Friday returned to Eastport, where I expect to preach on the Sabbath. About two hundred have been added to the temperance societies this week, and things appear favorable. Women walk five or six miles to attend meeting, and bring a child in their arms, and return home at 10 o'clock at night in the same way."

He proceeded to *St. Johns, in the province of New Brunswick*, where he wrote to Rev. Mr. Gale, his brother-in-law, at Eastport, Aug. 24: "Through the kindness of the Lord I arrived here, after a pleasant passage, on Saturday evening at half past 10 o'clock. On Sabbath morning I called on Rev. Dr. Burns, and preached for him in the afternoon on the worthiness of Jesus Christ. Rev. 5:12. On Monday morning I called on Rev. Dr. Gray, on the mayor, and on Mr.

McLeod. They all received me kindly, and seemed to be gratified at my arrival.

"The mayor said, that the people of New Brunswick 'beat the people of the United States all hollow' as to drinking; that the people of the United States drank only about *five gallons* a year to each individual; whereas the people of New Brunswick used more than *seven* to every man, woman, and child in the province. He said they had about 50,000 inhabitants, and it cost the consumers, upon an average, about one dollar per gallon, which would make $500,000 a year, paid out for that which does no good, and which causes a loss in idleness, dissipation, etc., of more than $500,000 more. They have about two hundred and fifty persons licensed to sell ardent spirits in St. Johns.

"I found the mayor received the Journal of Humanity," (a temperance paper which had been established at Andover,) "and is prepared to favor the temperance cause. Any of the public rooms, he said, should be at my service at any time when I chose. He wished, however, that they might have till next week to notify the people, so that they might have a large assembly. I have concluded therefore, with the leave of Providence, to take the steam-boat to-morrow for Fredericton, with a letter from the mayor of this city to the governor and others. My expectation is to return here on Monday, speak on Tuesday evening, and return to Eastport on Thursday of next week."

He soon entered on the prosecution of the temperance enterprise in the middle states and the District of Columbia, to which he devoted *a half year* of uninterrupted successful toil, making brief allusions to his proceedings, and their results, in letters to his family and friends.

To his brother-in-law, Dea. Daniel Safford, of the Salem church, Boston, he wrote from New York, November 2, "It would give me great pleasure to be with you at Salem church to-morrow," (at the installation of Rev. Dr. Blagden as pastor,) "but the Lord seems to direct another way, and our safety and interest and usefulness, you know, consist in following him. My dear wife, I hope, will be with you, and that you all will enjoy much of the presence of God."

"BALTIMORE, Nov. 15, 1830.

"MY DEAR WIFE—From New York I went to Princeton, spent a night with Rev. Dr. Miller, and the Sabbath at New Brunswick. On Tuesday night attended, with the Hon. Mr. Frelinghuysen, the annual meeting of the New Jersey State Temperance Society, at the state-house in Trenton. On Wednesday went to Philadelphia, and on Friday came to this city. Yesterday I preached twice on the subject of temperance; expect to preach again on Thursday evening, and then, if the Lord will, twice on the coming Sabbath. On the Thursday following is their annual meeting, and I shall probably stay here two or three weeks, and then go to Washington."

The Rev. Dr. Miller, President of the New Jersey State Temperance Society, says, in a letter apologizing for unavoidable absence from their anniversary, and encouraging the friends of temperance:

"There is one thought on this subject, which I will take the liberty of expressing. It is, that I seriously doubt whether our *female friends* are aware how much is in *their* power in reference to the cause of temperance. I am fully persuaded, that if *they* with one accord should all unite in expressing, on all proper occasions, their abhorrence of the use of ardent spirits in any form, as a common drink; and if they should resolutely frown upon all whom they may see using ardent spirits on any occasion, they would do more to banish this dreadful destroyer from our land, than almost any other human means that could be used. Indeed, I cannot doubt that if our respected countrywomen were unanimous and firm in taking this course, the use of distilled liquors would be speedily banished from all decent society. And when I consider what a peculiar interest females have in preserving their nearest and dearest relatives from that gulf of infamy and destruction to which the sin of intemperance is daily leading thousands, I cannot help feeling equal surprise and regret that they do not take a more decisive stand against *all use* of ardent spirits; for the longer I reflect and inquire on this subject, the deeper is my persuasion that it is only in the way of *total abstinence* that the path of safety lies; and that the idea of indulging in the 'guarded' and 'temperate' use of this deceiver without danger, is one of the greatest and most fatal of all delusions."

The above having been kindly copied by the Rev. Dr. James W. Alexander, and sent to Dr. Edwards, to the care of the lamented Rev. Dr. Nevins, Baltimore, Dr. Alexander adds, that the directors of the Delaware and Hudson Canal Company had discontinued the use of ardent spirits among their workmen; and gives "the following impressive anecdote.

"When the contractors were closing their engagements with the company last week, one of them complained of this condition, and stated this as his experience: When he had a contract upon a Pennsylvania canal, he gave every hand eight or nine drams a day, upon this condition, that he should work to the utmost limit of his strength. 'And,' said he, or to this effect, 'I got a fourth more work out of them; but in two years they were absolutely *worn out, burnt up;* indeed a man would last just about as long as his tools.' You may depend upon this statement as substantially correct."

From Baltimore he writes to Mrs. Edwards, December 2, "I recollect as I write, that December 2d was the day that I was ordained at Andover, eighteen years ago. I hope that in the next eighteen years, if my life shall be spared, I may be disposed and enabled to do a great deal more good, than I have for the eighteen years past.

"I had three meetings on the Sabbath, and have had one every day since, and am to have two more this week. On Tuesday I went to Annapolis, thirty miles below this, on the Chesapeake bay. A Temperance Society was formed of about a hundred, and one in Baltimore last night. Another is to be formed here to-night, and another to-morrow night.

I have visited the state-prison, containing about 330 prisoners, about 300 of them brought there by intemperance; and the almshouse, containing 1,138, of whom 1,076 were brought there by intemperance."

On the 21st he was at Washington city, where he wrote to Mrs. Edwards' brother in New York, "This morning one of the Senators, and also one of the Representatives called on me to know whether I would consent, if invited, to preach in the capitol, and make a statement on the subject of temperance to the members of Congress, and I have consented to do so.

"Mr. Lumpkin, of Georgia, informs me that in his part of the country the change on temperance has been so great, that should any candidate for office offer ardent spirits to the electors, it would defeat his election. About a dozen members of Congress called the first evening after my arrival, and all seemed very favorable to temperance. At a late party of the French minister, they had no ardent spirits; and they have none at quite a number of the boarding-houses.

"It is, as you may well suppose, a great self-denial for me to be absent so much from my dear family; but we ought to be willing to take that course in which we can do most good. That was a noble resolution of President Edwards:

"'Resolved, That I will do whatsoever I think to be most to the glory of God, and my own good, profit, and pleasure, *in the whole of my duration*, without any consideration of the time, whether now, or never so many myriads of ages hence; and to do whatever I think to be my duty, and most for the good and advantage of mankind in general, whatever difficulties I meet with, how many soever and how great soever. And resolved, that I will live so as I shall wish I had done when I come to die.'

"May the Lord give both you and me, my dear brother, grace that we may do the same."

The next day he wrote to the American Tract Society in New York, recommending as a tract the able address on temperance delivered at Washington by Dr. Sewall, an eminent citizen, an ornament to the medical profession, and an active and influential member of the Methodist Episcopal church. He stated that "many of the members of Congress were wishing to obtain copies of it, to circulate among their constituents;" and also requested a grant of $20 worth of temperance tracts for his own distribution. He soon transmitted the tract, prepared for the press by himself and Dr. Sewall, and it constitutes No. 249 of the series.

"The temperance cause," he adds, "is shaping well. I yesterday preached in the capitol; and though it was very stormy, I was told by a man who has been twenty years in this city, that he never saw more of the members out; and they listened with attention. Many of them take a deep interest in the subject. I am expecting this week to see the President and the Secretary of the Navy; and then to visit Annapolis, at which place we expect to form a State Society."

To Mrs. Edwards' brother in New York.

"PHILADELPHIA, March 3, 1831.

"MY DEAR BROTHER—I arrived here to-day from Wilmington, Delaware, where they yesterday formed a Delaware Temperance Society. They have also formed a State Society in Maryland, and about twenty others in Baltimore, Annapolis, and other parts of the state. Thirteen also have been formed in the District of Columbia, embracing in all more than three thousand members.

"*As I have been absent nearly six months*, it gives me much pleasure to set my face again towards home. I have had great cause to be thankful that I have travelled in safety, met with a very kind reception, and I hope been instrumental in some good. The people have assembled in great numbers, and listened with deep attention, and apparently with much feeling; and I cannot but hope that it will be seen at some future time, that much good has been done through the grace and mercy of the Lord Jesus.

"I understand that there is more than usual attention to religion in your city, and I cannot but hope that you and many others will know the blessedness of living not unto yourselves, but unto Him who died for us and rose again; that to live is Christ, and to die is gain.

"Truly and affectionately yours,

"J. EDWARDS."

At this time Dr. Edwards received a cheering letter from the venerable Hon. JOHN COTTON SMITH, of Sharon, Connecticut, in which he says,

"You overrate my powers, but not my zeal in promoting the cause of temperance. I feel with you, in all its extent, the importance of enlisting the whole of our American youth in this sacred enterprise. They, and they only, possess the means of finishing the work so auspiciously begun; and we cannot be too diligent in impressing this truth upon their minds. Let them see the magnitude of the evil, and *their* efficiency in removing it. Let them feel that the welfare of their country is at this moment suspended, under God, upon their efforts. In a word, 'show them the enemy,' and unless I mistake the character of my young countrymen, the battle is won, gloriously won for them, and for the world.

"Of the present generation our hopes are less sanguine. More, however, much more has been accomplished in giving a new direction to public opinion, and in breaking down habits heretofore deemed incorrigible, than we could have imagined; and we are urged by irresistible motives to persevering exertion.

"I had supposed the moderate use of wine allowable; but from a more careful scrutiny of the word of God, I am convinced that inebriating liquor of whatever kind is clearly prohibited, excepting for medicinal and religious purposes. You and other good men, I doubt not, have entertained the same sentiment for a much longer period. Whether it is expedient to press the subject thus far at present, deserves mature consideration.

"I have marked your progress, my dear sir, the past year with no common interest. Your labors and success in this noble cause entitle you, in my judgment, to the lasting gratitude of your country and of mankind."

From Norwich, Connecticut, where there were evident manifestations of the presence of the Spirit, he wrote to the compiler, April 29, "God is doing wonders in our land, and giving us all the utmost encouragement to be humble, to hold on, and to look up; knowing that our poor endeavors will not be in vain in the Lord. I hope he will be with you and all friends in New York, at that *joyful, dangerous* time, the anniversaries, and teach you all to please him."

On the 18th of May, 1831, the American Temperance Society held their anniversary in Boston, when Dr. Edwards, as Corresponding Secretary, presented the able Fourth Annual Report, which constitutes the first of the well-known and widely circulated "PERMANENT TEMPERANCE DOCUMENTS" from his pen, which have exerted so powerful an influence on our country and the world. He says in this document:

"The Corresponding Secretary, since his reäppointment, August 27, 1829, has continued uninterruptedly his labors in the service of the Society. He has visited various parts of the British province of New Brunswick, and the states of Maine, New Hampshire, Massachusetts, Connecticut, New York, New Jersey, Pennsylvania, Delaware, Maryland, and the District of Columbia. He has travelled more than six thousand four hundred miles, and preached and addressed public bodies *three hundred and eighty-six* times. He has assisted in the formation, and attended the anniversaries, of numerous Temperance societies; written a number of articles for publication; conducted the correspondence, and superintended the general concerns of the Society.

"On the first of May, there had been reported one hundred and forty societies in Maine, ninety-six in New Hampshire, one hundred and thirty-two in Vermont, two hundred and nine in Massachusetts, twenty-one in Rhode Island, two hundred and two in Connecticut, seven hundred and twenty-seven in New

York, sixty-one in New Jersey, one hundred and twenty-four in Pennsylvania, five in Delaware, thirty-eight in Maryland, ten in the District of Columbia, one hundred and thirteen in Virginia, thirty-one in North Carolina, sixteen in South Carolina, sixty in Georgia, one in Florida, ten in Alabama, nineteen in Mississippi, three in Louisiana, fifteen in Tennessee, twenty-three in Kentucky, one hundred and four in Ohio, twenty-five in Indiana, twelve in Illinois, four in Missouri, and thirteen in Michigan territory; making, in all, more than two thousand two hundred, and embracing more than one hundred and seventy thousand members. These members have been constantly increasing, and have, in many cases, been more than doubled since they were reported. There are also numerous societies which have been formed, and some of them embracing large districts of country, not contained in the above list, and from which no returns have been received. The number belonging to societies which are not reported, in the state of New York, are supposed, by the Committee of the State society, to amount to more than thirty thousand. In other states from which the returns have been less general and complete, the number in proportion is still greater. In Kentucky, in which but twenty-three have been reported to us, containing only about sixteen hundred members, a correspondent writes, that they have, in his opinion, nearly one hundred societies, and not much short of fifteen thousand members. So it may be in other states; and from the best information which has been obtained, the Committee conclude that there are now formed in the United States, on the plan of abstinence from the use of ardent spirit, more than *three thousand temperance societies, containing more than three hundred thousand members.*

"From the influence of these societies, and other causes, three hundred thousand more may have adopted the plan of not using it, or furnishing it for the use of others. Connected with these, six hundred thousand children, and persons in their employment and under their control, may be as many more. And thus one million two hundred thousand may already have been brought under the influence, and may now be experiencing the benefit of the Temperance reformation. Among these, should they continue to refrain from intoxicating drink, there will never be a drunkard; whereas, had they continued in habits which prevailed five years ago, fifty thousand of them might have come to the drunkard's grave.

"So that, should this reform now be merely stationary, and make no further progress, it may have saved fifty thousand from the drunkard's doom; and how many it would save of their children, and children's children, none but God can determine.

"In one case, as our Secretary was informed, a father adopted the plan of using a little ardent spirit every day. He was never intoxicated, and never thought to be in the least intemperate. He only took a *little*, a *very little*, because he thought that it did him good. For the same reason his children took a *little* daily; and so did their children. And now, no less than forty of his descendants are drunkards, or in the drunkard's grave.

"Another man adopted a different plan: he would

not use ardent spirit; he would not purchase it, nor would he suffer it to enter his house. He taught his children to treat it as a poison, a mortal poison; and they taught their children. And now, there is not a drunkard among them; nor has one of his descendants ever come to the drunkard's grave. Long, long may it be, before any one ever shall. And when the long lines of descendants of these two men, through all future ages, shall rise up before them, and before the universe, in the blazing light of eternity, who can estimate the difference of results of the different courses adopted and pursued by their progenitors? None but He who seeth the end from the beginning, and to whom they have both now gone to render their account."

"From a town in Connecticut a gentleman states, 'We succeeded in forming a large Temperance society. Several of the drunkards ceased to use spirituous liquors. They appeared like new men, and O, their families appeared to be in a new world. The change was wonderful. But they have, almost all, gone back. And we cannot help it, so long as *one of our deacons will sell rum*. They say, 'If it is not wrong for the deacon to sell it, it is not wrong for us to buy it. He thinks that a little does good, and so do we.' And thus they go down to ruin. And O, their families, their wretched families—but we cannot help them, so long as the deacon will sell rum.'

"No; if deacons and church-members and sober men will continue, for the sake of money, to sell rum and make drunkards, and thus become their tempters and destroyers, good men and the friends of humanity cannot help it. Nor can they, but to a small extent, furnish relief to their wretched families. Though they go with an angel's kindness, and with an angel's freeness pour it out upon them, the deacon, or the church-member, or some other retailer, for twenty-five cents will throw that whole family, for days, into all the agonies, the heart-rending, heart-breaking agonies, of having a drunken and an infuriated maniac for a husband and a father! Yes, for twenty-five cents, he will hear the scream of the children, and see them run away and hide, and hear the groans of her who cannot get away; and though she comes, when the storm is over, and beseeches him with tears, not to sell her husband the madman's poison, for she and her children—and her tongue falters as she says, *children*—cannot endure it; yet, for twenty-five cents, he will sell it yet again and again, till, as was the case in one instance, the husband and the father went home from the deacon's store, and under the influence of what the deacon had given him, murdered his wife! She will never again beseech him, for her children's sake, and the Saviour's sake, not to sell her husband rum. No; she will not complain, nor will she beseech him any more. But his own children may do both. One of them, on hearing of this murder and the circumstances, said, 'Father, do you not think, that in the day of judgment, *you* will have to answer for that murder?' And must not conscience, when awakened, echo, '*Murder, murder!*' Why? did he murder that woman? No; but he gave her husband that which excited him to do it; when he knew, from the testimony of judges and jurists, that it caused more than three-fourths of all the murders in the United States. And why did he do it? For money. How much? A sum so great that a man could not withstand it? No; for less than twenty-five cents! Yes, for less than twenty-five cents those children were made orphans; and their father, when our agent passed through that part of the country, was in prison, to be tried for his life for murdering their mother! And all his excuse was, he was excited to do it by what he received from the deacon. No wonder his child should beseech him to give up the traffic, and warn him with tears, that if he did not do it, he would be, at the day of judgment, stained with the guilt of blood.

"It is an established principle of law, for the violation of which men have been hanged, that the accessory and the principal in the commission of crime, are both guilty. If this principle is correct, and applies to divine as well as human law, and the drunkard cannot enter heaven, what will be the condition of him who is accessory to the making of drunkards; who furnishes the materials, and for the sake of gain, sends them out to all who will purchase them, when he knows the nature and effects of this employment? Can he enter heaven?

"The Committee do not ask these questions concerning those who were engaged in this traffic when its nature and effects were not known, and when it was supposed to be consistent with the Christian religion; but only concerning those who, since its nature and consequences are known, and known to be ruinous to the temporal and eternal interests of men, still continue it. And they do not make such inquiries concerning them, but with the kindest feelings, both towards them and the community.

"But when it is known that more than two murders in a week, upon an average, are committed in the United States, through the influence of ardent spirit, and that more than five hundred persons in a week are killed by the use of it, they cannot but present this subject, kindly and plainly, to the consideration of all sober men.

"It is now known, that hundreds of thousands have ceased to use this liquor, and that their health and comfort, and those of their families, have been greatly improved; that the amount and severity of sickness have lessened, and the number of paupers, crimes, and deaths been diminished. It is known that while men continue to use this liquor, intemperance can never be prevented, and its evils never be done away. It is known too that it tends, when used even moderately, to hinder the efficacy of the gospel and prevent the salvation of men, and thus to ruin them, not for time only, but for eternity. All this is known, and known to the owners of ardent spirit. And if they, notwithstanding this, not only suffer it to go abroad, but sell it to all who will buy; send it out, and spread it through the community; let them know, let it be told, and let it echo through creation, that they, by Jehovah, will be held responsible at his tribunal for its effects. To the pauperism, crimes, and wretchedness, the sickness, insanity, and deaths, which it occasions, and to the ruin, temporal and eternal, they are knowingly and voluntarily accessory. And of all the obstructions which the friends of temperance now meet with, which stand in the way and hinder the progress of that mighty movement which God has awakened, and which takes hold on the destinies of unborn millions for eternity, these men, yes, the men who traffic in ardent spirit, present the greatest.

"And if this movement is ever to be stayed, and that deluge of fire again roll, unobstructed, through the length and breadth of this land, scorching and withering, consuming and annihilating, all that is fair and lovely and excellent, and glorious in possession and in prospect, these men, the men who continue to traffic in ardent spirit, are to bear a vast and ever-growing portion of the odium, the guilt, and the retribution of this tremendous ruin. They not only sin themselves, but they tempt others to sin. They stand at the fountain of death, and open streams which may roll onwards after they are dead, and sweep multitudes to the world of woe.

"But we do not believe, and we shall not admit, till we behold it, that this mighty movement which God has commenced, and hitherto carried forward with a rapidity and to an extent altogether unexampled in the history of man, and which is now spoken of, in both hemispheres, as one of the wonders of the world, is ever to stop, till the use of ardent spirit, and the traffic in it as an article of luxury or diet, is abandoned by every good man in our country. We cannot believe that any good man, or any man that expects to render an account for the influence which he exerts on the world, when he sees what he is doing, will consent, for the sake of money, to be actively instrumental in destroying the bodies and souls of men. We cannot believe that, for the sake of money, good men will consent, when they know what they do, to deal out the cause of pauperism and crime, sickness, insanity, and death—to raise a barrier against the influences of the Holy Spirit, and help the great adversary to people the world of woe. Even should human governments continue to license such a business, we cannot believe that good men, or any who regard the welfare of their fellow-men, will continue to consent to take out such a license, or to use it, for all the wealth of the world. That *light and love* which have already led more than one million to give up the use of ardent spirit, and more than three thousand who were engaged in the traffic, to renounce it, will, we trust, if kindly, universally, and perseveringly diffused, and attended, as they have been, by the mighty power of Him who worketh all in all, lead all good men to do the same.

"More than one thousand distilleries have already been stopped; and the owners of many would not again open them for the wealth of creation. In one town, in which were sixteen of these fountains of death, there are now but three; and those, it is believed, furnish a less quantity of the poison, destroy a less number of lives, and ruin fewer souls, than they did when the whole were in operation. One brass-founder states that he has bought thirty stills, and sold but one. In many towns, this destroyer is not even sold. Among more than one hundred thousand people, none, except keepers of public-houses, have license to sell it; and from more than one hundred public-houses it is excluded. The owners will not consent, for the sake of money, to poison even the traveller; and he finds, often to his amazement, that he can be received cheerfully, treated politely, and refreshed abundantly, by those who furnish nothing adapted to destroy him. And why, should these and similar facts be made known to all, and the Holy Spirit incline them to their duty, may we not expect this to be the case throughout our land, and throughout the world?"

A request having been presented to him that he would supply, "for a few Sabbaths or a few months," the Presbyterian church in Morristown, New Jersey, in reference to a settlement, he replied, July 8, "Were it consistent with duty, it would give me great pleasure to be with my family more than I can in my present business as Secretary of the American Temperance Society; and were I to settle again in the ministry, no part of the country would be more pleasant to me, on account of the climate as favorable to my health, and on account of its being a region which the Lord hath blessed, than the state of New Jersey. But so far as I can judge, the great interests of our country and the world, and the greatest success of the gospel in the salvation of men, seem to require that I should continue, for the present, my connection with the Temperance Society."

To his family, at the opening of the new year.

"Boston, Jan. 2, 1832.

"My dear Wife—Rev. Mr. Mead of East Hartford, Rev. Mr. Mitchell of Norwich, Rev. Mr. Sanford of Philadelphia, and Rev. Mr. Jenkins of Portland, all ministers in the midst of life, have died within a few weeks. So frail is human life, that man in his best estate is altogether vanity. 'He cometh forth as a flower, and is cut down;' but the word of the Lord endureth for ever. Blessed, truly and for ever and supremely blessed, are all those who trust in him, and who delight in keeping his commandments. Though they die, it is but to live with Christ and angels and good men, free from pain, from sickness, from sorrow and from sin, for ever and ever. They would not wish to come back to this world if they could; for to be with Christ is far better.

"All the feelings, thoughts, words, and actions of the last year, and of our whole past lives, are now written in the book of God's remembrance, and closed up for the judgment of the great day, then to be exhibited before the assembled world. Happy, unspeakably happy, are all those, and those only, who have Jesus Christ for their friend. Better, infinitely better, to have Christ, than to have all the world besides. Let us this year resolve to live wholly *for him*, to act as in his presence, and seek in all things to please him, daily and heartily to commune with him, listen to his voice speaking in the Bible, give him our hearts, do good as we have opportunity, and keep our end continually in view; that when absent from the body, we may be present with the Lord."

CHAPTER VIII.

LABORS IN THE TEMPERANCE REFORMATION—CONTINUED.

TWO YEARS—1832, 1833.

EARLY in 1832, Dr. Edwards wrote a powerful "NATIONAL CIRCULAR, addressed to the head of each family in the United States," which was issued in tens of thousands of copies, not only by the American Temperance Society, but by the American Tract Society at Boston and at New York. Having presented a cheering view of the wonders God had wrought in the Temperance reformation, and many motives which should induce all individually to adopt the pledge of total abstinence from ardent spirit, he proceeds:

"*It destroys the soul.* It makes sinners more sinful, and prevents them from experiencing God's illuminating and purifying power. It tends directly and strongly to make men feel—as Jesus Christ hates—rich spiritually, increased in goods, and in need of nothing; and for ever to prevent them from feeling as men must feel, in order to be interested in the blessings of his salvation. The Holy Spirit will not visit, much less dwell with him who is under the polluting, debasing effects of intoxicating drink. That state of mind and heart which this occasions, is to Him a loathing and an utter abomination. Not only does it darken the understanding, sear the conscience, pollute the affections, and debase all the powers of the soul, but it counteracts the merciful designs of Jehovah, and all the overflowing kindness of an infinitely compassionate Saviour for its deliverance, binds the soul in hopeless bondage to its destroyers, awakens the 'worm which dieth not,' and the 'fire which is not quenched,' and drives the soul away in despair, weeping and wailing, to be punished with everlasting destruction from the presence of the Lord and the glory of his power.

"And yet these evils, great as they are, rising up to heaven, and overwhelming as, if continued, they certainly will be, may nevertheless, *with perfect ease, all be done away.* Let each individual cease to use intoxicating drinks, and intemperance with all its abominations will vanish; and temperance, with all its blessings to body and soul, will universally prevail. Our three million children may come forward into life without the habit of using intoxicating liquor, without any appetite for it, or any expectation of benefit from the use of it. And such a generation they may be as this world never saw; to show, by their blessings, the glory of free institutions, and the brighter glories of the gospel of the Son of God, and to spread a light which shall cause ignorance and vice, desolation and wretchedness, over the whole earth, for ever to flee away. We therefore cannot but confidently anticipate that you, and your family, will cheerfully, for the sake of doing good, add to the pledge which is annexed the influence of your names.

"But some may say, 'Why sign a pledge? Why is it not as well, and even better, for each one to abstain, take care of himself, and let all others do the same? What is the benefit of visible, organized union?' Do you remember the time when your fathers and mothers could not drink tea, without sanctioning that odious principle, taxation without representation? And what did the men of '76 say? Let each one take care of himself? Let us have no visible agreement, no pledge? Hear the voice of the delegates of Virginia, assembled at Williamsburg, August 1, 1774:

"'Considering the article of *tea* as the *detestable instrument* which laid the foundation of the present sufferings of our distressed friends in Boston, *we view it with horror;* and therefore,

"'*Resolved, That we will not, from this day, import tea of any kind whatever, nor will we use it, nor suffer such as may now be on hand to be used in any of our families.*'

"They invited others throughout the country to join them. They did so; and the effects were felt across the Atlantic. They are felt throughout our country, and they will be felt in every land, to the end of time. What was the benefit of that combination, that visible agreement, that universal pledge? *Strength, action,* SUCCESS. Suppose each man, when the armies of oppression were poured in upon our country, had said, I will abstain from helping them; and I will abstain too from all visible agreement with others to oppose them. I will make no pledge; and when I fight, will fight single-handed, and do my own fighting in my own way. Then had the enemy triumphed, and we never had been free. And if we could not conquer Britons without visible organized union, can we conquer that before which, not only Britons, but Americans too, have fallen? and in vastly greater numbers than fell for their country's independence?

"But why, it is asked, should *women* belong to temperance societies? Because, under the light of the gospel, which raises women in excellence of character and ability to do good to an equality with men, every association composed of both will more than double its influence over the public mind, especially over the minds of *youth and children.* And the grand object of efforts for the promotion of temperance is, the salvation of the children. And to accomplish it, we need, and must have, the influence of *mothers* as well as fathers, *sisters* as well as brothers.

"There is another reason why all women should unite with temperance societies. More than a hundred thousand of the lovely daughters of the last generation were doomed to the tremendous curse of having drunken husbands, and rearing their little ones under the blasting, withering influence of drunken fathers. But there is no need of it. Let the fathers and mothers, the brothers and sisters of this generation, all cease to use intoxicating drinks, and unite their influence in temperance societies, and the daughters of the next generation, and of all future generations practising on this plan, shall be for ever free.

"And there is another reason why women should belong to temperance societies. Multitudes of the last generation were made drunkards by the customs of society. Though the appetite for ardent spirit is not natural, and would never exist were it not formed by the use of it, it has been formed, not only in the cradle, but in many cases has been coeval almost with life itself. Even the mother, when her infant was unwell and she did not wish during the night to be kept awake with it, drank the poison herself, and the helpless babe slept like a drunkard, and for a similar reason; and the drunkard's appetite was formed there; and, as if that were not enough, as it lay in the cradle, she fed it with a teaspoon, and the drunkard's appetite was strengthened; and no sooner could it walk than the father, after he had been drinking, gave it the bottom of the glass, sweetened in the most enchanting manner; and the drunkard's appetite was confirmed. And before the heedless youth had entered upon manhood, he stumbled into the drunkard's grave, was covered up, and his destroyers were glad to forget him. But there is no need of it. Let the customs of society be changed, and each individual unite with others, to touch not, taste not, and handle not the abominable thing, and the evil will be done away. Generations yet unborn, to all future ages, saved, by simply ceasing to do evil and learning to do well, will rise up and call you blessed.

"PLEDGE.

"We whose names are hereunto annexed, believing that the use of ardent spirit, as a drink," [changed in a reissue of this circular in 1835 to read, "that the use of *intoxicating liquor as a beverage*,"] "is not only needless, but hurtful to the social, civil, and religious interests of men; that it tends to form intemperate appetites and habits; and that, while it is continued, the evils of intemperance can never be done away; do therefore agree that we will not use it, or traffic in it; that we will not provide it as an article of entertainment or for persons in our employment; and that, in all suitable ways, we will discountenance the use of it in the community."

On the 30th of May, 1832, another Temperance anniversary was held in Boston, and Dr. Edwards presented the Second Permanent Temperance Document, showing, by an array of facts and testimonies of the deepest interest, the moral wrong, not only of the *use* of ardent spirit as a drink, but of the TRAFFIC in it.

In one town which he visited, he says, "There was but one man who sold ardent spirit, and he was a member of the church. There were one-fourth as many drunkards in that place as there were families; and he supplied them all. He supplied, also, all moderate drinkers with that which is adapted to make them drunkards, to ruin their children, and to perpetuate a drunkard to every four families to all future generations. At one time his own son, in the house and business of his father, was dealing out this poison, and partaking of it himself, till he became so poisoned that he could not stand; and was carried home to his heart-broken wife and children, in a state of intoxication. This, you say, is horrible, horrible. It is, indeed. Yet it is the very business in which are many church-members, even in New England. Some of this character have, the last year, been admitted to the churches, who are as really accessory to the making of drunkards, as was this man. If they do not make drunkards of their own children, they do of the children of others. And the committee cannot but deeply regret that Boston, the metropolis of the pilgrims, exalted by blessings to heaven, and which ought to be a light and a glory to all lands, should have churches in which there are members who make it a business to stand at these poisonous fountains, and pour out streams of death over the community; thus teaching by their business, in the most impressive way, that for men to buy and use ardent spirit is right—a doctrine that has probably, during the past century, polluted more hearts, beggared more families, destroyed more lives, and ruined more souls, than any other heresy or crime whatever. And so long as the churches shall connive at such deadly evils in their members, may they expect to be visited with the withering curse of the Almighty. They cannot hold the protecting banner of the cross over such enormities, and escape the blasting indignation of Him who bled upon it, to redeem unto himself a peculiar people, zealous only of *good* works. Not only are they ruining men by thousands for the next world, but most unjustly and cruelly loading the community with tremendous burdens in this.

"As certainly as the nature of man continues the same, and light on this subject continues to increase, this conviction will extend, till it shall become universal. It fastens, even now, upon the seared conscience of many a retailer himself. Said one who during the past year renounced this traffic, laying his hand on his heart, 'You can't think what a load I have got off here.' He had been the whole round of excuses for continuing the business; had persevered in the contest between covetousness and conscience, until he had fought every inch of ground; but, 'I have lain awake,' said he, 'night after night, and night after night, thinking of it.' *Thinking of what?* That he was engaged in a work of death; that for the wretchedness, temporal and eternal, which he was occasioning, he must answer at the tribunal of God—thinking that it would profit him nothing to gain the world and lose his soul, or be instrumental in destroying the souls of others. Yes, he lay awake night after night, thinking of it. It is the determination of God that men shall *think* of it. His providence is pressing it upon their minds. Light has penetrated even the thick darkness which surrounds the distiller's conscience and the wholesale dealer's."

Going on to illustrate the enormity of the sin, by testimonies from judges on the bench, officers of the army and navy, and other sources; and then looking at the conquests already won, the thousands who had refrained from drinking and were rejoicing in hope of the glory of God; and thousands who, continuing to drink, had rejected "glory, honor, and eternal life," and many of whom were weeping and wailing beyond the boundaries of hope, he says, in burning words:

"And shall we be told, that temperance is only a *secular* concern; that it affects only the bodies of men, not their souls, and is a concern which relates to time only, not to eternity; and that it ought not to be discussed from the pulpit on the Sabbath? Should Satan cause this to be believed, he would perpetuate intemperance to the end of the world. Shall the fires which make this poison burn on the Sabbath, and the use of it tend to counteract all the merciful designs of Jehovah in establishing that holy day; shall Jehovah be insulted by the appearance in the sanctuary of men who use it on the Sabbath; and yet the Sabbath not be occupied, by light and love, to abolish the use of it? Shall it cause the word of the Lord, even from the pulpit, to fall as upon a rock, instead of being as the rain and the snow that come down from heaven and water the earth; and cause thousands who might be trees of righteousness in the garden of the Lord, to stand like the heath in the desert, not seeing good when good comes—and yet the pulpit be dumb? or speak only on week-days, when those who traffic in it have so much to do in furnishing the poison, that they have no time, and less inclination to hear? If Satan can cause this to be believed, and those who manufacture, sell, and use the weapons of his warfare, and multiply the trophies of his victory, not hear of their sin on the Sabbath, when God speaks to the conscience; or be entreated from the pulpit, his mercy's seat, by the tears and blood of a Saviour, to flee from coming wrath—the adversary will keep possession of his strong-hold. *There is no coping with him, but with weapons of heavenly temper from the armory of Jehovah, on the day when he goes forth, and creation, at his command, stands still to witness the conflict.* Then it is, as conscience kindled from above blazes and thunders in the heart of the enemy, that he is consumed by the breath of the Almighty, and destroyed by the brightness of his coming.

"Never was an idea farther from the truth, than that which represents the Temperance reformation as *only a secular concern*, affecting principally the body;

or confined in its influence to this world, or to time. Its principal influence, and that which in importance eclipses and swallows up every other, is upon the soul, and for eternity. And let ministers and churches do their duty, free themselves from all participation in, or connivance at iniquity, and let them, by light and love, poured out kindly and perpetually, labor to persuade all, from supreme regard to God and good will to men, to do the same, and the night and woe of ages will pass away, and the Sun of righteousness, rising in his glory, will pour round the globe the life and the bliss of universal and unceasing day.

"And when Ethiopia is rising and stretching out her hands, and the isles of the sea are receiving and obeying God's law; when China is struggling to keep off death from her people, Iceland in supplication for deliverance is melting, and the whole creation groaneth and travaileth in pain; when the Saviour, with a voice which pervades creation, is proclaiming, Who is on the Lord's side? Who? and the universe look with intense gaze to witness the result; and when a single individual, by coming out openly and decidedly on the Lord's side, and sacrificing, in a single instance, money to duty, may roll a wave of salvation on the other side of the globe—shall professed members of that church which Christ has bought with his blood, take part with the enemy of all good, and assist in perpetuating his dark and dismal reign over souls, to endless ages? If they do, God will write, for the universe to look at, *To whom they yield themselves servants to obey, his servants they are.* And the register, in blazing capitals, will be eternal. And though men who continue knowingly and habitually to do evil, and to hate the light, may, in this world, refuse to come to it, and when it approaches them may attempt to flee away; in the future world it will blaze upon them in one unclouded vision of infinite brightness, and show the hearts of all who persevere in wickedness to be more black than darkness itself for ever."

While his mind and heart were full of this subject, Dr. Edwards wrote the able document on "THE IMMORALITY OF THE TRAFFIC IN ARDENT SPIRIT," which is not only embodied in the Permanent Temperance Documents, but constitutes Tract No. 125 of the American Tract Society's series, and is a standard treatise, combining convincing argument and the most rousing and tender appeal.

Having constructed the body of the document, showing the nature of ardent spirit, and its destructive influence for the life that now is and that which is to come, and noticed the more common and plausible *excuses* for engaging in the traffic, he says,

"Suppose a man, when about to commence the traffic in ardent spirit, should write IN GREAT CAPITALS ON HIS SIGN-BOARD, to be seen and read of all men, what he will do: That so many of the inhabitants of this town or city, he will, for the sake of getting their money, make paupers, and send them to the almshouse, and thus oblige the whole community to support them and their families; that so many others he will excite to the commission of crimes, and thus increase the expenses and endanger the peace and welfare of the community; that so many he will send to the jail, and so many more to the state prison, and so many to the gallows; that so many he will visit with sore and distressing diseases, and, in so many cases, diseases which would have been comparatively harmless, he will by his poison render fatal; that in so many cases he will deprive persons of reason, and in so many cases will cause sudden death; that so many wives he will make widows, and so many children he will make orphans, and that in so many cases he will cause the children to grow up in ignorance, vice, and crime, and after being nuisances on earth, will bring them to a premature grave; that in so many cases he will prevent the efficacy of the gospel, grieve away the Holy Ghost, and ruin for eternity the souls of men. And suppose he could, and should give some faint conception of what it is to lose the soul, and of the overwhelming guilt and coming wretchedness of him who is knowingly instrumental in producing this ruin; and suppose he should put at the bottom of the sign this question: What, you may ask, can be my object in acting so much like a devil incarnate, and bringing such accumulated wretchedness upon a comparatively happy people? and under it should put the true answer, MONEY; and go on to say, I have a family to support; I want money, and must have it; this is my business, I was brought up to it; and if I should not follow it, I must change my business, or I could not support my family. And as all faces begin to gather blackness at the approaching ruin, and all hearts to boil with indignation at its author, suppose he should add, for their consolation, 'If I do not bring this destruction upon you, somebody else will.' What would they think of him? what would all the world think of him? what *ought* they to think of him? And is it any worse for a man to tell the people beforehand, honestly, what he will do, if they buy and use his poison, than it is to go on and do it? And what if they are not aware of the mischief which he is doing them, and he can accomplish it through their own perverted and voluntary agency? Is it not equally abominable, if *he knows* it, and does not cease from producing it?

"And if there are churches whose members are doing such things, and those churches are not blessed with the presence and favor of the Holy Ghost, they need not be at any loss for the reason. And if they should *never* again, while they continue in this state, be blessed with the reviving influence of God's Spirit, they need not be at any loss for the reason. Their own members are exerting a strong and fatal influence against it; and that too, after divine Providence has shown them what they are doing. And in many such cases there is awful guilt, with regard to this thing, resting upon the whole church. Though they have known for years what these men were doing, have seen the misery, heard the oaths, witnessed the crimes, and known the wretchedness and deaths which they have occasioned, and perhaps have spoken of it and deplored it to one another, many of them have never spoken on this subject to the persons themselves. They have seen them scattering firebrands, arrows, and death, temporal and eternal; and yet have never so much as warned them on the subject, and never besought them to give up their work of death. Every brother in such a case is bound, on his own account, to converse with him who is thus aiding the powers of darkness, and opposing the kingdom of Jesus Christ, and try to persuade him to cease from this destructive business. And the whole church is bound to make efforts, and use all proper means, to accomplish this result. And before half the individual members have done their duty on this subject, they may expect, if the offending brother has, and manifests the spirit of Christ, that he will cease to be an offence to his brethren, and a stumbling-block to the world, over which such multitudes fall to the pit of woe.

"Professed Christian, you have been redeemed, not with silver, nor with gold, but with the precious blood of Jesus Christ. When all were dead, he died that they who live should not live unto themselves, but unto him that died for them and rose again. In the manufacture or sale of ardent spirit as a drink, you do not and you cannot honor God; but you do, and so long as you continue it, you will greatly dishonor him. You exert an influence which tends directly and strongly to ruin, for both worlds, your fellow-men. Should you take a quantity of that poisonous liquid into *your closet,* present it before the Lord, confess to him its nature and effects, spread out before him what it has done and what it will do, and attempt to ask him to bless you in extending its influence; it would, unless your conscience is already seared as with a hot iron, appear to you like blasphemy. You could no more do it, than you could take the instruments of gambling, and attempt to ask God to bless you in extending them through the community. And why not, if it is a lawful business? Why not ask God to increase it, make you an instrument in extending it over the country, and perpetuating it to all future generations? Even the worldly and profane man, when he hears about professing Christians offering prayer to God, that he would bless them in the manufacture or sale of ardent spirit, involuntarily shrinks back, and says, 'That is too bad.' He can see that it is an abomination. And if it is too bad for a professed Christian to pray about it, is it not too bad for him to practise it? If you continue, under all the light which God in his providence has furnished with regard to its hurtful nature and destructive effects, to furnish ardent spirit as a drink for your fellow-men, you will run the fearful hazard of losing your soul, and you will exert an influence which powerfully tends to destroy the souls of your fellow-men. Every time you furnish it, you are rendering it less likely that they will be illuminated, sanctified, and saved, and more likely that they will continue in sin, and go down to the chambers of death.

"My friend, you are soon to die, and in eternity to witness the influence, the whole influence which you exert while on earth, and you are to witness its consequences, in joy or sorrow, to endless being. Imagine yourself now, where you will soon be, *on your death-bed.* And imagine that you have a full view of the property which you have caused to be wasted, or which you have gained without furnishing any valuable equivalent; of the health which you have destroyed, and the characters which you have demoralized; of the wives that you have made widows, and the children that you have made orphans; of all the lives that you have shortened, and all the souls that you have destroyed. O, imagine that these are the only 'rod and staff' which you have to comfort you, as you go down the valley of the shadow of death, and that they will all meet you in full array at the judgment, and testify against you. What will it profit you, though you have gained more money than you otherwise would, when you have left it all far behind in that world which is destined to fire, and the day of perdition of ungodly men? What will it profit when you are enveloped in the influence which you have exerted, and are experiencing its consequences to endless ages, finding for ever that as a man soweth so must he reap, and that if he has sowed death he must reap *death?* Do not any longer assist in destroying men, nor expose yourselves and your children to be destroyed. Do good, and good only, to all as you have opportunity, and good shall come unto you."

In a note to Mrs. Edwards, Feb. 14, 1832, he says, "You have probably heard before this, that Rev. Dr. Cornelius died, at Dr. Hawes' in Hartford, on Sabbath morning, of a brain-fever; brought on, probably, by excessive care, toil, and labor. His wife arrived there in the afternoon, and is a deeply afflicted widow. But the God of the widow, and the Father of the fatherless, will no doubt provide for her, and hers."

The Rev. President Davis, being about to retire, in advanced years, from the charge of Hamilton College, New York, wrote to Dr. Edwards, March 2, a full and earnest letter, spreading before him the history and claims of that institution, and its promise of future usefulness, and asking that he would allow himself to be a candidate for election to that office. To this application he felt constrained to reply:

"Yours of the 2d inst. has been made the subject of as much attention as my very numerous duties would permit. Considering the importance of my present situation to the great interests of the church and the world, and the difficulty of my leaving it, at present, without detriment to the Temperance cause; considering also, that my present employment appears to be highly favorable to the enjoyment of sound and vigorous health, and that you may probably unite in a man who has paid more attention, of late, to collegiate studies than I have, and might be more useful than I could be at the head of your college, it does not appear to me, at present, to be consistent with the will of Providence that I should consent to become a candidate for that very interesting, responsible, and important office."

The three following notes indicate some of the means which Dr. Edwards was employing, and how he was cheered on in his work by some of the worthiest of men.

"ALBANY, March 19, 1832.

"DEAR SIR—I have been confined to my chamber since November last by severe illness, which has incapacitated me to attend to business. You will please to receive this as my apology for not sooner attending to your communication. I will with pleasure be a contributor of one hundred dollars for a few years. We are making extra efforts here in our State Temperance Society, we think and hope successfully. May the Lord smile on our exertions, is the prayer of

"Yours sincerely,

"STEPHEN VAN RENSSELAER."

"BREMO, Fluvanna county, Va., Dec. 1832.

"DEAR SIR—Grateful for the benefit which the Temperance reformation is spreading throughout the Christian world, but especially for the happy effects I have seen resulting from it in my own neighborhood and county, I feel myself called upon to contribute some pecuniary aid to a cause which, excepting the propagation of the blessed gospel, in my humble opinion, stands second to none among the various Christian and benevolent enterprises of the day.

"I inclose you a check of the cashier of the branch Bank of the United States at Richmond, on the Boston branch of the same bank, for two hundred and fifty dollars. After deducting the cost of one hundred copies of the fourth, and one hundred copies of the fifth report, to be forwarded as herein after directed, add the balance to the funds of the American Temperance Society.

"Yours respectfully,

"JOHN H. COCKE."

He adds a list of about fifty distinguished clergymen and laymen at the south, to which he wishes a copy of both reports to be addressed, with an additional supply for the respected bishops of the Protestant Episcopal church.

"WASHINGTON, Jan. 18, 1833.

"DEAR SIR—I have just received your favor of the 15th inst., and thank you for the invitation to the anniversary of the American Temperance Society on the 7th May next. It will afford me great pleasure to enjoy the privilege of taking part in its exercises. A few of us, in Congress, contemplate the formation of a Congressional Temperance society on the 26th Feb. next. I hope we shall be enabled to carry such a plan into operation. There seems to be an influence resulting from sayings and doings *here*, that is peculiar, and I think we are bound to cast it all on the side of good principles. I trust the Lord will attend and succeed it with his blessing.

"Yours very truly,

"THEO. FRELINGHUYSEN."

In a communication to the committee of the New York City Temperance Society, February 1, 1833, he says, "I have attended in this city thirty-two meetings, and have four more engaged. The ward associations are all formed and in a course of successful operation. Eleven churches are free from all members connected with the traffic, and in seven others there is only one in each, who it is hoped will be out of the business soon. The members of the various Temperance societies in the city, I think, are now more than seven thousand."

He soon proceeded to Washington city, with a special view to organizing a Congressional Temperance society.

"WASHINGTON CITY, Feb. 15, 1833.

"MY DEAR SONS AND DAUGHTERS—I left New York on Friday, spent the Sabbath in Philadelphia at Mr. Henry Bird's, and arrived here on Wednesday. I have been up this morning to the Senate chamber, where are Mr. Webster, Mr. Clay, Mr. Calhoun, etc. Mr. Calhoun has to-day been speaking. He expects to finish to-morrow, and then Mr. Webster will speak.

"There is now in Congress one man, Mr. Choate of Salem, who, like Justin, was a little boy in the academy, long since I came to Andover. And if Justin lives he will soon be old enough, and so will each of his brothers, to be in Congress; and if they are good, they may be in a much more useful and honorable place, namely, the pulpit, or in some log-hut, or under some green tree, teaching men how to become, not citizens, or even rulers of an earthly kingdom, but citizens of heaven, and even kings and priests unto God, and to reign with him for ever and ever. *To be good, is to be great in the best sense; and to be useful from the love of doing good, is to be happy.*"

The next day he writes, "The prospect now is, of having a great Temperance meeting on the evening of the 24th, and of forming a Congressional Temperance society under favorable auspices on the 26th. A paper signed by ten of the Senators is now circulating in the House for the signatures of those who are disposed to unite in it.

"The chaplain of the House has to-day applied to me, in consequence of the application of members to him, to supply his place to-morrow in the capitol, which, with the divine leave, I now expect to do, and to reason with the members, 'of righteousness, *temperance,* and judgment to come.'"

Three days later he says, "I preached in the capitol on the Sabbath on the subject of temperance, and for

Rev. Mr. Post in the afternoon. Large assemblies, and many members of Congress in both places. Fourteen of the Senate have signed a paper declaring their readiness to join a *Congressional Temperance society* on the 26th, and the paper is now circulating for signatures in the House. Among the men in the Senate are Webster, Wilkins, Dallas, Grundy, Ewing, Tipton, Sprague, Tomlinson, etc. The prospect so far looks well. Col. Richard M. Johnson has engaged this morning to apply for the capitol in order to have in it a great Temperance meeting, and says he will carry it by acclamation. There are in the House a number who are no friends to temperance; but the cause is evidently rising, and is viewed by many as a cause more interesting to our country, and more important in its prospective influence, than any which has agitated Congress.

"One of the largest mail contractors in the United States has concluded to have no man drive any of his stages who drinks ardent spirit. Let that course be taken by all stages, steam-boats, and railroads, and on all public works, and thousands of lives will be saved, and if adopted by all who hear the gospel, thousands of souls too."

The "American Congressional Temperance Society" was organized, as proposed, on the 26th, under favorable auspices; and having returned to Boston, he writes, March 15, "On Wednesday, by invitation from the Speaker of the House of Representatives, I came down to attend a meeting of the members of the legislature of Massachusetts, which is to be holden in the Representatives' hall this evening, for the purpose of forming a '*Massachusetts Legislative Temperance Society*;'" which was also successfully organized.

On the 7th of May, 1833, a summary view of Dr. Edwards' labors for another year was presented to the American Temperance Society, whose anniversary was then held in the city of New York. The great principles and facts which had been spread before the country and the world in the first and second Permanent Temperance documents, had been received with favor, and were producing happy results. Of the first, issued in 1831, two editions of 10,000 and 5,000 copies were printed in this country, and two editions in England; in an abridged form 10,000 were issued, and of an abstract of the document 170,000 more. Of the second Permanent document, 14,000 were printed in this country, and it was reprinted entire in England; and of the "Immorality of the Traffic," included in that document, 40,000 were circulated separately; making of both documents, or parts of them, about two hundred and fifty thousand copies. Numerous periodical and other Temperance publications were issued in various parts of the country; agents were employed by state and county societies, and the work was rapidly advancing.

On the 26th of February, not only the *American Congressional Temperance Society* had been formed, but simultaneous meetings had been held extensively, both in the United States and Great Britain. The Secretary of War had abolished spirit rations in the army, substituting therefor sugar and coffee; and temperance had been introduced into several ships of the navy. The General Conference of the Methodist Episcopal church, and numerous other ecclesiastical bodies, had also taken action on the subject, the spirit of which is indicated in the language of the General Assembly of the Presbyterian church, who said,

"It is now a well-established fact, that the common use of strong drink, *however moderate*, has been a *fatal, soul-destroying* barrier against the influence of the gospel. Consequently, wherever total abstinence is practised, a powerful instrument of resisting the Holy Spirit is removed, and a new avenue of access to the hearts of men opened to the power of truth. Thus in numerous instances, and in various places, during the past year the Temperance reformation has been a harbinger, preparing the way of the Lord; and the banishment of that *liquid poison*, which kills both soul and body, has made way for the immediate entrance of the Spirit and the word, the glorious train of the Redeemer. But a great work is still to be effected in the church. The sons of Levi must be purified. The *accursed thing* must be removed from the camp of the Lord. While professing Christians continue to exhibit the baleful example of tasting the *drunkard's poison*, or, by a *sacrilegious traffic*, to make it their employment to degrade and destroy their fellow-men, those who love the Lord must not keep silence, but must lift up their warning voice, and use all lawful efforts to remove this withering reproach from the house of God."

At this time Dr. Edwards issued the able document, "LAWS WHICH AUTHORIZE THE TRAFFIC IN ARDENT SPIRIT AS A DRINK, MORALLY WRONG."

"The American Temperance Society," he says, "at the commencement, took the ground that to *drink* ardent spirit is morally wrong; and in their reports they have exhibited the reasons which demonstrate its truth. Millions in this country have embraced this truth, and are now acting under its influence. Its influence has also been extended to other countries, and great numbers in foreign lands are imitating our example.

"The next position taken by the society was, that it is wicked to *make* ardent spirit, or to *furnish it* to be drunk by others. This too they accompanied by legitimate and abundant proof; and it has been embraced, as whole counties in which it is now a violation even of human law to sell it, and a thousand churches in which there is not a man who prosecutes the business, and thousands of other churches that are struggling to throw off the mighty incubus, abundantly testify. It is shown also by the existence of more than six thousand Temperance societies, embracing more than a million of members, pledged to abstain from the drinking of ardent spirit, and from the traffic in it, and also to use all suitable means to cause this to become universal. The means by which such a result may be expected, is the universal conviction that the drinking of ardent spirit, or the furnishing it to be drunk by others, is sin; an offence against God, and injurious to the temporal and eternal interests of men. Whatever tends to produce this conviction, tends to promote the Temperance reformation; and whatever tends to prevent the one, tends to hinder the other.

"Perhaps nothing now stands more in the way of producing this conviction, and causing it to become universal, than the fact that the traffic in ardent spirit *is authorized by law;* and thus receives the sanction and support of legislation. This is a public testimony to the world that the sale of ardent spirit, and of course the drinking of it, are right: a fundamental and fatal error, destructive in its effects to the life that now is, and to that which is to come. The next thing to be accomplished therefore, is *by the universal diffusion of information and the exertion of kind moral influence, to produce throughout the community the conviction, that the laws which authorize the traffic in ardent spirit as a drink, by licensing men to pursue it, are morally wrong*, opposed in their influence to the laws of God; and that the public good, instead of requiring that some men should sell it, utterly forbids that this should be done by any; and that no men or body of men who understand, or have the means of understanding this subject, can be instrumental in making such laws without the commission of sin. And as such laws are *morally* wrong, they never can be politically right, or beneficial, or expedient. While Jehovah lives, righteousness, and that alone, will exalt a nation; sin in any form, and especially if sanctioned by law, will be a reproach and a nuisance to any people."

He proceeds to a calm, logical discussion of the subject, supported by acknowledged principles and facts, and adds,

"Over wide regions of country, where the facts are known, and a part of the people abstain from the use of ardent spirit, and from the traffic in it, and a part do not, as the committee behold ten times as many in proportion to the number, of one class enlisting apparently under the banners of Immanuel, as of the other; and see the number from one, as light increases, constantly and rapidly increasing, and from the other as constantly and rapidly diminishing, they cannot but feel, that the laws which sanction the traffic and use, and proclaim them to be right, are radically and morally wrong, offensive to the Saviour, and hostile to the temporal and eternal interests of men. And they cannot but *most respectfully and kindly, earnestly and perseveringly entreat* the legislators of our country, by the rich mercies which he has so bountifully bestowed upon it, and by the agonies which he so freely endured for our race, and the glories which he so graciously proffers them, no longer to sanction these iniquities, or say by legislation that they are either useful or right. As He poured out life to redeem them, and would have all men come to the knowledge and love of his truth, and be his obedient and glorified people, they would beseech legislators no longer to do what tends so powerfully, extensively, and fatally to hinder it."

CHAPTER IX.

LABORS IN THE TEMPERANCE REFORMATION—CONTINUED.

THREE YEARS—1833-1836

On the 24th of May, 1833, a National Temperance Convention, called by the American Temperance Society, was held at the Hall of Independence in Philadelphia, at which were assembled *four hundred delegates from Temperance Societies in twenty-one states*, embracing much of the intelligence, piety, and patriotism of the nation. The Hon. Reuben H. Walworth presided, and Dr. Edwards was chairman of the business committee. It should be recorded with gratitude to God, that this large Convention, one of the most influential bodies that ever assembled for such an object in our country, united in adopting twenty-eight resolutions which embodied in substance all the great principles and aims of the Temperance movement.

The resolution "that *the traffic* in ardent spirit, to be used as a drink, is morally wrong, and ought to be universally abandoned," received the most calm and solemn deliberation. "Many," says Dr. Edwards, "were anxious to know what the physicians, the jurists, and the statesmen, assembled from all parts of the country, thought upon this subject. As the discussion proceeded, and the manifest and enormous immorality of the traffic was exhibited, the Convention not only saw that it is an immorality, but that it was a duty which they owed to God, to themselves, and to society, to express their deep and solemn conviction of this truth, and to publish it as extensively as possible, for the benefit of mankind. And seldom has any act of a public body, designed to operate by moral influence, been hailed with greater gladness, or promised to do greater good. Passed as it was, after long and full discussion, in a body composed of men of all professions and employments, and of all Christian denominations and political parties, and from all parts of the country, and in accordance with the fundamental truth which the American Temperance Society and various other bodies of men had been propagating for years, its influence was felt throughout the land. Numbers who had not before done it, were now led to examine the subject in the light of the moral law; and the more extensive the examination, the more deep and general has been the conviction, that the sentiment expressed by the Convention is eternal truth, the belief of which is of infinite importance, and that it ought to be published, with its evidence, and proclaimed throughout the world."

So deeply impressed was the Hon. Stephen Van Rensselaer of the powerful influence which these proceedings were calculated to exert, that he bore the expense of publishing *one hundred thousand copies* of the proceedings of the Convention for gratuitous distribution.

Other large and influential Temperance conventions were soon held in different states of the Union, in most of which Dr. Edwards took part, and all of which concurred substantially in the action of the National Convention. At the *Massachusetts* State Convention, held at Worcester, more than five hundred delegates, embracing distinguished gentlemen of all professions, were present, and the Governor of the state presided. A similar convention for the state of *New York* was held at Utica, and for the state of *Connecticut* at Middletown. An *Ohio* State Convention was held at Columbus, at which the Governor presided, and a Legislative Temperance Society was soon after organized. A *Mississippi* State Convention was held at Jackson, which recommended not only to abstain from ardent spirit, but from wine. A *Kentucky* State Convention was held at Frankfort, and a Legislative Temperance Society formed on the principle of abstinence both from ardent spirit and wine, and the Governor was made president. A convention was held and a State Temperance Society formed in *Missouri*. A State Society was formed in *Alabama*. A *Pennsylvania* State Temperance Convention was held at Harrisburg, and a Legislative Temperance Society formed. A *Delaware* State Convention was held at Dover. A State Convention was held in *New Jersey;* another in *Vermont;* another in *Maine;* and a convention of cities was held in New York.

"Thus," says Dr. Edwards, "has the sentiment that the *traffic* in ardent spirit is an immorality and ought to be universally abandoned, been expressed by bodies embracing more than five thousand ministers of the gospel, and six thousand Christian churches; by the American Congressional Temperance meeting, by the United States Temperance Convention, by ten State Temperance conventions, and numerous other bodies and classes of men, in various ways and places throughout the land.

"The truth that the traffic is wicked, strikes the evil at the root, and with a blow so strong and deep that it will inevitably destroy it. If the traffic is not a violation of the law of God, and by him forbidden, if the friends of temperance do not believe this truth and publish it with its evidence to all people, vain are all expectations that it will ever be exterminated. *There is no force but that which from the throne of God fastens on the conscience, and binds man according to his deeds irrevocably to an eternal retribution*, that is strong enough to say to this ocean of death, Hitherto shalt thou come, but no farther; and here let thy violence be stayed. And while this sentiment ought to be expressed, as it ought ever to be held, *with great kindness*, so it ought to be expressed, *with great plainness;* and in such a manner as is best adapted to produce universally the deepest conviction, and the most active and persevering efforts."

Of the injustice of gaining money by the traffic, he says, "The article which is put into the miserable victim's hand to induce him to give up his money, is not merely worthless—it is destructive. Its direct, well-known, universal, and inevitable tendency is to kill—to kill soul and body. What the retailer wants is his customer's three cents! He does not wish to kill him. He only gives him what kills him, because that is the only way to get his three cents. He does not wish to destroy the man for the very sake of destroying him. He does not desire, on its own account, to ruin his character, and take away his property, and break his wife's heart, and beggar and starve his children. No, his object is only to get the man's money, and he does these things, because that seems to him the shortest way to secure his three cents. All the money he makes, is worse than taken dishonestly. *It is the price of blood!* Every dollar he receives, instead of being a certificate of the amount of good he has done, is a certificate of the misery and ruin he has spread around him. His coin should be inscribed, 'This certifies that the bearer has made a man beat his wife.' 'This half dollar is a memorial of four nights of wretchedness, which were given to a whole family in exchange for it.' 'This bag of money certifies that the possessor has sent two of his neighbors to the jail, and their wives and children to the poor-house.' What money for a man to hold in his coffers! IT IS THE PRICE OF BLOOD!"

In the autumn of 1833, Dr. Edwards proceeded to a laborious and successful *tour of several months in the western states*, of which he writes to his family and friends many instructive facts and pleasing incidents, that we should gladly give more fully than our limits allow.

"CINCINNATI, Oct. 23, 1833.

"MY DEAR WIFE—I left Albany on Monday, the 7th; arrived at Buffalo on Friday morning; visited Niagara Falls, and spent the Sabbath at Buffalo; in the evening had a large and interesting temperance meeting; on Monday took the steam-boat on Lake Erie for Cleveland, and arrived on Tuesday night. Wednesday took the stage, and went one hundred and eighty-three miles to Springfield, Ohio, where I arrived on Saturday evening and spent the Sabbath; then took the stage and arrived here, seventy-two miles, on Monday night, through the great kindness of the Lord, in good health.

"Cincinnati is a beautiful city, on the north side of the Ohio, which here runs to the west; and as the mountains were round about Jerusalem, so they are round about Cincinnati. How long I shall remain here is uncertain; perhaps a month or two, if circumstances favor it."

Again he says, November 2, "We have just finished the week of anniversaries, which has been a very delightful one, and so far as I can judge, produced a fine impression. Things here appear in a promising state. I now expect to preach here tomorrow; and on Monday, if the Lord will, go with Dr. Beecher and Dr. Cogswell, to Lexington, Kentucky, eighty-four miles, where next week is to be another series of meetings, and the commencement of Transylvania University."

At Louisville, he writes, November 20, "From Lexington I went, on Tuesday of last week, to Frankfort, the capital of Kentucky, and on Wednesday had a Temperance meeting. On Thursday came to this place. Had a meeting last evening, and expect another this evening. On Monday or Tuesday of next week expect to leave this, if the Lord will, for St. Louis, by water, about eight hundred miles; then perhaps visit Jacksonville, about one hundred and twenty miles, and then return to Cincinnati.

"I find enough to do to *bring these ten states in the valley of the Mississippi to be temperate,* each one of which is six times as large as Massachusetts, and all equal to sixty such states."

In the introductory paragraph to the Fourth Permanent Temperance Document, presented May, 1834, at the anniversary of the American Temperance Society, held in the city of Philadelphia, Dr. Edwards notices as "auspicious peculiarities of the present age," that increasing numbers of people are disposed to inquire with regard to every moral principle and practice, *Is it right?* That the standard of right and wrong, with increasing numbers, is *the Bible.* That the number is rapidly increasing, who, when they learn that the Bible condemns a practice, will renounce it; and who, when they learn that it requires action, will attempt, with the spirit which the Bible inculcates, to perform it, whether other men do this or not. That there is a deeper conviction of *individual, personal responsibility directly to God,* binding each one, in all situations, for the character and tendency of his actions, to the retributions of eternity. That it is becoming more and more common, if a man wishes to have good done, to engage in it *himself,* and to do it *now;* and to aim at *the root* of evils, instead of merely attempting to lop off the branches.

"A striking development of these principles has been made in the Temperance reformation. A vicious practice had obtained, had received the sanction of legislation, and the support of the example of nearly the whole Christian world. But it was followed, as its natural and necessary result, by loss of property, character, life, and the soul, to an extent which must fill every person who comprehends it, with amazement. And the question was started, no doubt by the Spirit of God, '*Is it right*' to continue a practice which produces such results; and which, if continued, will perpetuate and increase them to all future ages? The Bible was examined, and providences observed; divine teaching was sought, and the conviction was fastened on the mind, that the practice was *not right;* and that to prevent the evils which it produced, men must cease to perpetuate the cause."

Dr. Edwards at this time prepared an able document on THE IMMORALITY OF THE TRAFFIC AS PRESENTED IN THE BIBLE.

"The Bible," he says, "is not constructed on the plan of mentioning every practice by name, and saying in so many words, it is right, or wrong; but on the plan of revealing certain great principles of right and wrong, by which every practice in which men ever did or ever will engage, may be tried, and be seen to be right or wrong. The proper question is not, Does the Bible mention this or that thing by name; but, *Do the principles of the Bible approve or condemn it?* When the nature of the thing is seen in the light of its effects, is it found to accord with those principles, or to violate them? If it is found to violate them, it is forbidden; it is an immorality, and ought to be abandoned; and as certainly as the Bible shall govern men, it will be abandoned throughout the earth.

"What then are the facts with regard to the traffic in ardent spirit, to be used as a drink? What is the nature of this traffic, as manifested by its effects?

Does it accord with the principles of the Bible, or does it violate them? This is the question to determine its morality, or immorality. And it is *the only question.* What then are the principles of the Bible, by which this traffic is to be tried?

"One of them is in Matthew 6 : 13, '*Lead us not into temptation, but deliver us from evil.*' This is a principle so important that the Saviour of men, who was willing for their good even to die, would have them, in their supplications and conduct, *daily* regard it. Does the traffic in ardent spirit, to be used as a drink, tend to lead men into temptation; and give to temptation peculiar power to overcome them, so that they fall by it into sin, when they otherwise would not fall? And is this its natural tendency? If it is, the Bible forbids it; and to pursue it, is manifestly an immorality. What then are the facts?"

He proceeds by an array of facts to prove that the use of ardent spirit tends *to idleness—to crime—to murder.* He then discusses the great principle, "*Whatsoever ye would that men should do unto you, do ye even so to them;*" and then the command, "*Abstain from fleshly lusts, which war against the soul;*" and then the principle, "*As we have opportunity, let us do good unto all men,*" under which he recapitulates the ruinous effects of intoxicating drinks on the body and the soul, and says of the traffic, "Instead of doing good, it does evil, and nothing but evil. To all these tremendous and overwhelming calamities there is no countervailing benefit. And while the cause of them is continued, they never can be prevented. The Bible then *forbids* it. *It violates all those principles which require men to honor God or do good to mankind;* it is manifestly hostile to both; and no principle of religion, morality, or humanity, will justify its continuance." He adds:

"The Temperance reformation, which has scattered the darkness and broken the slumber of ages, and is now travelling in the greatness of mercy over the length and breadth of the world, *was begun by the influence of the Bible.* It was undertaken in prayer, and for the purpose of delivering souls from sin and death. It was to remove that mighty obstruction to the efficacy of the Redeemer's kindness, which, while continued, will keep millions in spiritual bondage; and to open the way for the speedy and universal triumphs of his grace. This it is, we believe, which has led him to favor it, and by his mighty power to crown it so extensively with his blessing. And this it is, which inspires us with the continually growing expectation, that if his friends do their duty, it will never stop till drunkenness has ceased from under heaven."

As the documents which had been issued showing that LAWS *which authorize the traffic in ardent spirit as a drink are morally wrong,* "proceeded a step farther than previous publications on the subject, and not only called in question the morality, but proved, as it was believed, the *immorality* of a part of legislation which had long received extensive sanction and support," they were submitted to a large number of distinguished physicians, divines, jurists, and statesmen, with the two following inquiries:

"1. Are the principles exhibited in these documents in your view correct, and the arguments sound?

"2. What would probably be the effect on the great interests of the community, *should the people generally, and legislators, choose* to have all legislation on this subject conformed to those principles?"

To these questions very able affirmative replies and discussions of the principles involved were received, which are worthy of the consideration of all who wish further to investigate the subject. See Fourth Permanent Temperance Document, 1834.

June 3, 1834, he writes to Mrs. Edwards' brother, a merchant in New York, on the occasion of his marriage: "I feel a strong desire that, as you are now beginning life as it were anew, you should begin it with the Lord. One half hour, morning and evening, spent by yourself in reflection, reading the Scriptures, and prayer, will be likely to have a very important influence upon your thoughts, feelings, and conduct, through the day. I have found it so with myself, and doubt not it must be so with others. God has been very kind to you in giving you property, and now a companion worthy of your confidence and affection, and who may be to you a rich and lasting blessing. Now is a favorable time to devote yourself and all that you are and have to him. Should you and your beloved wife daily unite your hearts in supplications before the throne of the heavenly grace, you would find that it would lighten all your sorrows, and double all your joys."

Under another date he writes to the same brother, suggesting the inquiry "whether it would not be well to devote from ten to twenty-five per cent. of his income to charitable and benevolent objects;" or to adopt any other system by which a substantial part of all his income might be devoted *by the steward to Him who is the owner* of all things. He urges this as needful to counteract that "*love* of money, which every person, if he lays up for himself all he can get, will always have, and which will be likely always to prevent him from coming under the saving influence of the gospel; and because those who thus habitually give a part of their income to save the souls of men, are so much more likely themselves to be saved."

Again he says, "In a late New York Observer, I saw a brief notice of my friend, that most accomplished merchant, Nathaniel R. Cobb of Boston. Might it not be well for all merchants to adopt resolutions* as to property, similar to his. He had the fairest prospects of happiness and usefulness, but sickness and death came at the age of thirty-five. Yet he had hopefully his treasure in heaven. His sickness was remarkably peaceful, and his death blessed, which is worth more than all earthly good. My highest wish for you is, that your life may be such that this blessedness may be yours."

* The remarkable resolutions adopted and practised upon by Mr. Cobb were:

"By the grace of God, I will never be worth more than $50,000.

"By the grace of God, I will give one fourth of the net profits of my business to charitable and religious uses.

"If I am ever worth $20,000, I will give one half of my net profits; and if I am ever worth $30,000, I will give three fourths; and the whole, after $50,000. So help me God, or give to a more faithful steward, and set me aside.

"N. R. COBB."

Some time after, as a son began to receive some proceeds of his labors, he wrote him, "You had better start on the principle of giving one-tenth part of your net profit annually to good objects: The other nine parts will then be more likely to benefit you, than if you lay up the whole. 'A wise son heareth his father's instructions.'"

"BREMO, Fluvanna county, Va., Nov. 5, 1834.

"MY DEAR WIFE—I am now at the mansion of Gen. Cocke, who called on you with Mr. John Tappan when I was absent. He has five hundred acres of the best meadow land, in full view of the window from which I am writing, lying on the banks of James river. The meeting of the Temperance convention at Charlottesville was an intensely interesting one, and closed very happily. On Friday I expect to start for Richmond. My journey has hitherto, through the divine kindness, been interesting and pleasant, and my health is quite comfortable. This, if there were none but freemen in it, would be a delightful region of country; and when the glorious gospel of the blessed God shall universally prevail here, joy and gladness shall universally abound, thanksgiving and the voice of melody. That is the only effectual remedy for the ruins of the fall, and for the ills of human life."

On March 31, 1835, Dr. Edwards was unanimously elected as Associate Secretary of the Presbyterian Education Society, located in the city of New York. The acceptance of this appointment was urged upon him by many esteemed brethren in New York, from the great need of additional laborers in the ministry, and the belief that Dr. Edwards' singleness of purpose, devoted piety, sound discretion, kind and catholic feeling, and far-reaching views as to the character of men needed, and wisdom in guiding them in a course adapted to the highest usefulness, might be of incalculable benefit to the churches, to our country, and the world. It was believed that in his extensive communications with pastors and with the officers and members of literary and theological institutions, he would exert a most salutary influence which would be felt by all evangelical Christian denominations, and that in no way perhaps could he more usefully employ his powers.

But the early champion of Temperance, the author of the "Six Sermons," then located in the great West, came in with his plea, that that battle was not yet fought, and many triumphs remained to be won. His reasons against a transfer to another agency were mainly these three:

"1. Because, so long as you continue to act as an agent, it is all loss and no gain for you to take another sphere. A great amount of experimental knowledge in your present sphere cannot be transferred to the other, and must be acquired by time, of which in this short life we have little to spare.

"2. Because the Temperance movement, though progressive, is not past the dangers of falling back, through want of a constant energetic supervision and system; or of shipwreck by ultra, headlong violence which shall divide our forces. And you are the only man to whom God has given the wisdom and energy and influence over public opinion, to guide the experiment safely through.

"3. Whatever may be true of the East, we are by no means sufficiently enlightened and organized and consolidated at the West, to hold on and advance to a sure victory. Before you resign your Temperance agency, you ought to come to the West and do the work up here, at least as far as it has been done at the East. You can accomplish at the West, in two or three years, as much as your entire agency has done at the East; and *no other man can do it* in the same or double the time."

Mr. Delavan, the champion of the New York State Temperance Society, which was circulating by the hundred thousand, papers advocating abstinence from all intoxicating drinks, and battling the brewers for the use of poisonous drugs, also came in with his earnest plea. "I should feel much distressed at the idea of your leaving your present situation *for any other*. I know no other man fitted to fill the important station. If we make mistakes here, we affect only a single state; but should the National Society make a misstep, the whole nation would feel it. I do hope, dear sir, that you will stay where you are, and by your wisdom *keep us all steady*."

Dr. Edwards' reply to the request of the Education Society was, that "so far as he could judge, it did not appear to be consistent with the present indications of Providence for him to accept the appointment."

At the same date he also replied in a similar manner to a request that he would engage in the service of "the American Union for the Relief and Improvement of the Colored Race."

About the same time renewed overtures were made to him from the Western Reserve College, Ohio, and he was requested to consent to accept the office of professor of theology in that institution; but he felt it to be his duty to discourage further proceedings in that direction.

It was deemed advisable at the outset of the Temperance movement to call attention simply and distinctly to the evils attending the use of *ardent spirit* as a drink. But the principle involved evidently applied equally to *all intoxicating drinks*. The Fourth Permanent Document had been closed, in 1834, with the understanding that it would be the last; but in connection with the Temperance anniversary, May 26, 1835, another document was prepared, the primary topic of discussion being *the nature of alcohol*, which was shown to be produced by *vinous fermentation*. Of course it exists in *fermented liquors;* and every man might readily draw the inference, that if the use of fifty-three per cent. of alcohol in brandy and rum was wrong, the use of twenty-four per cent. in Madeira wine, seventeen per cent. in claret, thirteen in champagne, and from five to nine in ale, cider, etc., was at least questionable. From this date onwards Temperance papers and documents speak more generally of the evils, not of alcohol or ardent spirit merely, but of *all intoxicating drinks*.

"That intoxicating principle, which has in this country been the chief cause of drunkenness, is not," he says, "the product of creation; nor is it the result of any *living* process in nature. The animal kingdom, in all its vast variety of existence, and modes of operation, saith, 'It is not in me;' and the vegetable kingdom responds, 'It is not in me.' It cannot be found, and it does not exist, among all the *living* works of God. Those substances, however, which contain or which will produce sugar, after they are *dead*, and have become subject to those laws which *then* operate on inanimate matter, in the incipient stages of decomposition, undergo a process which chemists call *vinous fermentation*. By this process a new substance is formed, called alcohol. This is the means of intoxication. It is composed of hydrogen, carbon, and oxygen in the proportion of 13.04, 52.17, and 34.79 parts to a hundred; and is in its nature, as manifested by its effects, an exceedingly subtle and diffusive *poison*. The elements, by the combination of which this is formed, existed before; but the substance, which this combination forms, did not before exist. It is an entirely new substance, and is altogether different in its nature and effects, from what existed before.

"We are the more particular on this point, because there is much error in the public mind with regard to it. Many suppose that there is some portion of alcohol in all vegetable substances; at least in all whose fermentation, after death, will produce it. But this is an entire mistake. Not a living vegetable under heaven, so far as has yet been discovered, contains a particle of it. It does not exist in any living substance. It is formed *only* by *vinous fermentation*. After it is formed, it can be extracted from fermented liquors, as in common distillation."

He proceeds to state that alcohol was probably

first extracted from fermented liquor eight or nine hundred years ago. It was soon ascertained to be a *poison*, and no one thought of its ever being used as a drink. About the year 1234, however, it was introduced, in the south of Europe, as a *medicine*, and "in 1581 was introduced by the English as a kind of cordial for their soldiers in the Netherlands war." He then shows the reasons why men, from the pleasure and excitement which alcohol at first occasions, *think it does them good, and continue to use it;* and then why, from its exhausting influence on the system, they are led to *increase the quantity*, and so go on till they "commit suicide as really as if they did it with arsenic, a pistol, or a halter."

Believing that the testimony of distinguished men to the benefits they had themselves received by "*entire abstinence* from the use, as a beverage, of *all intoxicating liquor*, would be of service, especially to young men," Dr. Edwards, in November, 1835, addressed to numerous highly respected gentlemen in the various departments of life, the three following inquiries:

"1. What, in your case, has been the effect of abstinence from the use of intoxicating liquor, on health?

"2. What has been the effect on the capability of making great and continued efforts of body and mind?

"3. What has been the effect on the feelings, as to cheerfulness, uniformity, etc.? with any other particulars which may occur to you as important to be known by the human family."

The answers to these inquiries were in many cases very full, and abundantly corroborative of the salutary influence of entire abstinence from all intoxicating drinks. Thirty-four of them were embodied in the report presented at the Temperance anniversary held at Saratoga Springs in August following, and were added to the permanent Temperance documents. They are at once an admirable testimony to the value of Temperance, and to the high excellence, moral worth, patriotism, and benevolence of many of our eminent fellow-citizens, the living and the dead.

Of the first three Temperance documents, or parts of them, about 325,000 copies had been put into circulation before the fourth was issued; and when subsequent parts were added, vigorous and persevering efforts were made to supply the volume "for every preacher, lawyer, physician, magistrate, officer of government, secretary of a Temperance society, teacher of youth, and educated young man throughout the United States; and also for sending a copy of it to foreign missionaries and distinguished philanthropists in all parts of the world." The substance of these documents was issued, in 116 pages 8vo., as a "Temperance Manual for the Young Men of the United States," with the hope also of supplying it to every accessible family of immigrants who read our language. The substance of the documents was also published by the American Tract Society in *German* and in *French*, in which languages, by the activity of the Rev. Dr. Baird, who was then in Europe, it was translated, issued, and widely circulated both in Germany and in France.

In a letter to the king and the crown-prince of Prussia, written in the hope of extending the Temperance reformation in Germany, Dr. Edwards says, "The number of Temperance societies formed in this country, is more than *seven thousand;* and the number of persons who have united with them, more than *twelve hundred and fifty thousand.* More than *three thousand distilleries* have been stopped; and more than *seven thousand merchants have abandoned the traffic* in spiritous liquors. More than *a thousand vessels* sail from our ports in which no such liquors are used; and more than ten thousand persons, who, a few years ago, were *drunkards*, now use no intoxicating drink. They are all sober men; many of them are industrious, respectable, and useful; and not a few of them truly pious men. In those parts of the country in which these Societies are most general, industry, economy, morality, and religion have been greatly revived; sickness and mortality have been much diminished, and pauperism and crime have been almost entirely done away."

Mr. JOHN TAPPAN, chairman of the Executive Committee of the American Temperance Society, says:

"I was placed on the Committee of the American Temperance Society with Dr. Edwards at its formation in 1826, and acted with him during the whole period of his agency, and continued on the Committee with him until the close of his life. In forming its constitution, conducting its correspondence, employing its agents, attending conventions, drawing resolutions as chairman of the business committees in nearly all the public meetings, in the capitol at Washington, and the capitols of most of the states of the Union, he was the pivot upon which all moved. His gentleness of manner, 'speaking the truth in love,' disarmed opponents, and the light he threw upon the subject in debate, convinced and made friends of those who came to oppose. Never was there a more lovely exhibition of the Christian character, than was displayed by him in conducting this great movement, from its earliest conception to its all-pervading influence through this and other lands—an influence continually extending, especially in these United States.

"He looked forward to great results, in the further spread of the gospel, when men should universally abandon intoxicating beverages; and with this object in view, he was instant in season, and out of season, that he might save not *some* only, but *many* of the deluded unhappy victims of intemperance, made such, in many cases, more by injudicious parents and friends, than by any other cause. Never, in our day, should we have rejoiced in the enactment of the laws prohibiting the traffic, with all their countless blessings, and have seen them extending their influence through the United States, had it not been for his efforts in laying the foundation on which they rest. That foundation was the word of God. *To cause men universally to be temperate, that they might become Christians*, was the one great object for which he labored and prayed.

"With the same singleness of purpose, he afterwards engaged in efforts for the promotion of the better observance of the Sabbath, and there also his influence extended over our land. When the increased facilities for travel in railroads and steam-boats, with the increase of wealth which was flowing into our country, alarmed the friends of the Sabbath lest it should be more extensively desecrated, his influence was greatly felt in putting a stop to public travelling, and conveying the mails on the Sabbath, throughout a large portion of the land. In the cause of the Sabbath, as in that of Temperance, the influence of his efforts will extend to remote time.

"The present generation have lost a leader who lived what he taught, and whose record is on high. Never has a brighter combination of wisdom in counsel, energy in action, and humility in life shone forth, than in our revered friend; and to have so often met him in prayerful consultation and familiar intercourse, during a period of nearly thirty years, has been one of the highest of my privileges."

To Mrs. Edwards he wrote, "Let us daily *pray for our children*, and especially on the birthday of each. That day, if you please, we will, as far as circumstances permit, devote as a day of special supplication to the Father of all mercies, that they may be partakers of his rich grace in Jesus Christ, be disposed to serve him and do good on the earth, and be prepared to glorify and enjoy him for ever in heaven."

He again writes, "I should be glad to have all the members of the family, every night before they go to sleep, repeat that delightful hymn,

'Glory to thee, my God, this night,' etc.,

and when we awake in the morning, that other,

'Awake, my soul, and with the sun,' etc.

I like these hymns very much, and mean daily to

repeat them myself. We shall then be able to sing them without the book; and however we may be separated, shall all be repeating the same things at nearly the same time."

To his youngest son, then residing for a time in New York, he wrote, March 30, 1836, "Your brother Jonathan is now anxious, and we hope seeking his salvation. Numbers in the academy have become hopefully pious. A temper to be happy in doing the will of God, is *essential;* and every person who has not such a temper, should fix it in his mind, that without a change he will be wretched. This then is more important than learning, wealth, and every thing else. It is indeed 'the one thing needful.'"

Again he says, "Do not forget that the great business for which you were made, and on which your happiness for both worlds depends, is to serve God, love and obey him. Read daily a portion of his word, with humble, believing prayer for the teaching of his Spirit. You are now in the most interesting part of your existence, and forming a character for endless being. Strive daily to give your heart, and all that you are and have, to Jesus Christ, whose favor is life, and whose loving-kindness is better than life."

To his eldest son in New York he says, "I send you a copy of Baxter's Saints' Rest, which I should like to have you treat as a friend—read it through with care, and with fervent prayer to God that it may be to you, as it has been to thousands, the means of preparing them for that heavenly rest on which he, and multitudes of others through his instrumentality, there is reason to believe, have entered."

Writing from Pittsburgh, May 8, 1836, he says to his little daughters, "This morning when I awoke, just as it began to be light, I heard the birds singing their Maker's praises most sweetly. And it made me think of you, and hope that you and all the children will do so too. The Lord is good to all. All his works praise him. But especially should those do it who have reason, and have been redeemed by the sufferings and death of his own dear Son. I hope you do not forget the way to be happy. Love the Lord, and do good, be kind and obliging, hate and forsake all sin, and trust in Jesus Christ, and strive to be like him."

In August, he attended a Temperance Convention at Saratoga Springs, where he wrote Mrs. Edwards, "I see no objection to Jonathan's being admitted to the church as soon as the way is prepared for it; or to his attending commencement at Yale College and offering himself for admission, if his teachers think it best. I hope he will daily listen to the Bible, and seek heartily the divine guidance, protection, and blessing; be humble and diligent, and do all the good in his power."

We close this chapter with the substance of a glowing, Christ-exalting address by Dr. Edwards, at a foreign missionary meeting in Masonic Hall, New York, February 11, 1835, having special reference to the violent death of the missionaries, Rev. Messrs. MUNSON and LYMAN, in Sumatra, and the sudden death of the Rev. Dr. WISNER, secretary of the Missionary Board.

"Nothing," he said, "except the contemplation of God fills my mind with greater awe than the contemplation of the human soul—its amazing power, its endless duration, its capability of for ever rising from glory to glory, or sinking from woe to woe.

"But the points suggested by this occasion, are, That souls have begun a course of departure from God, the fountain of all being, and excellence, and blessedness; and that from this course they must return in this life, or they will continue on it for ever and for ever; and that nothing but the gospel will ever induce them to return."

He proceeds to show the darkness of the heathen; the pollution of their gods—that the more they worship them and pray to them, the more they become like them; and that not only the heathen must perish without the gospel, but we need *on our own account* to send it to them, to "live not unto ourselves, but unto Him that died for us and rose again." Christ made the one great sacrifice in bearing our sins in his own body on the tree: he never faltered or shrunk back till he could say, "It is finished." It is now for us to do our duty. It is not the way of *love* to wish the object beloved to make all the sacrifices, while he who loves lives supremely to himself.

"It was not so with Paul. He did not wish to have Christ, or any other one, do all or suffer all. The love of Christ constrained *him* to count all things but loss, that he might proclaim the great salvation in places in which the name of Jesus had not been known. He rejoiced even in his sufferings, 'that he might fill up that which was behind of the afflictions of Christ, for his body's sake, which is the church.' This he did, not on the ground of merit, but as the fruit and evidence of love; because God, and his own salvation, and the salvation of the heathen, required it.

"So with Brainerd, and Martyn, and Mills. As MILLS came one day and took my arm, he said, that no young man redeemed by the blood of Christ, and living in the nineteenth century, ought to intend to die, or to live, without an effort to make *his influence felt round the globe.* Hall, and Newell, and Judson, and Parsons, and Fisk, whose tongues, moved by the love of Jesus, I have often heard plead for dying heathen, did not wish to have all the labors performed, and all the privations and sufferings endured by others. They chose to do and suffer a part themselves. Their salvation required it, Christ required it, and the joy which they wished to excite in heaven required it. I remember hearing the modest, but heavenly-minded FISK once say—and his form seems now to rise up before me, as if it were only yesterday when he spoke it—'O what a privilege it is to live in this day. The way is open; a man may do as much as he chooses. O, it is an unspeakable privilege to live in such a day.' Fisk gave not only his money, but he gave himself. And do you think, as he stood on Calvary, or lay gasping in death, or as he rose to glory, that he altered his opinion? No. Nor was he alone. There were Richards, and Robbins, and Warren, and many others, whose love to Christ, and to souls, carried them to the other side of the globe; yes, and farther too, it carried them to heaven.

"ROBBINS is a name not often mentioned among

missionaries, but in heart and soul he was a great missionary; by whose mighty instrumentality, and that of others, was prayed into existence the whole system of American missions. His bones slumber in a southern clime, and his spirit, we trust, mingles sweetly with that rapidly increasing band of perfect missionaries, before the throne of God.

"I could tell you too, of MUNSON and LYMAN, who began privation and sacrifices while in the midst of overflowing abundance, that when called, in Java, or Sumatra, or Siam, to make them, they might, not only by the strengthened love of Christ, but also by the power of habit, be rendered more easy and more sweet. Precious youth—they loved not their lives, but they loved Christ, unto the death.

"'But,' it is said, 'they died by the hand of violence.' So did Stephen, though full of the Holy Ghost. So did Peter, though he could say, even to the Searcher of hearts, 'Thou knowest all things; thou knowest that I love thee.' And so did Paul; and though to live was Christ, to die was gain. By the hand of violence? Mr. President, where had been your hope, and mine, and the hope of other sinners, if no one had been willing, for the salvation of men, to die by the hand of violence, and to make his grave with the wicked? Thanks, everlasting thanks to Him who was willing, when it was needful, to die by the hand of violence. 'I, if I be lifted up,' said he, 'will draw all men unto me.' Therefore we, and this dying world have hope.

"'But they died so soon,' it is said. Yes, and it was probably because that prayer which Jesus, when about to taste death for them, put up, was so soon answered: 'Father, I will that they whom thou hast given me, be with me where I am, that they may behold my glory.' Robbins, as when dying he was reminded of his friends, raised his eyes, and smiling, whispered, 'I have friends there, I hope; and go *to* them, not from them.'

"'But those poor widows without a guide, or protector, what will become of them, and that little fatherless child?' Without a guide, or protector? a little child, too, in a land of strangers, among heathen, and fatherless? Whose voice do I hear, so much sweeter than the voice of angels, so divinely tender, and yet all-pervading, echoing, wherever the Bible goes, down to the end of time, 'Leave your fatherless children, and let your widows trust in me.' Which is best, to have an earthly father and protector, such as Munson, or Lyman, or any other mortal man, or to have the Lord God, gracious and merciful, slow to anger and abundant in kindness, saying, 'I will never leave thee, nor forsake thee?'

"'But the heathen are perishing, we have not half as many missionaries as we need; and what can God mean in taking so many so soon away?' What can he mean? He means that Christ shall have 'the heathen for his inheritance, and the uttermost parts of the earth for his possession;' that 'all nations, and kindreds, and people shall serve him.' When Christ raises up missionaries, and fits them for his service by pouring into their minds the light of heavenly truth, and shedding abroad in their hearts richly of his love by the Holy Ghost; and they come to us, and urge upon us with the living voice, and the corresponding living example, the last great command of the Saviour, and we do not obey, but hug our children, hoard our treasures, and live for this world, and will not hear the voice of their *life*, then he speaks to us in their *death*. And in this way, he does not speak in vain.

"HARRIET NEWELL, though we had then few missionaries, did not live to go to the spot where the mission was to be established. She died, but her death was the seed of missions. I found her life on the shelf, away off at the south, in a place where, I believe, they did not see missionaries, or hear missionary sermons. But Harriet Newell, speaking in accents of death, and pleading for dying heathen, with a tongue and a power to which when living she was a stranger, went and preached to them. Though she sleeps on the other side of the globe, she has raised her voice so as to be heard almost throughout Christendom, and it is not spent, she does not become fatigued; her voice has awakened many a minister in our own land to his duty; and many a daughter and son have been devoted to the service of God among the heathen. But Oh, I tremble when I recollect that we have been so backward to do our duty, and that God has found it needful to add so many other dying voices to hers, in order to awaken us from our slumbers, and lead us to obey him. *Ten times*, by the death of missionaries, God hath spoken to us the past year. O may we hear the voice, and awake to our duty.

"Said JEREMIAH EVARTS, in one of the last conversations that I had with him, '*There is nothing in this world like being a benefactor of minds;*' a sentiment worthy of being inscribed on the annals of the universe. So said Evarts, not in words only upon one occasion, but habitually and perseveringly in deeds. And when he came to die, as they wiped the cold sweat from his face, he opened his glimmering eyes, and looking upward, said, 'Infinite glory, infinite glory!' Yes, 'infinite glory' is before the man that lives for Christ, and is a benefactor of minds: glory which eye hath not seen; and into which, when he leaves the body, he will enter and will shine as the brightness of the firmament, and as the stars for ever and ever.

"Young men, I speak to you—you who are, or may be, blessed with grace, talents, and education. There is nothing in this world like being a benefactor of minds; and nothing that more surely or rapidly fits the soul for heaven, than making known, from love to Christ, the gospel of his grace to dying men. This may be one reason why those who engage in it with all the heart, are so soon prepared, through grace, to be with Christ, beholding his glory, and made perfectly like him; where 'they hunger no more, neither thirst any more, but the Lamb himself leads them to fountains of living water, and wipes away all tears from their eyes.'

"When I have seen brother WISNER, during the past year, stand and plead as for his life for perishing heathen, as his bosom heaved and his eye swelled with tears, I have often thought of what a minister said to me once of brother CORNELIUS, six months perhaps before his death, a minister with whom he used to take counsel, and unite in prayer: 'It appears to me he is fast preparing for heaven.' And that dying woman, too, on whom I once called, at whose bed-side Cornelius had been offering up his supplications, said to me—and she was on the borders of heaven, when such persons sometimes have peculiar spiritual discernment—'I think he is ripening for a bright crown of glory.'

"And may we not hope, must we not hope, that this was also the case with Wisner? When I met him in Tremont-street two weeks ago yesterday, he hastened and took my hand and said, 'Where have you been that I could not find you? I have been wanting to see you. I wrote you a letter about it before I got home.' And what did he want? To tell what he had thought about a plan for more speedily evangelizing the world. And if, through boundless grace, he was thus prepared for a bright crown of glory, why should he not wear it; especially when it would be for the glory of Christ, and swell the joy of that great band of missionaries who had gone before him to glory, to see him, after all the tossings of this tempestuous world, landing in safety on the heavenly shore? And more especially when we may hope that his death too will start into life many a precious missionary who may do more for God among the heathen, than even he could have done, had he lived. As the voice by his death waxeth louder and louder, saying, 'Whom shall I send, and who will go for us?' methinks I hear one, and another, and another, from the East, and the West, and the North, and the South, saying, 'Here, Lord, am I; send me!'

"Missionaries will be greatly increased, but we

must not depend upon them. No, their very foundation is in the dust, they dwell in houses of clay, and they are crushed before the moth. We must look upward to God; yes, one and all of us must look up, with hearty submission, unwavering confidence, and transporting hope. In the closet, in the family, morning and evening, every day; as we walk the street, and sit in the house; at the monthly concert especially, let every man, woman, and child that loves Christ, or wishes for the salvation of those for whom he died, cry mightily unto God, and rest not from prayer and action, till 'the kingdoms of this world are become the kingdom of our Lord and of his Christ.'"

In January, 1837, the "American Temperance Union," consisting of the officers of the American Temperance Society and of the several state societies, commenced its operations in the city of Philadelphia, when its present secretary, Rev. John Marsh, entered on his official labors in connection with that institution. As secretary of the Connecticut Temperance Society, though still pastor at Haddam, Mr. Marsh had long and actively coöperated with Dr. Edwards; and as early as 1829, published his rousing Temperance appeal, "Putnam and the Wolf," No. 240 of the Tract Society's series.

CHAPTER X.

HIS PRESIDENCY IN THE THEOLOGICAL SEMINARY.

SIX YEARS—1836-1842.

DR. EDWARDS, in February, 1836, was elected Professor of Theology in the Seminary then recently organized in *the city of New York;* and on the 9th of March he wrote the Directors of that institution: "The subject is of great importance; and when the facts connected with it shall have been fully laid before me, I shall endeavor to give it that attentive and prayerful consideration, which a subject so intimately connected with the prosperity of the Redeemer's kingdom and the salvation of men, appears to deserve."

While the question of accepting this appointment was pending, he applied by letter to many esteemed brethren for their counsel, and the question had not been decided when, on the 21st of April, he received the following note from the Hon. Samuel Hubbard of Boston, a member of the Board of Trustees of the Theological Seminary at Andover.

"I have said nothing to you in relation to your invitations to the Western Reserve and to New York. As to the first, I never had the least doubt. As to the second, our doings at Andover," (at a meeting of the trustees, just held, electing him President of the Theological Seminary there,) "will assure you *what my most deliberate judgment is* as to your appropriate sphere of usefulness in the service of our divine Master."

The venerable Mr. Bartlet, one of the founders, and a member of the Board of Visitors, already the largest donor to the seminary, uniting in the judgment of Mr. Hubbard and others, had agreed to pay the salary of Dr. Edwards for five years, should he be elected President—an office which had existed in the seminary only during the last six years of the life of Rev. Dr. Porter, the senior professor, from 1828 to his death in 1834; and which has since been filled only during the time it was occupied by Dr. Edwards. It was the quenchless desire of Mr. Bartlet, Mr. Hubbard, and others, that the seminary should be preserved a pure fountain sending forth pure streams; and they had great confidence, that the hallowed influence of Dr. Edwards in the station assigned him, and virtually as pastor of the seminary, of the academy, and of the schools and families connected with them, would be wisely and powerfully exerted for that end.

In view of all the light he was able to obtain, he felt constrained to decline the appointment at New York, and to accept that of the seminary of whose board of trustees he had for sixteen years been an active member.

"To the Reverend and Honorable the Trustees of Phillips Academy, in Andover.

"Gentlemen—The appointment to the Presidency of the Theological Seminary in Phillips Academy, which I had the honor to receive from you, I have considered, with a portion at least of that desire for divine guidance and attention to the indications of the divine will, which the great importance of the subject seemed to require. The subject has not been without difficulty, nor have I been free from painful solicitude with regard to it. It has at times appeared to me doubtful whether I shall probably enjoy as good health in the situation to which you invite me, as in the one which I now occupy; and if I should, whether I can be as useful to the world. But after all the light which I have obtained, by application to the Father of lights, and attention to those indications by which he ordinarily, on such occasions, manifests his will, I have come to the conclusion to accept, and I hereby do accept, the appointment to the Presidency of the Theological Seminary under your care; and will, with the divine permission, enter upon the discharge of its duties at the commencement of the next term. * * *

"Wishing you at all times the divine guidance and blessing, and asking an interest in your prayers, that I may be faithful and useful, that the seminaries under our care may be eminently instrumental in advancing the kingdom of our Redeemer, and that we may all, after having served God and our generation according to his will, meet as trophies of grace before his throne, and mingle with that blest assembly who through faith and patience are now inheriting the promises, I am with great respect and esteem,

"Truly and gratefully yours,

"J. EDWARDS.

"ANDOVER, July 16, 1836."

On the 7th of September, 1836, he was inaugurated President of the Theological Seminary, on which occasion he delivered an address to the young men about to leave the Seminary, on the sacred work of the gospel ministry.

In August previous, he had been unanimously elected Chancellor of "the University of Western New York," for which a location had been selected at Buffalo, and an endowment of "two hundred and twenty-five thousand dollars" had been subscribed; but the communication from the Rev. John C. Lord and others, announcing this election, reached him after he had accepted the appointment at Andover.

In tracing the life of Dr. Edwards while laboring in the Temperance reformation, we have had the most abundant materials, in public documents, and in appeals which he must necessarily issue in order to reach the minds of individual men throughout the community. As President of the Seminary; as a member of the Board of Trustees, or Chairman of their Committee of Exigencies; in his consultations with members of the respected Board of Visitors, or with the Faculty, or with individual members of the Seminary or Academy, or in regard to all the varied, responsible, and often complicated interests requiring his patient, laborious attention and care, his deliberations and counsels were to a great extent official and confidential. He neither wrote, nor reported them verbally, to any one. Those who consulted him as to official duties, or their individual interests, had a right to know that it was in a confidence ever to remain sacredly inviolate. Of this portion of his life and labors while in the Presidency, however rich it may have been in lessons of wisdom or instruction, we have of course no record. Those who knew most intimately the labors and responsibilities devolving on him at this period, believe that they were not less arduous than in other portions of his life, and that their blessed results will appear in the revelations of the final day.

In an official report at the end of his first year in the Theological Seminary, he says, "I have prepared and preached, during the year, twenty-three sermons on the great principles and duties of the Christian religion. I have endeavored to exhibit them in an experimental and a practical, rather than in a scientific and scholastic form, as I considered them in this form best adapted to promote the spiritual interests of the Seminary.

"I have attended the devotional exercises of the chapel daily, through the year, in the morning; and have taken my proportion with the other officers, who have not been excused from this service, in the evening. I have spent one evening in a week, most of the year, with one of the other officers, in prayer and religious conversation upon some experimental and practical subject, with the members of the seminary; and have taken my proportion in the criticism of the sermons of the Senior class.

"I have also had one exercise a week with the resident licentiates on the composition and delivery of sermons, and the performance of the various duties of the ministry. One evening in a week has been devoted to conversation with all who wished to see me on the subject of religion. I have taken the charge of the pulpit, and of the monthly concert, and have had one meeting in a month for the families belonging to the congregation.

"All the members of each of the seminaries who wished for the privilege, have had access to my study for an hour and a half in a day, for the purpose of making inquiries on any subject with regard to which they wished for counsel and advice. Much time has often been employed in this service; and I have endeavored, as far as circumstances would permit, to act the part not only of a pastor, but of a father; and from the frequent expressions of gratitude which I have received, I am led to believe that this exercise may have been useful to many.

"I have also conducted the correspondence of the seminary; which, with the numerous letters of inquiry from individuals, churches, literary and benevolent institutions, for pastors, teachers, agents, etc., and also for advice with regard to their concerns, has required much time and labor."

At the end of the second year he reports, that there had been an addition of forty-three students, making the whole number one hundred and two; that "during the winter term there was an increasing attention to the subject of religion, and several cases of hopeful conversion among the members of the academy and others belonging to the congregation;" that members of the seminary had performed much faithful labor during the spring vacation, in places visited by the special influences of the Holy Spirit; that he had devoted one evening each week to conversation and prayer with all who wished to meet to make inquiries on the subject of religion, and once in three months had attended a meeting for the mothers and the children; that in the morning prayers of the seminary, which he had uniformly attended, he had found opportunity to speak to the members on subjects to which at any time he thought their attention ought to be turned; and that three hours in each day his study had been open, for consultation and advice, "not only to the one hundred young men in the seminary, but more than two hundred youths in the other institutions, many of whom," he says, "are without parents, most of whom are at a distance from their friends, and not a few of whom are laboring under pecuniary and various other embarrassments, and are greatly needing wise parental advice;" which gave "the best opportunity to become intimately acquainted with many in the morning of life, and under circumstances peculiarly favorable to exerting upon them a salutary influence."

At the end of the next year, he says, "The number of students who have entered the Seminary during the year, exclusive of the advanced class, has been *fifty-two*, and *ten* who had been absent have returned; *twelve* entered the advanced class; making an addition to the number of students in the Seminary of *seventy-four*, the whole number being *one hundred and twenty-five*. The state of religion in the Seminary has been, in view of the Faculty, comparatively favorable; and the character of those who now finish their course of study is such as to give good reason to hope that, with the divine blessing, they may be rendered eminently useful to the world. A number of them are devoted to the work of missions among the heathen; and it is the opinion of the Faculty, that the prevalence of the missionary spirit has been, and promises to continue to be, highly salutary to all the great interests of the institution."

Addressing the students of the Seminary, October, 1837, on the responsibilities and duties of the ministry, he gives the following *hints as to a minister's conversation and conduct*, which we record not only as inherently valuable, but as having been faithfully exemplified in his own life as pastor.

"The conversation and conduct, and the whole example of a minister, at all times, and in all things, should be such as will strengthen and confirm the influence of his preaching. Ministers are a spectacle not only to God, and to angels, but to men. All eyes are upon them, and all ears open to their words. In the stage, in the steam-boat, in the parlor, in the public concourse, in the private circle, or when conversing with individuals—anywhere, everywhere, 'the priest's lips should keep knowledge.'

"No man can measure his influence for good, concerning whom it can in truth be said, he utters no improper *words*. And no one can express the pain which is sometimes given to the sensitive and discreet mind, or the injury that is done, by the unsavory, ill-judged, frothy conversation of a thoughtless, vain, indiscreet, or even hypochondriacal minister. Does he travel? you hear of his remarks, from the mouths of the thoughtless and the profane, all along his journey; and among his own people, they become the current coin of conversation—counteracting, and often more than counteracting, the good which he might have done, if his conversation had been 'in simplicity and godly sincerity,' as became his office. He is a minister of Him, who so spake that men 'wondered at the gracious words which proceeded out of his mouth;' and in this he hath left us 'an example, that we should follow his steps.'

"A minister may sometimes converse so much about *himself*, as to lead all to conclude that he thinks more about himself, than he does about God; sometimes so much about his friends, as to show that he idolizes them; sometimes so much about the rich and the great, as to show that he seeks supremely to be like them.

"He may converse so constantly and in such a manner about *property*, especially when buying and selling, as to make the impression that his treasure is on earth—that there is nothing he loves above gold. So far as all transactions with regard to property are concerned, it is ordinarily wise for a minister first to ascertain the value of the thing in question, so as to prevent imposition, and then to do his business in the kindest way, and with as few words as practicable. Let him see to it that he does not in reality love the world; and that he does not make the impression that he loves it.

"A minister's manner of speaking about *persons* may be such as to make the impression that he does not speak of others, as he would wish and ought to wish that they should speak of him; and of course that he is not governed by the spirit of the gospel.

All that is trifling or frivolous in his conversation—all that is unmeaning and apparently adapted only to flatter his hearers, or to make them think highly of himself—all that is not an exemplification of the truths which he inculcates in the pulpit, will tend to prevent their good effects. Nor is it enough that it should not be positively in opposition to the truth; it must be in favor of it: here it is emphatically true, that he that gathereth not with Christ, scattereth abroad.

"I do not mean that a minister must speak only upon the subject of religion, and never converse with freedom on the things of this life; but that he should do it at such times, and in such a way, as is adapted to leave the impression that life is a vapor, that eternity draweth nigh, that 'one thing is needful,' that 'now is the accepted time;' in such a way as shall say, in moving and persuasive accents, 'O that they were wise, that they understood this, that they would consider their latter end.' In all his intercourse with his people, this should manifestly be his great object, that to which his time, his talents, his influence, his all of body and mind, should be habitually and perseveringly devoted. His heart's desire, his prayer to God should manifestly be, that they may be saved.

"I might also urge a strict regard to *simple truth* in all his professed narrations of facts, so that all who hear him, or hear of his statements, may with confidence and safety conclude that the things stated are really so. If a man prevaricate, or exaggerate in conversation, and others find that they cannot rely upon him *out* of the pulpit, it tends directly and powerfully to destroy their confidence in what he says in the pulpit, and thus to cripple his power of producing conviction, even when he declares the truth. 'Let your communication be yea, yea; nay, nay'—simple verities in all things; that none need ever doubt the correctness of your representations."

December 29, 1838, he preached to the Theological seminary from the text, "Worthy is the Lamb that was slain;" presenting Christ as a willing, an unchangeable, an almighty Saviour.

"Do you doubt," he says, "whether the great apostle justly spoke of him as 'God over all, blessed for ever?' Look into heaven, and see written by the finger of God in great capitals for the universe to read, 'Worship the Lord thy God, and *him only* shalt thou serve.' Then listen to the heavenly song, 'Blessing, and honor, and glory, and power, be unto Him that sitteth upon the throne, and unto THE LAMB, for ever and ever.' Do they not worship Christ? If so, they break the first command, or Jesus Christ is God. And if men cannot, or will not view and treat him as such here, what can they do in heaven?

"Do you say he was *a man*, he looked like a man, and acted like a man? He ate, and drank, and labored, and died; and in all, appeared like a man? No doubt, for he *was* a man; in all respects like other men, except sin. But *why* was he a man? I know that he who 'in the beginning was with God, and was God—by whom all things were created that are in heaven and that are in earth, visible and invisible, whether they be thrones or dominions, or principalities or powers, and without whom was not any thing made that was made'—was himself 'made flesh, and dwelt among us;' that 'he took not on him the nature of angels, but the seed of Abraham,' 'was found in fashion as a man, and humbled himself, and became obedient unto death, even the death of the cross.'

"But *why was he a man?* To die for you, and for me, and thus open a way in which God might be just, and yet save us from an eternity of sinning, and an eternity of suffering; change us into his own blessed image, and raise us to seats of glory at his right hand. Had it not been for his love to us, and his desire to save us, he never had been a man; but had reigned, in the glory which he had with the Father before the world was, to everlasting ages, and no being in heaven had doubted who he was.

"But he loved sinners, and gave himself for them. Shall they on this account withhold from him their hearts, and refuse to give him their lives? While angels and cherubim and seraphim veil their faces, and cast their crowns at his feet, and raise the highest ascriptions of glory 'to him that sitteth upon the throne, and to the Lamb for ever and ever,' shall they who have been redeemed to God by his blood stand mute, or say in their hearts, 'We will not have him to reign over us?'"

At the time of the prostration of his health in Boston, May, 1829, Dr. Edwards resigned his membership of the Publishing Committee of the American Tract Society at New York. In September, 1839, he was reëlected to that office; but as he still believed that the pressure of his official and other public duties forbade his resuming the labors required, a special committee of the Society, consisting of S. V. S. Wilder, Esq., president, Rev. James Milnor, D. D., chairman of the Executive and Publishing Committees, and Rev. William A. Hallock, secretary, addressed him on the subject, in a note written by Rev. Dr. Milnor.

"REVEREND AND DEAR SIR—The Executive Committee of the American Tract Society have received with great regret your letter declining the appointment which they had hoped you would accept, as a member of the Publishing Committee.

"Under a deep sense of the importance of having a gentleman of the Congregational denomination on that committee, who with other required qualifications should have so established a reputation in that body and in the community as to give weight to our publications by his revision and sanction of them, and believing that divine Providence directs us immediately to yourself as that person, we are induced to ask of you the favor to reconsider your determination.

"The interest you have heretofore taken in the Tract cause, and the valuable contributions you have made to our series, together with the great importance, in the view of the resident members of the Publishing Committee, of having associated with them an eastern colleague in whom they could so entirely confide as yourself, induce them to hope that you may still feel yourself at liberty to engage in this interesting service.

"We are persuaded that the duty will be less arduous than you imagine, as the Publishing Committee will only forward you for examination such Tracts as the resident members have previously approved, and of course you will be spared the reading of a large quantity of manuscript which they have had the labor of examining, and have been obliged to reject.

"Be assured, it will afford great pleasure to the Executive Committee, and they believe essentially promote the good cause in which they are engaged, if you can, though it be at some sacrifice of personal convenience, unite with them in their labor of love."

Dr. Edwards soon consented to act again on the Publishing Committee, and continued to discharge the duties of that office until his death.

Mrs. Edwards' brother in New York, in whose spiritual welfare he had felt so deep an interest, having obtained hope in Christ, he wrote him May 14, 1838: "It has rejoiced our hearts, and I trust led us to praise the Lord, that through his kindness and grace, you have been led to hope in his mercy. Next to the gift of a Saviour, the gift of a heart to trust in him, is the greatest which God ever bestows upon the children of men. If the Lord has granted you this blessing, he has, my dear brother, done more for you than if he had given you all the kingdoms of the world.

"If your hope is that which will not fail, but will be as an anchor to the soul, sure and steadfast, it will lead you to make it your great object to be in temper like our blessed Saviour, and in all things to do his holy will. You will see more and more clearly, and feel more and more deeply your own unworthiness and guilt, your indebtedness for all your comforts to God's unmerited grace, and will strive to honor him in body and spirit, which are his.

"Seek, my dear brother, in all things to set a holy example, and *to do good* as you have opportunity to all. Your conversion may be in answer to the prayers which have been offered by many for this event. Pray much yourself for the salvation of others, and forget not our dear son Justin, and the other dear children which God has given us and you."

A few weeks later he writes this beloved brother, requesting him to join in a concert of private prayer, in which the parents and a few friends had "agreed," for the conversion of absent sons and each of the children of the family. He adds by way of encouragement, "Did we know how ready Jehovah is to hear and answer prayer, we should no doubt pray much more than we now do, and with much more faith, earnestness, and perseverance. It may have seemed strange that you should be brought to hope that you know the truth, believe in and love the Saviour. But when it shall be told, in eternity, how many times your beloved mother has made this her last petition at night, and her first petition in the morning, how much others have prayed for you, and how faithful God is to answer prayer, the mystery may be unfolded."

His two younger sons being now in Yale College, he prepared for them the following

HINTS TO A STUDENT AT COLLEGE.

"Make it your first object to discharge your duty to God, to love him supremely, and obey his commands; and daily read a portion of his word, with prayer for the teaching of his Holy Spirit.

"Keep holy the Sabbath, statedly attend public worship, avoid the reading of worldly books, and attention to wordly business, conversation, or amusement.

"Be regular and diligent in your studies. Pass over nothing which is required in college without thoroughly understanding it. Be punctual and constant in your attendance upon all college duties; and treat all the officers of college uniformly with politeness and respect.

"Choose the sober and the good only for your companions; and never associate with those who are in any way vicious. Never be afraid to say to any one who solicits you to do an improper thing, 'No.'

"Engage in no business, or reading, or amusement, or any thing which will hinder you from attending every recitation, and being thoroughly prepared. Never think it a mark of genius to be idle, or of dulness to study hard. Never be found in opposition to the government. Though all college should go wrong, let it be seen and known by all, that you on this point will go right.

"In your dress be plain, simple, neat; and in your manners easy and dignified; be respectful to superiors, kind and affable to inferiors, and open, frank, and generous to equals. Never feel uneasy at hearing others praised, or try in any way to disparage them. Rejoice that others can do so well, and strive yourself to do better.

"Take good care of your health; exercise at least two hours in a day; rise and retire early; use cold water freely in washing every morning, and apply a coarse towel briskly to the skin; and do the same whenever there is an inability to sleep during the night. Eat regularly and slowly, masticate thoroughly, and always be accommodating and polite at the table.

"In journeying, be as circumspect as you would be at home; treat all with politeness; never differ with any one, should he take your seat in the stage or the car, and never dispute with any one by the way. Show that you can bear an affront, or if need be an injury, without condescending to notice it. Ever delight to show a kindness, and do all the good you can.

"Let the consequences be what they may, never do what you know to be wrong, or neglect what you know to be right. In all things strive to *be*, rather than seem to be; and to do that which you will most approve for ever.

"Daily ask God for Christ's sake to guide you in all your views, feelings, words, and actions; for he that trusteth to his own wisdom, or goodness, or, in the language of the Bible, 'to his own heart,' is a fool. 'The fear of the Lord is the beginning of wisdom, and a good understanding have they who keep his commandments.' 'Hold thou me up, and I shall be safe;' guide me, and I shall go in the right way."

He afterwards says, "Among the most common baits which the devil puts upon his hook, in order to catch young men in college, are wine, cards, profaneness, and tobacco. Whoever nibbles at either of them, may expect to be caught. Avoid soda, mead, confectionary, and every thing which tends to generate *an artificial appetite* of any sort. Keep your natural appetite, and you will find that nothing quenches thirst so well, or tastes so good as pure water, a beverage as perfect as infinite power can make."

Again he says, "Mr. Webster and all such men are now experiencing the benefit of their thorough attention to science when young; while many are exerting far less influence than they might have done, had they not while in college neglected their studies for that which they thought would in future life be to them of more advantage."

To a son in College.

"ANDOVER, Feb. 24, 1840.

"MY DEAR SON—There is much more than usual attention to religion in many places, and a number have become hopefully pious. At such times, God may be said to be peculiarly near; and it gives special emphasis to his direction, 'Seek ye the Lord while he may be found, call ye upon him while he is near.' It often appears to be much easier to secure the salvation of one's soul at such times than at others. But it must be made the object of *chief* attention. A heart to see and feel one's own sins, to abhor and forsake them, to behold the infinite beauty, loveliness, and excellence of Jesus Christ, to trust in him as a Saviour, and to delight in obeying him, is infinitely better than all wisdom, knowledge, or wealth, without it.

"The coming Thursday is a day which is very generally observed as a day of special prayer for colleges and other seminaries of learning. I suppose you have public exercises on that occasion. All such seasons I should be glad to have you attend, feeling that every thing is of small importance compared with the salvation of the soul."

A week later he says, "I feel especially desirous that you, my dear son, should *now* make this your great concern. Without a heart to choose God as your portion, to give him your supreme, your best affections, and make it your great object in life to honor him and do good, you are not fitted to live or prepared to die; and you are constantly robbing him of what is most justly his due. You know from your acquaintance with the word of God, that you must experience a change in the temper of your mind, or you cannot see his kingdom. And you know also, from your own consciousness, that without it you cannot be happy here. As you must at some time make this your great concern, or it had been better for you not to have been born, and you can never have a better time, is not the present a peculiarly favorable time? it may be your only time. Does not duty, interest, safety, blessedness, every thing dear and every thing dreadful, urge you to give yourself, and all that you are and have, without delay, to Him who hath said and sealed it with his blood, 'Him that cometh unto me I will in no wise cast out.'"

Again he says, "Contemplate, my dear son, your character and condition as a sinner in the sight of God. Go to him habitually, and tell him honestly and freely how you feel, and what you need; beseech him to grant you his Spirit—who convinces of sin, of righteousness, and of judgment; who takes of the things of Christ, and shows them unto men; who opens blind eyes, unstops deaf ears, softens hard hearts, and brings those that were afar off nigh by the blood of Jesus. And forget not, that Jesus is now '*exalted to give repentance and forgiveness of sins.'* He intercedes for you, invites you to come to him, guilty as you are, and will delight to receive you; and there would be great joy in the presence of all the angels of God. *Give them this joy,* my dear son, and let that Saviour who freely gave up his life for you, have your soul for a jewel in his crown of glory."

To the compiler he wrote in reference to this son, "If convenient and pleasant for you and your friends to remember him before your heavenly Father, and to ask that he may be furnished to be an instrument in preparing jewels for the crown of Him whom the Father delighteth to honor, you will lay me under many and great and new obligations by doing so, and may be instrumental in saving not only one, but many souls from death, and hiding multitudes of sins."

To his eldest son in New York.

"ANDOVER, March 7, 1840.

"MY DEAR SON—I am glad to hear of so much attention to religion in New York, and hope you will ever feel that the blessings of the Holy Spirit are the greatest and most to be desired of all blessings. If persons feel their need of Christ and his salvation, give up themselves to him, trust in him, and choose to serve him, he has promised that they shall not want any good thing. He will keep them from the dangers to which they may be exposed, will guide them in the right way, will give them as much of this world as shall be best for them, will order all things for their good, and when they leave this world will receive them to himself. They, and they only, are safe, and in the way in which alone it is possible to be either excellent or happy, in this life or the life to come.

"The Bible is the expression of His will. And persons may know something how they feel towards Him, by knowing how they feel towards that. If they love the one, they will love the other. And if you do not find delight in daily searching the Scriptures, you should fix it in your mind that your heart is not right with God, and that without a great change you cannot see his kingdom. Daily spread out your feelings to him, and beseech him to grant you the teachings of his Spirit. May the Lord guide and bless you, my son, and make you a blessing."

To his sons in college he wrote, June 11, recording the wonderful preservation of the life of their elder brother: "We yesterday received a letter from Justin, dated Galena, Illinois, June 5, saying that he was on board a steam-boat in the Missouri river, which struck a snag and sunk." He says,

"'She sunk in three minutes. Six persons were drowned; two women, three children, and an old man. In the afternoon four or five of us had been talking about the bursting of boilers, and other accidents of steam-boats upon these waters. We all concluded that the stern of the boat, on the hurricane deck, would be the safest place should the boat strike a snag. While talking, the supper-bell rang. Just after we were seated we heard a tremendous crash, and knew that the boat had struck. The dishes were all knocked off the table, and some of the persons from their seats. I sprung for my life-preserver, which I had in my berth already filled. I took that and was on the hurricane deck in less than a minute; two others followed, one of them was the old man. All the others who could, got into the small boat, which was immediately filled, and sunk before it reached the shore, but all got safe to land. The steam-boat careened, and threw us who were on the deck into the water. The current was strong, and it was nearly two hours before I reached the land, and when I did I was out of sight of the place where the boat sunk. I was cold, and ran as fast as I could up the river, till I came to the passengers. The one who stood on deck with me was on the opposite side of the river safe, but the old man was drowned. I immediately left the spot, and after walking about four miles, found a wagon and went back to St. Louis.'

"He had $1,400 with him when in the water, but so secured that it was not injured. He will be kept out, should he live and be able to travel, a number of weeks longer than he expected. The goodness of God in his preservation should be devoutly acknowledged, and that life which God has so graciously spared, be devoted to his service."

To his son so kindly preserved, he wrote, "We rejoice and desire to be grateful to God, the author of all good and the giver of every mercy, for his kindness in your preservation, and that having obtained help of him you are permitted to continue, as we hope, in the land of the living. So true it is, that we do not know, and we cannot know, what a day or an hour may bring forth. The merchant is unwise who does not get his goods insured. How much more he who does not, by believing in the Saviour and loving him, secure the everlasting interests of his soul, when that is so much more exposed than goods, and so much more valuable, and the loss of it so much more irreparable.

"It must have been a solemn time to you when in the water, your companions sinking by your side, and you not knowing but that soon you would follow them. No one, without experience, can know the value at such a time, of having a good hope through grace of an interest in the Lord Jesus Christ, and a joyful assurance that if called to be absent from the body the soul will be present with the Lord, beholding his glory and rejoicing in his love. Had you then, my dear son, closed your probation, where would now have been your soul? Nothing of this sort occurs by chance. It is under the wise and good direction of God. It is a call to you, in his providence, to give him your heart, and devote that life which he has so kindly preserved, as an offering of gratitude, to his service. Pray daily for his Spirit, that you may hearken to his voice, love him, and trust in him. And may that love which led God to give up his dearly beloved Son to die for you, constrain you to live henceforth not unto yourself, but unto Him who died for you and rose again."

To a son who for a short time assisted in a post-office he wrote, January 21, 1841, "Do nothing in connection with the post-office but what is strictly legal, and be as careful not improperly to deprive the government of their just revenue, as you would be not to deprive an individual of his just due. There is sometimes much looseness of conscience on this subject, even among professed Christians, and they seem to think it less wrong to defraud the government than to defraud an individual. But this is not right. We experience great blessings through the medium of our government, and we should conscientiously and cheerfully pay our proportion of taxes, customs, postage, etc., for its support."

Writing to a relative a few days later, he says, "I have had more than twenty students to examine this week, preparatory to their being licensed to preach; and sometimes it takes two or three hours to examine one and say all to him which seems important before he begins to preach. It is a great thing for a minister to preach even one sermon, and have all that is said strictly true, and so said that it will *convey* nothing but truth to others."

About the same date he wrote to a Christian friend, who he perhaps feared might awaken prejudice or opposition in the young and tender mind by too anxious endeavors for immediate spiritual results:

"'First the blade, then the ear, after that the full corn in the ear.' 'The husbandman hath patience for the early and latter rain.' So must we have patience. The husbandman who keeps all the time handling the little tender blade, and pulling it with his fingers, and trying to make it grow faster, and bring forth fruit *now* before it is half grown, will not help it any, or have any greater harvest, than he who prepares the ground, keeps out the weeds, and goes to sleep at night, while it springs up and grows he knows not how. And 'he that goeth forth and weepeth, bearing precious seed, shall doubtless come again with rejoicing, bringing his sheaves with him,' and giving all the praise to the God of the harvest, who giveth 'seed to the sower and bread to the eater,' for ever."

Reporting to the compiler his approval of the treatise on "Love to God," by the excellent Joseph John Gurney, of the society of Friends, he says, "It is a very sweet work, with which the soul is delighted as with marrow and fatness," and adds, "We ought to be grateful that there are some servants of Christ who, through grace, are tall enough to walk over the denominational walls which men have placed around them."

In a letter of February, 1841, Dr. Edwards records the death of the Hon. WILLIAM BARTLET, the princely donor to the Theological Seminary, who had added to his other gifts, provision for the salary of Dr. Edwards in the presidency, for five years from 1836 to 1841. He died at his residence in Newburyport, February 8, 1841, at the great age of ninety-three years. Besides all his munificent charities while he lived, he bequeathed, chiefly to children and grandchildren, upwards of half a million of dollars. At the age of twenty-one he was a shoemaker, and he was strong and vigorous till within a very short period of his death. A tribute to his memory was delivered at Andover by the Rev. Daniel Dana, D. D., April 19, 1841, in which, after referring to his deep interest in the benevolent institutions of the age, which, with other objects of philanthropy, received his liberal support, he says,

"It is a singular and memorable fact, that when, about thirty-four years since, several opulent and large-hearted individuals were meditating the establishment of a theological seminary in this place, an assemblage of the same description, in a distant part of the county, were, without any mutual knowledge or communication, engaged in a design entirely similar. When the respective parties became acquainted with each other's intentions, a most interesting question arose: Would the cause of God and the interests of the churches be best promoted by a *separate* or a *united* organization? The question received a long and ample discussion. In the issue, difficulties vanished, minor differences were merged, the spirit of union and of mutual concession prevailed; and as the result, this theological institution rose into existence amply endowed, and powerfully sustained. The founders at Andover," (Samuel Abbott, Esq., the widow of Lieutenant-governor Samuel Phillips, and Hon. John Phillips, Jr.,) "having been first in maturing and arranging their plan, it was agreed that the other party should unite with them under the appellation of Associate Founders. Messrs. Brown (of Newburyport,) and Norris (of Salem,) made each a donation of ten thousand dollars; Mr. Bartlet the same; adding, at the time, another ten thousand, and soon after increasing his subscription by a similar additional sum. These contributions, so liberal and ample, were but a mere introduction to subsequent displays of his liberality. To this liberality we owe the elegant and commodious chapel in which we are now convened. To this we owe a spacious and convenient hall for the residence of students. To this we owe no small part of our select and invaluable library. Having from early time adopted the Seminary as the child of his affections, he has followed it, in every subsequent stage, with spontaneous and unintermitted kindness, crowning all former favors by a very liberal provision in his last testament."

September 8, 1841, Dr. Edwards preached before the American Board of Commissioners for Foreign Missions, in Philadelphia, his published sermon, "Christ, the Builder of the Spiritual Temple," from Zechariah 4 : 6, "Not by might, nor by power, but by my Spirit, saith the Lord of hosts." This spiritual temple is the church, "built upon the foundation of the apostles and prophets, Jesus Christ himself being the chief corner-stone." "It is to be composed of all true believers who shall ever have lived, from the first morning of creation to the last moment of time. They may not belong to the same denomination, or spend life on the same side of the wall which they have set up; but if they believe on the Son of God, and are so joined to him as to be 'one Spirit,' they shall form a part of his spiritual temple. Europeans, Asiatics, Africans, Indians—all, of every age, and color, and kindred, and people, and nation, and tongue, who believe on the Lord Jesus Christ, shall thus be builded together for an eternal habitation of God through the Spirit."

"The greatness of the work which it was necessary to perform to lay the foundation—the foundation itself," the Son of God, the brightness of the Father's glory, and the express image of his person—"the materials out of which the temple is to be made," fallen and apostate man—"and the object for which it is to be erected," to make known "the manifold wisdom of God, and the exceeding riches of his grace in his kindness towards men through Jesus Christ"—all show that it must be built, not by might, nor by power, but by the Spirit of the Lord of hosts. That divine Spirit has chosen to work by blessing his own truth in answer to prayer, and has commanded his followers to make known that truth to every creature. "The grand business of every one is to embrace the gospel himself as the power of God unto salvation, and exert his influence to have this done by every man, woman, and child in Christendom, and throughout the world. From the discharge of this duty no man can be excused. Let him be a merchant, a manufacturer, a mechanic, or a farmer; a professional man, a man of leisure, or a man of business—whoever, wherever, whatever he may be, he is bound by obligations which he can never throw off, to go himself, or assist others to go, and preach the gospel to all people, and to use his influence to induce all to embrace it."

Fired with this theme, when the members of the Seminary reässembled, he solemnly laid before them the import of the Saviour's last command, in its practical application to foreign missions—a command demanding not prayer only, or the gift of money, but the gift of *themselves* to go at the bidding of the Lord. And here his mind reverted to Mills, and Hall, and Richards, and Robbins, his companions in college, whose consecration of themselves to missions, in the dark period thirty years before, had been blessed in the cheering results then witnessed. He records that while the best pastors who had long been praying that the gospel might be preached to the heathen, were advising the young men "*to give up such visionary projects*," one of the little band wrote to another as follows:

"'I trust that our brethren will stand at their several posts, determined, God helping them, to show themselves *men*. Perhaps the fathers will soon arise, and take the business into their own hands. But should they hesitate, let us be prepared to go forward, trusting to that God who hath said, 'Lo, I am with you alway, even to the end of the world.' O that we could *enter at a thousand gates; that every limb were a tongue, and every tongue a trumpet*, to spread the gospel sound. Let us, my dear brother, rely with implicit confidence upon those great eternal precious promises contained in the word of God: 'There is no man that hath left house, or brethren, or sisters, or father, or mother, or wife, or children, or lands, for my sake and the gospel's, but he shall receive a hundred-fold, now in this time, with persecutions; and in the world to come, eternal life.' Be strong therefore, and let not your hands be weak, for your work shall be rewarded.

"'Come then, and, added to thy many crowns,
Receive yet one, the crown of all the earth,
Thou, who alone art worthy; it was thine
By ancient covenant e'er nature's birth;
And thou hast made it thine, by purchase, since,
And overpaid its value with thy blood.'"

"Such were the feelings of four young men in 1809. Their reliance was on God, and their determination was, that, let others do as they might, they would attempt in this matter to obey Christ, and do what they could to cause the gospel of his salvation to be preached to every creature. They resolved, if they could, to form an association in this country to assist them. And if they could not, to go to some other country and form one there, if they could. And if they could not do this, then to work their way to some portion of the heathen world, and make known to the dying people, as far as they could, 'the unsearchable riches of Christ.' *This is the spirit which God delights to bless.*"

January 27, 1842, he wrote to relatives in Boston, who had kindly supported his second son throughout his college course, informing them that the son had entered the Theological Seminary, and requesting them to procure a copy of "The Way of Life" to be presented to him by his sister. He adds:

"J—— appears to be in fine health; he entered immediately into the Junior class, and appears to be devoted to his studies. And if the Lord shall grant him the teaching of his Spirit, I cannot but hope that your many labors and prayers and sacrifices for him, may not be in vain in the Lord; but may, through his rich abounding grace, redound to his glory, to the honor of that Saviour to whom we owe all our friends, all our comforts, and all our hopes; and to whom we shall be indebted for all, for ever. It is good to serve him; and in proportion as our young ministers, and old ones too, learn to follow him, they will not walk in darkness, but have the 'light of life;' a light compared with which, the light of reason, of learning and science, of wealth and power, of reputation and influence and popularity merely, are as that of the glowworm compared with the light of the sun. It is a light from the Sun of righteousness, which causes those who receive and enjoy it, not only to have light, but to *become light* in the Lord."

To his youngest daughter, who was with friends in Boston, where were some special indications of the presence of the Spirit, he wrote, March 17, 1842, "We are willing that you should stay; hoping that your great desire is to become reconciled to God, and be prepared to serve him. He is good; he has been very kind, all your days, to you; and it is right that you should, without delay, serve him. For this end, trust not to yourself, or to ministers, or Christian friends, as they cannot help you, except as Jesus Christ shall, by his Spirit, use them for this purpose. He is everywhere present, and he can do for you what you need. Go directly to him, tell him all your unworthiness and all your wants; and that he must save you, or you must perish. Tell him how you feel, and what you need, remembering that he would be just, if he should show you no mercy, but leave you, on account of your sins, to perish; and yet, that he died to save you; and invites you, guilty and unworthy as you are, to put your trust in him. He is all our hope, and we are under everlasting obligations to him for dying in our stead, that God might be just, and yet sanctify and save with an everlasting salvation all who trust in him."

A few months later, under her father's kind and faithful counsel, this daughter publicly professed

Christ, and joined herself to his people. Having connected herself with Bradford academy, an institution identified with the early history of Mrs. Ann H. Judson and Harriet Newell, her father wrote to her, "Daily read the Bible, and ask God to teach you by his Spirit all his holy will. Endeavor in all things to set an example which is lovely and will benefit all who shall follow it. Endeavor to keep the Sabbath-day holy from the beginning to the end, and to do to others as you ought to wish they should do to you. Trust in Jesus Christ for all that you need, and strive to imitate him, that you may find rest to your soul. Cultivate cheerfulness and piety as the balm of human life, which is nourished and increased by doing good to all."

In a letter to Mrs. Edwards' brother in New York, April 25, 1842, he announces his retiring from the presidency: "When I accepted the appointment of President of the Theological Seminary, provision was made for my support for only five years, and I knew that I might be liable to close my connection with the institution at the close of that time. Nevertheless, I thought it best to accept the appointment, even if that should be the case. The five years closed last September. The trustees then appointed a committee to see if means could be appropriated to my support from funds which we now have. But they find that they cannot do it without taking them away from other objects, from which none of us wish to take them, and I have of course resigned my office as president, still retaining that of trustee of the institution.

"I am this day fifty-five years old. May the Lord

make me truly grateful for all his kindness, and teach me evermore to rejoice in him. I hope he will open some door of usefulness for me, and provide in kindness for my family. He has hitherto been unspeakably kind, and I cannot but hope that he will give me a heart to trust in him, and to do his will."

Many worthy and successful pastors, and others in stations of eminent usefulness in the church of God, bear a grateful testimony to the hallowed and abiding influence exerted by Dr. Edwards upon their own minds during his presidency—an influence which they value the more as they have become acquainted with the practical wants of men, and the power of the simple gospel of Christ as the remedy for sin and woe. His influence was practical and biblical, rather than theoretic, literary, or scholastic; and was enforced by a living example of what the man of God should be. His prayers and other devotional exercises are remembered as breathing "an unction from the Holy One;" his brief practical expositions of the Bible as refreshing to the spirit that loved to draw divine instruction from the inspired fountains; and his kind counsels as indicating that he had himself been taught of God, and as guiding to the course of true wisdom and usefulness. Often has the remark been made, that all he did in his presidency for the best good of individuals brought into connection with him, and for the highest spiritual interests of the kingdom of Christ, will never be fully appreciated till the fruits into which it ripened shall be garnered in a brighter world.

An esteemed pastor, who was a member of the seminary, says, "His counsels to the young men about to enter the ministry, in the weekly conference, and on other occasions, were very valuable; and his kind, peaceful, evangelical influence was felt on the seminary, and through the academies, in nameless ways. I have a distinct impression of the singular appropriateness and force with which he commented on the passages of Scripture read at the devotional exercises of the seminary. He seemed neither to say too much nor too little; his words were 'fitly spoken.' He was preëminent as a counsellor. His study was the resort of students perplexed and 'troubled about many things,' and he was the *father* of them all."

Another, after expressing a wish that he could have acted as Professor of Pastoral Theology, and from the professional chair "imparted to the students his varied experience and wise counsels respecting pastoral duties," says, "He exerted a powerful and beneficial influence, of which no record can be made. Among the eminent men whom I gratefully remember as my teachers, there is not one whom I remember with more gratitude than Dr. Edwards. It is good to be permitted even to know such a man, and to love him."

CHAPTER XI.

HIS LABORS FOR THE SANCTIFICATION OF THE SABBATH.

SEVEN YEARS—1842-1849.

DR. EDWARDS having resigned the presidency of the Theological Seminary, April 19, 1842, we mark the workings of his mind on the question, WHAT GOD WOULD NOW HAVE HIM DO; and his humbly seeking the guidance of the *word*, the *providence*, and the *Spirit* of God, which at length was manifestly imparted.

April 26, he wrote to the Rev. Dr. Brigham, Secretary of the American Bible Society, a letter of inquiry touching a department of usefulness to which his thoughts had long and often been turned:

"For a number of years, when reading the Bible, and finding it to be sweeter than honey or even the honey-comb, and that a knowledge of it is more to be desired than gold or even *fine* gold, and that in understanding, believing, and obeying it, there is indeed a *great* reward, I have had many thoughts floating about my mind as to the best mode, in the least time, of giving it to all who can read, and who would not otherwise receive it. You may perhaps recollect a letter which I wrote to you from Saratoga thirteen or fourteen years ago. What it was I do not now distinctly recollect; but I remember that it was designed, should the Lord give opportunity, to open the way for some further communications with regard to this subject. But other objects intervened, and it has rested to the present time. What should you think of a systematic, united, general, and *persevering* effort, *to induce each individual who has the Bible*, DAILY *to read some portion of it;* and to *do something to extend it*, IN THE LEAST POSSIBLE TIME, *to every individual who can read*, and who would not otherwise obtain it? And should you be disposed, without any noise, to consult further with regard to it; or are your plans now as well constructed, and in as general, vigorous, and efficacious operation as in the present imperfect state of things they probably can be?"

To this letter Dr. Brigham replied, May 4, that it had awakened much interest; that "the Board felt more and more the importance, not only of *distributing* a greater number of Bibles, but of having them more generally and faithfully *read;*" that "after consulting two committees, of which the Rev. Dr. Milnor and the Rev. Dr. DeWitt were chairmen, it was resolved to invite him to give an address at the Society's anniversary to be held on the 12th instant, embodying all the wisdom he had on the subject of the universal *distribution* and *perusal* of the word of God."

On the day in which Dr. Edwards wrote the above note to the Bible Society, the secretaries of the American Tract Society at New York addressed him, inquiring "if he would listen to any proposition that Society could make for gaining his coöperation more immediately in the Tract department of benevolence;" to which he replied, May 10, that he was not then prepared to decide with regard to his future course; that he "*did not intend to be idle, but to keep his eyes and ears open, and take suitable measures to ascertain the will of God, and in dependence on him, as fast as he learned his will, to attempt to do it.*"

Near the close of the month, during the anniversary week in Boston, he invited the compiler to a walk on the Common, and stated that his attention had been especially directed to three objects—TEMPERANCE, the BIBLE, and the SABBATH. To the first he had devoted seven years; the other two were now more especially before him, and he wished to see clearly to which of the two God called him to consecrate himself.

While these subjects were under consideration, the committee of the American Temperance Society, June 4, 1842, reappointed him for the service of that Society, though with the understanding, that should he feel that he was called to combine with it or even relinquish it for labors in behalf of the Sabbath or any other kindred object, he should be at liberty to follow what he might believe to be the indications of the divine will. And here we have brief memoranda from his own pen for a few days, in a little book for the pocket, chiefly filled with business items of the work on which he was to enter.

"JUNE 13, 1842. On the 4th inst. I received an appointment from the Executive Committee of the American Temperance Society, and on the sixth I accepted the appointment. During the week I prepared two communications for the press: one on the nature, author, object, progress, and results of the Temperance movement, and the duties of the friends of God and man with regard to it; the other an appeal to ministers of the gospel in the state, with reference to the Massachusetts Temperance Union.

"To-day I undertake to prepare a discourse, to be preached as I may have opportunity, on Psalm 24:1: '*The earth is the Lord's, and the fulness thereof; the world, and they that dwell therein;*' designed to make the impression upon my own mind and the minds of others, that GOD IS THE OWNER OF ALL THINGS; that men are and can be only stewards, and that to be *honest* they must be disposed to render Him his due; and designed to point out to all people who may hear it, what honesty requires.

"May the Lord guide me by his Spirit, and make me instrumental of honoring him, and doing the highest good of which I am capable to the children of men. I feel, or think I feel, more and more my constant need of his presence and blessing; and that *the entrance of his word, accompanied by his Spirit*, or *the Spirit speaking by the word*, giveth light; it giveth understanding to the simple; it indeed shineth as the day. And the amount of light which He, through his truth, can communicate *at once* on spiritual subjects, is truly wonderful; so that through Him, as our day is, not only our strength, but also our light, our consolation, and all other needed blessings, shall also be. 'Trust in the Lord,' therefore, 'with all thy heart, and lean not to thine own understanding. In all thy ways acknowledge him, and he shall direct thy paths. Be careful,' over-anxious, 'for nothing; but in every thing by prayer and supplication let your requests be made known to God. And the peace of God, which passeth all understanding, shall keep your mind and heart through Christ Jesus.' May I ever feel this and act accordingly, and so seek Thee, thou source and fountain of light and love, wisdom, strength, and consolation, that I shall not want any good thing.

"*Afternoon.* Had several hours very interesting conversation with a friend on the means of the moral renovation of this world; particularly the promotion of *Temperance*, the observance of the *Sabbath*, and the proper treatment of the *Bible;* and concerning God as the author, Christ as the foundation, the Holy Ghost as the producer, and faith and love and Christian effort as the means, of all good to the children of men. May the Lord bless it to him and to me, and make it the means of great good to millions for ever."

On the 19th he preached the sermon on Psalm 24:1, in Newburyport, and then proceeded to Portland, where on the 21st he says, "I addressed the Maine Conference on the subject of *Temperance*, the *Sabbath*, and the *Bible*. Had an interesting and very pleasant time. The Lord seemed to be there.

"At seven P. M. took the boat for Boston. Arrived fifteen minutes too late to take the cars for Hartford, and soon saw, or thought I saw, the goodness of God in my disappointment. May I always rejoice in his will, and say, not in words merely, but in feeling and conduct, 'Not my will, but thine be done.' Left at three P. M. and lodged at the Exchange, (Hartford,) where the proprietor keeps a Bible in each lodging-room, and does not sell the drunkard's poison to be drunk even by sober men. This is as it should be, and I trust soon will be over all the earth, should the

Bible go everywhere, and be understood, believed, and obeyed by every soul.

"22d, (at the Exchange hotel in Hartford,) thought this morning of forming, or attempting to form, an AMERICAN AND FOREIGN BIBLICAL ASSOCIATION, the object of which shall be to induce every person who cannot read, to learn to read; every person who can read, and is destitute, to supply himself with a Bible, daily to read some portion of it, and seek the teaching of the Holy Spirit, that he may understand, believe, and obey it.

"23d, arrived at Wethersfield just in time to procure from the General Association of Connecticut the passage of three resolutions on *Temperance*, the *Sabbath*, and the *Bible*, the same as were passed on the 21st, by the General Association of Maine. I would devoutly acknowledge the goodness of God in bringing me here at the hour, and inducing the Association to give the resolution so favorable a reception. May he help me henceforward to notice his hand, his kindness and love in all things, and rejoice evermore in him and his holy will, so that I may pray without ceasing, and in every thing give thanks, because this is the will of God. Help me, O God, to trust in thee at all times, and to pour out my heart before thee, and in all my ways so to acknowledge thee that thou mayest in all things direct my paths. Give me clear and extended discernment, sound judgment, a pure and holy heart, an ardent thirst after knowledge, especially a knowledge of the 'only true God, and Jesus Christ whom thou hast sent;' an ardent love to men, and desire for their highest good; candor and kindness in view of their failings, and compassion in view of their sins; a deep abhorrence of every wrong thing; a rejoicing in others' prosperity, in their increasing influence, and ability and disposition to do good; and a heart to render to thee at all times all the glory. Open the way, I beseech thee, O Lord, for the sake of thy Son, for all people soon to bow to him and own him as Lord, to thy glory.

"25th, reached Boston, where I spent the Sabbath.

"27th, went to Andover and formed the Sabbath Association.

"29th, went to Westborough, and attended the General Association of Massachusetts, who adopted the resolutions on *Temperance*, the *Sabbath*, and the *Bible*."

On the 31st he is at New Haven raising funds for the *Sabbath* cause; then at Saratoga and at Mr. Delavan's in Ballston, then at Utica, then at Rochester at an interesting *Sabbath Convention;* then at Geneva, Auburn, Albany, Troy; then at Boston successfully conferring with gentlemen as to providing funds, and then in other parts of New England, and we find him *in the midst of a powerful agency for the cause of* THE SABBATH, to which he devoted seven years of his public life.

As in the Temperance reformation, when he was brought as it were *into contact with the millions of men*, in forming and executing plans of which the responsibility rested mainly on himself, he showed a giant power which none before knew that God had given him, we now seem to feel the renewed pulsations of his great and warm heart, as he launches forth among the works and people of God, with the grand aim of inducing *all men to pause* on the holy Sabbath, and *hear the voice of God* speaking to them the words of eternal life.

He had labored nearly one year, when, on the 4th of April, 1843, the AMERICAN AND FOREIGN SABBATH UNION was organized in Boston: Chief Justice Williams, of Connecticut, President; Dr. Edwards, Secretary; and Messrs. John Tappan, Moses Grant, Benjamin Smith, Jacob Sleeper, and Benjamin Howard, Executive Committee.

On the 17th April, 1844, their first anniversary was held, when we have a summary record of the labors of Dr. Edwards for nearly two years.

"The Secretary of this Union has visited ten different states, and travelled about twelve thousand miles." He has generally preached, or delivered public addresses, two or three times on the Sabbath, and often during the week; he has attended five general Sabbath conventions, and addressed a great number of all classes of people. "These conventions have been numerously attended, and with great unanimity have expressed and published their views with regard to the importance of the Sabbath, and the benefits which would result to individuals and to the community from its universal observance.

"He has also attended the meetings of twenty-five ecclesiastical bodies of various denominations, has addressed personally more than *thirteen hundred ministers* of the gospel and several hundred more by letter, procured the passage of numerous resolutions expressive of their views of the divine authority and perpetual obligation of the Sabbath, and has engaged many to preach on the subject, and in the various ways in their power to disseminate a knowledge of the reasons why all men should remember that day and keep it holy. He has also visited many colleges and seminaries, and addressed the students on the importance of the Sabbath, as a day of rest from their secular pursuits, and of special devotion to spiritual and eternal concerns. Wherever he has gone, he has been welcomed, and the subject of the Sabbath has been treated with the most respectful attention. Many distinguished men have expressed their conviction of its great importance to all the interests and prospects of our country; and applications for the services of the Secretary have been much more numerous than he could comply with. He has also published numerous articles in various periodicals, which have been extensively copied and circulated. Through his efforts and those of others, an increased attention has been awakened, and in many places a great change in sentiment and practice is taking place with regard to this subject.

"The transportation of the mails on the Sabbath has, on numerous routes, been discontinued; and stage-coaches, steam-boats, rail-cars, and canal-boats have, in many cases, ceased to run on that day. Stockholders, directors, distinguished merchants and civilians, have expressed their conviction, that, should this be the case universally, it would greatly promote the welfare of all. The number of those who go, or send to the post-office, who are disposed to labor, or engage in secular business, travelling, or amusement on the Sabbath, is diminishing; and the number increasing who are disposed to attend the public worship of God. Sabbath-breaking is becoming more and more disreputable, and is viewed by increasing numbers, as evidence of a low, reckless, and vicious mind. The conviction is extending that it is not only morally wrong, but is unprofitable and dangerous. And should all the facts with regard to this subject be known, and duly appreciated, that conviction, we believe, would become universal.

"Laborers, in many cases, refuse to work on the Sabbath. They view it, as it actually is, *a degradation* to be thus singled out from the rest of the community, and obliged to labor when others are at rest. They find it to be hurtful to themselves and their families. It injures their health, corrupts their morals, and increases the danger of their being abandoned to infamy and ruin. Some who, in consequence of refusing to labor on the Sabbath, had been dismissed from their employments, have afterwards been sought for and employed again, and warmly commended for their attachment to principle, and for their fidelity and success in the discharge of their duties.

"There is a growing conviction, founded upon experience and observation, that property and life are *more safe* under the care of those who keep the Sabbath, than under the care of those who violate it; and that the one class are more likely to be blessed and to be a blessing, even in this world, than the other. As principles and facts become known, all see new evidence that 'the Sabbath was made for man,' and that in the keeping of it, according to the will of God, there is great reward."

The FIRST of the well-known and still widely circulated PERMANENT SABBATH DOCUMENTS, prepared by Dr. Edwards, had now been issued: exhibiting the ends for which the Sabbath was appointed; the reasons why it should be kept; the benefits of observing it; and the evils which, by laws that no one can annul or evade, must come upon those who profane it. The Sabbath, with its attendant means of grace, is presented as "the great institution of Jehovah for communicating, preserving, and rendering practically efficacious the knowledge of himself, as the Creator, Preserver, Redeemer, Benefactor, Owner, Governor, and Judge of men. It is the institution which he appointed, and which he blesses for that purpose. And so efficacious is it for that end, that no people who have continued to observe it according to his will, have ever lost the knowledge of the one only living and true God, or ceased publicly to serve and adore him. And had all people continued from the beginning to observe it, they had in all ages been worshippers of Jehovah, and idolatry never have been practised upon the earth."

At the creation God established the Sabbath for the race of man, and ratified it by his own high and holy example in resting on the seventh day. "Time itself was to be divided, not merely into days, or months, or years, or into any periods measured by the revolutions of the earth or the heavenly bodies, but into *weeks*—periods of seven days; six for labor, and one for rest and special devotion to spiritual things. This division of time, measured by the conduct and will of God, and by the capacities and wants of men, was to be, in all ages and all countries, a sign of the covenant between God and his people; an emblem and a foretaste of the rest which remaineth for them, and a special season of preparation for its eternal joys.

"For this reason, Jehovah not only kept it himself, but he sanctified it, or set it apart from other days for this special purpose. He also blessed it, and with such a fulness of blessings, that they flow out to those who keep it, not only on that day, but through all the other days of the week. They are blessed in their bodies and souls, in their going out and their coming in, and in all their ways."

"When, on the morning of that blessed day, the sun rises and shines as brightly as on other days, the oxen graze as peacefully, the lambs skip as briskly, and the birds sing as sweetly—yet no man goes forth to his labor, no shop-door or window opens, no wheel rattles on the pavement, or vessel leaves the harbor, no stage-coach or canal-boat runs, no whistling or rumbling is heard on the railroad, or bustle is witnessed in any department of secular business, but universal stillness reigns throughout creation, except as broken by the voice of prayer and praise ascending to its Author: *that stillness is the voice of God to the moral nature of man*—his still, small, but all-pervading and efficacious voice, proclaiming his existence, his character, and his will."

"When the day comes, every man has *a right* to keep it holy to the Lord. This is the right of the *poor*, as really as of the rich; of servants, as well as of masters. All have a right to labor six days in a week, because God has given it. All have a right to rest one day in seven, because God has given that. This right comes from God. Like the right to live, to see the sun, and breathe the air, it vests in humanity, and is *inalienable.* No human government gave it, and no human government, without deep injustice, can take it away. There is not a laborer on the canal or railroad, in the manufactory or workshop, or in any department of worldly business, who has not this right."

And not only the law written on tables of stone, but "*another law written by the finger of God on the nature of man and beast,*" requires this. "They were not made for seven days' labor in a week, and they cannot endure it, without lessening their health and shortening their lives:" a principle which he supports by the most reliable and abundant testimony, showing that "the policy which seeks to gain by the violation of the laws which infinite wisdom and goodness have established, is selfish, short-sighted, and defeats its own end."

The SECOND Permanent Sabbath Document, issued the next year, considers *the change from the seventh to the first day of the week.* The original institution was the setting apart of one day in seven for the holy rest; and we have simply to learn the will of God as to which day of the week it shall be. The seventh day was originally observed in commemoration of Jehovah's resting from the work of *creation;* the first day is observed in commemoration of *the greater work* of *redemption*, as shown in the New Testament.

"No sooner does Jehovah appear as 'God manifest in the flesh,' than suddenly there is with the angels a multitude of the heavenly hosts, crying, 'GLORY TO GOD IN THE HIGHEST.' Why? Because that in six days he created the heavens and the earth? No; not that merely, or principally; but because there is 'peace on earth, good-will to men,' through those wondrous manifestations into which angels desire to look, of a JUST GOD, AND YET A SAVIOUR.

"The first creation made men creatures, and placed them where, by their voluntary rebellion, they became sinners, and exposed to endless death; the second creation makes them saints, and prepares them to be kings and priests unto God, and to reign with him for ever and ever.

"Ever since He who had power to lay down his life, showed that he had power to take it again, by bursting the bands of death, and rising triumphant, leading captivity captive, his disciples have assembled on the day of his resurrection to worship and adore. For eighteen hundred years has been sung, by the church on earth, *a new song*, and one which the physical creation merely could never inspire, 'Thou art worthy, for thou wast slain, and hast redeemed us unto God by thy blood, out of every kindred, and tongue, and people, and nation.' This is now their practice; and such it will continue to be, till this song of the church on earth is swallowed up in the song of the church in heaven."

After Christ's resurrection, when according to the prophecy he became the headstone of the corner, we hear no more of his going into the synagogue, or any other place of worship, or even meeting his disciples, on the seventh day, (the day in which he had lain in the grave;) but on the first day he met them from time to time with abundant blessings, and said, "Peace be unto you;" "Receive ye the Holy Ghost."

The THIRD Permanent Sabbath Document, issued two years later, is entitled, "THE SABBATH A FAMILY INSTITUTION," and shows that as God made *one woman* to be the help-meet of *one man*, so he made *the Sabbath* to be the help-meet of *the family*, without which, in neither case, would he have fulfilled his designs of love. The whole subject underlies the dearest individual, social, civil, temporal, and eternal interests of man.

"To bring glory to himself in the highest, and manifest most efficaciously and extensively good-will to men, God established, at the creation, two great, fundamental, and permanent institutions. The first was that of MARRIAGE, or the union for life of one man and one woman, as the head of one family. The next was THE SABBATH, or the day of weekly rest from worldly business and cares, and of special devotion to the worship of God and the promotion of the spiritual good of men. Both were established in paradise, before the fall, and were 'made for man.' Both are suited to his nature, adapted to his capacities, and essential to the supply of his wants. They were so at the beginning, they are so now, and they will continue to be so, in all countries, to the end of time. They are parts of one whole, and mutually aid and sustain each other."

He considers the family institution under the heads

of *government*, *instruction*, and *example*. Under the first he says, "Children are the creatures, and as such, the property of God. He commits them to their parents as his representatives and officers, to receive and train them for his service. For this purpose they are, from the beginning, to consecrate them to him, and early to teach them the first great lesson of his moral government, 'Not my will, but thine be done:' that they must not be permitted to have their own way, to govern themselves, or others. They are not qualified to govern. They have not lived long enough, they do not know enough, they are not good enough, they are not strong enough. Their interest, safety, excellence, and usefulness, their happiness, and the happiness of others, all require that they should not govern, but be governed. Parents are God's officers to teach them this truth, which lies at the foundation of his moral government, and the practical experimental knowledge of which is essential to the excellence, usefulness, and happiness of every human being."

The instruction they need, especially "the knowledge of God their Creator, Redeemer, and Sanctifier, and of themselves, their relations and duties, should be communicated, not in set forms, or at stated periods merely, but 'line upon line, and precept upon precept, here a little and there a little,' as they are able to bear it. In the house and by the way, when they lie down and when they rise up, parents must communicate knowledge as there is time and opportunity. And in order to secure the performance of these duties, parents must daily read the Bible *themselves*, and pray, not only in secret, *but in their families*. All the family must assemble and hearken to the voice of their common God and Father; bow before him in confession of their sins, and in humble supplication for his mercy; render thanks for his benefits, and ask of him the blessings which they need for the body and the soul, for time and eternity, especially the blessings of his grace, that they may all be made wise unto salvation through faith in Jesus Christ. And in the duties and events of the day, parents must manifest those feelings of supreme regard to God and good will to men, which they inculcate on their children; and must set them an example of living, not unto themselves, but unto Him who died for them and rose again.

"Under the influence of such government, instruction, and example, they may expect, with the blessing of God, that their children will know him, and Jesus Christ whom he has sent, and will become followers of those who through faith and patience are now inheriting the promises."

But there would be no such "family government, instruction, and example," as here inculcated, if the Sabbath, with its ordinances and blessings, had not been given, and the very terms of the command seem to present it as a family institution: "In it thou shalt not do any work, thou, *nor thy son, nor thy daughter, thy man-servant, nor thy maid-servant,* nor thy cattle, nor the stranger that is within thy gates," or under thy control. "God has made it the duty of the head of the family to see that it is observed. And one great object that he had in view in the establishment of family government was, that through its influence the observance of the Sabbath might be secured," and thus the two great primeval institutions of paradise be the mutual support and strength of each other.

The FOURTH Permanent Sabbath Document, issued the next year, shows, chiefly from scriptural authority, THE PROPER MODE OF KEEPING THE SABBATH. The divine command, as above intimated, secures rest on this day to all under one's care and control, not only men but beasts of burden, and requires that all things be so arranged as to give them this privilege.

"Though heaven and the heaven of heavens cannot contain him, and he has ten thousand times ten thousand round about him, God does not forget the poor or the dumb. Not a servant escapes his notice, nor a beast is beneath his care. He never for a moment overlooks the defenceless, who cannot protect themselves, or plead their own cause. He compassionates their condition, and sympathizes with their wants. When, after six days of labor, they need, in addition to the rest of the nights, the rest also of one day, he guarantees it to them. And it was with reference to them, as well as others, that he made the Sabbath, set it apart for sacred purposes, gave it to men, forbade them to labor during its hours, and commanded them to keep it holy.

"To keep the Sabbath-day, then, in a proper manner, oxen and owners, servants and masters, children and parents, workmen and employers, sojourners and citizens, all, on this day, must rest from worldly business, except so far as works of necessary mercy, and the best discharge of the appropriate duties of the Sabbath as a holy day, may require."

He proceeds to a careful analysis of *the directions of the Bible* as to the sacred observance of the day, and especially the teaching of Christ and the apostles; and then examines a great variety of cases, in all the principal departments of life, in which there may be *a supposed necessity for violating the Sabbath*, illustrating the subject by facts which had come to his knowledge. He considers very fully the case of *manufactories—haying and harvesting—the merchant, or banker—the lawyer—travelling—the mails—the sailing of packets—going into the country for health—ferries—livery stables—the butcher—the baker—the printer—arrangements of families—steam-boats—navigation of ships—whaling—secular reading, or conversation—ministerial exchanges*, etc., showing in all the safety, the wisdom, and the duty of sacredly and faithfully keeping the day holy unto God. He then renews the consideration of the benefits of observing the day, in the study of the Scriptures, public worship, prayer, gaining or imparting religious instruction, and other means of grace, and adds:

"Let all who would be the friends of their Maker and benefactors of their race, confine their secular business, travelling, and amusement to six days in a week, the only days which God has made or given to men for that purpose, the only days which they can take without taking what is not theirs, and thus showing themselves to be at heart, towards God, dishonest men. Let them remember the Sabbath-day, and keep it holy as the day of the Lord; devoting it from beginning to end cheerfully to his worship, private, social, and public, and to the promotion of the spiritual good of men. Let them cease from secular cares, from worldly, scientific, and literary reading, conversation, visiting, and pleasure. Let them hearken diligently to the voice of God in his works, his word, and his providence, and as echoed by their own conscience; let them make it a part of their employment every Sabbath, to study the Bible with attention, docility, and prayer; to hearken to it as illustrated, expounded, and enforced by the pious, learned, and faithful ministers of the gospel; and then let them search the Scriptures for themselves, and judge whether what they hear is confirmed by the unerring word of God; and if so, let them receive it, not as the word of men, but as the word of God, treasure it up in their hearts, and exemplify it in their lives. Then will they shine as lights in the world, holding forth the word of life, and letting their light so shine that multitudes will be led to glorify their Father in heaven. Life will be pleasant, death will be peaceful, and eternity glorious. Their children who walk in their steps will rise up and call them blessed. Posterity will honor their memory, and unborn generations to all future time reap the benefit of their labors, and add to their exceeding and eternal weight of glory."

The FIFTH, and last Permanent Sabbath Document, DEVELOPMENTS OF PROVIDENCE ON THE SABBATH, comprises one hundred and thirty-four well attested, instructive, and in many cases intensely interesting facts; illustrating the blessedness, even in this life, of keeping the day holy, and the folly and sin of presumptuously rebelling against God by its profanation.

"These facts," he says, "are not stated to *prove* that the Sabbath is a holy day; but, as a part of the history of providence with regard to the day, they serve to illustrate and enforce the truth, that when men, in opposition to the known will of God, openly trample down a great institution of his appointment, the observance of which is essential to the promotion of his glory and the welfare of men, he will in his providence so often thwart their plans and disappoint their expectations, that for them to pursue such a course is not wise. It is not good policy for this world. It does not produce a good influence on a man's own mind while he pursues it; and it does not work well on his children. It is not the best way to obtain property, and receive from it the greatest benefit; and it does not end well."

These admirable "Permanent Sabbath Documents" were joyfully welcomed by the Christian community, both in this and the mother country, as they successively appeared, and they are still the standard work for general circulation on the sanctification of the Lord's day.

On the 27th of November, 1844, a NATIONAL SABBATH CONVENTION was held at Baltimore, attended by upwards of *seventeen hundred delegates,* from eleven different states, at which JOHN QUINCY ADAMS, late President of the United States, presided. This convention adopted with great unanimity twenty resolutions, expressing their sense of the sacredness, the divine authority, the obligations, and the benefits of the Sabbath; and also adopted three able and forcible public appeals for the true and proper observance of the day: one *to the people of the United States;* one to *canal commissioners;* and one to the *directors of railroads*—all of which, with the proceedings of the convention and valuable letters from gentlemen of distinction who could not be present, were published and extensively circulated. Within the first three years of Dr. Edwards' labors, fifteen general Sabbath conventions were held, of which seven were state conventions, each attended by from one hundred to five hundred delegates.

On the adjournment of the National Convention at Baltimore, he entered on one of those extensive and laborious tours by which he exerted so effective an influence. The brief record is: "He visited Washington, and addressed six public assemblies in the District of Columbia. He then proceeded westward, spending a week or two, and attending various public meetings, in the principal places from that city to St. Louis, where he addressed seven public meetings, and then proceeded to Alton, Peoria, Chicago, and Detroit, and returned by way of Buffalo to Albany. In the course of his tour, he attended about *sixty public meetings*, and had opportunity to address many members of the courts and other distinguished individuals, and members of the legislatures of Ohio, Indiana, Illinois, Michigan, and New York. He was listened to by crowded audiences, and with great attention. And not a few expressed the opinion, that could information be spread, and Sabbath observance receive, from *good men*, the united influence of a uniformly consistent *example*, it would ere long become universal.

"Railroad directors, in increasing numbers of cases, confined the running of their cars to six days in the week; locks on canals were not opened, and official business not transacted on the Sabbath. Stage-coaches and steam-boats in many cases had ceased to run; and more than eighty thousand miles of Sabbath-breaking mails had been stopped."

The last Sabbath report he presented, May, 1850, states that he had travelled more than forty-eight thousand miles, through twenty-five of the United States, "addressing various classes of men through the pulpit and the press, and pointing out the reasons why, as individuals and as a nation, we should, in obedience to God, 'remember the Sabbath-day to keep it holy.'"

"About *forty railroad companies*," he says, "stop the running of their cars on that day, on about *four thousand miles of roads*. The communities through which they pass, and whose right to the stillness and quiet of the day had for years been grossly violated by the screaming and rumbling of cars in time of public worship, are now free from the nuisance, and are permitted to enjoy their rights and privileges without molestation. No good reason can be given why this should not be the case universally, throughout our country. The running of rail-cars on the Sabbath is giving sanction to its public desecration, and openly setting at defiance the will of Jehovah. It is undermining the efficacy of his laws, and encouraging the vicious to break them. If one class of men may violate one of the ten commandments, those great, fundamental, permanent moral laws, engraven with the finger of Jehovah on tables of stone, another class may violate another, and so on, till all are disregarded. Thus an example is set which tends powerfully to universal profligacy, and to the destruction of that virtue on which all our social, civil, and religious institutions depend. That railroads are to be the principal mode of conveyance on all our great thoroughfares, is now settled. From morning to evening, and from evening to morning, one incessant and mighty rush of human invention, activity, and enterprise will, year after year, sweep from ocean to ocean, through the six working days of the week. If then, at the bidding of Jehovah, the giver and preserver of all good, the fire of our engines is extinguished, and our millions of wheels cease to roll—if the rising Sabbath sun, unobscured by the smoke of our fires, casts his cheering rays on every iron road, and as he passes over our widely extended and extending country, sees in our cities, towns, and villages, the whole people congregating for prayer, thanksgiving, and praise, then shall our peace be as a river, and our righteousness as the waves of the sea. The difference between the Sabbath and other days will be seen and felt by every child in our nation, and they will grow up instinctively exclaiming on its approach, 'This is the day which the Lord hath made; we will rejoice and be glad in it. Let us come before his presence with thanksgiving, and make a joyful noise unto him with psalms. O come, let us worship and bow down; let us kneel before the Lord our Maker; for he is our God, and we are the sheep of his pasture and the people of his hand.'"

CHAPTER XII.

LABORS FOR THE SANCTIFICATION OF THE SABBATH—CONTINUED.

1842-1849.

HAVING presented a brief view of Dr. Edwards' more public and official labors for seven years in behalf of the Sabbath, we return to gather some gems from his correspondence during the same period.

To his eldest son, who was about to travel at the South and West, he gave the following hints:

"Commit yourself and your way to the Lord; acknowledge him with gratitude as the first duty of the morning, and seek his guidance, protection, and blessing through the day. These we always need, and especially in travelling, for then it is especially true that we know not what a day may bring forth. Keep a little pocket Testament as your daily companion, and endeavor to read some portion of it every day, though it be but a few verses. Avoid travelling on the Sabbath, and wherever you may be, endeavor to keep it holy, and always attend public worship. It is the way to prosper during the week.

"Avoid gaming of every sort, even for amusement, at public-houses, on board the steam-boat, and in all other places. I have seen young men on the western steam-boats induced '*just to begin,*' and having once begun, unable to stop till they had lost all, and were deeply in debt. Many of the boats and public-houses abound with men who are constantly watching, and who make it a business to ingratiate themselves into the confidence of the young, in order to seduce and ruin them.

"Do nothing on your journey under the idea that you are a stranger, and that it will not be known. Treat all persons with courtesy and kindness, but never commit yourself to any stranger in such a manner that he may injure you, should he prove to be a bad man. Have no difficulty or personal altercation with any one, however badly he may treat you. If a man takes your berth in the boat or your seat in the coach, and refuses to give it up when politely informed that it is yours, then take another. Be above having any difficulty with such a man, and have nothing to do with him except to 'overcome evil with good.' This is the way to make all treat you with kindness and respect.

"Keep your eyes and ears open, see every thing, and hear every thing, and learn as many valuable and important facts as possible while on your journey. Provide yourself with good pocket travelling maps and note-books, and make yourself thoroughly acquainted with the geography of the country through which you pass. Soon after you enter a city, like Cincinnati or St. Louis, it is well to go upon the highest elevation in the neighborhood which overlooks the city, and get as perfect a view as possible fixed in your mind of its exact location, size, shape, etc. You will thus get correct and permanent impressions of every place you visit.

"Be as regular as possible in meals and sleep: avoid overloading the stomach, especially in the evening; and above all, avoid wines, beers, and all intoxicating liquors. Be careful not to be out at night or in storms. This is more hazardous at the West than at the East. Avoid as far as possible great fatigue, which will expose you to fever and ague, and bilious fevers. When sick do not travel, but lie by, and send for the best physician, if possible a Christian physician, for such a one may be more safely trusted. Above all, look to the great Physician of body and soul, who is always able and willing to hear and to do for those who truly and heartily apply to him. When getting up from sickness, be careful not to set out on your journey too soon. A relapse thus caused will be more dangerous than the first attack, and many have thus lost their lives.

"If called to lay your body among strangers, or in the rolling deep, commit your soul in penitence and faith into the hands of Him who hath said, 'Him that cometh unto me I will in no wise cast out.' 'He that believeth on me shall never die;' and 'though he were dead, yet shall he live.'"

He adds a list of thirty or forty worthy clergymen and laymen in the principal cities and towns, connected with the several evangelical Christian denominations, who, in case his son should be sick and need their aid, would gladly render it.

In October, 1842, having taken part in a public deliberative meeting of the Board and friends of the American Tract Society in New York, he wrote to the compiler: "The meeting will, I trust, do great good, and several of the documents read might with great advantage be put into a volume, or circulated in some other form, to all the friends of Zion. The idea that *every Christian*, wherever he goes or stays, should be a colporteur to the destitute, should be extended and impressed universally.

"The paper read on the divinely appointed methods of spreading the gospel, is *a fundamental document*, and could the New Testament be fairly and fully exhibited on that subject, it would sweep away many powerful obstructions to the most extensive good. It is earnestly hoped that the Christians of this country, and other countries, will not wait till they are, by persecution, violently scattered abroad, before they will, wherever they go, preach the word; and testify that by which men may be saved. If making known divine truth is preaching, all may bear a part in preaching the gospel to every creature; and all may have souls for their hire. There never was a people on the face of the earth who had greater facilities, or were under stronger obligations to do this, than the people of these United States; especially to evangelize, in the least possible time, *every nook and corner of our own country*.

"God is furnishing instruments for the battle of the great day. Our Leader is invincible, and ultimate victory certain. Let us be strong in the Lord, and in the power of his might; not weary in well-doing; not stop by the way to contend which shall be the greatest, or whose course the most important; but do good as we have opportunity to all, and rest assured that if any man serve Christ, him will the Father honor."

Being in the city of New York, April 29, 1844, he wrote to Mrs. Edwards: "Last evening I attended a meeting in the Tabernacle, and heard a son of Rev. Dr. Scudder, who is to sail on the 6th of May as a missionary to India. He has three other sons, who are preparing to be missionaries. One of them spoke after his brother, and the father closed. When he rose, he told the audience that he had *eight* sons and two daughters; that he gave all up to be missionaries, to go anywhere, or to any place to which God might call them. He then addressed other parents, and urged them to give up their children to the same blessed work; then called on the young merchants, doctors, and lawyers to dedicate themselves to Jesus Christ, and go to the heathen, or make money to help others to go; as a work infinitely more noble, dignified, useful, and blessed, than living merely for dollars and cents."

About the same time he wrote from New York to Mr. Delavan: "I am becoming most strongly impressed with the *immense influence* which a man of the right sort, stationed in this city, might exert, by keeping his eye on all the papers, and preparing weekly for each a short paragraph adapted to meet the wants of the public mind, and to exert a transforming power on the press of the country.

"I have proposed to Dr. Nott to prepare an address for a great public meeting in Boston and then in New York, *on the importance of the Sabbath to the laboring classes of the community*. I hope he will do it. It might then be printed, and scattered on the wings of the wind."

Mrs. Edwards being at Saratoga Springs when her venerated mother died, at the age of eighty-six, he wrote her from Andover, August 6, 1844: "Our dear mother died on Wednesday, at three o'clock, P. M. We have great reason to be thankful that she lived so long, and was enabled and inclined to set so good an example; that she had such a peaceful, quiet old age; such a calm and merciful departure from this world; and that we have such good reason to believe that she is now in glory, where no one saith, I am sick; where there is no sin, and of course no suffering, or disappointment, or sorrow, or evil of any description; but where all are holy, and beautiful, and perfect, and blessed.

"Every day probably, for many years, and especially for several of the last years of her life, she prayed for all her children and grandchildren. It was her custom, when she lay awake at night, to spend the time in mentioning her children and grandchildren to the Lord; and in beseeching him to grant them the blessings of his grace. Her prayers are now ended. And it becomes more and more important, that they should pray daily for themselves, and endeavor, all of them, to become followers of them who, through faith in Jesus Christ and obedience to him, are now inheriting the promises which God has made to all that love him.

"Some of her excellences were, good common-sense, a charming temper, great kindness towards all, uniform consistency of character, steady devotion to the appropriate duties of her station, and persevering obedience to the known will of God. May her children and grandchildren all imitate her as far as she imitated Christ. It is a great blessing to have had such a mother and grandmother."

December 2, he wrote Mrs. Edwards, from Washington city, "It is to-day thirty-two years since I was ordained at Andover. 'So teach us to number our days, that we may apply our hearts unto wisdom.' Life, when it is finished, will have gone in the same way like a dream when one awaketh.

"'Well, if our days must fly,
We'll keep their *end* in sight;
We'll spend them all in wisdom's way,
And let them speed their flight.
They'll waft us sooner o'er
This life's tempestuous sea;
Soon we shall reach the peaceful shore
Of blest eternity'—

provided we spend life in learning and doing the will of God. We shall then enjoy much comfort in this world, and do much good; and when called, shall, through grace, be prepared to leave it and enter into that 'rest which remaineth for the people of God.' The Sabbath was designed to be an emblem of that rest, and a season of preparation for it. And when it shall be kept by all the people according to the will of God, many, very many will be preparing for heaven."

On the thirty-fourth anniversary of his ordination he wrote again from Boston, "I recollect that ten years after I was settled, I had a very impressive view of the shortness of human life. I was then thirty-five years old, one-half of seventy; and I could see very plainly that twice the term I had then lived would be very short. I am now within a little more than ten years of seventy, and about nine years older than Rev. Dr. Armstrong, who, you have heard, died last week, in the wreck of the Atlantic. A week ago this morning he was here at the Marlboro' hotel, and led in family prayer, as I did this morning. After prayer, I had conversation with him on the subject of missions. He left Wednesday afternoon. His thanksgiving-day, and that of the crew, tossing on the waves, was very different from ours. He has left a wife and five children. On Sabbath morning they hauled up the Atlantic on the dry dock, and spent the Sabbath in repairing her. But these Sabbath-day repairs do not end well. Before the next Sabbath she was in fragments on the rocks, and forty-five of her passengers had bid adieu to earth."

Writing while on a long journey, he says, "My health is good, and I am as comfortable as can be expected away from home, until I grow better, and learn to be more happy in God, and doing his will."

He says again, "My present mode of life is in some respects that of *exile*, and no one who has a good home and kind friends knows the privations of being absent from them, and living on the winds and the waves, in bar-rooms, stages, rail-cars, and steam-boats, but from experience. Yet as no great good can be accomplished without many sacrifices, and as we have but one life to live in this world, it is best to make the most of it, and do what we can for HIM who has done and suffered so much for us."

His letters to his family, in his long, laborious, and successful tours at the West and South, indicate untiring perseverance in his work, gratitude for the Christian kindness and coöperation received, and buoyancy and cheerfulness in meeting the ever-varying incidents which occurred. He often made journeys of hundreds of miles by stage, travelling slowly day and night in almost impassable roads; notices of which in his letters are mingled with descriptions of the growth of cities, interesting intelligence of passing events, and all the variety of kind paternal counsels which he would have wished to give verbally at home.

On one occasion he writes to his eldest daughter, "I went up the Kentucky river forty-five miles, from Frankfort to Munday's landing, and wishing to come about ten miles to Harrodsburg, it being very muddy, a gentleman offered me his horse. Asking him what I should pay, 'O, nothing,' said he. 'Well, what shall I do with the horse?' 'O,' said he, 'my boy' (a large colored young man) 'will go with you and take care of the horse: I suppose you have no objection to his riding with you.' 'No,' said I, 'not at all.' So we started off together, with the colored man behind me on the same horse, and thus arrived, through the mud, at Harrodsburg."

He adds, "As I came up from Louisville, about sixty miles on the Ohio, and about seventy on the Kentucky river, to Frankfort, in the evening, at one end of the cabin were a number of men playing cards. At the other, was a man with a violin, and a number of men and women dancing. I sat between them, looking, as I suppose they thought, very sober, thinking how light-headed and empty-hearted persons must be who have no more substantial, elevating, or purifying employments. When they were not dancing, they were, women and all, playing cards on board a public steam-boat.

"It is one of the devices of the adversary to get ladies to patronize card-playing by their example. Though perhaps they do not play for money, or only play for a *very little*, a few bright little silver pieces, yet it opens the way for others, judges, jurists, statesmen, merchants, farmers, mechanics, young, old, middle-aged, black, white, and all classes, to be caught in Satan's snare, and led captive through its bewitching influence, down to ruin. I should rejoice should each one of my children be able to say, at the close of life, that they *never knew how to play cards*. That is one of those things with regard to which it is a great honor to be ignorant.

"I am glad you have had opportunity to see all your brothers; and hope that they and their sisters will often be permitted to meet, and will love God and one another so heartily and fervently, that their meetings will always be seasons of *exceeding great joy*."

To his two eldest daughters, who were members of the Mount Holyoke seminary, he wrote with a father's love and care for their highest temporal and eternal good.

"I hope," he says, "that you find your situation increasingly pleasant, and that you do all you can consistently with health to improve the advantages you enjoy. Some privations must of course be experienced while pursuing study, but they are more than paid for by the increase of useful knowledge, which with suitable diligence and self-denial you may obtain. I wish all my daughters, as well as sons, as soon as they can, to get a good education, so that, should their parents die, or be unable to support them, they can, with the blessing of God, support themselves. The *time* of young persons who have a good opportunity for an education, is more valuable than they can well imagine. It is in fact the seed-time of life. And what a man soweth, that must he also reap."

In March, 1845, he wrote to his eldest daughter, whom he had recently left in Boston, a full and serious letter in reference to her own salvation: "I have thought of you much since I left, and cannot but feel that the present is a time of great interest with regard to your happiness and usefulness on earth, and your salvation in heaven. That salvation, as you know, to be enjoyed *there*, must be begun *here*, in the conversion of the soul to God. And blessed be God, he has opened the way for this, freely, of his own accord, and determined to do it, even before any one had ever asked him, though it cost him the sacrifice and death of his own beloved Son. And Jesus Christ consented to bear the effects of our sins in his own body on the cross, as he did when he suffered, for our sakes, agonies such as no other ever endured, and such as none but himself can fully conceive. This shows that he is *love*, and desires not the continuance in sin, or the death of any one, but that they may all forsake it, be delivered from it, and enjoy his presence and favor on earth, and everlasting life and glory in heaven.

"In pursuance of this same love and mercy, and as the manifestation of his desire to seek and to save the lost, he has opened the way for the Holy Spirit to convince men that they are sinners, and without his mercy and grace must perish; that they have something to do to be saved, and that the present is the time in which to do it. All such feelings are the fruit of the Holy Spirit operating on the mind, and are the voice of God to the soul, in pursuance of that same love which led him to give up his Son for our redemption, saying with infinite kindness, 'Turn ye, turn ye; why will ye die?'

"If God should, of his infinite mercy, light up in your soul the flame of love to him, kindled by the full-orbed glory of his love to you, as it shines in the face of Jesus Christ, that you might not perish, but wonder, admire, praise, and adore for ever, it will not be, and it ought not to be, solely or principally, that you may be saved, but that you may be instrumental, by the manifestation of a portion of that same love which was in Him, in saving others. Do not fail daily to study the Bible, asking God, as you proceed, to teach you by his Spirit, who takes of the things of Jesus Christ and shows them unto men, that you may rightly apprehend his truth and feel right in view of it; especially that you may *know him*, that is, have right views of his character and right feelings towards him—have spiritual discernment of his beauty, excellence, loveliness, and glory, that you may be changed into his image. It is right, it is safe, it is blessed to give up body and soul for time and eternity to Jesus Christ, and to trust in him for all that we need; for pardon of sin, for the Holy Spirit to work in us both to will and to do what he requires, and what is our duty and most reasonable service. Go then, my dear daughter, to him, cast all upon him, put yourself under his teaching, and learn of him who is meek and lowly in heart, and you shall find rest to your soul."

Two months later he writes to one of his sons, "*Your sisters have, I hope, chosen that 'good part which shall not be taken from them.'* If they have chosen God for their portion, and shall live to serve him and do good, he will provide for them, and be their everlasting Father and friend. My great desire and prayer to God is, that this may be the case with you, and all my children, that when the few days of this life shall have passed away, we may meet, *an unbroken family*, in heaven."

Dr. Edwards' two eldest daughters, a few weeks after this, publicly professed their faith in Christ and joined themselves to his people.

To his second son, entering on theological study, he writes, "Live near to God, and make it your great object to learn his will as revealed in the Bible. The more you make of the Bible in your preparation for the ministry, the more able and successful you will be as a minister. That is the voice of God, while other books are the voice of men."

In another letter, having alluded to theological controversies as to original sin and the atonement, and recommended to get the views of distinguished theologians, "not by hearsay, but by a careful perusal of their works," he says, "The *Bible*, on these and other subjects, is all *just right;* and that is the only book, in matter and manner, probably, that is so. All human standards and human works partake of the imperfections of their authors. To the law and the testimony every thing is to be brought, and by them to be tried. If they speak not according to that word, they are to be rejected. It is important to be biblical *in manner* as well as in matter, to catch *the spirit and aspect* as well as the sentiment or truth of the Bible. The truth may be held in unrighteousness, and spoken in contention, hatred, variance, wrath, emulation, and strife, instead of love, joy, peace, long-suffering, gentleness, meekness, goodness, faith, and temperance. Let a minister be truly mighty in the Scriptures, not in the letter merely, that killeth, if alone; or in the literature and critical verbal philology, that puffeth up; but in the *spirit*, that giveth life: let the word of Christ and the Spirit of Christ dwell in him richly in all wisdom and *spiritual* understanding, and then will he find it mighty through God to the pulling down of strong-holds. *Make God your principal teacher*, if you would become godlike in temper, teaching, and success."

To his youngest son, in Augusta, Maine, he wrote from Richmond, Virginia, November 21, 1845, "If you have a good opportunity, I think it well for you to get a knowledge of German; and were I in your situation, I would also learn Spanish and Italian, which are so much like the Latin that they are easily obtained. It is best when young to avail ourselves of all practicable means of acquiring knowledge; as knowledge is power, and power to do good. This was one trait in President Dwight, in which every young man would do well to imitate him—his diligence and perseverance, even to the end of life, in acquiring knowledge; and not merely from books, but from men. He freely mingled with men of all classes, and made inquiries, especially on subjects with which they were particularly acquainted—of shoemakers concerning shoes, of gardeners concerning gardens, of mechanics concerning their business, of mercantile men concerning theirs, etc. He spent his vacations in journeys for such purposes, which kept him in good health; and his History of New England is the result, while his Lectures on Theology, a book worthy of the *attentive study* of every young man, are probably better than they otherwise would have been.

"*The book of God*, a portion of which should be attentively read daily, with prayer for the teaching of the Holy Spirit, and *the works of God*, are the great sources of the most important knowledge, even that knowledge of himself which is *life* to the soul."

He writes again, January 17, from Louisville, Kentucky: "I send you herewith a pamphlet written by Prof. Hodge, concerning the late Prof. Dod, which I think is very interesting. Prof. Dod was one of the ablest men of New Jersey. I read from his pen, in the Princeton Repertory of October last, a review of the 'Vestiges of Creation.' It was the last thing which he wrote, and is very able. I should like to have you read it, if you have opportunity. He takes occasion to remark on mesmerism. Perhaps Dr. Tappan may take the work, and will lend it to you. The remarks which he makes about the kind of minds that embrace mesmerism, phrenology, etc., are deserving of attention. It is ordinarily not wise to occupy our minds or devote our energies much to those unaccountables which tend to weaken, bewilder, darken, and perplex, rather than to invigorate, strengthen, purify, and elevate. There are *boundaries* to human knowledge, and very much of real improvement depends upon seeing distinctly what those boundaries are, and keeping, in all our efforts, within them.

"Many things which are true, we in this life can never know. Life is too short to acquire the knowledge, or we may not need it here. It is needful therefore, if we would turn life to the best account, to make a selection, and employ our energies upon those subjects with regard to which we may obtain real knowledge, and knowledge which we can make useful, and which tends to benefit our own minds and the minds of others. In the case of Prof. Dod, we see very clearly what is, in the hour of trial, '*the one thing needful,*' and that in comparison with which, all others may be said, in a sense, to be needless. That you, like him, may have in your last days that 'peace of God' which passeth all understanding, is the prayer of

"Your affectionate father."

To his eldest son, then a merchant at New Orleans, he wrote, February 8, 1847, prudent counsels as to his business and worldly concerns; advising him to such a distinct written agreement with his partner, that in case of the death of one of the firm there should not be ground for litigation, and to *make his will*, on which point he says:

"Some people have a reluctance to making a will, as it seems as if they were going to die. But they will not die any sooner, on account of having a will; and it may prevent many evils, after they are dead. Among the worst contentions in families, have sometimes been those which have arisen about the property of deceased relatives. And where they do not differ, they often feel dissatisfied.

"With a good knowledge of business, diligent and economical habits, and a virtuous character," he adds, "a man may get as much money as will be likely to do him any good. We should not expect to be made happy by the things of this world. All that they can do for us is, to supply our temporal wants as we pass rapidly through it. We need to be in such a state of mind as to be happy, when we leave this world and all that there is in it, in that endless state of being which is to follow this short and uncertain life. And as we know not, and cannot know when we shall come to the close of life, preparation for that should, with each one, be the first and great concern.

"I feel very desirous that you should daily think of the goodness of God, and cultivate towards him an increasingly *grateful* spirit. Ingratitude is a very hateful sin, and exceedingly injurious to the soul; while gratitude is not only a duty, but a source of the purest joy. 'What shall I render unto the Lord for all his goodness?' is a question proper for us all; and nothing can be more suitable, than that we should daily praise him for his kindness to ourselves and our fellow-men.

"I feel that we, *as a family*, have great reason to praise him, that he has preserved the lives of all, healed them in sickness, rescued them in danger, and continued them till grown to men's and women's estate; that he has rendered them kind and affectionate to their parents, and to one another, and is giving them opportunity and disposition to be diligent in some useful business, and to provide for themselves in the world; that he has led four of them to hope that they have experienced of his grace, and to acknowledge him as their Saviour before the world. If he should lead the other two to believe on Jesus Christ as their Saviour, and to devote their lives to honoring him, and doing good by the keeping of his commands, *our cup of blessings would seem to be full;* and we should be under renewed obligations to bless him for ever.

"Never till you are a parent will you know how much pleasure it gives us to hear from you."

To the compiler he wrote, August 18, 1846: "My object in preparing a 'NATIONAL SABBATH MANUAL' was to write, if possible, in such a manner as should be *attractive*, *true*, and *convincing*. The accounts which I receive from various parts of the country, give me increasing reason to hope that the object which I had in view will, through grace, be in some measure accomplished. A distinguished civilian informs me that his friend, and I believe not a religious person, told him that after beginning to read the Manual, it was impossible to leave it till it was finished. I hope it may be found so with many. Mr. Bliss told me the other day that he should want ten thousand a month.

"I have now just prepared a 'NATIONAL TEMPERANCE MANUAL,' after repeated requests from distinguished individuals to do so. Should the Committee think proper, I have thought that it might be well to have it printed by the Tract Society, in the same form with the Sabbath Manual, to go with it into every family in the nation. The object is to set the public conscience right on that subject, with a view to an *enlightened, permanent, kind, ever-growing moral influence*, till no one, not abandoned, shall think of making money by the sale of that which corrupts and destroys his fellow-men. My object has been to embody principles, and illustrate them by facts in such a manner that every child as he grows up may become acquainted with them and act accordingly; and we wish, *in all practicable ways, to get them out before the mind of the nation.*

"Perhaps when we get ready, if Providence permit, they may to great advantage be followed by a 'NATIONAL BIBLICAL MANUAL,' the object of which shall be, to point out in a kind, plain, convincing manner, the reason why *every person who has a soul should be taught to read, and own a Bible*, and also the manner in which he should treat it, in order to be saved."

In the winter of 1847–48, Dr. Edwards made a tour of some months in the southern and south-western states, laboring chiefly in the cities and principal towns of Alabama, Louisiana, and Mississippi, meeting legislatures, the conference of the Methodist Episcopal church and other clerical bodies, and preaching and delivering addresses. When at Montgomery, Alabama, he wrote to the American Tract Society, January 21, 1848:

"In passing over the southern and south western parts of our country, I have been more and more deeply impressed with the vast importance of the *Colporteur* enterprise. Without being scattered abroad by persecution, as were the first disciples, yet, like them, the colporteurs go 'everywhere, preaching the word,' and like apostles preach it 'from house to house.' If they were *obliged* to be scattered 'everywhere' by persecution, we should rejoice in their doing this; that is, talking of Jesus Christ and the way of salvation through him, and even entreating men 'with tears,' to be reconciled to God, and thus preaching the gospel to 'every creature' in every kitchen and parlor to which they should be invited. Much more may we rejoice when well-qualified men are found to do this only from love to Christ and to souls.

"While there are thousands and tens of thousands who are, and till they die must be destitute of the stated preaching of the gospel from educated, regular, and ordained ministers, who would not say, let them have statedly, till they can get better, such preachers as Baxter and Bunyan, Doddridge and Flavel, and Paul? No colporteur should pass a house that is not supplied, without leaving the works of *inspired men*, who spoke and wrote as they were directed by the Holy Ghost. And not a family, on the mountain or in the valley, should be suffered to continue without being visited by some man of God, who, like his Master, is 'going about doing good.'

"The *Sabbath Manual* I find in many families; and in view of what I see, I have often wished that the *Temperance Manual* had gone with it; for rum, whiskey, and brandy drinkers will break the Sabbath, and Sabbath-breakers will neglect the Bible, and neglecters of the Bible will disobey God.

"My ears have often been greeted with the encomiums which have been bestowed in different places on the colporteurs who passed that way, and my heart delighted to hear it so often repeated, in widely distant sections of country, 'I presume the one who came along here, was *one of the best of them.*' Thousands will bless God for ever for the colporteur, who left his home and wandered far over mountain and vale, through forest and flood, to visit the parent and the child, to sell them good books, if they could buy, and if not, to give them, especially that book of books the Bible.

"Let men cease to poison themselves with the drunkard's drink, confine their secular business and cares to six days in a week, and keep the seventh holy; let each one that has a soul be taught the art of reading, that speaking-trumpet of the Almighty, and let him hear daily his Father in heaven speaking to *him* 'words by which he may be saved;' let him look up for the Holy Spirit to Him who hath said, 'Ask, and it shall be given you,' and each one may become wise to salvation, and learn the heavenly art of living, not unto himself, but unto Him who died for him, and of doing to others as he ought to wish that

21*

others should do to him. Then will all live together *as brethren;* tasting and seeing that the Lord is good, and feeling that he doth indeed 'magnify his word above all his name.'"

Visiting New Orleans, where he met his eldest son, and enjoyed the hospitality of his pastor Rev. Dr. Scott, he says, "Nothing but the mercy and grace of God can save us from sore and desolating judgments; for the wickedness of men is great, and their sins cry to heaven. But the Lord is good, his tender mercies are over all, and thus far he waits, not willing that men should perish, but come to repentance. Many are the indications that he is working with us. Let us therefore be steadfast, immovable, always abounding in the work of the Lord, inasmuch as by faith we know that our labor shall not be in vain in the Lord."

Proceeding from Memphis, Tenn., up the Ohio river, he wrote Mrs. Edwards from Cincinnati, March 7: "I arrived here on Saturday. The weather was cold and snowy. I had been somewhat threatened during the day, and went to the Broadway hotel. Before morning I was attacked as at Lowell," (in October, 1847, with an internal inflammation,) "though in a much milder form. In the morning sent for Dr. Mussey, and in five minutes was relieved; have since been gaining, and am now about as comfortable as I was about a week after I came from Lowell. Six ministers and a number of others called to see me on Monday, and had me removed from the hotel to Mr. Funk's in Vine-street, where I have every accommodation which I can desire. Mr. Funk says he heard me preach eight or ten years ago, and the next day made terrible havoc among the whiskey barrels, and in a month there was not a whiskey seller in their church."

On the 7th of September, 1848, Dr. Edwards had the high satisfaction of uniting with his beloved brethren in the ministry, in the ordination and installation of his second son, Jonathan, as pastor of a large and important church, in Woburn, ten miles from Boston, on which occasion he delivered the charge to the pastor, commending to him THE BIBLE as the fountain of all truth, the theme of his preaching, the guide of his ministry and his life.

CLOSING WORDS ON THE SABBATH, AND ON TEMPERANCE.

In the autumn of 1848, he wrote the compiler, sending fifty dollars, for stereotyping the Temperance Manual in *Spanish*, and said, "We have put a copy of the whole of both the Sabbath and Temperance Manuals into every family in Andover, and given one to every young man who is at work for himself and disconnected from the family of his father; making in all, with one to each member of the seminary and academy, *eighteen hundred copies of each*."

Again he writes from Boston: "A copy of the Temperance and Sabbath Manuals, and a New Testament, I hope may yet be put into the hand of *every immigrant* that reaches our shores; especially every one who can read; together with a *Biblical Manual*, showing them the nature of the Bible and the manner of treating it, which will prepare them for, and carry them to heaven. The same should be done for every family visited by colporteurs or missionaries. And I hope that the time will soon come, when the Tract Society will furnish all the books which they through their agents can circulate. I wish to see them in a race with all others, as to the furnishing of the above for every family in the United States. If you have not room enough to furnish all fast enough, why not put on another story on your building, and multiply your presses and workmen accordingly? The 'American Messenger' comes richly freighted, and is doing a great and good work. Hold on, look up, and move onward.

"Yesterday was a beautiful day, and all seemed to rejoice greatly that they are henceforward to have in Boston an abundance of good, clear, fresh water. And they have reason to rejoice. It is a greater blessing than any imagine. Yet he that drinketh of this water shall thirst again: but he that drinketh of the water which we may be instrumental in communicating to as many millions as there were thousands in Boston yesterday, *shall never thirst;* and it shall be in him a well of water springing up unto everlasting life."

February 5, 1849, he wrote from Washington city: "Our meetings here yesterday, both in the morning and at night, were intensely interesting;" and, in the name of several gentlemen, he requests that a copy of the Sabbath Manual might be sent to each member of Congress. "They think," he says, "that the facts would be of great service; and that the book coming after the subject has been presented to an overflowing congregation in the capitol, would be read, be carried home, or sent by members of Congress to influential constituents, and thus do great good. I suppose that there are about sixty Senators, and two hundred and thirty members of the House. There has evidently been a great change for the better within a few years in this city, with regard to the keeping of the Sabbath; adding another to the very numerous evidences, that wherever this subject is presented, as in that Manual, it commends itself to every man's conscience in the sight of God."

"Mr. Delavan, of Albany," he again writes, "has concluded to print one hundred thousand of the Sabbath Document, to be distributed to stockholders and those who travel on the railroads from Albany to Buffalo, to prepare the way for all the cars to stop running on the Sabbath."

At another date he says, "Might it not be well to have prefixed to the Temperance Manual," (similar to what had been already prefixed to the Sabbath Manual,) "something like the following, namely:

"'Every minister of the gospel into whose hands this Manual shall come, is respectfully requested, should it appear to him to be adapted to be useful, on the Sabbath to preach a sermon to his people, and exhibit the biblical principles in their application to the subject of Temperance, in its connection with righteousness and judgment to come; and to open the way to put a copy of this Manual into every family in his congregation.'

"In that way might we not secure the preaching of ten thousand sermons forthwith on the Sabbath *from the ministers;* which is just what the Temperance cause now needs, and thus open the way for the circulation forthwith of one hundred thousand Temperance Manuals. And if you cannot afford to send a Manual to every minister gratis, then print it on a sheet like the Messenger, and send it to them, and we will pay $100 to circulate it in that form; and we will also pay $100 to circulate part first of the Sabbath Manual in the same way." He suggested also, that students from theological seminaries might employ their vacations in circulating these documents.

To Rev. O. Eastman, and Rev. R. S. Cook, Secretaries of the Tract Society, he wrote frequently, encouraging the widest circulation of the Sabbath and Temperance Manuals in all the channels of the Society's distributions, partly at the expense of the Sabbath Union.

"Should it be consistent," he says, "for the Committee to say to me, that for every hundred dollars which I shall pay them for that purpose, they will put in circulation ten thousand copies of the Sabbath Manual, to the amount of one, two, or three hundred thousand copies a year, perhaps I may be able to raise some money for that purpose, and in that way we may perhaps enlarge the circulation. The Sabbath effort is like the purifying of the air of a great country, in its influence on the health of the people. It is better to purify the air, and so keep the people well, than to let them get sick, and then send in the doctors to cure them. In proportion as we get the Sabbath observed, we increase the number of readers of the Bible, tracts, and all good books; and the number also who attend public worship, hear the gospel, and come under the divinely appointed means of grace; and the efficacy of all other means will thereby be greatly increased. Of course, to make *special efforts* for the universal observance of the Sabbath, is in the highest degree *philosophical*, *biblical*, and *economical*, with reference to the salvation of men."

On the 23d of January, 1850, he wrote again: "The object of the American and Foreign Sabbath Union, in the donation of $1,000, which they have this year made to the American Tract Society, and in the donation of $1,320, which they have previously made, for the distribution of the Sabbath Manual, was, to enable the Tract Society so to supply all their colporteurs with it, that they might place a copy of one or more of the parts of that Manual in every family, at the cost of it wherever the receivers are able and willing to pay, and gratuitously where they are not; with a few words of good advice as to the benefits that will result to them and their children, from the keeping of the Sabbath. The same also, as far as practicable, they wish to have done by all home or domestic missionaries; that in the least possible time, through the various modes of circulation, every family in the United States, especially in the new settlements and on the frontiers, may be supplied with a copy. Should all the children of our country grow up with a knowledge of the principles and facts embodied in that Manual, exhibiting the will of God, as manifested in his works, his word, and his providence, with regard to the Sabbath-day, we cannot but hope that through his blessing, this will be a Sabbath-keeping nation to the end of time."

The Tract Society coöperated in all these plans, and reported to him that of different parts or numbers of the Sabbath Manual, they had circulated 684,741 copies in English, 8,277 in German, 1,718 in French, and 5,146 in Spanish, making a total circulation of 699,882 copies; and that these included *grants* to the value of $2,421 77, for the supply of emigrants at Buffalo, Pittsburgh, and other great thoroughfares, and for missionaries, clergymen, and others, exclusive of grants by their colporteurs; and that it was believed the colporteurs had circulated gratuitously not far from an equal amount.

In a circular letter written by Dr. Edwards, January 24, 1851, requesting funds to aid in circulating the Sabbath Manual, he states that of the first part 541,000 had been printed, and of all the other parts in four languages 634,000, making *one million one hundred and seventy-five thousand copies.*

During the whole of Dr. Edwards' labors for the Sabbath, he lent his aid, in all practicable ways, to the cause of *Temperance;* acting on the Committee of the Temperance Society, and identified with its interests from the time of its formation till his death.

Of the *Temperance Manual*, which had been translated into German, French, and Spanish, the Hon. JOHN MCLEAN, judge of the Supreme Court of the United States, wrote him, December 17, 1847, "I feel the greatest interest in saying, that I have never perused a treatise on the subject which condensed in so few pages so many facts and arguments so unanswerable, against intemperance. No one can read this little work, who wishes well to his species and his country, and not ardently desire to see a copy of it in the hands of every family in the United States. It would have a powerful effect to render odious, to the rising generation, the ruinous vice of intemperance; and indeed, its influence would be salutary on all whose sensibilities are not blunted or destroyed by a criminal indulgence in the use of ardent spirits."

At the close of the years 1847 and 1849, Dr. Edwards wrote brief reports of the American Temperance Society, which were published in the religious papers, and in which we have *his mature judgment and testimony* on the subject of that enterprise, after abundant labors and careful observation for thirty years.

"The Temperance reformation," he says, "*was begun for the purpose of removing that mighty obstruction* which the using of intoxicating liquors as a beverage occasions *to the efficacy of the gospel and the means of grace.* It was carried forward for years principally by religious men, and urged by religious motives. It then received the manifest approbation of heaven, and the efforts which were made were crowned with great success. Such motives must always lie at the foundation of this great moral reformation. They are *the only motives that go deep enough* to produce permanent, ever-growing results. They are also the only motives which we can expect will be so attended with the influences of the Holy Spirit, as to be rendered in the highest degree successful."

Acknowledging the good service which many *reformed drunkards* had done in their narratives of their own appalling history, and the influence they might still have in reforming others, yet he says, "Wherever the work has been left solely or principally to them, its progress has soon ceased to be onward. Sober men who never were drunkards, educated men, professional men, ministers of the gospel, and all sorts of good men, must come up to the work. The Bible must be put in requisition, and the sanctions of religion as well as morality, of eternity as well as time, must be brought to bear upon the hearts of men. The voice of God, as well as of men, must be heard by drunkards, and drunkard-makers, and those who use the drunkard's drink. The motives which He has revealed, as manifested in his works, his word, and his providence, drawn from heaven, earth, and hell, must urge upon them his heartfelt entreaty, 'Turn ye, turn ye from your evil ways; for why will ye die?'

"Men may crowd temperance meetings to be *amused*, or to enjoy the luxury of strongly excited feelings. They may hear the statement of the drunkard's follies and woes, and the agonies of his starving wife and dying children; or they may hear the follies of the drunkard, and the pretended ardent friendship for temperance of the drunkard-makers held up to *ridicule*, while the mind is not enlightened, the conscience not aroused, and the heart not healthfully or permanently impressed. There must be truth, the truth of God, and it must be spoken in love. It must be attended by the Holy Ghost sent down from heaven, and convince men of the *sin* as well as the folly of intemperance, and of aiding and abetting it in any way. The motives which are urged to induce men to cease from this, as well as other sins, should be drawn from, and presented in the light of the cross.

"It should also be understood by all, that the people in their *civil* capacity, who do not wish longer to suffer the evils of the liquor traffic, *have a perfect right, through the legislature, that right arm of the people which God has provided for that purpose, to defend themselves against the nuisance.* This mode of self-defence is in accordance with the Bible, with the constitution of the nation, and of the several states. It is required by a due regard to the great interests of the people, and their children. Nor have liquor-sellers any right, in opposition to the wishes of the people, to force the evils of this ungodly traffic upon them. It is a violation of the rights of humanity, and a vicious way of making money. Every people who have the power, have also the right to defend themselves and their children against this evil. And those who do their duty to themselves or their children, their country or their God, will not draw back till this work be accomplished."

September 1, 1851, he wrote to E. C. Delavan, Esq., "If we can keep at work, all hands, we shall *in due time secure effectual legislative defence;* but in order to this, there must be a steady, regular, and long course of wise, 'patient continuance in well-doing,' by the old, substantial, and long-tried friends of temperance, who 'in all their ways acknowledge God,' and act in the spirit and under the influence of the gospel, and for the purpose of honoring God in the salvation of men."

Mr. Delavan, in enclosing the above, says, "This

letter was the last of the many which I received during the past quarter of a century from my dearly beloved departed friend. Under God, I owe to him, and to a few others of the same nobility of soul, a deep debt of gratitude. And now, at this important crisis of the same reform to which he devoted so many years of his life, and in which I feel it to be my duty and privilege still to labor, I miss, and that greatly, the counsel and advice, always so full of wisdom, which he was, when asked, so ready to give. He has been to me a faithful friend and wise counsellor. I feel that I have lost a brother. I always looked forward to his yearly visits with great pleasure: he brought and left a blessing."

CHAPTER XIII.

HIS COMMENT ON THE BIBLE, AS GOD'S GIFT FOR ALL MEN.

FOUR YEARS—1849–1853.

WE have seen that to give THE BIBLE to all, with the best incitements and helps to read and understand it, had long been a prominent object before the mind of Dr. Edwards. When earnestly seeking his own salvation without the knowledge of any minister or private Christian, the word of God was precious to him. It was so in pursuing theological study; it was so in his labors as pastor, and in his Bible-classes; and at the turning-points of his life, both in 1829 and 1842, he seriously considered the question of devoting his undivided energies to the object of its being universally *circulated*, and prayerfully and profitably *read*.

We are now to see how, as a child of Providence, he was led to give the effective energies of the closing years of his life to this design, second in importance perhaps to none in which he had been engaged, though in a way somewhat different from that which he seems to have planned.

In his visits to all parts of the country he saw prevailing *destitution* and *neglect* of the Bible; and while pushing the circulation of his own Sabbath and Temperance Manuals, and enlisting the Tract Society's colporteurs and other agencies to circulate them by hundreds of thousands of copies, the idea still pressed itself upon him, that God's inspired word had yet higher claims. He urged upon colporteurs as he met them, and upon the officers of the Society, that every family found destitute should be supplied with *the Bible;* and when he learned the fact that the colporteurs of that Society, on whose Committee he was still acting, were turning away from tens of thousands of families whose distant abodes they had reached, and leaving them unsupplied, from the difficulty of procuring Bibles, his soul was stirred within him. In all delicate and proper ways, as his correspondence shows, he sought to remove this obstacle, and ultimately to effect the more universal circulation of the Bible, and at the same time to call attention to its pages, and to "assist common readers to understand the meaning of the Holy Spirit" therein conveyed.

While in the midst of his labors for the sanctification of the Sabbath, June 11, 1846, he wrote to an officer of the American Tract Society at New York:

"It appears to me that the time is near, when it will be well to make *a general effort* to instruct every person in this land in the art of reading, and to induce every person who can read *to own a Bible*, and to treat it in such a manner that it will be 'a lamp to his feet and a light to his path.' The American Tract Society may, by that time, have in the field five hundred colporteurs. Among the books they circulate might be, and should be, Bibles and Testaments of all descriptions, and as low as they can be printed. If each colporteur should put in circulation one thousand copies annually, they might thus aid in giving the

Bible each year to half a million of families. I hope for the time when every man, bond and free, shall exercise his inalienable right to hear the voice of his heavenly Father, and in the words which 'the Holy Ghost teacheth;' and when that foul libel against God, that the daily reading of his word would tend to make any one worse, will for ever cease.

"If the London convention (the Christian Alliance) should do nothing more than to commence *forthwith* an effort to induce every person on earth who can read *to own a Bible*, they would do a great work.

"The way would then be open to send out among all who do own a Bible, *specific directions* as to the manner in which it should be treated, in order to guide each one who has it to heaven, through that way of pleasantness and path of peace. It appears to me that some presentations might be made on this subject, which might be carried out in their practical application, through the medium of colporteurs and others, with great advantage to the world."

Two years and a half later, in December, 1848, he wrote again: "Every body in this country that has a soul and can read, should as soon as possible have a Bible, and a brief, lucid statement of the nature of the book, the right manner of treating it, and the effect which such treatment will, through grace, have on him for both worlds; and then a few words in the margin, or in brief notes, which may express the meaning of the Holy Ghost more plainly, where the language is obscure; and we may all expect, that in the moral renovation of this world, the Lord will 'magnify his word above all his name.' The Tract Society has been too long sending out for Bible truth, the works of uninspired men merely. It is time, high time, while they increase the works of good men a thousand-fold, that they should send with them to every man who has it not, *the word of God*, perfect as its author, the standard and test by which all the works of men are to be tried: that each one, while reading the works of men, may 'search the Scriptures,' and under the influence of their divine Author, become wise unto salvation through faith in Christ Jesus."

Dr. Edwards having a table in the office of the American Tract Society at Boston, where he usually wrote when in that city, conferred freely on the above subject with the officers of that Society; and their Executive Committee, December 6, 1848, appointed the late lamented Hon. Simon Greenleaf, and Rev. E. N. Kirk and Rev. Seth Bliss a special committee "to consider the importance of the American Tract Society's publishing a Bible and New Testament with brief explanatory notes, in order to supply their colporteurs with this book for circulation." The report of the special committee, in favor of the object proposed, was adopted December 13; and on the 19th the Rev. Mr. Kirk, in behalf of the Society in Boston, commended the subject to the most serious attention of the Executive Committee of the Society in New York, who again referred it to a special committee, consisting of their chairman the Rev. Dr. Knox, the Rev. Dr. John S. Stone, and Rev. William A. Hallock.

While this special committee were seeking light, frequent communications were held with Dr. Edwards, who wrote from Albany, January 1, 1849:

"I rejoice that the Committee are taking up the subject of the New Testament. It is high time that we were all engaged, heart and hand, in furnishing each one who can read, with a copy.

"If the Lord will, I shall be in New York on Saturday next, and shall bring what I shall be willing that the Committee should adopt as a preface for the New Testament, if they think proper. I do not wish, in the Testament which we shall print, to have a commentary, but only a *glossary*, or dictionary, or rather an instructor to teach the reader, as he goes along, the *meaning* of certain words and phrases which he might not understand, such, for instance, as repentance, faith, justification, sanctification, Pharisees, Herodians, concision, etc. But you can print the first hundred thousand *immediately*, with only the preface, and by the time those are gone, the notes may be ready."

As Dr. Edwards was proceeding from Albany to the city of Washington in his labors for the Sabbath, he stopped in New York, conferred on the subject of the comment, prepared some specimen notes, and submitted the following draft of a *preface*, such as might perhaps be prefixed to the New Testament.

"This book is the word of God. In it he makes known to men his character and will. It is all given by inspiration of the Holy Ghost, and is profitable; teaching men what to believe; showing them in what they are wrong; instructing them in what is right; and leading them, through the grace of God, to do it. Although written by men, God directed them what to write and how to write it, that as a rule of human faith and conduct it might be perfect. Having been all written, not in words taught by the wisdom of men, but the wisdom of God, it is 'perfect, converting the soul; sure, making wise the simple; and right, rejoicing the heart.' Of course a knowledge of this book is more to be desired than gold, even much fine gold; because in understanding, believing, and obeying it, there is great present and great future reward.

"Hence, every person who can should own a copy of it, and should read some in it every day; asking God to teach him, by his Spirit, rightly to understand, cordially to believe, and faithfully to obey it. It will then be spirit and life to his soul, and make him wise to salvation. It will be a lamp to his feet, and a light to his path; guiding him in the way of righteousness, that way of pleasantness and path of peace. He will be wiser, in the things of God, even than his teachers, if they do not understand, believe, and obey the Bible. Through it he will get understanding and will hate every false way; and by it he will be furnished thoroughly for every good work.

" On the Sabbath he should study this book in its divinely inspired aspect and connection; not merely that he may obtain a greater knowledge of it himself, but also that he may be better qualified to communicate this knowledge to others. He should also, as he may be able, avail himself of the assistance of his fellow-men, that he may receive from the treasures of revelation things new and old.

"For this purpose he should confine his worldly business, cares, travelling, and amusements, to six days in a week, and should rest on the Sabbath and keep the day holy. He should not only, as on other days, pray to God, morning and evening, himself in secret and also in the family, but he should meet with others and worship God in public; hearken to the preaching of the gospel by the ministers of Jesus Christ; and when he goes home, and has opportunity, he should examine the Bible and see whether what he has heard is according to it. If it is, he should receive it and treat it as the truth of God. If it is not, he should reject it; for if any one preaches contrary to the Bible, he does not preach the truth, and is not to be believed. Each one should therefore study this word of God for himself, that he may be able rightly to judge whether what he hears is according to it or not. Every true minister of Christ will wish to have his hearers do this; and like Paul will rejoice, (see Acts 17 : 2,) when he learns that they are searching the Scriptures, to satisfy themselves whether what he preaches is true. By this law and testimony of God all human teaching from the pulpit and the press should be tried. If men speak not according to this word, there is no light in them.

"Reader, make this book your own. By it try your faith, and your practice. Hearken to it daily, as the voice of God speaking to you, telling you words by which you may be saved, and by which you may also be instrumental in saving others. Follow its heavenly teachings, and all things shall work together for your good. God will guide you by his counsel through life; he will support and comfort you in death; and after death, he will receive you to glory;

where with him, and all his people, you will rise from glory to glory for ever and ever.

"N. B. Some words and phrases which might not otherwise be understood, are explained in the notes at the bottom of the page; and a specimen given of some of the instructions which the Scriptures afford."

In the mean time, the Secretary at Boston procured and transmitted to the special committee a letter from the venerable Rev. Dr. JENKS, who had labored long in preparing the "Comprehensive Commentary," giving his kind suggestions as to the character of a comment best adapted for the object proposed—whether the text should be issued as a "Paragraph Bible," or possibly in a chronological arrangement like that of Townsend; whether the references in Bagster's Bible, "prepared by the diligent and lamented Mr. Greenfield," should be adopted; to what length notes and practical remarks should be extended; and the desirableness of inserting a sketch of the events which occurred "between the closing of the Old Testament canon and the opening of the New."

On the 10th of February, Dr. Edwards, having returned to New York, presented a specimen of brief notes on the first chapter of Matthew, to give an idea of the kind of Commentary which he "wished somebody to publish, for all our population who should not be otherwise supplied."

On the 10th of March, he wrote: "From this time forward I hope that all colporteurs will be so furnished with Testaments, that each family, found destitute, shall be supplied with a copy, and each child in each family, who can purchase it, or whose parent or friend will purchase it for him; also that colporteurs enough be forthwith employed and furnished, to offer a copy to every family of *immigrants*, and to as many of their children as they will purchase for, well bound and *in their own tongue*. No foreigner should get into our southern or western country, without having had the offer of a Bible or Testament as soon as possible after he steps on our shores: so that it may be understood, over all the world, that *no body is to live in this country without a Bible*, or a Testament, unless through his own rejection of it. If they can have *the Bible*, the great object is accomplished, whether they have the comments of men, or not; and every soul that shall be sanctified and saved through the influence of a Bible which without us he would not have received, will *bless the Lord for ever*, that we did not put off and delay doing good 'as we had opportunity,' till after he was dead. What thy hand findeth to do, do with thy might; for in the grave to which thou art hastening there is no work."

On the 23d of April, the report of the special committee was received and adopted; recommending, "that the comments be such as are needful to assist the common reader rightly to understand the word of God, without lengthened human expositions. Where, from a change in the meaning of terms since the received version was made, from the obscurity of the meaning of words or phrases, from ignorance of ancient customs, from the prevalence of false interpretations, (as in the notes appended to the Douay version, or in the multiform teachings of men denying the Lord that bought us,) or from any other cause, the common reader would be likely to fail of apprehending the mind of the Spirit as revealed in the sacred volume, it seems desirable to add such explanations, notes, or comments, and perhaps occasional practical reflections, as may guide the reader to a reception of the great evangelical truths revealed, all centering in 'HIM, of whom Moses in the law, and the prophets did write,' 'THE LAMB OF GOD, which taketh away the sin of the world.'"

The following minute was also unanimously adopted:

"Whereas the Rev. Dr. Edwards, who has been long and intimately connected with this and the American Tract Society at Boston, has for years had his attention called to the momentous importance of bringing the truths of the Bible, in their divinely inspired aspects and connections, into contact with the minds of all our population:

"Resolved, That he be requested to prepare and submit to this Committee a comment and notes on the gospel by Matthew, as a specimen of what he proposes, with a view to aid the Society in reaching a definite conclusion upon the whole subject."

He entered immediately on the work thus assigned him, and, May 17, wrote to the Publishing Committee: "In compliance with your request, I herewith send you a specimen of what I suppose it may be proper for the Tract Society to publish on the gospel of Matthew. The object of the work is to express to laboring people, common unlearned readers, in the plainest manner, the meaning of the Holy Ghost in the gospel of Matthew, and some of the instructions which it affords. I have therefore endeavored to avoid all attempts at learned criticism, and to give the results of sound judicious interpretation, without giving the steps by which we reach those results.

"The *Instructions* I have added for the purpose of helping all persons, when they read the Bible, to form the habit of drawing from it such instructions as will tend most to their growth in knowledge and in grace, and furnish them thoroughly for every good work."

Though Dr. Edwards originally contemplated only a *glossary*, or the briefest explanation of terms and phrases, yet as he proceeded through the gospel of Matthew, the work grew upon his hands, especially in the rich practical instructions suggested, till it became evident that the comment would be larger than was designed, and he proceeded carefully to abridge and condense it into the form in which, under the revision and sanction of the Committee, it was stereotyped.*

* We annex the last three verses of Matthew as a specimen of the comment, though both the notes and instructions are longer than in the work generally, which contains the references and marginal readings of Bagster's Polyglott Bible, and maps.

MATTHEW 28:18–20.

18. And Jesus came and spake unto them, saying, All power is given unto me in heaven and in earth.

19. Go ye therefore, and teach all nations, baptizing them in the name of the Father, and of the Son, and of the Holy Ghost:

20. Teaching them to observe all things whatsoever I have commanded you: and lo, I am with you alway, *even* unto the end of the world. Amen.

While the best form of publishing the work was under consideration, he wrote: "I think there are serious objections to intermingling the instructions with the notes; or turning off the attention from what God has said, until the reader has spent as much time in attending to it as he thinks to be suitable. Then, if he has time, and is disposed to look at the instruction which God's communication has suggested to a man, he can do so; or he can write down, or think

NOTES.

18. *All power;* power is here used in the sense of authority. *Is given unto me;* as mediator, God and man.

19. *Teach;* disciple all nations; proclaim to them the gospel, for the purpose of persuading them to become my disciples. *The Father, the Son, and the Holy Ghost;* the one only living and true God.

20. *I am with you;* in this work, to guide, comfort, sanctify, and sustain you; to render you successful in awakening the attention of men, convincing them of sin, and turning them from darkness to light, and from the power of sin unto God. I will be with you and all who succeed you in preaching the gospel, to the end of time. *Amen;* so let it be, and so it shall be.

INSTRUCTIONS.

18. As Christ has authority over all, and power to direct and govern all, they who put their trust in him will be for ever safe.

19. The making of all nations the disciples of Christ should be the great object of all. Some should labor for it in one way, and some in another, as the Lord shall call them; but all should strive together that the Scriptures may be translated into every tongue, and the gospel be preached to every creature.

20. Christ, with his divine presence and aid, will be with his people in doing his will, to the end of time; and after having inclined and enabled them to serve him and their generation according to the will of God, will receive them to himself, that where he is they also may be, to behold his glory, the glory which he had with the Father before the world was. John 17:24.

out the instruction which the divine communication suggests to his own mind.

"I do not intend to insert any introduction to each book; but to the Bible or Testament perhaps it might be well to have an introduction, stating to the reader the peculiar nature of this book, the manner in which it should be treated, and some of the good it will do him, if he treats it in that way."

He says again, "It is very difficult to make any one work best suited to all classes of people. The very passages which to ministers and learned men are about as plain as they can be, are not so to the unlearned and to children, to whom simple explanations of the word of God are *very attractive.* The Bible about which learned doctors have so long differed, the unlearned millions exceedingly desire to have made plain to them.*

"If this work is to have a general circulation among all classes of people, and be best suited to all, it appears to me there must be different editions, and some comprehending more than others. Might it not be best then first to prepare an edition best suited for colporteur distribution among those who would not be likely to get the Bible, except through their instrumentality? and then, as time, experience, observation, and the providence of God may point the way, prepare it in other forms and sizes and varieties for other classes of people?

* "'*Machinations*'"—a term which some one had proposed in revising the notes—"is a long hard word, which unlearned laboring men do not use, and which many of them do not understand, or know how to pronounce."

"As to references, if the Committee think that the comment will be sought after by ministers and Sabbath-school teachers and experienced Christians, and that it would be better for them to have more references, I have no objection, provided they do not call upon me to make them. The reason why I should be reluctant to perform that labor is, it appears to me that the little time which I have to stay on earth, may, in another way, be employed to better advantage. I have always supposed that a number of tables containing such information as common people need, and which they would not be likely to get except from this Bible, might be embodied, and add much to the attractiveness and value of the work.

"My attention is now fully occupied in endeavoring *rightly to apprehend and rightly to express the meaning of the Holy Ghost in those passages of Scripture which I am called upon to examine.* This employment is delightful. The weeks slip away with amazing rapidity, and will soon be all gone—it may be before I get through the Bible, or such parts of it as may be thought desirable. If they should not, and I should be here and able to do it, and nothing else should more urgently call, I will attend to references or any thing else to which Providence may direct me. What my hands find to do, I ask an interest in your prayers and those of the Committee, that I may be enabled to do and with my might, according to the will of God; and I hope that through your and their assistance, and the divine blessing, great and lasting good will result to mankind."

The stereotyping of Matthew having been unavoidably delayed, he wrote, December 3: "It is no doubt best that the Committee and all concerned should, in this and all things, take all needed time to learn the divine will and to do it. He that believeth, while he will be diligent in business, and what his hands find to do, will do with his might, and heartily unto the Lord, will not '*make haste*,' or wish to pluck the fruits of Providence before they are ripe. Unripe fruits are unhealthy; and though they often look beautifully, and are very tempting, yet God causes them to ripen slowly, on purpose, I suppose, to try our patience, and let us know that unless we let patience have its perfect work, we can never be perfect and entire, but shall ever be wanting."

In a letter, April 4, 1850, he says, "I sometimes please myself with the hope, that somebody at some time may be enabled to prepare a *Biblical Manual*, to go with the Bible, which shall contain what its common readers may need to know about the nature of the book, the proper mode of treating it, and the effects of treating it in this way; all needful tables of weights, measures, distances, coins, titles, offices, etc., together with history, chronology, geography, etc.; in a word, whatever is needful to enable the people to understand the Lord's meaning in all the words which he uses.

"It may contain also a dissertation, briefly stating the *right* which every man who has a soul has to own a Bible, to read some in it daily, to judge himself of its meaning, and when he learns what the will of God is, his right and duty to do it; and the unspeakable importance of every man, woman, and child, especially in this country, taking this course.*

"It might be called the 'BIBLICAL MANUAL,' and go out with the Temperance and Sabbath Manuals, and the Bible, to every soul that will receive it, and thus aid in preparing the way for the Lord to 'magnify his word above all his name,' and to make the light of the moon like the light of the sun, and the light of the sun as the light of seven days."

Again he says, "No words can express my constantly growing convictions of the importance and the necessity of men becoming, in their proper place and

* Dr. Edwards having written to the aged antiquarian, Rev. Thomas Robbins, then at Hartford, for information as to the Bible published by recommendation of our American Congress, he replied, that "Mr. Robert Aitken, a printer at Philadelphia, finding that there was a great scarcity of Bibles in the time of our revolutionary war, made application to Congress to patronize the object, January 21, 1781. His memorial was referred to a committee, of which James Duane was chairman. The work went on slowly, a great work for that day, and the committee reported, September 1, 1782, 'that Mr. Aitken has, at great expense, now finished an American edition of the Holy Scriptures in English; that the committee have from time to time attended to his progress in the work; that they also recommended it to the two chaplains of Congress to examine and give their opinion of the execution.'

"The chaplains, Dr. White and Mr. Duffield, reported their high approbation, and Congress then

"'Resolved, That the United States, in Congress assembled, highly approve the pious and laudable undertaking of Mr. Aitken, as subservient to the interests of religion, as well as an instance of the progress of arts in this country, and being satisfied from the above report of his care and accuracy in the execution of his work, they recommend this edition of the Bible to the inhabitants of the United States, and hereby authorize him to publish this recommendation in the manner he shall think proper.'"

in the right way, *workers together with God*, in promoting their own salvation and that of others. To induce them to do this, is one grand object of all that I am now doing."

He pressed forward laboriously with his delightful work, and on the last day of December, 1850, was enabled to announce the *New Testament completed.*

"My dear Sir—Through the great kindness of God, and by his continued assistance, I have finished the book of Revelation and the New Testament.

"I desire to express to you and to the dear brethren of the Committee, and to your fellow-laborer Mr. Rand, my grateful acknowledgments for the kind assistance which you and they have rendered me, and above all, to the God of all grace, the giver of all good, for enabling and inclining you and them to do it. I would also ask the continued aid of your and their prayers, that should my life and health be preserved, and I be graciously permitted to pursue this work, I may rightly apprehend and rightly express the mind and will of the Holy Ghost; that we may be instrumental in communicating a knowledge of it to multitudes of the present and future generations who would otherwise not so clearly or to so great an extent understand it. And may our daily prayer ascend to God, that his truth as communicated by us and others may, through his rich abounding grace, be the means of preparing many for glory and honor, immortality, and eternal life in heaven. With much love to you and all the brethren,

"I am truly and gratefully yours,

"JUSTIN EDWARDS."

His youngest daughter having, at the close of the year 1850, engaged for a time in teaching in Alabama, he wrote her kind and fatherly letters, giving valuable hints as to the management of the school, her own course of reading and study, the cultivation of piety in her own heart, her usefulness to those around her, and especially prayerful fidelity to the eternal welfare of the pupils under her charge.

January 1, 1851, he writes her, "'I wish you a happy new year,' by your remembering that all our happiness comes from that great and good God in whom we live and move and have our being, and that if we are ever truly and permanently blessed, it must be in learning and doing his will. All that we are, and all that we have, we receive from him. For our friends, and for all that is lovely in them, and all the comforts we receive from them, we are indebted to him; and they come to us as the fruit of our Saviour's kindness and condescension, his exile for more than thirty years from his Father's house and its manifold comforts, in a cold and pitiless world, where although the foxes had holes, and the birds of the air nests, he had not where to lay his head.

"I learn from Elizabeth's letter, for which we are all very much obliged to you, that you sometimes feel lonely. This I expected; for I have often, when absent from home and friends, especially when I was young, felt so myself. When my mother died, and I had to leave my father, brother, and sisters, and go to live with strangers, I had such feelings as I never had before, and which we should know nothing about if we did not experience them. Yet hundreds and thousands in different parts of the world, and many of them in situations much less comfortable than yours, are experiencing such lonely desolate feelings all the while. God wishes that we should think of them, sympathize with them, and pray to him for them; but we never should do it, if we never had any such feelings ourselves. Jesus Christ, knowing how much we should need his sympathy, left his home in heaven and took upon him our nature in body and soul, and willingly submitted to the temptations, trials, and distresses of this life, that he might know by experience what they are, and be better fitted to feel for, sympathize with, and succor those who are lonely and distressed, and need his help. He is near you, though we are not, and into his kind bosom you may pour out all your wants. When I have been far away from friends, and felt lonely and desolate, I have sometimes found great comfort in reading the epistles to the Philippians and Colossians. 'Cast thy burden on the Lord, and he shall sustain thee.'"

To his brother-in-law, Rev. Jared Reid, who had an attack of paralysis, which ere long terminated his life, he wrote, January 7, from Rockport, where he had been to attend the funeral of a little son of Rev. Mr. Gale: "We have here learned that you are prostrated by disease. We tenderly and deeply sympathize with you in your affliction, and hope that the Lord will be graciously pleased to be with you, and for Christ's sake grant you his presence and blessing, lift upon you the light of his countenance, and give you joy and peace in believing on him, who is, you know, able and willing to do exceeding abundantly above all that we can ask or think, for all who put their trust in him. As diseases are his servants, that go and come at his bidding, and as he does not afflict willingly or grieve the children of men, but for their profit, that they may be partakers of his holiness, we have always reason in the midst of our trials to say, It is the Lord, let him do as seemeth him good; he doeth all things well; and though the fig-tree should not blossom, neither fruit be in the vines, yet I will rejoice in the Lord, I will joy in the God of my salvation. I hope he will graciously direct to and bless means for your recovery, and raise you up to the glory of his name, and to the good of all concerned; above all, that he will be with you, and enable you so to trust in him as to be like mount Zion that cannot be moved, and so to seek him that you will not want any good thing.

"The good seed which you and your departed wife sowed in your ministry at Reading and at Belchertown, seems to be evidently springing up and bringing forth fruit unto life eternal. So I trust it may be at Tiverton, so that whether you remain, or go to be with your dear wife and those who through faith and patience, and often through much tribulation, are now inheriting the promises, you may see, in due time, that through rich grace your labors have not been in vain in the Lord."

To his eldest son, whose partner in New Orleans had been removed by death, and who had formed a new mercantile connection in New York, he wrote, January 21, 1852:

"MY DEAR SON—If I rightly recollect, it is thirty-three years since I first saw your face and heard your voice—almost one-third of a century. You have now lived to be half of sixty-six, and by looking back can see a little how sixty-six years of human life will seem to you, should you live to see them. You can also see about all which this world can do for men, as to making them happy. It can do, through our own efforts, and the blessing of God, what it has done for you and me: furnish food and raiment, and the means of support for the body, something with which to aid our friends, and if we are disposed, do good to our needy fellow-men. But as we brought nothing into this world, so we shall carry nothing out of it, except the character we here form. And it is on our character, our feelings with regard to God and our fellow-men, that our happiness depends.

"Especially will this be the case, when we leave this world, which we may be called to at any time; and the character we then have will continue for ever. Hence, with every wise man, the great inquiry will be, how his own mind may be brought into such a state as to be happy in loving and obeying God. There is a way, and that way is pointed out in the Bible; and each person may learn it, under the teaching of the Holy Spirit, which God gives to those who desire it and ask it of him. Matt. 7:11. To assist men in doing this, and in receiving the instructions which the Holy Ghost gives, is one object I have in view in writing notes on the Bible. An objection which persons sometimes think of is, that if they make it their great object to learn and do the will of God, they shall not obtain as much as they want of this world. But the answer to that is, God has promised that they shall have all that they need, all that will do them good, all that will not in the end be a curse to them. And what wise man, who looks upon himself as an immortal being, will wish for more. 'Seek ye first the kingdom of God and his righteousness, and all these things,' that is, all which you need, all which will be best for you, all you can have without injury, 'shall be added to you.' Matt. 6:33. I hope my notes may be instrumental in leading many rightly to understand such passages, and by taking the course pointed out, experience the blessings which are promised. To seek first the kingdom of God and his righteousness, is to treat him as our rightful King, seek to be governed by his will, do what we know to be right, and trust in what Jesus Christ has done for acceptance with God. In doing this, we shall have all that God sees to be best for us in this world, and enjoy much more happiness in it than we can in any other way, and be perfectly and for ever blessed with him and all his redeemed people in the world to come.

"Your ever affectionate father,

"J. EDWARDS."

CHAPTER XIV.

THE CLOSING LABORS OF HIS LIFE.

As soon as he had finished the notes and instructions on the New Testament, he began those upon the Old Testament, to which he consecrated his unremitting energies for nearly a year and a half, till he had reached the end of the first book of Kings, when, April 17, 1852, he wrote by an amanuensis:

"DEAR SIR—I am down with a fever, brought on, I suppose, by too long continued and intense mental excitement and effort. Though I trust not immediately dangerous, I am not able to employ my mind about any thing. You must make the first of Kings as perfect as you can, and go on and print it, or leave it to be examined by me, should the Lord permit, at some future time, as you may judge best."

This sickness, which he doubtless attributes to the true cause, "too long continued and intense mental excitement and effort," not only in urging forward the Comment, but fulfilling other public responsibilities, especially affected the brain, and for some weeks he was in a high state of mental and nervous excitement; prostrated by disease and yet apparently in great buoyancy of spirits, talking continually of the Comment, the Sabbath, the religious hopes of his children, and an endless variety of subjects, often displaying uncommon shrewdness and brilliancy; but as when in health and the full use of his reason, expressing no alarm at the approach of death, scarcely alluding to the subject of the state of his own mind or his preparation for eternity, and in no case speaking an unkind word of the absent. Two of his sons, one a merchant in New York, and one a lawyer in Augusta, Maine, came to him, and remained through the crisis of the disease; and for seven days and seven nights, in which they were with him, together or alternately, they believe he slept not a moment, but was almost constantly speaking, except when his tongue became paralyzed, at periods when his death was daily and almost hourly expected. Not only was there the influence of fever, but the biliary derangement, under which in the pressure of great labor and exhaustion he had formerly been prostrated, returned; and with it the chronic "internal inflammation" of which his letters speak, that at times had caused intense suffering—a complication of disease which seemed to indicate the will of God, that his work on earth should now be terminated. But prayer was made for him continually; his own prayers that he might be useful were with the great Intercessor before the heavenly throne; and after about forty days he became again comfortable, though reduced to a state of great weakness.

On the 12th of May, his son in Maine wrote: "I have been during the last ten days engaged with the other members of our family in attending on my father. He now seems to be slowly improving, and I think the impression of the physician is, that if no relapse should take place, he will recover.

"There is no doubt in the mind of the physician, or of the family, that the cause of the present illness was too severe and long continued mental effort. For two years, as he has repeatedly said during his illness, he has had no vacation. His daily biblical studies being of a nature which rendered it proper to think and read in connection with them on the Sabbath, I doubt if he has had even the relaxation and change of pursuit which make that day so valuable to other men. In addition to the Commentary, which required as much labor as he was able to perform, he has had various and laborious duties in connection with the Sabbath and Temperance interests, the Theological Seminary, and other matters. The brain was thus tasked beyond its power of endurance, and delirium ensued, which lasted some three weeks. His mind is still weak, and must have time to recover itself. His life is of so much value that we feel bound to use every effort to prevent it from being prematurely terminated by a return to the full burden of past labors."

June 3, his youngest daughter wrote: "The love and anxiety manifested on our behalf by sympathizing friends, has been most grateful to our feelings, and has contributed not a little to support and strengthen us in this day of doubt and trial. But thanks to our merciful heavenly Father, the clouds are now graciously dispersed, and we are allowed to look forward to the time when he who is so precious to our hearts, shall be raised up from his bed of languishing and distress to become again a blessing to the church, the world, and his family, and gladden the social circle by his counsel and example. I am rejoiced to be able to tell you that my father gains slowly, though *very* slowly, from day to day. For a week past he has been riding out a short distance every pleasant day, and though fatigued by the exertion, seems refreshed, after his long confinement, by the lovely attire in which spring is clothing our village."

June 24th, Dr. Edwards wrote, "For nearly three years I pursued a course of vigorous mental effort, without any substantial vacation, hoping to prevent the depressing effects by a course of daily vigorous bodily exercise; but both mind and body failed, and I have been affected with a violent inflammation of the brain, which for a time endangered my life. From that I am now slowly recovering, and hope in due time to be able to prosecute my duties. Some things about the Bible may be learned in sickness, which will not ordinarily be learned in health."

July 7, he says, "I am gradually but slowly gaining as to health, and hope in due time to resume my work. You can now stereotype all that you have, and must wait upon Providence for the rest. I rejoice that you have sent one hundred and fifty copies of the New Testament to foreign missionaries."

September 9, he wrote, "Had I taken two months' vacation in each of the three years I have been occupied with the Commentary, it might have saved me the long and severe illness I have suffered. But I did not take any, and even when absent on a journey took my manuscript with me, hoping that by exercising the latter part of each day I could continue my labor without any vacation. But in this I was mistaken, and have had to take nearly six months' vacation, all at one time. The knowledge thus acquired, I hope to make of use, if I live, in future time and labors. I am perceptibly but slowly gaining, and hope that on the approach of cold weather I shall gain faster. But that I leave with Him who bringeth down and raiseth up, and who doeth all things well."

As his strength gradually returned, he proceeded cautiously in the preparation of the Comment, the completion of which was now the one work to which Providence seemed to call him; and though he had little strength for any other service, the Bible grew more and more precious, and it was food to his soul to drink in its blessed truths, and draw out its practical heaven-inspired instructions for the benefit of others. On the 30th of October, he sent the second book of Kings, and on the 23d of December had finished the book of Esther.

About the middle of February, 1853, he had completed the book of Job, and reached the fortieth Psalm, when the complicated disease by which he had been prostrated ten months before reäppeared, though in a much milder form; and a lingering fever and nervous exhaustion again precluded all mental effort. After some weeks he wrote, April 18, "My health is slowly gaining. I ride out every pleasant day, and walk a little. To-day I finish the comment on the fiftieth Psalm, and hope to go on slowly with the work, but shall at present attempt to do but little." Within a few weeks, applying all his remaining strength, at short intervals, to his endeared work, he carried it forward to the end of the *ninetieth Psalm*.

He resorted to all means of relaxation: riding,

exercise in his garden of which he was fond, and even ventured to take a little journey, beyond his strength, to visit his relatives in Westhampton; but he found that no means he was using had any essential recuperative influence upon his health: when his esteemed friend General Cocke of Virginia visited him, and after cheering conversation on their old favorite subject of Temperance, recommended his visiting the Virginia Springs, agreeing to meet him at Richmond, or Philadelphia, and accompany him, first to his own residence and then to the Springs, and if desirable, to take him in the ensuing winter to his plantation in Alabama.

Hoping against hope that his formerly successful remedy of a change of scene in a somewhat extended tour might restore his energies; and though with lurking disease manifestly prostrating his system, yet seeing no prospect of health if he remained at home, he resolved to accept the General's invitation, and June 1, wrote to the compiler in New York:

"I should think well of printing forthwith the comment to the end of Job, as volume first of the Old Testament. It would be a great convenience to me to have it. How long before the whole will be finished will depend much on my health.

"I now think, if Providence permit, of visiting the Virginia Springs. If so, I shall be in New York next week. I would thank you to see Dr. Bliss, and tell him I am just getting up from a forty days' fever; but am feeble, have no appetite, and am not able to get any. I daily ride out in pleasant weather, but the circulation in the system is low, and I am very easily tired with very little effort, and do not seem to gain. My old difficulty for which he visited me, continues to trouble me some, but not more than it has ordinarily for several years past. If you will ascertain his views as to my going to the Virginia Springs for a few weeks, so that you can inform me when I reach New York, you will oblige me."

On the same day Mrs. Edwards wrote, "He has attended church half the day for two or three Sabbaths. Last Sabbath being very warm, and the air of the church becoming close, he fainted, but on coming to the fresh air revived again, and has seemed since quite as well as before."

Having made all arrangements as if he might never return—which was usual in his preparation for a journey—he, on the 8th of June, left Andover accompanied by his youngest daughter, and on the second day reached the city of New York, and found a home in the family of the compiler. So great was his weakness, that he was unable to converse continuously on any topic, or even to lead in family devotions; and the singing of his favorite hymn,

"O could I speak the matchless worth,
O could I sound the glories forth
Which in my Saviour shine,"

was more than his prostrated nervous system could bear; yet occasionally his tender beaming eye and flashes of spiritual thought showed the heavenly fire that glowed in his public appeals when in the vigor of his pastoral life.

Though the physician in New York feared that the internal disease upon him was incurable, and regarded the attempt to reach the Virginia Springs as hazardous, he left on the morning of the 13th, accompanied by his daughter and his eldest son, for Philadelphia; and one week later he wrote Mrs. Edwards from the mansion of General Cocke, that he had safely arrived there, and his health "seemed to be improving." He wrote again, June 27, and June 30, that his health was "rather more comfortable than when he left home;" that his appetite, though poor, was somewhat improved, and "the swelling in his feet much lessened;" that he frequently rode out, and every thing was done for his comfort; that they were having "the warmest summer weather for Virginia, the thermometer ranging from ninety-four to ninety-eight degrees, but he did not feel oppressed by it more than by the warm weather at the north."

One week later, he and his daughter were accompanied by General Cocke, by way of the Natural Bridge, to the Rockbridge Alum Springs. They here spent four days, when the General was called home on business, and Dr. Edwards and his daughter proceeded sixteen miles to the Bath Alum Springs; being still ten miles distant from the "Hot Springs," which he wished to reach, hoping to receive benefit from bathing in the waters. At the Rockbridge Springs, "he went to meals every day leaning on the General's arm, though he seemed to relish little or nothing that he ate," and the night he arrived at the Bath Alum Springs, Wednesday, July 13, he was taken sick. We give the brief narrative that follows, in the words of his daughter in a letter to her mother, "Sabbath morning, July 24, 1853:"

"MOTHER DEAR—Pa went home to heaven yesterday morning at half past seven o'clock. I believe he heard the harps of the angels before he died, for the sweetest smile is on his face. I'm so happy to think he's done with sickness and pain for ever; and if one is made perfect through suffering, then I'm sure he is tuning his harp very near the throne of God this beautiful Sabbath morning. I wrote you on Thursday night after the doctor came, but pa was so debilitated by his loss of appetite and distress, that the physician could only make use of the most simple remedies. He gradually failed till Friday night, when we thought him dying. I held his head on a pillow from twelve o'clock until four Saturday morning, when his breathing, which had been difficult, became as calm as an infant's, but gradually grew shorter and shorter, till the last was over.

"I had prayed most earnestly that the agony of his disease might not accompany him to the hour of death, and when I found my prayers were answered in granting him so calm an exit, I could not ask for more, for his death was the same peaceful, quiet scene that his life has ever been. And, dearest mother, if you could look on the lovely expression of his countenance, I am sure you must feel comforted in knowing that every thing was done for him, that under the circumstances, human aid could afford.

"I have always thought I should have a dread of death, but shall never feel it again. I could kiss the death-dew from his brow, and sing his favorite hymns—thinking that though so nearly lost to the outward world, he might still be able to *hear* what he loved in health—all through Friday night, though the moon shining over his bed was my only company. The doctor had asked me if I would not have some gentlemen from the house called in; but I told him not unless they could do some good, for it was my greatest comfort to stay alone with him and feel that I was committing his spirit from my care to that of his God.

"Although my trial was a most bitter one, to lose so dear a friend, and among strangers too, yet when the struggle was over I could feel that Virginia was as good a place from which to go home to God and glory, as Massachusetts could ever be. I had none of the desolate, lonely feelings one might expect. I could calmly select the clothes in which to dress him as though they were only for the journey of the next day, as I have so often done before; and kissing him after he was dressed, seemed like bidding him good-by only for a little while. I made arrangements to leave the same afternoon, though they begged me to stay till the next day; but I told them, no, for my business was done: I could no longer comfort my father, and must hurry home to console my mother by telling her how much we have to be thankful for. I had a plain box made in which to bring pa as far as Lexington, where I could get a metallic case. The doctor insisted on accompanying me as far as Richmond. I have found so many kind friends—every body is good to me.

"I began this at Rockbridge, where we stopped for breakfast, but am finishing it on the boat going down James river. I have no fear but I shall get on well, and never can distrust again when I have been so wonderfully sustained so far."

At Richmond, her eldest brother met her, and they arrived at Andover on Monday, where the daughter says, "I found the consoling grace of God had reached home before me, and wonderfully sustained the bereaved and aching hearts waiting there. The children were all gathered together, with uncles, aunts, and cousins, that sorrowful but still rejoicing Monday night. On Tuesday, August 2, at eleven o'clock, Professor Phelps read the Scriptures and offered prayer at the house with the relatives. Then we proceeded in procession to the Seminary chapel, where the Scriptures were read, prayer offered by Rev. John Taylor, and hymns sung, the last of which,

'How blest the righteous when he dies,'

was one of those I sung to him the night he was dying. In the chapel burying-ground we laid him down to rest, 'with kings and counsellors of the earth,' and what is more, with 'kings and priests unto God.'"

As a distinguished friend called to tender his sympathy to the bereaved widow, he found her tearful eye lifted in thanksgiving and praise, saying, "I feel that to mourn would be ingratitude to God for his rich and abounding grace." And when regret was expressed that her departed husband had not said more of his own feelings in view of death, she replied, "That would not have been like him; he never talked about his own feelings."

A few days after, she wrote, "For more than a year, I have thought it probable that his stay on earth might be short; and he seemed to live as if he might be called away at any time, and yet as if he had *much* work still to do here, and was not ready to go till it was finished. Trying as it is to part with him, I would not call him back; he has found a far better home in heaven, where Jesus is, and where he can be *fully employed* without fainting or tiring, freed from suffering and from sin, and where he has, all his life, been preparing to go. I can feel that the Lord is good and kind in *giving*, and kind in taking away. I have not been left to regret that he went south. Had he stayed through my means and died here, I should have reproached myself, thinking that if he had gone as he wished, he might have lived. And how kindly was he taken care of, by friends he loved, all his journey through; and if he must die from home, what better place could he have chosen?—a large airy room, all things still and quiet, with *one* to attend upon him. Consoling as it would be to me to have been there, I am constrained to say, HE doeth all things well, and blessed be his holy name."

When he arrived at the Rockbridge Springs, and again when he reached the Bath Alum Springs, he asked for the volume of Dr. Scott's Commentary containing the Psalms, which assisted his meditations when his strength allowed, and was under his pillow when he died. Though, on leaving home, he arranged every thing as if he were not to return, he took with him the original Hebrew and best helps for continuing the Commentary; and on opening his trunk, it was found that he had carried it on from the ninetieth to the close of the one hundred and nineteenth Psalm. His daughter supposed this was done in the calm early morning hours of the oppressively hot days while he was at General Cocke's, though he was then too weak to bear continued conversation on any subject—so intent was he on finishing the work which he believed God had called him to do. He was cheered by the fact that his comment on the New Testament was in such demand that no less than *seventy thousand* copies had been already printed; that it was received and read with great interest, especially in family worship; that *the idea* of preparing *simple notes and instructions for the masses of men* was owned by the great Master, and would probably produce results more than realizing his expectations; and he was daily expecting to receive from the press the first volume of the Old Testament, Genesis to Job. At the time of his death it was supposed that his closing words on the ninetieth Psalm were the last he had written: "God is the author and finisher of all good works. With his presence and blessing, they will continue to prosper. Men must die, and leave many things unfinished, but God lives. His cause will extend, and by such instruments as he shall raise up, will ultimately prosper."

The physician who attended him from the commencement of his severe sickness a year before he died, says, "At my first visit, in April, 1852, on hearing his plain, clear, and graphic description of his antecedent symptoms and sufferings, and the treatment he had received by distinguished physicians, I was struck with his remarkable calmness, firmness, and acquiescence in whatever might be the will of divine Providence. He was of the nervous-bilious temperament, favorable to activity, strength, and endurance both of body and mind. The nature of his disease was such as to cause, at times, extreme suffering; yet he was never known to express any other view than that all was wisely ordered for good. Under all circumstances, he was uniformly kind, gentle, charitable, faithful, peaceful, firm, and patient. On one occasion of great suffering, I asked him if he had fear of death. He answered, 'None. It is nothing fearful to die and go to heaven'—adding, after a pause, 'I love my family and friends of course, and it would give me pleasure to be able to finish my commentary—for these I could desire life; but the Lord will provide, and do what is best.' In this severe illness he was many days deranged, in which state he disclosed much hidden treasure. His usual caution and reserve in speaking disappeared; and he became communicative, free, and lovely as the morn of spring: showing, in his constant conversation, wonderful stores of knowledge and wise reflection; speaking of all kindly, hopefully, charitably, and prayerfully; and exhibiting the loveliest phases of Christian character—thus dispelling the deep gloom often pervading families in such circumstances, and making his own sick-room really cheerful."

An excellent pastor, who resided some time in his family, says, "I knew him well and loved him much; and am much indebted to his advice, suggestions, and wise hints, for the degree of usefulness with which God has favored me in the ministry. He had sterling common-sense, and the most knowledge about the most subjects pertaining to all the *realities* of life, that I have discovered in any one man. Of his devoted piety there was but one impression among those who knew him. His was the religion of deep, unbending *principle*. These qualities combined rendered him eminently competent to *advise*, and to advise in such a way as to make his suggestions impressive and useful. Once he said to me, on telling him of some sacrifice to observe the Sabbath, 'That is right; put honor on God's institutions, and he will put honor on your instructions.' At another time, speaking of the difficulty of getting along peaceably in the midst of conflicting religious opinions and interests, he said, 'Hold fast to your principles; but with a limber elbow.' So always he had a word in season, appropriate, striking, sententious, lucid. I loved him as a father, and would say much, were I competent to speak of such a man."

Another intelligent and successful pastor, who was long in Dr. Edwards' family, and gratefully acknowledges his wise counsel and persevering fidelity in guiding his studies and preparing him for usefulness, says, with brevity, but judicious accuracy and discrimination:

"The following occur to me as among *the prominent traits* of his character as they developed themselves in my intercourse with him: A calm, constant determination to do all the good possible, to all the world. Patient, undeviating trust in God. Remarkable self-control; as perfect a command of his temper as I ever saw in any human being. Uncommon fairness of mind, willing to allow the weight of opinions opposite to his own, not dogmatizing, or seeming to desire to force his opinions on any one. Decided clearness of mind, seizing the strong points of a case. Singular discretion and sound judgment. Minding his own business. Honorableness of treatment towards all men. Kind and tender feelings. Great energy, perseverance, and self-reliance; an independence of other men, both in thought and in action, doing things in his own way. A constant endeavor to gain knowledge. An unusually *well-balanced* mind."

Of his *influence in his family*, the same pastor says, "It was characterized peculiarly by *kindness;* which showed itself, not in caresses or affectionate expressions, but in actions rather than phrases, in tones rather than sentences, in looks rather than declarations, in the general aspect and mien and intercourse, rather than in particular forms. If you asked him any thing, he listened to you carefully, and took time and pains to meet your wishes; ready to give his thoughts, his energy, and his wisdom for your welfare. In his family intercourse he retained his personal dignity, which rather repressed than invited familiarity. He seemed to be pleased with the happy sports of his children at proper times, but he never romped and sported with them, except with the greatest moderation. He was not stern; but a sort of calm moral grandeur seemed to pervade his whole life, a loftiness of thought, and plan, and labor, which left him little time and less disposition for mingling in childish sports. I believe he thought, in his later years, that it would have been better to have unbent more in familiar intercourse in his family. His bow seemed always to be stretched to its utmost tension; and had he allowed himself more relaxation, his strength might have continued longer. His conversation however was often entertaining and sprightly. He had inherently a vein of native wit, as appears sometimes in his writings, especially when replying in a single line to some fallacious objection; but I think he was a little afraid of it, and not only took no pains to cultivate it, and no pride in exercising it, but was sparing and careful in the use of it.

"His conversation was always *instructive:* he was all his life accumulating knowledge, a reader on agriculture, physiology, natural philosophy, politics, as well as on what more directly concerned his profession; and from the stores of information thus gathered, he not infrequently both entertained and instructed his household. He had the most perfect authority and control over his children, yet there was very little *show* of authority: he had a rare power of personal influence which answered all purposes, and quite forestalled any contest as to the question whose will should govern. That influence commenced so early that no one's memory ran back of it; and it continued so discreetly, so constantly, so calmly, that no one saw any breach made upon it: it was conceded from the first, so that though he punished his children almost never, he controlled them always. One ground of this result was, I think, his deference to the proper opinions and desires of his children. He took care to be in the right himself; not commanding, in haste, what he might afterwards wish to recall. He rarely commanded any thing; but when his will was known, it was expected to be, and was promptly obeyed. In a matter of doubt, he gave the child every opportunity to consider the reasons bearing on the case, and its own responsibilities; thus cultivating the exercise of individual judgment and discretion. The fairness of mind with which he weighed and balanced great public questions of the day, extended quite as much to the common affairs of the household.

"His *religious influence* over his family was not that of conversations with them personally at particular times and seasons, so much as the general and commanding influence of his life, evidently controlled, both at home and abroad, by the law of doing good as in the sight of God. His prayers sprang naturally out of such a life, not as a formal appendage, but an inherent part of it. It was clear to those who lived most with him, that he was calmly, industriously, wisely, with full purpose of heart, with strong and vigorous common-sense, continually consecrating himself to obedience to God—not fitfully, but steadily, perseveringly, right on, through the whole of life."

It may help to present him as he was, to add from a most intimate friend, "It was sometimes wished that he had been less reserved, and more familiar with his children and others, especially in expressing his own feelings; that he had indulged himself more in pleasant relaxation; and given more attention to minor external graces and attractions, while his mind was filled with subjects of great and momentous interest. His words were indeed few, but they were well chosen, and he was always ready to give advice upon any subject when asked. He was mild and kind, uniform and punctual, and careful as to making trouble, or finding fault. He trained his children to industry and energy in overcoming obstacles, in which he set them an example; making himself useful in the vigorous exercise he daily took to preserve health and prepare himself for mental labor. All that was to be done was done promptly and cheerfully, without noise or bustle, and nothing seemed a burden. He seemed to have gained the heavenly art of having his hands employed here, and his heart in heaven. He never joined in trifling conversation at home or abroad, or in worldly conversation on the Sabbath. He was calm, self-possessed, not over-anxious, trusting that Providence would order all things well; and though persevering, independent, and decided in his plans and purposes, when any thing occurred to show that the will of God was otherwise, he came into it as cheerfully and as cordially as if he had had no plans of his own. In sickness, he was patient and forbearing, cheerful and uncomplaining. In giving reproof he was gentle, and spoke in a low, mild voice. His early friends, though at a distance from him, seemed always to have a place in his heart, and he was ever mindful of their wants. He appeared to have a sympathy for all, from the king on his throne to the beggar in the street. He envied not the rich, nor despised the poor. His one great object, from first to last, seemed to be to advance the kingdom of Christ and get souls to heaven."

An intelligent theological professor says, "I knew him intimately, and hold in my sweetest remembrance those hours of friendship that I have enjoyed in his kind home. To the stranger, there was a sort of dignity and distance in his bearing, while the deep and low intonation of his voice seemed to awe rather than win to an acquaintance; but to those who knew him more intimately, these first impressions were lost in the ready and uniform kindness and courtesy that pervaded his social intercourse. He was in his family the truly Christian father. His household was eminently a happy one, made so by the steady, uniform influence he shed over it. The morning and evening devotions constituted a part of the order of the household, and came regularly with a still and quiet grace; making these services a bright and beautiful illustration of social religion. Grave in manner, reverent towards God, he opened the Bible, read a portion, often made some pertinent remark, and with deep solemnity offered a brief prayer, in which the relations and wants of all were definitely expressed. In earlier years, at the opening of the service he invoked the blessing of God, and at a later period the family united in singing a few verses. In conversation, it was his habit often to make obvious some great principle of duty; to illustrate some obscure passage of Scripture; to speak of events, political and moral, the passing scenes of daily life, however dark and adverse they might seem, as items only in the providence of God, who worketh all things after the counsel of his own will. Few men had such a readiness in pertinent scripture illustration: he often surprised you by a passage from the Bible revealing the truth under discussion with a fulness and force that no uninspired language could convey. The Sabbath evenings in his family will live with me till life is over. When the public duties of the day were past, his views of divine truth, expressed in his own happy manner, were rich with instruction, and doubly impressive as they were felt to be but the utterance of his own deep Christian life. We love to say of him, that in his private and family relations there was nothing which we should wish to forget. Always open, sincere, serious, he was a Christian gentleman; truthful, honest, he was a wise adviser in private counsel; he was an honored father, a beloved husband, whose memory shall long refresh those who knew him, 'as the dew of Hermon, and as the dew that descended upon the mountains of Zion, where the Lord commanded his blessing, even life for evermore.'"

The editor of an able and widely circulated journal, who was early associated with Dr. Edwards in the Temperance reformation, said in an article at the time of his death, "A great man is fallen in Israel. In his boyhood he manifested an extraordinary desire for the acquisition of knowledge, especially in the profoundest subjects of thought. His ministry was greatly blessed and honored. It was he, more than any other, that studied out and promulgated the doctrines of the great Temperance reform—the moral wonder of the age—everywhere seeking to fix the true doctrines and practice of Temperance deeply in the consciences of the best portions of society. His 'Permanent Temperance Documents' constitute a series of linked logic and powerful appeal that can hardly be equalled in the English language. His Family Comment on the Bible shows how perfectly original and unique his mind was both in conception and execution.

"The most striking traits of his character were greatness and integrity. He grasped the greatest subjects to which he turned his attention, and had them in his mind in all their relations. And the powers with which he was endowed, he cultivated and put forth with wisdom, and employed them to the utmost for the advancement of the best objects. Few men could present the great truths of salvation with such transparent clearness and such tremendous cogency, and in such varied, potent applications, as he was wont to do in his preaching as a pastor. Rare is the man who could lay such far-reaching and all-comprehending plans, having every step of the process so entirely in his mind, and carry them forward with such calm certainty of the result, and yet admit nothing into the process inconsistent with the spirit and example of the Saviour. He did nothing which even jealousy could imagine was designed for display, or to 'make an impression,' or to exhibit himself. The breaking down of his health during his pastorate in Boston, weakened the physical vigor of his giant frame, which before had few equals; but his extraordinary mental power in the investigation of truth, and in simplifying great truths to the general understanding, remained unimpaired. And the uprightness and integrity which marked his whole career of life, will make him a pattern to all other great and good men who shall be called to fill stations of peculiar difficulty and responsibility in the service of Christ."

About the same time, an eloquent pastor at the South wrote in a public journal, "Indomitable energy and perseverance were developed from the commencement of his college life. No soft indulgences marked any point of his career. Out of deep poverty was he to enrich those for whom he labored. With a thoughtful, investigating, reasoning mind was united the spirit of a practical philanthropy. He contemplated truth always with a view to results. Enamored of her excellence, he strove to impress a sense of it on others. One could not help being charmed with the beauty of his reasoning on subjects which are usually considered as demanding impassioned appeals. A singular combination of gentleness and energy characterized his mind. He sought to *persuade* by *convincing*. Inscribing on his banner LIGHT and LOVE, he elevated it, and never suffered it to be trailed in the dust. His plans for the good of men being adopted with great judgment, and carried out with a steady perseverance, were uniformly crowned with success. It is not usual that one so eminent as a student, a preacher, a teacher, becomes, when past the meridian of life, so aggressive and effectual a laborer in untried spheres. But the activity of his spirit could never be repressed. He could not 'live to himself.' To do good was the element of his being, the life of his happiness."

The "World's Temperance Convention," held at New York, September, 1853, dropped a tear over his departure, expressed their "high and grateful appreciation of his services in the cause of Temperance," and "deeply mourned the loss from their ranks of so efficient and faithful a laborer." The gentleman in the chair and others traced to his influence and early labors their own enlistment in the Temperance reformation. "I heard him in Maryland," said a veteran in the Temperance service, "and the words he used became riveted upon my heart. I had the honor of being with him on the business committee in the National Convention, held in 1833, in the Hall of American Independence. There, and in subsequent conventions where I was with him, whenever adverse thoughts and views were presented, a word or two from his clear mind was like oil from the troubled waters. His memory will last while ages last. Generations yet unborn will rise and call him blessed."

A late professor in the seminary at Andover says, "I first became acquainted with Dr. Edwards in 1811, when he was a member of the seminary. I remember well the high character he bore in the seminary, and increasingly abroad, as his high promise became rapidly known. He took a lively interest in the cause of missions, both at home and abroad, and lent his commanding influence in the seminary to the promotion of that cause. It was at that heart-stirring period when our first foreign missionaries were ordained and sent abroad, and when the projects were on foot for exploring our Western and Southern frontiers by Mills and others; and from that eventful day to his death, Dr. Edwards' heart was ever ready to exult in any new and wise movement for the promotion of Christ's kingdom. While a student at the seminary his health and vigor were remarkable, and his severe and successful application to study was enough to break down the strongest constitution. He was called to the church in Andover at precisely the grand crisis for orthodoxy in Eastern Massachusetts, when no one could predict the result. But the people, however variously they might regard his theology, all perceived a life, and power, and substance in his preaching, which was also much admired by the students; and the results have been most propitious to the interests of the Redeemer's kingdom. When, after the lapse of years, he was made president of the seminary, he came into that station with the same steady and glowing piety, sound judgment, and aim at practical wisdom, though the duties devolved on him, in their minute and ever-varying details, were far from being such as to give him the same prominence in the public eye that he had held in his previous life. As a presiding and executive officer, he was all that could be desired. Every thing belonging to the department was attended to promptly and well. It was from an intuitive knowledge of his fitness for these duties, that Mr. Bartlet was so anxious he should be appointed to the office, and so willing, year by year, till he died, to furnish, by special donation, the requisite funds for his support. His usefulness in this office will be fully known only at that final day when not only his general care of the seminary and the academy, but his prayers and the extent of his truly pious influence on the students, and through them on the world, shall be unveiled."

An officer of one of our prominent benevolent institutions writes: "Dr. Edwards' mind appeared to me to be comprehensive and far-reaching beyond that of most men. In the public enterprises in which he engaged, he laid the foundation of success in first securing the adoption, in the public mind, of simple and almost self evident principles that no one could question, and thus gained the results with more ease than most men are wont to do, winning his victories before the enemy was fairly aroused.

"His influence in intelligent deliberative assemblies, when he took an active part in them, was remarkably effective. The sanctified self-control, for which he was always distinguished, was one element of this influence. The unbounded confidence reposed in his integrity, was another. There was something, also, in his grave and commanding person, and in the deep tones of his voice. But these served only as auxiliaries to a high attribute of his understanding: I mean, *his power of stating facts*. In this he was preeminent. Never in haste to speak, when he did speak in deliberative assemblies it was generally in some simple, lucid statement, that placed the principal facts of the case in their true form and natural relations, making them all bear directly on the point at issue; and when once he had laid himself out in this manner, there was afterwards little real occasion for debate. In this power of effective argumentative statement of facts, he resembled Daniel Webster. This was indeed his forte; and it was delightful, while listening to him, to see the spirit of controversy visibly subsiding under the influence of truth presented, in its simplest forms, by a great and good mind.

"I never saw so remarkable an instance of sanctified self-control as on one occasion, when Dr. Edwards resigned a public charge, as he believed in accordance with the will of divine Providence. With solemnity, and with the same calmness and deliberation as when stating important cases in which he was not personally interested, he went into a historical view of his position, and of the matter as it then stood. And I must say that in all my intercourse with good men in similar circumstances, I never saw any thing equal to what I then beheld in Dr. Edwards. It was a great, magnanimous, and uncommonly sanctified man rising calmly out of painful perplexities, with his eyes intent on the divine Being ordering all things for his own glory. It was the sublime in character, and I delight ever to retain it in my memory."

CONCLUSION.

In reviewing this outline of the life of Dr. Edwards, which we have endeavored to present in simplicity and in truth in view of all the light that has come before us, and adoring the grace and mercy of God manifested in him, we notice,

The elements which were combined to form his religious character. Like Martin Luther, and John Bunyan, and John Newton, and James Milnor, he saw himself "plucked as a brand from the burning," and he longed to rescue others from the same doom. It was not immorality, or violence and crime, from which he was rescued, but the equally fatal "neglect" of "the great salvation," in which he and the community, including many of the churches around him, were gliding securely on, though practically denying the work and grace of Christ, and the necessity of the new birth by the renewing of the Holy Ghost. The spiritual death from which he had been redeemed, and the riches of grace revealed to him, were fresh in his mind till his dying day; and he felt bound by infinite motives, to make them known to others as far as the ruins of the fall had spread. In the revival of the work of God about the beginning of the present century, in which his religious character was formed, the distinguishing truths and doctrines of salvation by grace were perhaps as clearly preached as in the great reformation, or in the days of Baxter and Flavel in the seventeenth century, or of President Edwards and other worthies in the middle of the eighteenth; and to this there was superadded *the missionary spirit*—the sense of obligation to convey a knowledge of "the gospel to every creature"—which had not to the same extent appeared since apostolic days. The union of these two elements—clear views of the doctrines of grace, fired by the missionary spirit—is *the key that fits the wards of Dr. Edwards' life, and unlocks his character,* from the hour when he began to study for the ministry, till from the Virginia Springs he ascended into rest. Here we find the LIGHT and LOVE which characterize his efforts—light from on high, and love to perishing souls. Hence,

"*Jesus Christ, and him crucified,*" was his great theme. He had felt its constraining power, and knew that in it centre the hopes of men. Not only was this the theme of his ministry, but in his efforts for Temperance and the Sabbath he did not think any other motive *strong enough* permanently to control the heart and life. He saw too, that intemperance and Sabbath-breaking benumbed the hearts and closed the ears of men to the overtures of divine mercy, and that both were appalling obstacles which must be taken out of the way of the chariot of salvation. Hence too,

His life of prayer and trust in Providence. Did ever a circle of Christians, great or small, in any circumstances, bow with him before God in the spirit of prayer, when by his leading their devotions, they did not feel that they were brought nearer the throne of grace? "I never heard him preach," said a godly minister in New Hampshire, "but he once offered a prayer that I shall never forget." We have met him in his study when it seemed as "the gate of heaven," filled with the presence of God. A venerable lady of his church states that a few years after he was settled, as he was offering prayer in the sanctuary on a Sabbath morning, the shock of an earthquake was perceptible by all the congregation; but the tones of his voice were unchanged, and he immediately proceeded in thanks to God that "though the earth be removed," they that trust in him are safe. His looking for light and direction from above was habitual, and observed by all who knew him. A young clergyman, hearing that his health was prostrated, and fearing that death was near, wrote him, "I almost daily bless God for what you have done for me. If I have had any wisdom to follow the indications of Providence—not to contend with men, or set up my little self and determine always to have my own way, or attempt to carry measures by management—and not to be alarmed but trust in God when prospects look dark, I owe it in a great degree, under God, to you; and I beg still to ask an interest in your prayers." When he was asked by a young secretary who had just received interesting intelligence from abroad, whether to publish it at once, or keep it for the annual report, "Let it go," said he, "Providence will provide for the report." Hence too,

His love of the Bible, God's own revelation of truth in its inspired aspects and connections, in which there could be no defect, nor shade of error, and his desire that all men should have it and study and understand it. For this object he seems to have planned efforts like those he made for Temperance and the Sabbath—to visit legislatures and clerical bodies and churches throughout the land, and ultimately to prepare a Bible Manual presenting the subject in its momentous import and practical bearings; and though he did not live to execute these plans in the manner proposed, yet the notes and instructions for common minds, which he was providentially led to prepare on the New Testament and half of the Old, when carried to their completion, with auxiliary helps such as he designed, may yet happily realize the beneficent results he had in view.

He presented divine truth *in great clearness and simplicity to the common mind.* In preaching, he seemed to feel, like Dr. Archibald Alexander, whom in keen discernment, strong common-sense, wisdom in counsel, and love to the masses of men, he much resembled, that the pulpit was too sacred, and souls too precious, for him there to display himself in literary terms, or nice abstract disquisitions, while the souls of the great body of his hearers were hungering for the bread of life. In all Dr. Edwards wrote which has met our eye, we do not remember his using an obscure word of foreign origin, when a plain Anglo-saxon term would give the idea; nor have we met any argument in favor of the denomination with which he stood connected, to the prejudice of other denominations who embraced the great substantials of the gospel "in spirit and in truth."

He fixed on *the strong point* of a subject. He knew the common mind, and how to rouse it with prodigious energy. He worked out the plain practical thought on which a subject rested, and when he presented it, others seemed to see it as clearly as himself. To a great extent this was illustrated in every sermon he preached, or address he made. That *all the temperate* should practise total abstinence—God's *right* to the Sabbath, and the *right* of every laboring man and beast of burden to its rest—and that every man should learn what God has said in *the Bible* and obey it—are ideas as simple as, in the phases in which he presented them, they were original and profound, underlying the great objects to which nearly twenty years of his life were consecrated.

His patient endurance and laborious self-denial. Having given himself to Christ, with his firm physical powers strengthened by cultivating a rocky New England soil; parting with the caresses of his mother at the age of five, and compelled to work his way to manhood as it were alone—hardship and toil had no terror for him. Of all that his tender, sensitive heart endured, in the trying events to which human life is subject, and of the bodily pain he suffered, we have said little, for the reason that he neither wrote of them, nor spoke of them, even on the bed of death. The aim of life was to glorify God in doing good, and he could silently and uncomplainingly toil on, practise economy, endure self-denial, and bear burdens. Such was his punctuality, that in the seven years of his Temperance labors he did not remember being *in any case too late;* and his financial affairs were conducted with a promptness and accuracy, that left his mind unembarrassed for his great work.

He was uniformly kind. His natural reserve, cherished perhaps by the early removal of his mother and other circumstances of his early life, ripened into that "keeping his tongue from evil, and his lips from speaking guile," which was a beautiful trait of his character. The writer has discovered in all he wrote no spirit of retaliation, nor has he heard from his lips an unkind word concerning any human being. To a friend who submitted to him a sharp letter to one with whom he felt aggrieved, he replied, "The enclosed I have read with care, and now, according to your request, return it. He who was more wronged than any other, 'when he was reviled, reviled not again,' and when 'led as a lamb to the slaughter, opened not his mouth.'" The writer once applying to him for counsel, in some alarm at an obstacle to usefulness which another seemed to be interposing, the burden was rolled off in a moment as he replied, "O well, if he is determined to stand there, let him stand—it is not best to quarrel with him—pass right round him, and go on and do the Lord's work." There was in his counsels a remarkable absence of his own personal interest, and largeness of view for the prosperity of the Redeemer's kingdom.

His constant preparation for death. Our narrative of his last days and hours is but like that of the ancient scripture worthies, "And he died;" while his life shows that the future of the present and of the coming world was viewed by him, as it was seen in visions of the prophets, at one glance. When he should be transferred from one world to the other, was known only to God; and the idea that preparation was the peculiar work of a dying hour seems not to have entered his thoughts. In the spirit of his own rules of life, found in his pocketbook, he seemed to "act for God, for the universe, and for eternity;" to "trust habitually in Christ Jesus for all he needed both for this life and the life to come;" to "seek the teaching, the illuminating, and purifying influences of the Holy Spirit that He might dwell in him;" and to do what would "give him the greatest joy at the judgment-day." The language of his life was, "For me to live is Christ, and to die is gain." "Whether we live, we live unto the Lord; and whether we die, we die unto the Lord: whether we live, therefore, or die, we are the Lord's."

A neat, enduring marble monument has been erected at his grave, enclosed by an iron railing, with this inscription:

REV. JUSTIN EDWARDS, D.D.

BORN IN WESTHAMPTON, MASS., APRIL 25, 1787.
DIED JULY 23, 1853.

HE WAS SUCCESSIVELY PASTOR OF THE SOUTH CHURCH, ANDOVER, AND THE SALEM CHURCH, BOSTON; SECRETARY OF THE AMERICAN TEMPERANCE SOCIETY; PRESIDENT OF THE ANDOVER THEOLOGICAL SEMINARY; AND SECRETARY OF THE AMERICAN AND FOREIGN SABBATH UNION. THE LAST FOUR YEARS OF HIS LIFE WERE DEVOTED TO THE PREPARATION OF A FAMILY COMMENTARY ON THE BIBLE.

THE MEMORY OF THE JUST IS BLESSED.

www.ingramcontent.com/pod-product-compliance
Lightning Source LLC
LaVergne TN
LVHW021240110826
845150LV00002B/365

* 9 7 8 1 4 2 5 5 6 1 8 5 7 *